Constructing Borders/
Crossing Boundaries

Constructing Borders/ Crossing Boundaries

Race, Ethnicity, and Immigration

edited by Caroline B. Brettell

LEXINGTON BOOKS

A DIVISION OF
ROWMAN & LITTLEFIELD PUBLISHERS, INC.
Lanham • Boulder • New York • Toronto • Oxford

LEXINGTON BOOKS

A division of Rowman & Littlefield Publishers, Inc.
A wholly owned subsidary of The Rowman & Littlefield Publishing Group, Inc.
4501 Forbes Boulevard, Suite 200
Lanham, MD 20706

Estover Road
Plymouth PL6 7PY
United Kingdom

British Library Cataloguing in Publication Information Available

Library of Congress Cataloging-in-Publication Data

Constructing borders/crossing boundaries : race, ethnicity, and immigration / edited by
Caroline B. Brettell.
    p. cm.
  ISBN-13: 978-0-7391-1569-5 (cloth : alk. paper)
  ISBN-10: 0-7391-1569-3 (cloth : alk. paper)
  1. Minorities—United States—Social conditions. 2. Immigrants—United States—
Social conditions. 3. Ethnicity—United States. 4. Ethnic barriers—United States. 5.
United States—Race relations. 6. United States—Emigration and immigration—Social
aspects. I. Brettell, Caroline. II. Title: Constructing borders, crossing boundaries.
E184.A1C596 2007
304.8'730089—dc22   2006013876

Printed in the United States of America

∞™ The paper used in this publication meets the minimum requirements of American
National Standard for Information Sciences—Permanence of Paper for Printed Library
Materials, ANSI/NISO Z39.48-1992.

Contents

Part III: Ethnicity as a Resource

Preface and Acknowledgments

Josh DeWind, Program Director, and Jennifer Holdaway,
Associate Director, International Migration Program,
Social Science Research Council

The editor of this volume, Dr. Caroline Brettell of Southern Methodist University, came together with the contributors through a fellowship program organized by the Social Science Research Council's International Migration Program. The central theme of the book—an exploration of the variety of ways in which international migrants construct and cross social and geographic borders as they adapt their lives to American society—was identified and developed at a three-day conference held at the Asilomar Conference Grounds in Pacific Grove, California, in January 2004. The Andrew W. Mellon Foundation provided the funds for the fellowships, conference, and editing of the manuscript to advance its goal of strengthening international migration as an interdisciplinary field in the social sciences. We are indebted to scholars who have participated in the program, both as fellows and as members of the pre- and postdoctoral selection committees (listed below), as well as to Harriet Zuckerman at the Mellon Foundation and Katie Funk of Lexington Books. Their separate and joint efforts in facilitating the crossing of intellectual and disciplinary boundaries have made this volume possible.

Members of the Predoctoral Awards Committee

Caroline Brettell	Marilyn Halter
Leo Chavez	Sherrie Kossoudji
Louis DeSipio	Karen Leonard
Gary Freeman	Sarah Mahler
Manuel Garcia y Griego	Alex Stepick
Gary Gerstle	Marcelo Suarez-Orozco
Luis Guarnizo	Abel Valenzuela

Members of the Postdoctoral Awards Committee

Susan Carter	Luis Laosa
Luis Falcon	Colin Leach
Nancy Foner	Zai Liang
Donna Gabaccia	John Logan
Steve Gold	Sarah Mahler
James Hollifield	Nestor Rodriguez
Mathew Jacobson	Min Zhou

Introduction

Race, Ethnicity, and the Construction of Immigrant Identities

Caroline B. Brettell

The essays in this volume tackle the construction and significance of race and ethnicity as boundary-making processes among diverse immigrant populations in the United States. They emphasize the fluidity of racial and ethnic identities that are shaped, negotiated, and contested in specific contexts and situations. They capture the range of spaces in which ethnicity and race become salient— the university, the immigrant enclave, the detention center, the workplace, the nightclub, and even in trans-Atlantic passage. Sometimes these identities differ between the immigrant generation and their offspring. These differences are also explored by several authors who represent, through their essays here, the recent and growing interest in studies of the second generation.[1]

As boundary-making processes race and ethnicity can either unite or divide. Ethnic enclaves are communities with clearly defined boundaries that often set a particular immigrant group off from mainstream society. Some African and Caribbean immigrants mark boundaries between themselves and African Americans. However, equally, some African and South Asian immigrants may attempt to cross borders of nationality to construct a common identity with African Americans with whom they may share a common religion such as Islam. Immigrant children often broker the crossing of boundaries for parents, but at the same time immigration can also heighten cultural boundaries between immigrant parents and their children. Many of the debates within the field of immigration studies center on the rigidity or permeability of various boundaries (including national borders), how they are marked, and how and why these markings change over time (Donnan and Wilson 1999). The individual scholars contributing to this volume model, deploy, and explain notions of "borders" and "boundaries" in various ways, but collectively they engage the theoretical debates on borders as sites of cultural production (Anzaldua 1987; Ganster and

Lorey 2005; Rosaldo 1989; see also Alvarez 1995) in addition to engaging the debates about situational identity/ethnicity and the construction of race (see Banks 1996; Barth 1969; Greenbaum 2002; Nagata 1974).

In this introduction I explore somewhat further the issues of race and ethnicity, and of the borders and boundaries that they create, sustain, or transgress in relation to the study of immigration. I then move to a brief discussion of the interdisciplinary and comparative enterprise of migration studies, particularly as it pertains to the study of ethnic and racial boundaries. I conclude with a description of the overall organization of the book and its contributors. Each section of the book begins with a brief introduction that further situates and compares the individual contributions.

POST-1965 IMMIGRATION AND THE PROBLEMATIZATION OF RACE AND ETHNICITY

In 1965 amendments to the Immigration and Nationality Act reopened the doors to immigrants after a forty-year hiatus. A seven-category preference system replaced the system based on national origins quotas and forever changed the face of U.S. immigration. The result of these sweeping changes was not renewed streams of northern, southern, and eastern Europeans, as had been the case during the third wave of immigration between 1880 and 1924, but incipient and subsequently burgeoning flows of people from Asia and Latin America. By 1990 immigrants from Latin America and the Caribbean comprised 42.6 percent of the foreign-born population in the United States and Asians 25.2 percent.[2] Mexicans alone accounted for 22 percent of the foreign-born, and Filipinos, the second largest group, comprised 4.6 percent.

Table1.   Top Ten Countries of Origen for Immigrants to the Unites States, 2000.

Country of Origin	Percentage of Foreign-Born
Mexico	29.5
Philippines	4.4
India	3.3
China (excl. Taiwan and Hong Kong)	3.2
Vietnam	3.2
Cuba	2.8
Korea	2.8
Canada	2.6
El Salvador	2.6
Germany	2.3

Source: U.S. Census, 2000.

Between 1990 and 2000 the foreign-born population increased by 11.3 million people (a 57.4 percent increase). By 2000, 51.7 percent of the foreign-born were from Latin America, 26.4 percent from Asia, 15.8 percent from Europe, 2.8 percent from Africa, and 2.7 percent from North America. Table 1 lists the top ten countries of origin in 2000.

A characteristic of the post-1965 migration that became increasingly important as the United States moved toward the twenty-first century is the high proportion of foreigners, particularly Mexicans, who came to this country without documentation. After 1968, and with the demise of the bracero program, the flows from Mexico were subjected to increasing numerical restrictions (Massey, Durand, and Malone 2002). As the visas for legal immigrants contracted, the number of illegal immigrants expanded. Scholars have estimated that in the period from 1965 to 1986 (when the Immigration Reform and Control Act [IRCA] extended amnesty to undocumented workers) approximately 28 million Mexicans entered the United States illegally (Massey and Singer 1995). Although the goal of IRCA was to halt illegal immigration, it did not have this effect, and throughout the 1990s the number of undocumented workers from Mexican continued to grow. It is this continued flow that explains the movement of Mexicans into parts of the country where they had not previously settled in any significant numbers. This includes New York City and North Carolina about which Fuentes and Rose respectively write in this volume.

When asked to describe their race, fully 43 percent of the foreign-born included in the 2000 U.S. Census reported it as white alone and another 22.5 percent reported it as Asian alone. In addition, 21.5 percent reported some other race alone, and 6.8 percent black or African American alone. Finally, 14.2 million foreign-born individuals reported a Hispanic/Latino origin, representing 45.5 percent of the total foreign-born population (31.1 million) and 40.2 percent of the total Hispanic/Latino population of 35.2 million.

Most scholars of migration agree that these new immigration streams have fundamentally altered not only the ethnic and racial composition of the U.S. population but also the meanings of race and ethnic identity. Race has been a concept central to African American Studies and ethnicity to the study of immigration, but addressing the question of racial identity in American immigration scholarship is a relatively recent development.[3] As sociologist Mary Waters (1994: 795) has argued, the increasing diversity of immigration flows to the United States since 1965 "challenges the dichotomy which once explained different patterns of American inclusion and assimilation—the ethnic pattern of assimilation of immigrants from Europe and their children and the racial pattern of exclusion of America's nonwhite peoples."

Before 1965, in a dichotomous black and white America, Asians, Latinos, Caribbean, and multiracial populations were largely invisible or were themselves racialized as "other" in those regions of the country where their presence was felt. Greenbaum (2002), for example, suggests that in Florida in the 1960s, black Cubans as a category were "unthinkable." But in the late twentieth century a "new racial and ethnic amalgam is changing perceptions of race and ethnicity as well as creating new alliances, relationships, and divisions" (Foner 2001: 19; see also Das Gupta 1997 and Sanchez 1999a, 1999b). In some disciplines, anthropology in particular, the concept of race was once rejected in favor of ethnicity. However, Faye Harrison has recently suggested that "to do justice to the experiences of all peoples, including those who are identified and who self-identify in racial terms, . . . concepts such as racism, racialization, racial stratification, and racial identity formation need to be included in our analytical lexicon" (Harrison 1998: 613). Nina Glick Schiller and Georges Fouron (1990) echo this point with regard to the study of immigrants in particular:

> Whether ethnicity is defined in terms of cultural distinctiveness, explained as a reaction to structural constraints, or approached as ideology, the concept . . . seems inadequate to deal with race. Race, on one hand, is a "social" category whose boundaries and meaning differ from society to society. Scholars have emphasized the ideological nature of race to combat arguments about biological determinism. . . . But in the United States, race cannot be reduced to an ideological category. As a product of historical construction, race has emerged as a category critical to the maintenance of the hegemony of the capitalist class. (332)

Scholars are beginning to document cases of post-1965 immigrants and their children who are reworking the racial and ethnic categories of the United States by asserting identities that have no historical precedent (Bailey 2001; see also Waters 1994 and Kibria 2002). This is nowhere more apparent than in the literature on Caribbean immigrants in the United States.[4] Stafford (1987) explores the shifting symbolic meanings of race and ethnicity among Haitian immigrants in New York City and their consequences for behavior and social relationships. Haitians, like other West Indians, can be, as Stafford suggests, "perceived and categorized either as a racial or an ethnic population." They are invisible to white Americans, who perceive them as black and of low status, but visible to black Americans as foreigners with a different language and culture. "Such multiple affiliations . . . give Haitians some flexibility, providing them with a number of social identities which they can choose—and manipulate—according to circumstances at hand" (Stafford 1987: 143).[5]

Stafford observes that in Haiti color can be altered by social class affiliation. But Haitians know that this is not so possible in the United States, where race is critical in determining social position and blackness carries a stigma of inferiority. She describes Haitians who evoke symbols of French culture and Haitian history to distinguish themselves from American blacks and to garner positive assessment from whites.[6] Stafford also found that the Haitians she studied preferred not to identify with other West Indian immigrants, particularly those of English-speaking heritage. Rather, they invoked their French heritage to claim superiority and they rejected the broad West Indian label as something imposed on Haitians by Americans. Glick Schiller and Fouron (1990) suggest that French culture and Haitian history are components of a transnational identity that not only offers Haitians an alternative to an ethnic or black identity, but also can encompass a life that transgresses national borders. Such an identity counters the "boundedness of race."

Stafford goes on to predict that for second-generation Haitians life may be different and that "a common racial identity will bring them together with black Americans. Unless their Haitian heritage is strongly reinforced by their parents, their primary identity will be as blacks within a white society, with their ethnic identity as Haitians playing a much less important role than it did for the immigrant generation" (Stafford 1987: 152).

Stafford's conclusions about the second generation are echoed by other scholars. Sociologist Mary Waters, who studied second-generation Caribbeans in New York City, claims that the key factor for youth is race:

> The daily discrimination that the youngsters experience, the type of racial socialization they receive in the home, the understandings of race they develop in their peer groups and at school affect strongly how they react to American society. The ways in which these youngsters experience and react to racial discrimination influences the type of racial/ethnic identity they develop. (Waters 1994: 802)

Waters identifies three types of identities among the second generation—a black American identity, an ethnic or hyphenated national origin identity, and an immigrant identity. She argues that these identities are influenced by the way that adolescents perceive and understand race relations in the United States. Those young West Indian and Haitian American adolescents in New York who identify as black Americans see more racial discrimination. Those who identify as ethnic West Indians see more opportunities and rewards for individual effort and initiative. Race and class, she suggests, complicate the process of assimilation. Those who come from middle-class backgrounds, and whose parents are upwardly mobile and involved in ethnic organizations or churches, maintain ties to their parent's national origins, while poor inner-city adolescents assimilate to black American peer culture.

The differences that Waters outlines are similar to those that Alex Stepick (1998) found among Haitian youth in Florida. Stepick describes two young Haitian boys, Phede and Herve, in the opening pages of his monograph. Phede quickly assimilated after his arrival at age twelve, covering up his Haitian identity by Americanizing his name to Fred. Becoming "Fred" and thus African American allowed Phede to be accepted by his peers in a largely African American neighborhood where he lived and went to school. One day, his sister arrived at school and blew his cover by addressing him in creole. The identity he had constructed for himself was shattered. Fred took his own life. Herve or Herb, by contrast, celebrated his Haitian heritage. He became a rapper but in his songs he identified his background and focused on hard work and success. Stepick encapsulates the different strategies pursued by Phede/Fred and Herve/Herb in the contrast between "pride" and "prejudice" — pride in Haitian roots and the prejudice against Haitians specifically, and blacks in general, that exists in the United States. Young people must struggle with these exterior definitions of themselves; sometimes they are successful in constructing a workable identity, but occasionally their efforts end in tragedy.

Kasinitz, Battle, and Miyares (2001: 294) come to similar conclusions about the complex identities of second-generation West Indians in their research on anglophone Caribbean immigrants in Florida. They observe that racial identity is stronger among the second generation than among the 1.5 generation (those born abroad but who came to the United States as young children). The second-generation West Indians' perceptions of themselves as victims of discrimination, "combined with the lack of a distinctly West Indian residential or economic enclave, point to a growing, if predictably ambivalent, identification with the broader African American community."

Working on Jamaicans in New York City, Vickerman argues that even for the immigrant generation ethnic identity (as an "alternative self-definition") develops as a response to a racialized America. Race may be a uniting factor; but ethnicity is a dividing factor:

> Whereas Jamaica's history, culture, and social structure, and the very act of immigration, lead Jamaicans to idealize achievement, the realization that blacks — including Jamaicans — experience routine discrimination in the United States makes them understand that this achievement cannot be divorced from the larger struggle for social justice for all blacks. (Vickerman 2001: 205)

Jamaicans not only attempt to distance themselves from the unflattering assumptions that are made about blacks, they also ally themselves with Grenadians and Barbadians whom they would see as different if they were in Jamaica. Similar observations were made earlier by Nancy Foner (1987) who described "Jamaicanness" or "West Indianness" as a way to draw difference with black Americans, to express ethnic pride, and, she adds, to claim superiority. This ethnic distinctiveness is, Foner suggests, expressed and reinforced by their social networks, and by the transnational connections they maintain. But Foner also acknowledges that Jamaicans recognize the difference in the meaning of color at home and in the United States. "Education, income, and culture, do not, as in Jamaica, partially 'erase' one's blackness. Nor are whites sensitive to shade differences, as people were [in Jamaica]" (Foner 1987: 203). Bobb (2001) suggests that there are two ways for West Indians to rationalize

> the reality of racism in the United States. On the one hand, most cope with racism by deciding to "overlook" it or "ignore it." On the other hand, although many feel that they can safely ignore racist acts, some devise strategies for avoidance. (219)

All this research underscores not only the importance of integrating the study of race and ethnicity in the study of immigration, but also of understanding the conceptual differences between them. Race, as Kasinitz (1992: 4) and many others have pointed out, is a social construct. The meaning of race changes across time and space and it is often imposed from the outside. Ethnicity, on the other hand, is about self-definition that may or may not be invoked and that certainly can be mobilized for economic, political, or social ends.

Recently, historians looking at the third wave of immigration have lent nuance to our understanding of the mutability of race by exploring the concept of "whiteness" (Frankenberg 1993; Roediger 1991).[7] In the period prior to the Civil War, Irish immigrants were defined as a racial other, but by the end of the century, when others who looked more different began to arrive, the Irish were extended membership in the white category (Allen 1994; Ignatiev 1995; Warren and Twine 1997). On the West Coast people feared the "yellow peril" of Chinese and Japanese immigrants and in response the United States enacted various forms of legislation to restrict their entry and movement. On the East Coast, Eastern and Southern European immigrants became the new, nonwhite, racial other, assigned to this status by the state and by popular culture and frequently were referred to as "the Chinese of Europe" (Gabaccia 2002: 121).[8]

Karen Brodkin (1998) suggests that the employment sector was one foundation for the racial "othering" of these new immigrant populations:

> The temporary darkening of Jews and other European immigrants during the period when they formed the core of the industrial working class clearly illustrates

the linkages between degraded and driven jobs and nonwhite racial status. Similarly, the "indianness" of Mexicans and Asians, as they became key to capitalist agribusiness, stands as another variant on the earlier constructions of blackness and redness. (60)

Foner (2000) outlines the racial terms that were used to describe Jews and Italians in New York at the turn of the twentieth century:

Italians were often described as swarthy, and a common epithet for them, guinea, had long referred to African slaves. . . . "You don't call an Italian a white man?" a member of a congressional committee asked a West Coast construction boss. "No sir," he answered, "an Italian is a dago." (147)

The empirical question for those studying these groups is, then, how they became white? Smith et al. (2001: 6) suggest that as the social, economic, and political position of particular groups improved they became whiter. If this is so, it makes the recent argument made by historian Thomas Guglielmo, based on his research on Italians in Chicago in the period between 1890 and 1945, quite significant: "While Italians suffered greatly for their putative racial undesirability as Italians, South Italians, and so forth, they still benefited in countless ways from their privileged *color* status as whites" (Guglielmo 2003: 9). Class background, high human capital, has not necessarily helped the Caribbean immigrants discussed above because their color status is black not white. They are bounded by race in a way that the Irish, the Italians, and the Jews, ultimately, were not. Indeed Guglielmo argues that Italians were not only racialized and discriminated against, they were also privileged by their whiteness. As they moved into what Richard Alba (1981) has referred to as "the twilight of ethnicity" and mobilized around a white identity, they became the ones racializing others.

Particularly illuminating to this discussion of class, color, and race is the research on South Asian immigrants, who have become an increasing presence in the United States since 1980, although immigrants from India have been in the country since the end of the nineteenth century. Leonard (1997) describes Punjabis in California who intermarried with Mexicans and Mexican-Americans because, as people of color, this was their only legal option.[9] In the 1920s, the Supreme Court *Thind* decision barred Punjabi men in California from U.S. citizenship and pronounced people from India to be "Caucasian but not 'white persons' in the popular meaning of the term" (Leonard 1997: 48).

Asian Indian immigrants today do not see themselves as anything less than white although, phenotypically, some are very dark skinned. And they have largely been accepted as white, although there are incidents of discrimination and racism which members of the community have experienced, some in the aftermath of 9/11.[10] According to Lessinger (2001),

> the first generation of Indian immigrants tends to see itself as white because of its pre- and post-migration class privilege and has been in some degree insulated by money, professional jobs, and suburban residence from some of the most direct expressions of U.S. racism and nativism. (168)

Rangaswamy (2000), based on research in the Asian Indian community in Chicago, equally recognizes the importance of class. However, she also emphasizes that nationality or country of origin (i.e., ethnicity) rather than race is the identifying factor for Asian Indians in the United States. Asian Indians are

> not classified outright as "colored" as they are in Britain. . . . Chicago's white communities have a deep-rooted fear of "losing" their neighborhood to the blacks. But Indians seem to have avoided the consequences of this attitude because they are seen more as an ethnic group than as a racial group. (Rangaswamy 2000: 94)

Lessinger (2001: 168) argues that these experiences of class privilege and of ethnic rather than racial location are somewhat different for the American-raised children, "whose lives in school and college, as well as their entry into the work force, may have given them close encounters with U.S. racial realities." Second-generation Indian Americans are "slowly developing a more sophisticated sense of self, less afraid to acknowledge a nonwhite identity." This point is made most dramatically by Maira (2002), who identifies a "racial project" among Indian-American youth that responds to the black/white racial binary:

> As youth of color who, unlike their parents, grew up in the United States, these young people have been molded by the ethnic identity frameworks available to them and by their experiences of growing up as minorities. The question is whether these youth can build a racial politics that will allow them to participate in spheres based both on ethnicity and on alliances with youth of color, and whether they can resist the ethnic chauvinism of South Asian student organizations that view other group allegiances with suspicion. (68)

Perhaps what Maira is capturing here is a complicated and multifaceted system of racial categorization. As Espiritu (1997: 109) has noted, in the early part of the twentieth century Asians in the United States were "almost black but not blacks," but in the late twentieth century they have become "almost white but not white."

The research on Asian Indians, as well as on other groups, reinforces the argument that identity is fluid and that categories are mutable. Racialization is related not only to the broad categories of white, black, Asian, and Latino, but also to national origins, class position, and undoubtedly also gender and immigration status. It is these complexities that led sociologist Douglas Massey (1995: 645) to the conclusion that "rather than a slow, steady, and relatively coherent progression of ethnicity toward twilight, it will increasingly stretch from dawn to dusk."

As an example of the complexity Massey points to the different identifiers that the U.S. Census has used for people of Spanish origin— Mexican, Mexican American, Hispanic, and Chicano. Indeed such labels (and especially panethnic labels) are themselves hotly contested and, while sometimes generated from within (Flores 1999), they have also equally been applied from outside (Espiritu 1992; Lieberson and Waters 1988; Melville 1983, 1989). Oboler (1999: 46) observes that before the 1970s people of Latin American descent were not officially homogenized into one ethnic group nor were they identified as such by the State. She goes on to explore the consequences of labels for shaping identities, behaviors, and expectations, suggesting that panethnic labels are often more than convenient bureaucratic methods of categorization. Sometimes they are sources of social stigmatization that not only define people as "non-white" but also undermine the differences within Latino populations (see also Lopez and Stanton-Salazar 2001). As Omi and Winant (1996: 472; see also Winant 1995) have argued, "both a politics of inclusion and exclusion are involved in panethnicity, as racial and ethnic definitions and boundaries are contested." These references to inclusion and exclusion, to self-definition or imposed categorization, and to boundaries lead directly to the question of ethnicity as a theoretical concept.

ETHNICITY: THE SIGNIFICANCE OF BOUNDARIES IN OTHER/SELF-DEFINITION

Early conceptualizations of ethnicity focused on the boundedness of groups and an almost crass either/or distinction between being ethnic or nonethnic. Ethnic identity was thought to emerge from deep primordial attachments to a group or culture (Banks 1996; Jenkins 1997). But in 1969 the anthropologist Frederik Barth published an edited volume titled *Ethnic Groups and Boundaries: The Social Organization of Cultural Difference*. This book revolutionized thinking about ethnicity and the ethnic group. Barth (1969: 10) argued that ethnic groups are "categories of ascription and identification by the actors themselves, and thus have the characteristic of organizing interaction between people." Barth conceptualized "boundaries" not as something that circumscribes but as a locus of social interactions that mark difference and shape identity. He called on scholars to focus on the conscious use of ethnic identity by individuals across these boundaries, rather than on the "cultural stuff" of some sort of bounded social unit. In short, Barth shifted attention away from an external definition of ethnicity and toward an insider and subjective definition. Some have encapsulated Barth's paradigmatic shift more simply— he moved the discussion from a conceptualization of ethnicity as an aspect of culture to ethnicity as an aspect of social organization:

> Ethnic groups are not simply the automatic by-product of pre-existing cultural differences, but are the consequences of organizational work undertaken by their members who, for whatever reason, are marked off and mark themselves off from other collectivities in a process of inclusion and exclusion which differentiates "us" from "them." (Donnan and Wilson 1999: 21)

In an early article that reviewed the impact of Barth's work, Ronald Cohen (1978: 387) also referred to these processes of inclusion and exclusion based on "a series of nesting dichotomizations." But he further argued, somewhat contrary to Barth, that ethnic group boundaries, rather than being stable and continuous, are "multiple and overlapping sets of ascriptive loyalties that make for multiple identities" (387). Although Williams (1989) thinks that this approach by Cohen replicates old-fashioned structural functional lineage segment thinking, I disagree. What Cohen allows us to consider is the multiple identities that any single person can draw upon or, to put it in more contemporary theoretical terms, the various social locations from which they operate. Depending on context, individuals will invoke one or more of these nested identities or social locations.

The impact of Barth's formulation was particularly important for scholars of assimilation and acculturation, the two reigning theoretical models for social and cultural change into the 1960s. It allowed them to accept that rather than break down in situations of contact—ethnic boundaries might in fact be reinforced or even newly created. While Barth was not speaking to migration scholars at the time (indeed all the contributors to the volume were working on the more traditional societies studied by anthropologists—Laotians, Lapps, Pathans, Sudanese, Ethiopians, Mexican peasants in Chiapas, Norwegian peasants), clearly his reconceptualization of ethnicity was of enormous importance for those trying to understand the impact of immigration on those who displaced themselves to live, work, and raise their families in a new country. Of particular significance in Barth's formulation was the emphasis on the situational and fluid aspects of ethnicity and ethnic identity. Ethnicity could be constructed in specific social contexts, and often was in order to achieve certain ends. As Castles and Miller (2003: 35) have recently argued, ethnicity only becomes socially and politically meaningful "when it is linked to processes of boundary drawing between dominant groups and minorities." However, we should add that such boundaries also exist between one minority group and another, again depending on the parameters according to which they are drawn.

In a recent reevaluation of Barth's contribution, Jenkins (1997: 40) outlines four elements of what he calls the "social constructionist" model of ethnicity:

1. ethnicity emphasizes cultural differentiation (with the caveat that identity is always a dialectic between similarity and difference);
2. ethnicity is cultural—based in shared meanings—but is produced and reproduced in social interactions;
3. ethnicity is to some extent variable and manipulable, not definitively fixed or unchanging; and
4. ethnicity as a social identity is both collective and individual, externalized and internalized.

In discussing the difference between "race" and "ethnicity" Jenkins emphasizes that while race relations are hierarchical, exploitative, and conflictual, ethnic social relations are generally not. And while race is a question of social categorization, ethnicity is about group, and one might also add individual, identity. More broadly, however, both concepts stress the boundaries between "we" and "they." The question is who does the defining and whether the emphasis is on forging internal solidarity, contrasting solidarity, or both (Eriksen 1995).

It is in relation to this question that the issue of structure and agency can be brought into the debate and indeed it is for his lack of appreciation of structural constraints that Barth has been most criticized (Donnan and Wilson 1999; Jenkins 1997). Actors may have a lot of freedom in constructing particular identities in particular situations, but ultimately their choices are constrained by the broader society within which they operate. It is precisely this dilemma that shapes the way that the Haitian immigrants discussed above operate—trying to manipulate their Haitian and French identity in the context of a social and economic order that evaluates and hierarchizes based on phenotypical markers like skin color. Susan Greenbaum (2002: 9) has perhaps captured the issue most imaginatively. "Race," she writes, "is a uniform you wear, and ethnicity is a team on which you play."

BORDERS AND BOUNDARIES IN THE STUDY OF IMMIGRATION

By definition, international migration involves crossing legal/political borders that can be closed or open; guarded or unattended; effective or penetrated. Equally people meet and mix in borderland areas, forming what some have described as hybrid cultures or hybrid identities (Alvarez 1995; Anzaldua 1987; Donnan and Wilson 1999). Migration studies itself operates in the liminal space of disciplinary borderlands. Indeed scholars in different disciplines conceptualize borders and boundaries in a variety of ways.

Economists often measure the economic impact of the geographic displacement of labor across borders. They calculate the benefits and costs of migration to individual migrants who often incur significant debt as part of their decision to move; to sending societies that may experience a brain drain or a significant infusion of resources through emigrant remittances; and to receiving societies that can take advantage of cheap labor and/or the high human capital of newcomers, but must also assume the responsibility of caring for and/or educating the children of immigrants (Borjas 2003; Borjas and Trejo 1991; Chiswick 2000; Funkhouser 1995; Kelly and Tran 1989). Zuhniser (2000) captures the complexity of this work by writing of "one border, two crossings" while Engel and Rogers (1996) ask "How Wide Is the Border?" in their effort to measure how political borders disrupt the flow of goods and services. Some economists have addressed the economic impact of social boundaries, racial, ethnic, or religious. For example, Model and Lin (2003) ask about "the cost of not being Christian" for Hindu, Sikh, and Muslim immigrants in Britain and Canada.

Political scientists are interested in the implications of border control for various issues ranging from the rights of citizenship to national sovereignty (Cornelius, Martin, and Hollifield 1994; Hollifield 2000; Jacobson 1996). Some scholars challenge the efficacy of tighter border controls. For example, Cornelius (2001) argues that U.S. government restrictions since 1993, rather than reducing illegal entry, have simply resulted in more "deaths at the border" and escalating costs of smuggling. Taking a somewhat different approach, Soysal (1994) argues that the global discourse of human rights crosses national borders and impacts the efforts of states to fortify boundaries through the implementation of restrictive border controls. This research addresses the "battle of the border" so aptly described by Rodriguez (1996a):

> The battle for the border . . . is about the changing significance of nation-states in the global order, and thus of the changing relevance of nation-state boundaries. It is a struggle to maintain nation-state borders in a global context made increasingly fluid by heightened transnational migration of capital and labor. (23)

Political scientists have equally become interested in the legal boundaries that states construct and manage that separate citizens from immigrants and the implications of these for political participation and political incorporation

(Aleinikoff and Klusmeyer 2002; Bloemraad 2002, 2003; Gerstle and Mollenkopf 2001; Hammar 1990). Finally, there are those who are beginning to explore how immigrants negotiate extraterritorial (beyond border) citizenship and hence engage in political transnationalism (Fitzgerald 2000; Guarnizo 2001).

Transnationalism is of course a concept that is shared by migration scholars in a host of disciplines, but perhaps addressed most energetically by anthropologists and sociologists (Castles 2003; Glick Schiller 1999, 2003; Glick-Schiller, Basch, and Szanton-Blanc 1992; Levitt 2001; Mahler 2001; Portes 2001; Smith and Guarnizo 1998; Vertovec 1999). It invokes an idea of "blurred borders" (Goldring 1996). "Transnational communities," Rodriguez (1996a: 29) writes, "carry out functions of social reproduction across international boundaries as if these boundaries did not exist." Kearney (1991) has argued that because transnational migrants are able to operate in a borderless world that transcends the nation-state,

> native, non-ethnic white citizens avail themselves of the only totemic capital that they have available to form an identity from an inevitable dialectic of opposition with non-nationalist communities which are forming on and within their boundaries. And that totemic capital is of course nationalism (with a strong dash of racism). (59)

He suggests that having lost the battle of geographic space, they wage the battle of identity in social and cultural space, with English-only laws, Proposition 187, and the like. Migrants, on the other hand, in reaction to the economic necessity of migration but the denial of legalization in the United States, adopt a transnational identity that Kearney labels ethnicity, "the supremely appropriate form for collective identity to take in the age of transnationalism" (62). While Kearney applies this to an analysis of the Mixtecs in particular, it has broader application as a way to understand issues of race, ethnicity, and immigration in the context of borders and boundaries that are constructed or transgressed. Thus we return to the idea of border as a social relation that is rooted in subjective identities.

OVERVIEW OF THE VOLUME

The essays in this volume span historical time. They engage different methodologies, ranging from close textual analyses, to quantitative analysis with large data sets, to more qualitative approaches. Some have comparative dimensions and others are in-depth analyses of a single immigrant population. The volume, like migration studies itself, is multidisciplinary; the contributing authors include historians, sociologists, political scientists, and anthropologists.

In order to address broadly the questions raised by this introduction, the book is divided into three sections. In the first section two authors tackle the construction of racial/ethnic categories, and hence identities, in an historical context. Alexander X. Byrd writes about Gustavus Vassa (Olaudah Equiano), an enslaved African who wrote a memoir. Byrd argues that the identity of African slaves like Vassa was forged in passage and shaped by the institution of slavery. Indeed, his essay reminds us of many discussions about the hierarchal and situational nature of identity construction among migrants, whether internal or international. David Manuel Hernández tackles the role of the state through the agent of detention centers and detention practice in constructing immigrant identities. He outlines the racialized basis for distinguishing the citizen from the noncitizen in twentieth- and twenty-first-century America.

The chapters in the second section of this book focus on intergroup relations. Each author begins with groups that have something in common and explores shared or differential experiences, as well as the way that identities are shaped and boundaries are constructed to emphasize commonality or difference. Norma Fuentes analyzes the intersection of immigration, gender, and household structures (or class) among two Latina populations in New York. She argues that these constructs contribute to the formation of a racialized identity for Dominicans and an ethnicized identity for Mexicans. Jamillah Karim asks whether Islam creates solidarity between immigrant Muslims and African American Muslims. She describes the complex class and color lines that exist within the American Muslim *ummah* (community) and the multiple ethnic expressions of Islam that are the result. But she equally addresses the common Islamic commitment to justice that facilitates border crossings within this same community. Alana Hackshaw examines differences in racial identity among Caribbean blacks and African Americans, contrasting attitudes of the first generation with those of the second. She is particularly interested in what the differences mean for a common political cause (race politics) among blacks in America. Finally, Mariel Rose explores the shifting racial and ethnic boundaries among Mexicans, Blacks, Whites, and Indians in western North Carolina, a region of the United States where immigration is something new. Rather than focusing on workplace integration, Rose tackles the intimacies of racial/ethnic border crossings in the context of a nightclub where men and women from different backgrounds gather each weekend. Like Karim, she introduces the concept of class which, in this case, facilitates rather than deters interaction because no matter what the racial and ethnic differences everyone shares a similar working-class background.

The chapters in the final section of the book explore how race and ethnicity shape the economic lives of immigrants. More specifically, each author addresses the question of whether making ethnic identity salient works to advantage immigrants (i.e., it is a strategic resource) or to disadvantage them. Johanna Shih discusses how white women and Asian men and women in the Silicon Valley use their social capital to job-hop when they think they have encountered discrimination in the workplace. Zulema Valdez examines the effects of both social capital and residential concentration on entrepreneurship, noting that one allows immigrants to transgress boundaries while the other constructs them. She problematizes the supposedly positive effects of enclave economies to economic and social incorporation. Aviva Zeltzer-Zubida is also interested in how race and ethnicity, as organizing principles of the labor market trajectories of immigrants and their children, affect economic mobility and social incorporation. She too emphasizes that while co-ethnicity can be a safety net for individuals in some groups, it is a springboard for those in others. Finally, Cynthia Feliciano who, like Zeltzer-Zubida, focuses on the second generation, draws on a large data set to address immigrant selectivity and its impact on outcomes for the children of immigrants. She captures the less tangible forms of capital that vary from one group to another.

The dramatic demographic changes brought by the growth and diversification of the immigrant population since 1965 has transformed race relations in the cities and smaller towns of urban America. We can no longer conceive of race as being based on the binary opposition between black and white. Rather we must, as Rodriguez (1996b: 111) has suggested, consider the "multidimensional axes of ethnicity, immigrant status, nationality, race, and other social identities." The essays in this volume make both substantive and theoretical contributions to this multidimensional understanding of race, ethnicity, and the incorporation of immigrations.

NOTES

1. See, for example, Portes and Zhou (1993); Portes (1996); Portes and Rumbaut (2001); Rumbaut and Portes (2001); Levitt and Waters (2002).

2. All figures are from the U.S. Census, 1990 and 2000.

3. Historian Marilyn Halter stressed this point in her role as the discussant for the opening panel of the final International Migration Fellows Conference sponsored by the Social Science Research Council. The essays in this book were all initially presented at this conference and have been revised for this volume. See also Halter (1993). It is worth noting that equally the study of race relations has come late to the acknowledgement of diversity within the black population in the United States (see Foner 1987).

4. Undoubtedly research on African immigrants might also yield similar results but these populations have not, as yet, been well studied.

5. Glick Schiller and Fouron (1990) make similar observations.

6. Greenbaum (2002: 21) describes a similar process among Afro-Cubans in the Tampa area who accentuate their Cubanness in order to "minimize their blackness."

7. Whiteness has also been taken up by literary scholars (Morrison 1992). Mark Twain scholar Shelley Fisher Fishkin (1995) suggests that in the early 1990s "our ideas of whiteness were interrogated, our ideas of 'blackness' were complicated, and the terrain we call 'American culture' was remapped."

8. This "Chinese" label was equally applied to the French Canadians who migrated south of the border to work in the textile mills of New England. Of particular interest is Loewen's (1971) book on the Chinese in Mississippi who became white by defining themselves as not black in the most rigidly dichotomized social system in the country.

9. The California laws prohibiting marriage between people of different races were not repealed until 1948. See the discussion in Leonard (1997). Lee (1993) notes that the census classification for South Asians has shifted over the course of the twentieth century. They have been categorized as Hindu, White, Other, and Asian.

10. See the discussion in Rangaswamy (2000: 296–97). For a somewhat different perspective see Morning (2001). See Kibria (2002) for a discussion of the racialization of ethnic labels for Asian immigrants in the United States.

REFERENCES

Alba, Richard. 1981. "The Twilight of Ethnicity among American Catholics of European Ancestry." *Annals of the American Academy of Political and Social Sciences* 454: 86–97.

Aleinikoff, T. Alexander, and Douglas Klusmeyer (eds.). 2002. *Citizenship Policies for an Age of Migration*. Washington, DC: Carnegie Endowment for International Peace.

Allen, Theodore W. 1994. *The Invention of the White Race*. London and New York: Verso.

Alvarez, Robert. 1995. "The Mexican-US Border: The Making of an Anthropology of Borderlands." *Annual Review of Anthropology* 24: 447–70.

Anzaldua, G. 1987. *Borderlands/la Frontera: The New Mestiza*. San Francisco: Aunt Lute.

Bailey, Benjamin. 2001. "Dominican-American Ethnic/Racial Identities and United States Categories." *International Migration Review* 35: 677–708.

Banks, Marcus. 1996. *Ethnicity: Anthropological Constructions*. London: Routledge.

Barth, Frederik. 1969. "Introduction." Pp. 9–38 in *Ethnic Groups and Boundaries: The Social Organization of Cultural Difference*, ed. Frederik Barth. London: George Allen & Unwin.

Bloemraad, Irene. 2002. "The North American Naturalization Gap: An Institutional Approach to Citizenship Acquisition in the United States and Canada." *International Migration Review* 36: 193–228.

———. 2003. "Institutions, Ethnic Leaders, and the Political Incorporation of Immigrants: A Comparison of Canada and the United States." Pp. 361–402 in *Host Societies and the Reception of Immigrants*, ed. Jeffrey Reitz. San Diego: Center for Comparative Immigration Studies.

Bobb, Vilna Cashi. 2001. "Neither Ignorance nor Bliss: Race, Racism, and the West Indian Immigrant Experience." Pp. 212–38 in *Migration, Transnationalization, and Race in a Changing New York*, ed. Hector R. Cordero-Guzman, Robert C. Smith, and Ramon Grosfoguel. Philadelphia: Temple University Press.

Borjas, George J. 2003. "Welfare Reform and Immigrant Participation in Welfare Programs." Pp. 289–325 in *Host Societies and the Reception of Immigrants*, ed. Jeffrey Reitz. San Diego: Center for Comparative Immigration Studies.

Borjas, George J., and Stephen J. Trejo. 1991. "Immigrant Participation in the Welfare System." *Industrial and Labor Relations Review* 44: 195–211.

Brodkin, Karen. 1998. *How Jews Became White Folks and What That Says about Race in America*. Brunswick, NJ: Rutgers University Press.

Castles, Stephen. 2003. "Transnational Communities: A New Form of Social Relations under Conditions of Globalization?" Pp. 429–45 in *Host Societies and the Reception of Immigrants*, ed. Jeffrey Reitz. San Diego: Center for Comparative Immigration Studies.

Castles, Stephen, and Mark J. Miller. 2003. *The Age of Migration*. 3rd edition. New York: Guilford Press.

Chiswick, Barry R. 2000. "Are Immigrants Favorably Self-Selected?: An Economic Analysis." Pp. 61–76 in *Migration Theory: Talking across Disciplines*, ed. Caroline B. Brettell and James F. Hollifield. New York: Routledge.

Cohen, Ronald. 1978. "Ethnicity: Problem and Focus in Anthropology." *Annual Review of Anthropology* 7: 379–403.

Cornelius, Wayne. 2001. "Death at the Border: Efficacy and Unintended Consequences of U.S. Immigration Control Policy." *Population and Development Review* 27: 661–85.

Cornelius, Wayne A., L. Philip Martin, and James F. Hollifield, eds. 1994. *Controlling Immigration: A Global Perspective*. Stanford, CA: Stanford University Press.

Das Gupta, Monisha. 1997. "'What Is Indian about You?: A Gendered Transnational Approach to Ethnicity." *Gender and Society* 11: 572–96.

Donnan, Hastings, and Thomas M. Wilson. 1999. *Borders: Frontiers of Identity, Nation and State*. Oxford: Berg Publishers.

Engel, Charles, and John H. Rogers. 1996. "How Wide Is the Border?" *American Economic Review* 86, no. 5: 1112–26.

Eriksen, Thomas Hylland. 1995. "We and Us: Two Modes of Group Identification." *Journal of Peace Research* 32: 427–36.

Espiritu, Yen Le. 1992. *Asian American Panethnicity: Bridging Institutions and Identities*. Philadelphia: Temple University Press.

———. 1997. *Asian American Women and Men*. Thousand Oaks, CA: Sage Publications.

Fishkin, Shelley Fisher. 1995. "Interrogating 'Whiteness,' Complicating 'Blackness': Remapping American Culture." *American Quarterly* 47: 428–66.

Fitzgerald, David. 2000. *Negotiating Extra-Territorial Citizenship: Mexican Migration and the Transnational Politics of Community*. San Diego: Center for Comparative Immigration Studies, University of California at San Diego, Monograph Series No. 2.

Flores, Juan. 1999. "Pan-Latino/Trans-Latino: Puerto Ricans in the 'New Nueva York.'" Pp. 107–32 in *Identities on the Move: Transnational Processes in North America and the Caribbean Basin*, ed. Liliana R. Goldin. Albany, NY: Institute for Mesoamerican Studies, University of Albany.

Foner, Nancy. 1987. "The Jamaicans: Race and Ethnicity among Migrants in New York City." Pp. 195–218 in *New Immigrants in New York*, ed. Nancy Foner. New York: Columbia University Press.

———. 2000. *From Ellis Island to JFK: New York's Two Great Waves of Immigration*. New York: Russell Sage.

———. 2001. "Introduction: New Immigrants in a New New York." Pp. 1–31 in *New Immigrants in New York*, ed. Nancy Foner. New York: Columbia University Press.

Frankenberg, Ruth. 1993. *White Women, Race Matters: The Social Construction of Whiteness*. Minneapolis: University of Minnesota Press.

Funkhouser, Edward. 1995. "Remittances from International Migration: A Comparison of El Salvador and Nicaragua." *Review of Economics and Statistics* 77: 137–46.

Gabaccia, Donna R. 2002. *Immigration and American Diversity: A Social and Cultural History*. Oxford: Blackwell Publishers.

Ganster, Paul, and David E. Lorey (eds.). 2005. *Borders and Border Politics in a Globalizing World*. Lanham, MD: Scholarly Resources Books.

Gerstle, Gary, and John Mollenkopf. 2001. *E Pluribus Unum? Contemporary and Historical Perspectives on Immigrant Political Incorporation*. New York: Russell Sage.

Glick Schiller, Nina. 1999. "Transmigrants and Nation-States: Something Old and Something New in the U.S. Immigrant Experience." Pp. 94–119 in *Handbook of International Migration: The American Experience*, ed. Charles Hirschman, Philip Kasinitz, and Josh DeWind. New York: Russell Sage.

———. 2003. "The Centrality of Ethnography in the Study of Transnational Migration: Seeing the Wetlands Instead of the Swamp." Pp. 99–128 in *American Arrivals: Anthropology Engages the New Immigration*, ed. Nancy Foner. Santa Fe: School of American Research.

Glick Schiller, Nina, Linda Basch, and Cristina Szanton-Blanc (eds.). 1992. *Towards a Transnational Perspective on Migration: Race, Class, Ethnicity, and Nationalism Reconsidered*. New York: New York Academy of Sciences.

Glick Schiller, Nina, and Georges Fouron. 1990. "'Everywhere we go, we are in danger': Ti Manno and the Emergence of a Haitian Transnational Identity." *American Ethnologist* 17: 329–47.

Goldring, Luin. 1996. "Blurring Borders: Constructing Transnational Community in the Process of Mexico-US Migration." *Research in Community Sociology* 6: 69–104.

Greenbaum, Susan. 2002: *More Than Black: Afro-Cubans in Tampa*. Gainesville: University of Florida Press.

Guarnizo, Luis Eduardo. 2001. "On the Political Participation of Transnational Migrants: Old Practices and New Trends." Pp. 213–63 in *E Pluribus Unum? Contemporary and Historical Perspectives on Immigrant Political Incorporation*, ed. Gary Gerstle and John Mollenkopf. New York: Russell Sage Foundation.

Guglielmo, Thomas A. 2003. *White on Arrival: Italians, Race, Color, and Power in Chicago, 1890–1945*. Oxford: Oxford University Press.

Halter, Marilyn. 1993. *Between Race and Ethnicity: Cape Verdean American Immigrants, 1860–1965*. Chicago: University of Illinois Press.

Hammar, Tomas. 1990. *Democracy and the Nation-State: Aliens, Denizens and Citizens in a World of International Migration*. Aldershot: Avebury.

Harrison, Faye. 1998. "Introduction: Expanding the Discourse on 'Race.'" *American Anthropologist* 100: 609–31.

Hollifield, James F. 2000. "The Politics of International Migration: How Can We 'Bring the State Back In?'" Pp. 137–86 in *Migration Theory: Talking across Disciplines*, ed. Caroline B. Brettell and James F. Hollifield. New York: Routledge

Ignatiev, Noel. 1995. *How the Irish Became White*. New York: Routledge.

Jacobson, David. 1996. *Rights across Borders: Immigration and the Decline of Citizenship*. Baltimore: Johns Hopkins University Press.

Jenkins, Richard. 1997. *Rethinking Ethnicity: Arguments and Explorations*. London: Sage Publications.

Kasinitz, Philip. 1992. *Caribbean New York: Black Immigrants and the Politics of Race*. Ithaca, NY: Cornell University Press.

Kasinitz, Philip, Juan Battle, and Ines Miyares. 2001. "Fade to Black? The Children of West Indian Immigrants in South Florida." Pp. 267–300 in *Ethnicities: Children of Immigrants in America*, ed. Ruben G. Rumbaut and Alejandro Portes. New York: Russell Sage Foundation.

Kearney, Michael. 1991. "Borders and Boundaries of State and Self at the End of Empire." *Journal of Historical Sociology* 4: 52–74.

Kelly, C. B., and B. N. Tran. 1989. "Remittances from Labour Migration: Evaluations, Performance, and Implications." *International Migration Review* 24: 500–525.

Kibria, Nazli. 2002. *Becoming Asian American: Second-Generation Chinese and Korean American Identities*. Baltimore: Johns Hopkins University Press.

Koc, Ismet, and Isil Onan. 2004. "International Migrants' Remittances and Welfare Status of the Left-Behind Families in Turkey." *International Migration Review* 38: 78–112.

Lee, S. M. 1993. "Racial Classifications in the U.S. Census: 1890–1990." *Ethnic and Racial Studies* 16: 75–94.

Leonard, Karen Isaksen. 1997. *The South Asian Americans*. Westport, CT: Greenwood Press.

Lessinger, Johanna. 2001. "Class, Race, and Success: Two Generations of Indian Americans Confront the American Dream." Pp. 167–90 in *Migration, Transnationalization, and Race in a Changing New York,* ed. Hector R. Cordero Guzman, Robert C. Smith, and Ramon Grosfoguel. Philadelphia: Temple University Press.

Levitt, Peggy. 2001. "Transnational Migration: Taking Stock and Future Directions." *Global Networks* 3: 195–216.

Levitt, Peggy, and Mary C. Waters. 2002. *The Changing Face of Home: The Transnational Lives of the Second Generation.* New York: Russell Sage.

Lieberson, Stanley, and Mary Waters. 1988. *From Many Strands: Ethnic and Racial Groups in Contemporary America.* New York: Russell Sage

Loewen, James W. 1971. *The Mississippi Chinese: Between Black and White.* Cambridge, MA: Harvard University Press.

Lopez, David E., and Ricardo D. Stanton-Salazar. 2001. "Mexican Americans: A Second Generation at Risk." Pp. 57–90 in *Ethnicities: Children of Immigrants in America,* ed. Ruben G. Rumbaut and Alejandro Portes. New York: Russell Sage Foundation.

Mahler, Sarah J. 2001. "Transnational Relationships: The Struggle to Communicate across Borders." *Identities* 7: 583–619.

Maira, Sunaina Marr. 2002. *Desis in the House: Indian American Youth Culture in New York City.* Philadelphia: Temple University Press.

Massey, Douglas S. 1995. "The New Immigration and Ethnicity in the United States," *Population and Development Review* 21: 631–52.

Massey, Douglas S., Jorge Durand, and Nolan J. Malone. 2002. *Beyond Smoke and Mirrors: Mexican Immigration in an Era of Economic Integration.* New York: Russell Sage Foundation.

Massey, Douglas S., and Audrey Singer. 1995. "New Estimates of Undocumented Mexican Migration and the Probability of Apprehension." *Demography* 32: 203–13.

Melville, Margarita B. 1983. "Ethnicity: An Analysis of its Dynamism and Variability Focusing on the Mexican/Anglo/Mexican American Interface." *American Ethnologist* 10: 272–89.

———. 1989. "Hispanics: Race, Class, or Ethnicity?" *Journal of Ethnic Studies* 16: 67–83.

Model, Suzanne, and Lang Lin. 2003. "The Cost of Not Being Christian: Hindus, Sikhs, and Muslims in Britain and Canada." Pp. 181–214 in *Host Societies and the Reception of Immigrants,* ed. Jeffrey Reitz. San Diego: Center for Comparative Immigration Studies.

Morning, Ann. 2001. "The Racial Self-Identification of South Asians in the United States." *Journal of Ethnic and Migration Studies* 27: 61–79.

Morrison, Toni. 1992. *Playing in the Dark: Whiteness and the Literary Imagination.* Cambridge, MA: Harvard University Press.

Nagata, Judith A. 1974. "What Is a Malay? Situational Selection of Ethnic Identity in a Plural Society." *American Ethnologist* 1: 331–50.

Oboler, Suzanne. 1999. "Racializing Latinos in the United States: Toward a New Research Paradigm." Pp. 45–68 in *Identities on the Move: Transnational Processes in*

North America and the Caribbean Basin, ed. Liliana R. Goldin. Albany, NY: Institute for Mesoamerican Studies, University of Albany.

Omi, Michael, and Howard Winant. 1996. "Contesting the Meaning of Race in the Post Civil Rights Movement Era." Pp. 470–78 in *Origins and Destinies*, ed. Silvia Pedraza and Ruben G. Rumbaut. Belmont, CA: Wadsworth Publishing Company.

Portes, Alejandro (ed.). 1996. *The New Second Generation*. New York: Russell Sage Foundation.

Portes, Alejandro. 2001. "Introduction: The Debates and Significance of Immigrant Transnationalism." *Global Networks* 1: 181–94.

Portes, Alejandro, and Ruben G. Rumbaut. 2001. *Legacies: The Story of the Immigrant Second Generation*. Berkeley: University of California Press.

Portes, Alejandro, and Min Zhou. 1993. "The New Second Generation: Segmented Assimilation and Its Variants among Post-1965 Immigrant Youth." *Annals of the American Academy of Political and Social Sciences* 530: 74–96.

Rangaswamy, Padma. 2000. *Namaste America: Indian Immigrants in an American Metropolis*. University Park: Pennsylvania State University Press.

Rodriguez, Nestor. 1996a. "The Battle for the Border: Notes on Autonomous Migration, Transnational Communities, and the State." *Social Justice* 23: 21–37.

——. 1996b. "U.S. Immigration and Intergroup Relations in the Late 20th Century: African Americans and Latinos." *Social Justice* 23: 111–24.

Roediger, David R. 1991. *The Wages of Whiteness: Race and the Making of the American Working Class*. London: Verso.

Rosaldo, Renato. 1989. *Culture and Truth: The Remaking of Social Analysis*. Boston: Beacon Press.

Rumbaut, Ruben G., and Alejandro Portes (eds.). 2001. *Ethnicities: Children of Immigrants in America*. New York: Russell Sage Foundation.

Sanchez, George J. 1999a. "Race, Nation and Culture in Recent Immigration Studies." *Journal of American Ethnic History* 19: 66–84.

——. 1999b. "Face the Nation: Race, Immigration, and the Rise of Nativism in Late Twentieth-Century America." Pp. 371–382 in *The Handbook of International Migration: The American Experience*, ed. Charles Hirschman, Philip Kasinitz, and Josh DeWind. New York: Russell Sage Foundation.

Smith, Michael Peter, and Luis Eduardo Guarnizo (eds.). 1998. *Transnationalism From Below*. New Brunswick, NJ: Transaction Books.

Smith, Robert C., Hector R. Cordero-Guzman, and Ramon Grosfoguel. 2001. "Introduction: Migration, Transnationalization, and Ethnic and Racial Dynamics in a Changing New York." Pp. 1–32 in *Migration, Transnationalization, and Race in a Changing New York*, ed. Hector R. Cordero-Guzman, Robert C. Smith, and Ramon Grosfoguel. Philadelphia: Temple University Press.

Soysal, Yasemin. 1994. *Limits of Citizenship: Migrants and Postnational Membership in Europe*. Chicago: University of Chicago Press.

Stafford, Susan Buchanan. 1987. "The Haitians: The Cultural Meaning of Race and Ethnicity." Pp. 131–58 in *New Immigrants in New York*, ed. Nancy Foner. New York: Columbia University Press.

Stepick, Alex. 1998. *Pride against Prejudice: Haitians in the United States*. Boston: Allyn & Bacon.

Vertovec, Stephen. 1999. "Conceiving and Researching Transnationalism." *Ethnic and Racial Studies* 22: 447–62.

Vickerman, Milton. 2001. "Jamaicans: Balancing Race and Ethnicity." Pp. 201–28 in *New Immigrants in New York*, ed. Nancy Foner. New York: Columbia University Press.

Warren, Jonathan W., and Frances W. Twine. 1997. "White Americans, The New Minority? Non-Blacks and the Ever-Expanding Boundaries of Whiteness." *Journal of Black Studies* 28: 200–218.

Waters, Mary C. 1994. "Ethnic and Racial Identities of Second-Generation Black Immigrants in New York City." *International Migration Review* 28: 795–820.

Williams, Brackette F. 1989. "A Class Act: Anthropology and the Race to Nation across Ethnic Terrain." *Annual Review of Anthropology* 18: 401–44.

Winant, Howard. 1995. "Dictatorship, Democracy, and Difference: The Historical Construction of Racial Identity." Pp. 50–76 in *The Bubbling Cauldron: Race, Ethnicity and the Urban Crisis*, ed. Michael Peter Smith and Joe R. Feagin. Minneapolis: University of Minnesota Press.

Zuhniser, Steven S. 2000. "One Border, Two Crossings: Mexican Migration to the United States as a Two-Way Process." Pp. 242–76 in *Immigration Research for a New Century: Multidisciplinary Perspectives*, ed. Nancy Foner, Ruben G. Rumbaut, and Steven J. Gold. New York: Russell Sage Foundation.

I

RACE AND ETHNICITY

Categories, Labels, and the Construction of Identity

Introduction to Part I

The two chapters in this section address the topic of how racial and ethnic categories are constructed. Both authors adopt an historical perspective, thereby establishing continuities between the past and the present. Both focus on the role of coercive institutions—whether the economic institution of slavery or the politico-legal institution of the detention center—in defining who people are. Both demonstrate the power of racialized labels in situating individuals and groups in a social hierarchy and thus legitimizing a particular set of attitudes or corpus of behaviors directed toward them. Both focus on how boundaries are constructed or transgressed as part of the process of defining who migrants are. And finally, both describe a process of alienation that characterizes migration—whether the alienation from home that occurs as the migrant moves from sending to host society or the alienation that accompanies being defined as foreigner and non-citizen once the migrant is abroad.

In his chapter, Alexander X. Byrd engages in a close textual reading of *The Interesting Narrative of the Life of Olaudah Equiano* (1789), also known as Gustavus Vassa, to argue that Igbo identity was forged in the process of migration from the interior of Africa to the coast and during the middle passage to North America. It was not simply transported and transplanted from one specific place to the New World. Rather, Byrd argues that Eboe (or Igbo) identity emerged in the "holding pattern" of the coastal towns of West Africa as people from the interior were assembled and categorized with a single label that indicated their foreignness—as being from the interior. Byrd's argument lends nuance to Eric Wolf's (1982: 380) argument that racial categories are the outcome of the subjugation of populations in the course of European mercantile expansion by stressing that subjugated populations themselves learned how to adapt to these circumstances and, in the process, were able to preserve some sense of their own personhood. The extreme and prolonged violence of enslavement and Africans' human response to that violence, argues Byrd, was fundamental to creating and shaping African ethnic identity in the Americas.

Byrd's chapter is innovative for several reasons. First, it links the forced migration experience of slavery to broader migration studies, but stresses that it was a particular kind of migration. His essay should be seen as a contribution to recent efforts to integrate the African American experience with other migration experiences. Quite recently, for example, Pedraza and Rumbaut (1996) have included the "Great Migration" of African Americans from the rural south to the cities of the north, in the interwar period and later, with the broader history of immigration to the United States. The challenges to personhood and identity that the first black African immigrants to the United States faced, or that internal African American migrants have faced, have much in common with the challenges faced by other immigrants, albeit they were often more dehumanizing and more harshly racializing. But becoming something that one has never been—Igbo, West Indian, South Asian, Hispanic—is a common outcome of geographical displacement and/or the amalgamation process that occurs as people from diverse places gather in urban centers throughout the world.

Second, Byrd demonstrates that identity is as much imposed from the outside as it is constructed from the inside. First the slave traders collectively referred to the tens of thousands of Africans gathered in the port cities of West Africa as "Heebo" lumping together what were undoubtedly people from different points of origin. Second, Africans in the Biafran interior used the term to describe strangers and foreigners; that is, imprecisely identified others from other points in the interior. And third, captives came to identify themselves as Igbo because in the context of the shared experience of slavery and migration they needed to find and found connection. "The serial displacement and violence inherent to slave trading in the interior," Byrd writes, "prepared the way for people who previously would not have known themselves as Igbo to begin to identify themselves as such." Here Byrd's argument resonates with similar arguments made, for example, by scholars of Italian migration who have described how people from Abruzzi or Calabrese or Palermo became Italian only after arriving in the United States. Migration involves a process of becoming, of, as Byrd puts it, uprooting and regrouping.

In a very timely essay, David Manuel Hernández focuses on the historical underpinnings of immigrant detention, something about which Americans have become increasingly aware in the aftermath of 9/11 as Arab, Muslim, and South Asian immigrants have been subjected to intense scrutiny. Hernández argues that contemporary detention policies emerge from the historical dialectic between immigrant detention and the racialization and "othering" of non-citizens. By examining the production and categorization of immigrant detainees, known as "aliens" in government discourse, as diseased, as criminal, or as state enemies, Hernández demonstrates how race functions historically in the statutory production of "lesser citizenship" through immigrant detention and a systematic denial of due process. He emphasizes how the nexus of race, non-citizenship, and national security unveils new categories of lesser citizens, while simultaneously buttressing existing inequalities. The border that Hernández explores is not, as he writes, "the militarized border between the U.S. and its North American neighbors, but the social and structural divisions between citizens and non-citizens."

Indeed, Hernández asks us to think deeply about the politics of citizenship. At many times during the twentieth century, and most recently in the aftermath of 9/11, legal immigrants as well as native-born Americans of immigrant ancestry have been denied their rights. In the liminal space of detention centers or concentration camps (different kinds of borderlands), immigrant loyalties are challenged and the status of individuals is redefined. The boundaries between alien other and full citizen are more sharply delineated and, as national borders are secured, the differences between those who are welcome and those who are not becomes more blatant, bringing into question the very meaning of the definition of America as "a nation of immigrants." Deportations of the "unwelcome" are increased. In his references to the criminalization of immigrants that is part of this process, Hernández adds another dimension to Peter Schuck's (1999) argument about immigration as a victimless crime. Like Byrd, Hernández stresses that identity, in this case as a citizen, is defined by both self and other. It is about more than legal status; it is about being recognized as someone who belongs. In times of national crisis, wars, and terrorist threats, this recognition is often denied. Theoretically, then, both these authors further our understanding of the double boundaries of identities, "those from within and those from without, self-identifying and being identified by others" (Isajiw 1997: 90).

REFERENCES

Isajiw, Wsevolod W. 1997. "On the Concept and Theory of Social Incorporation." Pp. 79–102 in *Multiculturalism in North America and Europe*, ed. Wselvolod W. Isajiw. Toronto: Canadian Scholars Press.

Pedraza, Silvia, and Ruben G. Rumbaut (eds.). 1996. *Origins and Destinies*. Belmont, CA: Wadsworth Publishing Company.

Schuck, Peter. 1999. "Law and the Study of Migration." Pp. 187–204 in *Migration Theory: Talking across Disciplines*, ed. Caroline B. Brettell and James Hollifield. New York: Routledge.

Wolf, Eric. 1982. *Europe and the People without History*. Berkeley: University of California Press.

Violence, Migration, and Becoming Igbo in Gustavus Vassa's *Interesting Narrative*

Alexander X. Byrd

Among the lettered classes in eighteenth-century Great Britain, Gustavus Vassa was perhaps the best known African in the Empire. He penned correspondence to the London press, petitioned the government against the slave trade, and was the one time commissary to the nation's first colonial experiment in western Africa (the British settlement at Sierre Leone). In his lifetime, Vassa's memoir—*The Interesting Narrative of Olaudah Equiano, or Gustavus Vassa, the African* (1789)—went through nine British editions and was reviewed in such journals as the *Gentleman's Magazine* and *The Analytical Review* (Equiano 2001: 206–97 see figure 1.1). Among today's lettered classes, Vassa is still widely recognized and very nearly as widely read. Yet as things presently stand, some of the most affecting and cited sections of Vassa's life story—the details of his African origins, his enslavement, and his experience as a captive in the transatlantic slave trade—have come unmoored. As Vassa's most careful contemporary editor has recently pointed out, Gustavus Vassa, the African, may not have hailed, as indicated in his memoir, from Eboe behind the Bight of Biafra in what we now know as southeastern Nigeria. Rather, he may well have been a native of colonial South Carolina, as was recorded on the muster roll of a ship on which the future author sailed, as an able seaman, in the spring of 1773 (Carretta 2003; 1999; 2005).

This is a moment of uncertainty as far as Vassa's origins are concerned.[1] But inasmuch as Vassa's *Narrative* recounted what the author knew and learned about the slave trade from the region he sometimes called Eboe—let alone what he may have actually experienced—*The Interesting Narrative* still speaks to pressing questions in American slavery studies.[2] The book's account of the slave trade alongside its treatment of people and things Eboe is

Olaudah Equiano;

or

GUSTAVUS VASSA,

the African?

Published March 1 1789 by G. Vassa

Figure 1.1. Frontispiece and title page from Olaudah Equiano, *The Interesting Narrative of the Life of Olaudah Equiano, or Gustavus Vassa, the African,* 8th ed. (Norwich: 1794).

Source: Courtesy of the Library of Congress.

THE

INTERESTING NARRATIVE

OF

THE LIFE

OF

OLAUDAH EQUIANO,

OR

GUSTAVUS VASSA,

THE AFRICAN.

WRITTEN BY HIMSELF.

*Behold, God is my salvation; I will trust, and not be
afraid, for the Lord Jehovah is my strength and my
song; he also is become my salvation.
And in that day shall ye say, Praise the Lord, call upon his
name, declare his doings among the people.* Isa. xii. 2. 4.

EIGHTH EDITION ENLARGED.

NORWICH:

PRINTED FOR, AND SOLD BY THE AUTHOR.

1794.

PRICE FOUR SHILLINGS.

Formerly sold for 7s.

[Entered at Stationers' Hall.]

especially germane to how students of the African diaspora have come to analyze African ethnicity in the context of forced migration. It is now widely
held that the ways that African slaves identified themselves ethnically cannot
be properly understood if approached simply as artifacts of their former lives.
Igbo slaves in colonial Virginia (Igbo being the modern rendition of Vassa's
Eboe) were probably not unfortunate exiles from an Igbo heartland in western Africa. It is more likely, as John Thornton has pointed out, that as social
formations "African nations in the New World were new and unique to the
Americas," though they became, Thornton also holds, "the locus for the
maintenance of those elements of African culture that continued on American
soil" (1998: 321).

As reportage, documentary, and history—if not as memoir—*The Interesting Narrative* offers insight into the process of being and becoming Igbo, and
thus a good vantage from which to consider how migration figured into the
creation and functioning of so-called African nations in the eighteenth-
century Atlantic world. Closely read and contextualized with this particular
goal in mind, Vassa's *Narrative* substantiates three important points. First, although Vassa attempted in his *Interesting Narrative* to present Eboe as a more
or less stable, eighteenth-century, sociopolitical reality, it was not. Second, in
the eighteenth-century Atlantic world, the formation of an Igbo self-
consciousness depended first on Africans who did not formerly identify themselves as Igbo to begin to do just that. The violent, plodding, socially trans-
formative migration that was the slave trade from the Biafran interior to the
littoral catalyzed this process of identification (the origins of which are readily apparent in *The Interesting Narrative* even if the ways that Igbo identification became Igbo self-consciousness are less obvious). Third, consequently,
though John Thornton's ideas about the origins and nature of African nations
in the new world are both productive and provocative, the converse of Thornton's argument also merits careful consideration. As social formations, the
African nations associated with slave communities in the Americas—new
though they were—could and did indeed originate in Africa. But in spite of
their potential African origins, nations such as Vassa's Eboe were as much a
locus for and evidence of the destruction and transformation of African culture and society (if by African culture and society we mean the culture and
society of captives caught up in trade) as they were a locus for its maintenance and re-creation.

THE ENIGMATIC IGBO

Beginning in the 1740s, merchants and slave traders along the Biafran littoral
and their connections in the interior succeeded in consolidating long-existing

trade networks while aggressively forging new ones (Nwokeji 1999: esp. ch. 3; Northrup 1978: 54 and ch. 4). In the resulting commercial transformation, the trading men and women of the area began funneling more captives toward the Atlantic than at any other time in the region's history. From the turn of the eighteenth century to about 1740, for instance, Biafran slave traders provided, on average, less than 4,000 captives per year to Europe's premier slavers, the British. In the six succeeding decades, Biafran traders packed British ships with, on average, more than 14,000 captives per year (Richardson 1989: table 7). Counting slave deliveries to European slavers of all flags clarifies just how massive the trade became. In the second half of the eighteenth century, it appears that traffic from three Biafran towns—Bonny and Elem Kalabari (also known as New Calabar) in the eastern Niger Delta, and Old Calabar in the Cross River—accounted for a greater share of the total transatlantic traffic in slaves than any other three ports in western Africa (Eltis and Richardson 1997:

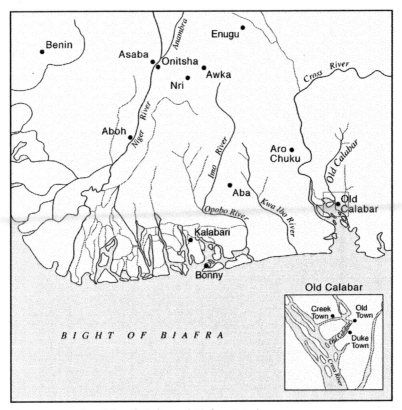

Figure 1.2.   The Bight of Biafra and Biafran Interior.

Source: Map drawn by the Cartographic Laboratory, Department of Geography, University of Wisconsin.

18–19, 29). Between them, quite simply, Bonny, New Calabar, and Old Calabar formed a nexus of trade, transport, and communication that helped to establish and then to sustain the Niger Delta-Cross River basin as one of the premier slaving regions of the second half of the eighteenth century (see figure 1.2).

Contemporaries had little doubt concerning the tens of thousands of Africans bound for the Americas from the Biafran coast. Most of the slaves sold at Bonny, Elem Kalabari, and Old Calabar, calculated slave trader John Adams, "are natives of one nation, called Heebo" (1966: 129). American planters engaged in the Africa trade adapted a similar descriptive nomenclature. Thus in a telling turn of phrase concerning the eighteenth-century British slave trade, Jamaican planter Simon Taylor called slave ships that arrived from the Biafran littoral "Eboe Men," instead of the more general Guineamen (Taylor 1789).

In spite of this contemporary certainty, however, there is good reason to doubt that many of the Africans who were called Eboe actually understood themselves as such (at least originally). In retrospect, this point became increasingly clear to Europeans who ventured beyond the Biafran coast in the nineteenth century or who were able to quiz so-called Igbo people on the matter themselves. The missionary and explorer Samuel Crowther had such an experience during a journey on the Niger in 1854. At a market near the confluence of the Niger and Benue Rivers, for example, he came across a "fancy cloth" said to be produced by the Igbo. Determined to find the manufacturers of the textile, Crowther continued downstream into the region his informants told him was the approach to their territory. Near the town of Onitsha, when Crowther inquired about the Igbo and the origins of the cloth he had in hand, a local trader answered him that the Onitsha people were indeed the manufacturers of the cloth and that the people upriver "not knowing the difference" tended to apply Igbo indiscriminately to all their southern neighbors (1970: 167–68, 173–77).[3] Even as late as the first decades of the twentieth century, the situation was not much changed when an enterprising, if somewhat overreaching, British colonial officer wrote as follows of his study of Igbo life in the area surrounding Onitsha:

An examination of the term Igbo shows that it belongs to the same category that the following words do in English. Viz. Kafir, Heathen; Barbarian, Welsh. All of these terms used in English are, with the exception of Heathen and Welsh, alien words used in alien languages to describe foreigners: i.e., persons not of the same race and language as the speaker. It would seem that Igbo is from a Sudanic root which means "bush" or people of the bush and its analogue in English would be Heathen, i.e., people of the heath. It is thus clear that as there is no heathen race or nation per se, so actually there is no Igbo race [or] language and none of the peoples described today as [Igbo] by the European will admit the term as descriptive of his race or language nor will he use it of himself. (Jeffreys 1937)

The author of this report was not correct in all matters, but he was quite on target concerning one important point: Historically, Igbo was a term that people in the Biafran interior tended to apply to strangers and foreigners, not to themselves (Shelton 1971: 6–7; Henderson 1972: 40–41; Forde and Jones 1962: 9).

CRUCIBLES OF IGBO IDENTIFICATION: SLAVERY AND THE SLAVE TRADE FROM THE BIAFRAN INTERIOR TO THE LITTORAL

Today, among scholars of the African diaspora, there is little argument about whether Igbo slaves in the New World exported an Igbo consciousness from some original Old World domicile (Chambers 2001; 2002; Northrup 2000).[4] Most, in all likelihood, did not. Still, efforts to sketch the means by which captives from the Biafran interior became Igbo have only just begun. Douglas Chambers has pioneered much of this work. He has argued that the roots of Igbo consciousness lie in various political, cultural, and material similarities that characterized life in the Biafran interior. According to Chambers, "An 'Eboan' collective identity developed, as slaves, once thrown into the diaspora, discovered ways of doing and of being which Igbo-speaking and Igbo-acting slaves shared" (2000: 57).[5] This is a sensible explanation, but inasmuch as it elides the fact that the development of Igbo consciousness was all but forced on enslaved Africans from the Biafran interior, the explanation risks a too benign understanding of the origins and meaning of Igbo consciousness in the Atlantic world.

For captives exported from such ports as Bonny, New Calabar, and Old Calabar, their experiences as enslaved migrants in the Biafran interior began in earnest a process of becoming Igbo. The slave trade, to be sure, did not turn men and women who may have formerly known themselves as Aboh people or Mbofia, for example, into Igbo in one fell swoop. What it did do and could do was begin a process of identification, a process by which captives from the Biafran interior were called and began to call themselves Igbo. Such identification was critical to an eventual shift in how they understood themselves and how they organized their subsequent society.[6] That this process was founded in violence and migration cannot be stressed enough, and this context has important consequences for our understanding of the development of Igbo consciousness and ethnicity.

In the popular imagination, the middle passage stands out as the defining moment of the Atlantic slave trade. Yet in perspective of time, the overseas voyage from the African littoral to the Americas represented perhaps the shortest leg of a captive's whole degrading odyssey. On average, for instance, English Guineamen calling at the Bight of Biafra sailed nearly seventy days to reach Jamaica. These same ships anchored at Biafran ports an average of 103 days collecting their human cargo (Klein 1978: 35). And even before reaching the ships, slaves from the interior could be many months moving from their former homes to the coast.[7]

The consequences of this trek through the interior should neither be overlooked nor underestimated. The trails captives followed in the interior were characterized by grinding, disjointed movement, and profound alienation whose total effect was to separate enslaved Africans from the physical and social moorings of their homelands. The trade forced captives into new connections and it attenuated former locally based ties and senses of self. In the end, the serial displacement and violence inherent to slave trading in the Biafran interior prepared the way for people who previously would not have known themselves as Igbo to begin to identify themselves as such.

The story Gustavus Vassa told of his enslavement in the Biafran interior, whether it represents his own experience or what he came to know about the slave trade, brings this process into clear view. One day, while the adults of his village were in their fields or otherwise engaged, the eleven-year-old Equiano and his sister were set upon in their father's compound by two men and a woman who, as Vassa put it, "got over our walls, and in a moment seized us both." Moving with expert stealth, the kidnappers bound and gagged the two children and dragged them out of the compound before either one was able to call for help or to offer any real resistance. The trio carried the children through the surrounding woods until nightfall, when they took refuge in a small house to eat, which the children refused, and to sleep, which the young captives welcomed (Equiano 2003: 47).

The next morning the thieves continued with their contraband. "For a long time," wrote Vassa, "we had kept the woods, but at last we came into a road which I believed I knew." The familiar road sparked hope in Equiano that they might yet be saved. Seeing a group of people on the byway, but at a distance, he cried for help. In response, his captors tied his limbs tighter, reapplied a gag, and placed him in a sack in which they carried him until nightfall. Once more they stopped for rest and sustenance but the children again refused to eat (Equiano 2003: 47).

The following morning the kidnappers stirred the two children from their slumber only to separate them. According to Vassa, though the siblings begged to be kept together, and though they held on to each other for dear life, the traders and the demands of the trade prevailed. "[S]he was torn from me and immediately carried away, while I was left in a state of distraction not to be described." Equiano's travels continued for many days afterwards, during which "he cried and grieved continually." For a time, he ate only what he was forced, and on this leg of his journey he changed masters frequently. His initial kidnappers passed him along the pathways of the interior; presumably, his sister suffered a similar fate (Equiano 2003: 47–48).

After some time in the trade, Equiano was at last purchased by a smith who employed the young slave in working the bellows of his forge and in assisting a slave woman with the cooking. He understood the dialect of the people, and though treated as an outsider—he was forbidden to eat with the free-born children and at times feared grave treatment at the hands of his master—he was at the very least finally set still. The stop, however, did not last. Before long he was sold away again (Equiano 2003: 48, 50). This time, the trader or traders who purchased Equiano marched him toward the sea. They carried him on their shoulders when he tired and could walk no further, and apparently he traveled in the company of others damned to similar fates. They marched and marched and marched, stopping only in the evenings to sleep. During this circuit of his journey, Equiano's path and that of his sister crossed once again. One evening when the traders who held him stopped for the night, those who had charge of his sister happened into the same way station. Their reunion lasted but one night. In the morning, they were again pushed separate ways (Equiano 2003: 50).

Following a great deal of travel through the interior, and after having changed hands at least three more times, Equiano was sold into a wealthy household somewhere in the Biafran wetlands, a town Vassa called Tinmah. He hoped it was his fortune to be adopted into this family, for they treated him more like a son than a slave. But after some two months, he was snatched from his bed in the early morning and sold away yet again. "The change I now experienced," Vassa wrote of the moment, "was as painful as it was sudden and unexpected." The overland journey that followed landed Equiano at "the banks of a large river, which was covered with canoes in which the people appeared to live with all their household utensils and provisions of all kinds." Here, he was placed into one of the dugouts "and continued to travel, sometimes by land, sometimes by water, through different countries and various nations, till at the end of six or seven months" he arrived at the coast (Equiano 2003: 52–54).

According to Vassa's account, the slave trade from the Biafran interior funneled captives from the uplands to the coast in spasms. The serial nature of the trade meant that captives were not only separated from their homes as time wore on, but they could not even count on remaining for long with fellow captives taken in the vicinity. For slaves, the consequence of such movement was the continuous introduction to new people and places. Moreover, though Vassa wrote little of the matter himself, the journey of enslaved Africans through the interior was characterized by levels of violence and denigration that compounded the inherent alienating effect of the movement itself. According to oral histories of the slave trade collected by Boniface Obichere, slaves were pushed hard through the elements and down the interior's roads and pathways, suffering all the while from hunger, disease, and maltreatment at the hands of their captors. When drivers encamped a slave coffle near a village or market for recuperation, the string of captives were usually held apart from the local population in adjacent areas designated for the use of slave traders and their prisoners. Slaves who perished on the way to market or at market were not buried. Rather, they were thrown to rot into the "bad bush," grounds used by local people to dispose of those who died tainted by some abomination. Slaves in transit, argues Obichere, suffered such harsh usage, in part, precisely because they were so far from home and thus so far from any potential protectors or relations. The slave coffles, quite simply, were full of the foreign born and strange accents. Slaves in transit were utter outsiders, pariahs, and they suffered as such (Obichere 1988: 48).[8]

In Vassa's *Interesting Narrative*, the effects of continual dislocation and the power slave owners held over captives is absolutely clear. Combined, the two phenomena dislodged captives from their former sense of society and place and encouraged them to work out and accept new connections. Relating Equiano's experience with the smith who was his first master, Vassa detailed this shift rather dramatically. After about a month in the smith's compound, Equiano was allowed some leeway from his betters. When trusted away from his master's compound, he connived constantly about how and whether he could make it back to his father's home. The information he gathered convinced him that if the right circumstances presented themselves, it was not out of the question to try to return home.

An opportunity soon arose. After having accidentally killed one of his master's fowls, Equiano ran to the thickets surrounding his owner's compound so as to escape punishment. While in hiding, he heard those seeking him suppose out loud that he was trying to make his way back to from where he came. They reasoned that "the distance was so great and the way so intricate" that the little slave would never reach his goal. He would die in the forest first. The conversation completely unnerved Equiano:

> I had before entertained hopes of getting home and I had determined when it should be dark to make the attempt, but I was now convinced it was fruitless and began to consider that, if possibly I could escape all other animals, I could not those of the human kind; and that, not knowing the way, I must perish in the wood. (Equiano 2003: 48–50)

Contrite and accepting what appeared to be his fate, the slave returned to his master.

Separated from his homeland by several months and many miles, Equiano resigned himself to the possibility that he might never again see his family. Thereafter, he attempted to insinuate himself into the ways and means of those among whom he was exiled. He mastered the dialects of his captors and whenever sold into another household tried in vain to make himself a transparent member of his new society. The sharp, serial displacement occasioned by the trade and the temporal separation it effected between Equiano and his home demanded as much (Equiano 2003: 51).[9]

In general, research on slavery in Africa reveals that the exigencies and transformations apparent in Vassa's *Interesting Narrative* are not at all uncommon to the condition. Reviewing more than fifteen local studies of slavery in Africa, Suzanne Miers and Igor Kopytoff have argued that enslavement and the internal African slave trade tended to inflict upon captives "a traumatic and sometimes violent withdrawal from kin, neighbors, and community, and often from familiar customs and language." So when first settled into new societies, captives were in a "state of marginality," their former senses of self and society necessarily enfeebled and new ones not yet fully determined (Kopytoff and Miers 1977: 14–15). In time, however, captives were often allowed to incorporate themselves into their new surroundings. Sometimes this incorporation led to captives achieving status as full members of their new society. More often it did not. But incorporation almost always entailed—and Vassa's *Interesting Narrative* provides but an eighteenth-century illustration—the slow recession of former social ties and the domestication of new ones (Kopytoff and Miers 1977: passim; Uchendu 1977: 121–32).

There is little evidence concerning what was on the minds of other eighteenth-century slaves pushed through the Biafran interior, but we do know that the displacement that formed Equiano's experience was not at all uncommon. Alexander Falconbridge—an abolitionist, formerly a surgeon in the Guinea trade, and familiar with affairs along the Niger Delta—believed that none of the slaves he saw boarded at Bonny were natives of the coast. He had quizzed several aboard the ships he served concerning their origins and was convinced from their replies that those loaded at Bonny came to port from a great distance and had passed "through several Hands" before arriving (House of Commons Sessional Papers 1975b: 48).[10] James Penny, himself the captain of a slave ship and no friend to abolitionists, conceded the same point in his testimony before Parliament. According to notes entered in the "Report of the Lords of the Committee of Council appointed for the Consideration of all Matters relating to Trade and Foreign Plantations," Penny attempted an icy precision in addressing the matter. "Mr. Penny believes," reads a summary of his testimony, "that some of the slaves are brought from Countries still more distant in the interior Parts of Africa":

> They sometimes find from the Slaves that they have travelled Two Moons (or Months) before they arrived at the Sea Coast. They may travel at the Rate of from Twenty to Twenty-five Miles a Day. (HCSP 1975a: 47)

Thus Penny conceded that he had regularly taken aboard his ship men and women who from appearances gave no reason to doubt that they had just been forcibly marched some 1,200 miles from the interior to the coast (HCSP 1975a: 47).

Penny's opinion is perhaps an exaggeration, but the assertion is useful because it directly confirms Falconbridge's claim concerning the great distances traveled by slaves loaded in the Niger Delta. Also, through its unintended allusion to the condition of slaves boarded at Bonny, Penny's testimony indirectly supports the contention that others loaded at Biafran ports had survived circumstances similar to those described in Vassa's *Interesting Narrative*. That is, during their journey toward the Atlantic they were *used* as slaves as well as *traded* as slaves. It is a point made more directly by a perceptive ship captain who, after waiting for slaves in the Bonny River for some two weeks with little to show for it, wondered whether the trade would soon pick up. In the interior, he reasoned, the harvest would soon be over. In all likelihood, farmers in the hinterlands would then release some of their slaves into the hands of traders, who in turn would funnel them toward the ships (Woodville 1791).[11]

After having passed through many hands in the hinterlands, slaves bound for the Atlantic were sold to the coast from markets on the outermost edges of the interior (Falconbridge 1788).[12] The arrival of enslaved Africans at these upland fairs marked their entry into the Atlantic world, and it is from the Atlantic that a clearer view emerges of not only how and why captives from the interior were described as Igbo but how they came to identify as Igbo as well. In contradistinction to circumstances in the interior, residents of the trading towns of the Biafran littoral held and articulated fairly well-developed notions of being Igbo. In a fundamental way, consequently, the origins of Igbo self-consciousness in the Americas probably owe a great deal to the nature of captives' sojourns along the Biafran coast—namely their continuing alienation within the urban contexts of such Atlantic towns as Bonny, Elem Kalabari, and Old Calabar and the commensurate expansion of internal and external pressures to identify as Igbo.

When European slavers anchored off Bonny, New Calabar, or Old Calabar, the principal traders of those towns dispatched people upriver to purchase slaves in bulk from the various trade fairs held on the near margins of the interior. As recalled by Alexander Falconbridge, preparations for such missions were "very considerable":

> From twenty to thirty canoes, capable of containing thirty or forty negroes each, are assembled for this purpose; and such goods put on board them as they expect will be wanted for the purchase of the number of slaves intended to buy. When their loading is completed, they commence their voyage, with colors flying and musick playing, and in about ten or eleven days, they generally return to Bonny with full cargoes. (Falconbridge 1788: 16)

The coastal traders loaded their canoes with goods acquired "on trust" from slave ship captains, and they were sometimes obliged to visit several markets before returning with a full complement. When demand was greatest, trading firms on the coast were capable of delivering enormous numbers of slaves. On a single day in April 1791, traders at Bonny busied themselves with the appetites of some thirteen ships then anchored in the river. All told, these vessels contained between them more than 4,000 slaves and were waiting for more (Woodville 1791).[13]

Laboring under such demands of volume, traders found it in their interest to expedite their missions upcountry. Under such conditions as prevailed at Bonny in April 1791, the more rounds a firm completed into the interior the greater its potential profits. In addition, canoe traders were under pressure to collect slaves from the interior before news concerning the number and/or status of ships at the coast reached the inland slave marts, for suppliers behind the coast set prices according to their perception of demand at the Atlantic (Falconbridge 1788: 17).

For slaves on sale at the fairs, these acute demands of the Atlantic African market translated into further degrees of degradation and alienation. Going upriver and back, traders gave only the slightest attention to the care of their cargo. A canoe trader was liable for the health of his slaves during the journey to the coast, but his responsibility expired eight to twelve hours after making a sale to a ship. Thus when at market, traders undoubtedly felt more pressure toward affecting a reasonable return time, acquiring a sufficient volume, and maintaining control over their cargo than anything else. To these ends, persons bought at the fairs were fastened tightly—many simply by the arms, the stronger by the legs as well—thrown into the bottom of a canoe, and spirited toward the sea.

By the time they made Bonny, New Calabar, or Old Calabar, slaves from the Biafran interior were deeply alienated. Almost every detail about their sojourn to the sea had served to separate them from the social details of their former homes. They arrived at the Atlantic strangers, and in the eighteenth century the residents of Bonny, Elem Kalabari, and Calabar had a specific name for such people. The foreigners brought down the river to be sold into waiting ships, whatever and whomever they used to be, were called Igbo.[14]

There is evidence from Bonny and Elem Kalabari that this nomenclature persisted throughout the eighteenth century. On a late seventeenth-century map giving the approach and soundings of the New Calabar River, for instance, the terra incognita beyond Elem Kalabari bears the label "The Hackbous Country is some Leagues above N. Calabar Town." James Barbot, who sailed to Elem Kalabari and Bonny in 1699 as supercargo aboard the slave ship *Albion*, referred several times in his journal to the people who lived beyond the littoral as Hackbous. In their deployment of the word, both the map of the New Calabar River and Barbot's journal undoubtedly followed the custom of the Bonny and Kalabari peoples from whose perspective European traders faced the interior (Hair, Jones, and Law 1992: plate 53, 702n5).

On one level then, people at the coast employed Igbo in a fashion similar to how it was probably used in the interior, as a way to refer to strangers and foreigners (Hair, et al. 1992: 693, 694, plate 54). But there were key differences too. In the polyglot, Atlantic trading towns of Elem Kalabari, Bonny, and Calabar, there are indications that Igbo referred only to certain kinds of strangers—not simply those from beyond the towns in general but those from beyond the littoral. At the coast, Igbo were not strangers from the pale, aliens abutting the territory and dependencies of the towns. Rather, they were the strangers beyond those strangers. Guinea sailors speaking in the manner of the African merchants with whom they traded for slaves at the coast understood the distinction quite well:

> The Slaves that are sold to the Europeans are generally procured by people that live in the Up Country, as it is called by the people of Bonny—supposed to be the country between the Sea Coast and the Ebo Country. . . . (HCSP 1975c: 19, 22, 46; HCSP 1975d: 299)

At the coast, Igbo took on a colonizing expansiveness mostly lacking from its use in the interior, and in the towns themselves there is evidence that people infused Igbo with meaning beyond the broad regional stereotypes apparent above. There were, for instance, settlements in the delta that traced their founding and lineage to Igbo progenitors from the interior, in ways distinguishing themselves from their neighbors (Alagoa 1972: 180–83). Further, in the ratcheting up of the slave trade in the eighteenth century, and the influx to the Niger delta of slaves, traders, laborers, and opportunists from the interior that this commercial explosion entailed, real and putative differences between newcomers from the hinterland and their progeny on one hand, and indigenes and more established residents on the other, took on an even more palpable meaning.

Work on the origins and social history of the trading towns of the Biafran littoral shores up the point. G. I. Jones, Robin Horton, and K. O. Dike have shown that key components of Kalabari, Bonny, and Calabar society were dedicated to the acculturation of Igbo immigrants from the far interior. At Elem Kalabari, the *koronogbo*, a subset of the Ekine fraternity of leading men, made it its business to roam the town on appointed nights accosting everyone they met. According to Horton: "If those challenged gave their names with a good Kalabari accent, they were allowed to go their way." If, however, "they gave their names with an accent betraying Ibo or Ibibio origin"—betraying that is, origins in the interior or the eastern delta—they might be assaulted as an object lesson for the poorly acculturated (Horton 1969: 54). At Calabar the Ekpe society played an analogous role, serving as a vehicle by which Igbo slaves and strangers from the interior could domesticate themselves into local society by mastering the language, customs, and associations of the town to which they now belonged (Jones 1956: 137–48).[15] At Bonny, the prevalence and tenacity of spoken Igbo, in the eighteenth century down to the present, suggests that acculturating institutions in operation there were in some matters no match for the volume of immigration from the hinterland (Dike 1959: 30).

Work on ethnicity formation and African cities suggests that the particular difference Igbo signified at Bonny, Elem Kalabari, and Calabar, in contradistinction to its more indiscriminate use in the interior, was illustrative of a kind of social and ethnic identification common in cities. Urban material conditions and politics encouraged people to ally with one another and to define others based less on distinctions operative from whence they came but to associate, rather, around issues and commonalities made pertinent by the peculiar conditions of urban life. For migrants to nineteenth- and twentieth-century African cities, for instance, frayed connections to their former homes and the insecurity and scramble of urban life combined with other exigencies to encourage, if not force, immigrants to associate on the basis of broad familiarities of language, culture, and "assumed kinship" to ameliorate their prospects in ways that gave rise and continue to give rise to new forms of ethnicity and ways of identification.[16] So too it must have been in the Atlantic trading towns of Bonny, Elem Kalabari, and Calabar—filled as they were with not just indigenes but with merchants, traders, and slaves from outlying areas near and far. Hunters, traders, refugees, smiths, and especially slaves, who in the interior understood themselves as Aro, Ngwa, Aboh, etc., were referred to at Bonny, Elem Kalabari, and Calabar—though not always indiscriminately—as Igbo.

More to the point, there is evidence that Bonny residents who originated in the interior came to internalize and act on the amalgamating ideology whereby matters of language, physiognomy, and practice that meant little in the social and ethnic geography of the interior could mean a great deal in the geography of the coast. At Bonny, European slave traders, town indigenes, and residents originating in the hinterland all understood what it meant to send an ailing Ebo slave from ship to shore to recuperate "in charge of one of her own countrywomen"—a declaration of kinship that would have made little sense in the interior (HCSP 1975c: 46).

UPROOTINGS, REGROUPINGS, AND THE SOCIAL CONSEQUENCES OF ENSLAVEMENT

Whether the story of Olaudah Equiano was an account of Gustavus Vassa's boyhood or was drawn from what Vassa came to know about the slave trade from the Biafran interior, when closely read and contextualized the account raises several key matters concerning the origins and nature of African nations in the Atlantic world. Among them, two issues should be considered in tandem because together they highlight a peculiar shortcoming in the recent historiography of the slave trade and black culture. They are, first, the apparent African origins of the Igbo nation of the Americas; and second, the combination of violence, despair, migration, and loss that apparently initiated among Africans from the Biafran interior a process of Igbo identification. Concerning the first issue, Vassa's *Interesting Narrative* and related materials suggest that Equiano was probably not born Igbo. But still, the process of his becoming Igbo most likely began in Africa with his enslavement, and had Equiano's travels ended along the Biafran littoral it is probable that he would have come to understand himself as Igbo as a slave in one of the coastal towns of the Bight of Biafra. Had he remained in the interior, however, it is quite unlikely that he would have developed any kind of Igbo self-consciousness. Thus John Thornton's position on the American origins of African nations in the New World is probably not universal. As a rule, African nations such as Vassa's Igbo were not unique to the Americas.[17] This ostensibly minor correction becomes important inasmuch as it necessitates paying attention to the African side of the process of becoming Igbo, especially to the violence, loss, and alienation that attended and initiated the process.

Violence, of course, is hardly a matter that has been ignored in the literature on the slave trade. It is, however, a matter that is more simply acknowledged as part of the experience of enslavement than approached as a formative component in the society and culture of slaves. Consequently, in some recent and influential studies concerning the slave trade and African ethnicity and society in the Americas, the violence and terror of enslavement is more cast as part of an ordeal that slaves overcame in the process of extending their former lives or in creating new ones. It is not ordinarily analyzed or understood as having a critical part in shaping African life. Thus Ira Berlin has argued that the linguistically dexterous, culturally plastic, and socially agile Africans (Atlantic creoles, he calls them) who arrived as slaves in seventeenth-century North America were probably not significantly affected by their enslavement and subsequent migration. "The transatlantic journey," writes Berlin, "did not break creole communities; it only transported them to other sites" (Berlin 1996: 267).[18] Elsewhere, writing of the first African slaves in French Louisiana, he holds, "Despite the long transatlantic journey, once in the New World, they recovered much of what they had lost in the Old. . . ." (Berlin 1996: 274). Berlin is cautious not to push his conclusions into the eighteenth century, but John Thornton believes that a similar argument can be made for this period as well. Writes Thornton:

> Although many scholars discuss the possibility of the survival of African culture into the present day, an important issue to be sure, the fact is that in the eighteenth century African culture was not surviving: It was arriving. Whatever the brutalities of the Middle Passage or slave life, it was not going to cause the African-born to forget their mother language or change their ideas about beauty in design or music; nor would it cause them to abandon the ideological underpinnings of religion or ethics—not on arrival in America, not ever in their lives. (Thornton 1998: 320)[19]

The analysis of Vassa's *Interesting Narrative* presented here indicates that there is good reason to reframe, if not reject, similar analyses concerning the impact of the slave trade, at least as far as being and becoming Igbo in the eighteenth century were concerned. Igbo society and self-consciousness in the Americas began in the crucible of migration and depended first on captives coming to identify themselves as Igbo (a process that began first in Africa, as I have argued here, but that must have continued in other legs of transatlantic movement as well). Studies of black culture and society in the New World that seize upon the African origins of blacks in the Americas without recognizing the ways in which those origins might themselves be related to the Atlantic slave trade cannot but underanalyze the social and cultural consequence of enslavement.

In this sense, slavery studies has arrived at the same place as many contemporary migration studies in the need to investigate more fully and theorize more rigorously the relationship between social origins, migrations, and destinations in ways that acknowledge the ironies and elisions that characterize these supposedly distinct categories.[20] "Being grounded is not necessarily about being fixed; being mobile is not necessarily about being detached," is how the editors of a recent collection on modern migration allude to the analytical problem at hand (Ahmed et al. 2003: 2). An important strand of recent scholarship on the slave trade and its aftermath fully accepts the second half of this formulation. The first half of the pronouncement, however, is equally important, and unless and until both halves of the proposition are considered equally it will be impossible to come to terms with the real experiences of enslaved migrants themselves.

Sara Ahmed, Claudia Castañeda, Anne-Marie Fortier, and Mimi Sheller (2003) argue that a present task of migration scholarship should not be simply

> to categorize "home" as a condition distinct from "migration," or to order them in terms of their relative value or cultural salience, but to ask how uprootings and regroundings are enacted—affectively, materially and symbolically—in relation to one another. (2)

In interpreting the significance of the slave trade, a not uncommon oversight in slavery studies has been to treat African social and cultural categories and practices as necessarily and by definition native to African slaves, and to do so in ways that occlude the kinds of uprootings and regroundings that were prime consequences of enslavement. John Thornton's claims that put the perseverance of African languages at the center of his argument concerning the perseverance of African culture and the negligible social and cultural consequence of the Atlantic slave trade illustrate this tendency. Writes Thornton:

> Of course, the Africans retained their native languages, and African languages were widely spoken in eighteenth-century America. There were more first-language speakers of African languages in many parts of America than speakers of English, French, Dutch, Spanish, or Portuguese. Many of these Africans developed a certain necessary proficiency in the colonial language, the European language of their masters and other European or Euro-American settlers, after some years' residence, but it was always a second language, spoken with an accent. They were like the runaway woman, described in a late eighteenth-century Jamaican newspaper advertisement, who "speaks not altogether plain English; but from her talk she may easily be discovered to be a Coramantee." She, like other African-born Americans, probably thought, dreamed, and communicated more often in her native language than in the colonial language. (1998: 320)

Here, Thornton's argument neglects the ways in which the language spoken by any particular enslaved Africans in the Americas was not necessarily their native language, but a language bequeathed them by the vagaries and demands of their captivity. This is the point that emerges from Vassa's account of the slave trade from the Biafran interior. The several languages that

Equiano acquired while enslaved in the interior were very likely related to the language spoken in his own town and perhaps even mutually intelligible. But Vassa is very clear that these languages were not *his* language. Though intelligible, they did not carry for him the same social and cultural meaning as the language of his town, his true native tongue.[21] Thornton's conflation of intelligibility with language and his reticence to consider the uprootings and regroupings necessitated by the slave trade result in his underinterpreting the relationship between language, in its fullest sociolinguistic sense, and the slave trade.

The question that should be asked and not assumed about African languages in the Americas is the degree to which they existed and functioned in the New World as they did in Africa. Vassa's *Interesting Narrative* suggests that linguistic differentiations even within what we might now consider a single language could nevertheless hold notable social, cultural, and ideological difference. Thornton brushes against the point but fails to engage it when he writes as follows of the development of African nations in the Americas:

> Indeed loyalties in their homeland were likely to be to a village, or perhaps one of dozens of independent, often hostile states, or to a leader of wealth and status—but not to a language group. Yet, in America these African distinctions were put aside, and linguistic loyalty formed a first order of contact and companionship. (1998: 322)

What this argument neglects is the fact that important facets of language can and do, in the parlance of linguistics, index all of the social and political statuses mentioned above. So the development of the kind of linguistic loyalty Thornton outlined would have necessitated, for many, the alteration of heretofore important aspects of their native tongues. Thornton argues that slaves spoke the colonial language as a second language and with an accent. It is probably also true that the so-called African language of their nation was a second language too—spoken with accents that their masters could not hear but that were probably quite relevant among their fellow captives.[22] The impetus for all of this linguistic change, of course, was the slave trade.

Thornton and Berlin suggest that the slave trade itself holds few significant consequences for the development of African culture and society in the Americas. A close analysis of Equiano's captivity, however, cannot help but delineate the ways that the slave trade—especially its violence—must have been essential to the creation of the eighteenth-century versions of Igbo society and culture that existed in the Americas (and in Africa for that matter). The violence of enslavement was not something that Africans necessarily overcame during and following their captivity on the way toward leading the fullest lives possible. The violence of enslavement, rather, was and could be a formative and fundamental part of captives' social and cultural lives. That there were Africans in the eighteenth-century Americas who claimed or accepted being Igbo is evidence, in and of itself, of the lasting and fundamental social and cultural transformations wrought by and in the context of Atlantic slave trade.

This is not to say that all expressions of African ethnicity in the Atlantic world can be explained as I have done here (though, no doubt, some can). It does not even mean that all Africans who identified themselves as Igbo across the Atlantic world necessarily came to acknowledge as much in the way that I have outlined above (though I think it likely that many did). The argument here has been that to understand the Igboness expressed in Vassa's *Interesting Narrative*, it is important to come to terms with certain social and historical factors which contributed to the eventual development of the kind of Igbo consciousness expressed in that account. Among these factors, the nature of internal African migration preceding the middle passage is particularly important. But because the experiences of Africans enslaved in the Biafran interior were not necessarily identical, and because the nature of the trade from the region changed over time, how the Igboness outlined in this essay compared to others is a matter that will require (and reward, I think) further investigation. Such work promises to shed light on how factors such as gender, age, time in transit, distance in transit, and transatlantic carrier, among others, shaped the experiences of enslaved Africans and related processes of Igbo identification, thus providing insight into how contrasting conditions may have contributed to different ways of being Igbo.

Two other points, however, require less qualification. First, that the origins, nature, and content of African ethnicity in the Americas—the so-called African nations—deserve to be deeply interrogated can hardly be contentious.[23] It should be less controversial still that more work that analyzes, rather than dismisses, the consequences of slavery's most salient aspects—its violence and catastrophe—can only improve our understanding of black society and culture across Gustavus Vassa's eighteenth-century Atlantic world (and perhaps beyond as well).[24] Second, the transatlantic slave trade was migration, and as migration it raises questions and issues relevant to analyses of contemporary migrant streams. This point should also not be controversial. David Manuel Hernández's contribution to this collection, though its subject is far removed in time and space from the matters taken up here, cannot help but underline powerful forces of external identification and violence (it must be admitted) that are very much in play in the "production of 'diseased,' 'criminal,' and 'enemy aliens'" in the modern migration history of the United States (especially in times of official national emergency). So although much distinguishes the experiences of captives thrown into the eighteenth-century slave trade and the detainees caught up in the post–9/11 dragnet described in the following essay, to understand either experience requires close attention to processes of alienation that all but defined the migrant experiences of both.

NOTES

1. In what follows, I refer to the author of *The Interesting Narrative* by the name he used most in public: Gustavus Vassa. When the paper describes incidents from *The Interesting Narrative* concerning Vassa's ostensive enslavement that do not concern Vassa as an author, I write of the experiences of Equiano. It is a choice that allows a useful distinction, I think, between Vassa the author and the events described in the African chapters of his *Interesting Narrative*. This usage is not meant to betray a position on whether Vassa was born in Africa, nor on whether his birth name was indeed Olaudah Equiano. On these matters I am, at the moment, agnostic (But see [Lovejoy, forthcoming] for a response to Carretta). In the notes and reference list, *The Interesting Narrative* is cited under the name Olaudah Equiano because this is how the book is cataloged in most libraries in the United States.

2. I have addressed this matter in more detail elsewhere (Byrd 2006). Carretta (2005: 319–20), Sobel (2002: 197–98), and Thornton (2003: 274 n 6) have also taken up the question of the sources of Vassa's *Narrative* in light of evidence suggesting that he may not have been born in Africa.

3. For a similar experience by another European in Africa, see Koelle (1963: 7–8).

4. As Kolapo has pointed out (2004), Chambers's body of work (1997, 2005, for example) is not always clear on this point.

5. Gomez (1998: 114–34) and Hall (2005: 130–36) have articulated similar takes on the development of Igbo consciousness.

6. I am concerned with what could be loosely referred to as the creation of Igbo identity. But the distinction between identification and self-understanding, I am persuaded by Brubaker and Cooper's "Beyond 'Identity,'" is a necessary and useful one to make. They argue that "Conceptualizing all affinities and affiliations, all forms of belonging, all experiences of commonality, connectedness, and cohesion, all self-understanding and self-identification in the idiom of 'identity' saddles us with a blunt, flat, undifferentiated vocabulary" and such a vocabulary, of course, has attendant consequences for any social analysis that depends on it (Brubaker and Cooper 2000) .

7. Joseph Miller (1988) and Joseph Inikori (1988) have addressed the disparity of attention to which I allude and have focused intensively on segments of the Atlantic trade preceding the actual sea voyage. Stephanie Smallwood's forthcoming book takes a similar tack (2007).

8. Such trials of the slave trade in the interior are less pronounced in Vassa's *Interesting Narrative*. For his part, Vassa indicated that the "sable destroyers of human rights" who forced Equiano from his home to the sea at no time offered any ill treatment to him or to the slaves who were his companions except for "tying them, when necessary, to keep them from running away" (Equiano 2003: 51). Given so much evidence to the contrary, however, it is likely that Vassa's point is largely rhetorical. A

prime object of his account was to indict European slave traders, not their African counterparts.

9. Concerning the acquisition of new dialects, Vassa wrote:

> From the time I left my own nation I always found somebody that understood me till I came to the sea coast. The languages of different nations did not totally differ, nor were they so copious as those of the Europeans, particularly the English. They were therefore easily learned; and, while I was journeying thus through Africa, I acquired two or three different tongues. (Equiano 2003: 51)

G. I. Jones believes this was because before Equiano began in earnest toward the sea, he was all the while not very far from home (1967: 67–68).

10. Hereafter, The House of Commons Sessional Papers will be cited as HCSP.

11. Wrote Woodville from the Bonny River: "some of the ships have been here from sixteen to nineteen weeks but as the provisions in the back country is now planted the times are much minded in respect to the briskness of the trade although the prices remain the same." Also see the evidence James Fraser gave the House of Commons. Fraser testified "that most of the Slaves we purchase at Bonny confess themselves to have been Slaves," a point of fact he took to mean that a "great many in the country are born Slaves." The observation, however, could just as well support the point I have made here (HCSP 1975c: 71: 19)

12. Vassa described with some awe this part of Africa. The people there "cooked in iron pots and had European cutlasses and crossbows." And they all but lived on the water. When Equiano arrived at the littoral, wrote Vassa, he was "beyond measure astonished" at what he saw (Equiano 2003: 54).

13. For more on trading "on trust," see Lovejoy and Richardson (1999).

14. Thus it is an act of rather confusing prolepsis to speak of the Igbo in eighteenth-century Africa as one would the Igbo of twentieth-century Nigeria. The Igbo of the era of the slave trade simply did not exist in the same way as did the Igbo of colonial and post-colonial Nigeria. Further, if Inikori's research on the slave trade from the Bight of Biafra pans out, it will have to be confessed that the majority of slaves exported from Biafra in the eighteenth and nineteenth centuries were not even the predecessors of the peoples now considered Igbo. That is, they were not from the present confines of Igboland, nor did they speak Igbo languages. Based on tenuous but intriguing demographic evidence, Inikori has argued that a majority of the slaves exported from Biafran ports must have been from north of the present confines of Igboland (Inikori 1988: 29–30, 34–36). More recently, Femi J. Kolapo has followed up on this line of argument (2004).

15. In Old Calabar, though, under the auspices of Ekpe, this was a painfully slow and uneven process compared to the custom at Bonny and Elem Kalabari.

16. See, for example, Hodgkin (1956: chs. 1–2), Cohen (1969; 1974), Mitchell (1987: ch. 5; 1956), Werbner (1984), Nnoli (1978, 1995), and Asiwaju (1995).

17. Thornton has argued that "African nations in the New World were new and unique to the Americas and did not correspond well to political or social units in Africa, in that they were based on language alone" (1998: 321). In America, he has argued, lo-

cal African social, cultural, and political "distinctions were put aside, and linguistic loyalty formed a first order of contact and companionship" (Thornton 1998: 322).

18. This was not necessarily the case, Berlin argues, for Africans transported to North America in the eighteenth century.

19. James Sweet is more reserved than Thornton on this point and he is in general more inclined to grasp the cultural and social significance of violence for interpreting African life in the Americas. Nevertheless his survey of the effects of enslavement for Africans bound for the Portuguese empire, at least from the fifteenth through the seventeenth centuries, though masterfully told, does not grant the ordeals of enslavement much lasting cultural or social consequence (Sweet 2003: passim, but see esp. 6–7, ch. 3, 115–17, 227). Similarly, Michael Gomez has vividly presented aspects of the Igbo response to the travails of slavery in the Americas. He does not consider, however, the ways that these travails may have been critical to the very formation and articulation of Igbo culture and society in the Atlantic world (Gomez 2003).

20. Though close and careful re-readings of excellent theoretical literature already produced by the field is also in order (especially Mintz and Price 1990).

21. See note 9 above.

22. My thinking in this paragraph has been influenced by the work of Judith T. Irvine (2002) and Irvine and Gal (2000).

23. Along the lines of Lovejoy (2003), Law (1997), Caron (1997), Morgan (1997) and Matory (1999).

24. Brown's recent essay on "Spiritual Terror and Sacred Authority" in Jamaica (2003) and the respective work of Painter (2002), Wood (1999), Hartman (1997), Dusinberre (1996), and Dirks (1987) are all fine examples.

REFERENCES

Adams, John. 1966. *Remarks on the Country Extending from Cape Palmas to the River Congo*. London: Frank Cass.

Ahmed, Sara, Claudia Castañeda, Anne-Marie Fortier, and Mimi Sheller. 2003. "Introduction: Uprootings/Regroundings: Questions of Home and Migration." Pp. 1–19 in *Uprootings/Regroundings: Questions of Home and Migration*, ed. Sara Ahmed, Claudia Castañeda, Anne-Marie Fortier and Mimi Sheller. Oxford: Berg.

Alagoa, Ebiegberi J. 1972. *A History of the Niger Delta: An Historical Interpretation of Ijo Oral Tradition*. Ibadan, Nigeria: Ibadan University Press.

Asiwaju, A. I. 1995. *The Birth of Yewaland: Studies and Documents Relating to the Change of a Yoruba Sub-Ethnic Name from Egbado to Yewa in Ogun State of Nigeria*. Ibadan: STATCO.

Berlin, Ira. 1996. "From Creole to African: Atlantic Creoles and the Origins of African-American Society in Mainland North America." *William and Mary Quarterly* 53: 251–88.

Brown, Vincent. 2003. "Spiritual Terror and Sacred Authority in Jamaican Slave Society." *Slavery & Abolition* 24: 24–53.

Brubaker, Rogers, and Frederick Cooper. 2000. "Beyond 'Identity.'" *Theory and Society* 29: 1–47.

Byrd, Alexander X. 2006. "Eboe, Country, Nation and Gustavus Vassa's *Interesting Narrative.*" *William and Mary Quarterly* 63: 123–48.

Caron, Peter. 1997. "'Of a Nation which the others do not Understand': Bambara Slaves and African Ethnicity in Colonial Louisiana, 1718–1760." *Slavery and Abolition* 18: 98–121.

Carretta, Vincent. 1999. "Olaudah Equiano or Gustavus Vassa? New Light on an Eighteenth-Century Question of Identity." *Slavery & Abolition* 20: 96–105.

———. 2003. "Questioning the Identity of Olaudah Equiano, or Gustavus Vassa, the African." Pp. 226–35 in *The Global Eighteenth Century*, ed. Felicity Nussbaum. Baltimore: Johns Hopkins University Press.

———. 2005. *Equiano, the African: Biography of a Self-Made Man*. Athens: University of Georgia Press.

Chambers, Douglas B. 1997. "'My Own Nation': Igbo Exiles in the Diaspora." *Slavery & Abolition* 18: 72–97.

———. 2000. "Tracing Igbo into the African Diaspora." Pp. 53–71 in *Identity in the Shadow of Slavery*, ed. Paul E. Lovejoy. London: Continuum.

———. 2001. "Ethnicity in the Diaspora: The Slave Trade and the Creation of African 'Nations' in the Americas." *Slavery & Abolition* 22: 25–39.

———. 2002. "The Significance of Igbo in the Bight of Biafra Slave Trade: A Rejoinder to Northrup's 'Myth Igbo.'" *Slavery & Abolition* 23: 101–20.

———. 2005. *Murder at Montpelier: Igbo Africans in Virginia*. Jackson: University Press of Mississippi.

Cohen, Abner. 1969. *Custom and Politics in Urban Africa: A Study of Hausa Migrants in Yoruba Towns*. London: Routledge.

———. 1974. *Urban Ethnicity*. London: Tavistock Publications.

Crowther, Samuel. 1970. *Journal of an Expedition up the Niger and Tshadda Rivers*. London: Frank Cass.

Dike, K. Onwuka. 1959. *Trade and Politics in the Niger Delta*. Oxford: Clarendon.

Dirks, Robert. 1987. *The Black Saturnalia*. Gainesville: University of Florida Press.

Dusinberre, William. 1996. *Them Dark Days: Slavery in the American Rice Swamps*. New York: Oxford.

Eltis, David, and David Richardson. 1997. "West Africa and the Transatlantic Slave Trade: New Evidence of Long-Run Trends." *Slavery & Abolition* 18: 16–35.

Equiano, Olaudah. 1789. *The Interesting Narrative of the Life of Olaudah Equiano, or Gustavus Vassa, the African*. 1st ed. Vol. 2. London: W. W. Norton.

———. 2001. *The Interesting Narrative of the Life of Olaudah Equiano, or Gustavus Vassa, the African, Written by Himself: Authoritative Text, Contexts, Criticism*. Ed. Werner Sollors. London: W. W. Norton.

———. 2003. *The Interesting Narrative and Other Writings*. Ed. Vincent Carretta. Rev. ed. New York: Penguin Books. [Original ed. 1794.]

Falconbridge, Alexander. 1788. *An Account of the Slave Trade on the Coast of Africa*. London: J. Phillips.

Forde, Daryll, and G. I. Jones. 1962. *The Ibo and Ibibio-Speaking Peoples of South-Eastern Nigeria*. London: International African Institute.
Gomez, Michael A. 1998. *Exchanging Our Country Marks: The Transformation of African Identities in the Colonial and Antebellum South*. Chapel Hill: University of North Carolina Press.
———. 2003. "A Quality of Anguish: The Igbo Response to Enslavement." Pp. 82–95 in *Trans-Atlantic Dimension of Ethnicity in the African Diaspora*, ed. Paul E. Love-joy and David V. Trotman. London: Continuum.
Hair, P. E. H., Adam Jones, and Robin Law (eds.). 1992. *Barbot on Guinea: The Writings of Jean Barbot on West Africa 1678–1712*. Vol. 2. London: Hakluyt Society.
Hall, Gwendolyn Midlo. 2005. *Slavery and African Ethnicities in the Americas: Restoring the Links*. Chapel Hill: University of North Carolina Press.
Hartman, Saidiya V. 1997. *Scenes of Subjection: Terror, Slavery, and Self-Making in Nineteenth-Century America*. New York: Oxford University Press.
Henderson, Richard N. 1972. *The King in Every Man: Evolutionary Trends in Onitsha Ibo Society and Culture*. New Haven, CT: Yale University Press.
Hodgkin, Thomas. 1956. *Nationalism in Colonial Africa*. New York: New York University Press.
Horton, Robin. 1969. "From Fishing Village to City-State." Pp. 37–58 in *Man in Africa*, ed. Mary Douglass and Phyllis Kaberry. London: Tavistock Publications.
House of Commons Sessional Papers (HCSP). 1975a [1789]. Shelia Lambert, ed., 69: 47. Evidence of James Penny. In "Report of the Lords of the Committee of Council Appointed for the Consideration of all Matters Relating to Trade and Foreign Plantations." Wilmington, DE: Scholarly Resources.
———. 1975b [1789]. Shelia Lambert, ed., 69: 120–21. Evidence of Alexander Falconbridge. In "Report of the Lords of the Committee of Council Appointed for the Consideration of all Matters Relating to Trade and Foreign Plantations." Wilmington, DE: Scholarly Resources.
———. 1975c [1790]. Shelia Lambert, ed., 71: 3–60. Evidence of James Fraser. In "Minutes of the Evidence Taken Before a Committee of the House of Commons being a Select Committee. . . . For the Purpose of taking the Examination of such Witnesses as shall be produced on the Part of the several Petitioners who have petitioned the House of Commons against the Abolition of the Slave Trade." Wilmington, DE: Scholarly Resources.
———. 1975d [1790]. Shelia Lambert, ed., 72: 293–344. Evidence of Alexander Falconbridge. In "Minutes of the Evidence Taken Before a Committee of the House of Commons being a Select Committee. . . . For the Purpose of taking the Examination of such Witnesses as shall be produced on the Part of the several Petitioners who have petitioned the House of Commons against the Abolition of the Slave Trade." Wilmington, DE: Scholarly Resources.
Inikori, Joseph E. 1988. "The Sources of Supply for the Atlantic Slave Trade Exports from the Bight of Benin and the Bight of Bonny (Biafra)." Pp. 25–43 in *De La Traite À L'Esclavage*, ed. Serge Daget. Nantes: Centre de Recherche Sur L'Histoire du Monde Atlantique.

Irvine, Judith T. 2002. "'Style' as Distinctiveness: The Culture and Ideology of Linguistic Differentiation." Pp. 21–43 in *Style and Sociolinguistic Variation*, ed. Penelope Eckert and John R. Rickford. Cambridge: Cambridge University Press.

Irvine, Judith T., and Susan Gal. 2000. "Language Ideology and Linguistic Differentiation." Pp. 35–83 in *Regimes of Language: Ideologies, Polities, and Identities*, ed. Paul V. Kroskrity. Santa Fe, NM: School of American Research Press.

Jeffreys, W. D. W. 1937. Awka Division Intelligence Report.

Jones, G. I. 1956. "The Political Organization of Old Calabar." Pp. 116–60 in *Efik Traders of Old Calabar*, ed. Daryll Forde. London: Oxford University Press.

———. 1967. "Olaudah Equiano of the Niger Ibo." Pp. 60–69 in *Africa Remembered*, ed. Philip D. Curtin. Madison: University of Wisconsin Press.

Klein, Herbert S. 1978. "The English Slave Trade to Jamaica, 1782–1808." *Economic History Review* 31: 25–45.

Koelle, Sigismund W. 1963. *Polyglotta Africana*, ed. P. E. H. Hair and David Dalby. Graz, Austria: Akademische Druck.

Kolapo, Femi J. 2004. "The Igbo and Their Neighbours during the Era of the Atlantic Slave Trade." *Slavery & Abolition* 25: 114–33.

Kopytoff, Igor, and Suzanne Miers. 1977. "African 'Slavery' as an Institution of Marginality." Pp. 3–81 in *Slavery in Africa: Historical and Anthropological Perspectives*, ed. Suzanne Miers and Igor Kopytoff. Madison: University of Wisconsin Press.

Law, Robin. 1997. "Ethnicity and the Slave Trade: 'Lucumi' and 'Nago' as Ethnonyms in West Africa." *History in Africa* 24: 205–19.

Lovejoy, Paul E. 2006. "Autobiography and Memory: Gustavus Vassa, alias Olaudah Equiano, the African." *Slavery & Abolition* 27: 317–47.

———. 2003. "Ethnic Designations of the Slave Trade and the Reconstruction of the History of Transatlantic Slavery." Pp. 9–42 in *Trans-Atlantic Dimension of Ethnicity in the African Diaspora*, ed. Paul E. Lovejoy and David V. Trotman. London: Continuum.

Lovejoy, Paul E., and David Richardson. 1999. "Trust, Pawnship, and Atlantic History: The Institutional Foundations of the Old Calabar Slave Trade." *American Historical Review* 104: 333–55.

Matory, J. Lorand. 1999. "The English Professors of Brazil: On the Diasporic Roots of the Yorùbá Nation." *Comparative Studies in Society and History* 41: 72–103.

Miller, Joseph C. 1988. *Way of Death: Merchant Capitalism and the Angolan Slave Trade, 1730–1830*. Madison: University of Wisconsin Press.

Mintz, Sidney, and Richard Price. 1990. *The Birth of African American Culture*. Boston: Beacon Press.

Mitchell, J. Clyde. 1956. *The Kalela Dance: The Rhodes-Livingstone Papers*. Manchester: Manchester University Press.

———. 1987. *Cities, Society, and Social Perception: A Central African Perspective*. Oxford: Clarendon Press.

Morgan, Philip D. 1997. "The Cultural Implications of the Atlantic Slave Trade: African Regional Origins, American Destinations and New World Developments." *Slavery & Abolition* 18: 122–45.

Nnoli, Okwudiba. 1978. *Ethnic Politics in Nigeria*. Enugu, Nigeria: Fourth Dimension Publishers.

———. 1995. *Ethnicity and Development in Nigeria*. Aldershot: Avebury.

Northrup, David. 1978. *Trade without Rulers: Pre-Colonial Economic Development in South-Eastern Nigeria*. Oxford: Clarendon Press.

———. 2000. "Igbo and Myth Igbo: Culture and Ethnicity in the Atlantic World, 1600–1850." *Slavery & Abolition* 21: 1–20.

Nwokeji, G. Ugo. 1999. "The Biafran Frontier: Trade, Slaves, and Aro Society, c. 1750–1905." Ph.D. diss., University of Toronto.

Obichere, Boniface. 1988. "Slavery and the Slave Trade in the Niger Delta Cross River Basin." Pp. 45–56 in *De La Traite À L'Esclavage*, ed. Serge Daget. Nantes: Centre de Recherche Sur L'Histoire du Monde Atlantique.

Painter, Nell Irvin. 2002. "Soul Murder and Slavery: Toward a Fully Loaded Cost Accounting." Pp. 15–39 in *Southern History across the Color Line*. Chapel Hill: University of North Carolina Press.

Richardson, David. 1989. "The Eighteenth-Century British Slave Trade: Estimates of Its Volume and Coastal Distribution in Africa." Pp. 151–95 in *Research in Economic History*. Greenwich, CT: JAI Press.

Shelton, Austin J. 1971. *The Igbo-Igala Borderland: Religion and Social Control in Indigenous African Colonialism*. Albany: State University of New York Press.

Smallwood, Stephanie. 2007. *Salt Water Slavery: A Middle Passage from Africa to American Diaspora*. Cambridge, MA: Harvard University Press.

Sobel, Mechal. 2002. "Migration and Collective Identities among the Enslaved and Free Populations of North America." Pp. 176–203 in *Coerced and Free Migration: Global Perspectives*, ed. David Eltis. Stanford, CA: Stanford University Press.

Sweet, James H. 2003. *Recreating Africa: Culture, Kinship, and Religion in the African-Portuguese World, 1441–1770*. Chapel Hill: University of North Carolina Press.

Taylor, Simon. 1789. Letter to Chaloner Arcedeckne (1 November 1789). Manuscripts Department, Cambridge University Library. Vanneck Manuscripts, Bundle 2/15.

Thornton, John K. 1998. *Africa and Africans in the Making of the Atlantic World, 1400–1800*. 2nd ed. New York: Cambridge University Press.

———. 2003. "Cannibals, Witches, and Slave Traders in the Atlantic World." *William and Mary Quarterly* 60: 273–94.

Uchendu, Victor. 1977. "Slaves and Slavery in Igboland." Pp. 121–32 in *Slavery in Africa: Historical and Anthropological Perspectives*, ed. Suzanne Miers and Igor Kopytoff. Madison: University of Wisconsin Press.

Werbner, Richard P. 1984. "The Manchester School in South-Central Africa." *Annual Review of Anthropology* 13: 157–85.

Wood, Peter H. 1999. "Slave Labor Camps in Early America: Overcoming Denial and Discovering the Gulag." Pp. 222–38 in *Inequality in Early America*, ed. Carla Gardina Pestana and Sharon V. Salinger. Hanover, NH: University Press of New England.

Woodville, William. 1791. Letter to James Rogers (20 April 1791). Public Record Office, Kew. CO 107/13.

2

Undue Process

Racial Genealogies of Immigrant Detention

David Manuel Hernández

> But the history of civil liberties in times of emergency suggests that govern-
> ments seldom react to crises carefully or judiciously. They acquiesce to the most
> alarmist proponents of repression. They pursue preexisting agendas in the name
> of national security. They target unpopular or vulnerable groups in the popula-
> tion less because there is clear evidence of danger than because there is little po-
> litical cost (Brinkley 2003: 45–46).

This essay examines the history and structure of immigrant detention in the
United States since the inception of the Bureau of Immigration in 1891. It
does so in order to clarify the structural and ideological components that led
to the widespread detention of Arab, Muslim, and South Asian immigrants
and citizens in the aftermath of the September 11, 2001 terrorist attacks on the
United States.[1] In presenting this history and analysis the essay's main concern is to highlight the social production and criminalization of "aliens" and
the juridical borders of U.S. citizenship and noncitizenship in the nineteenth
and twentieth centuries. Distilling the historical pattern of criminalization of
noncitizens and the production of "diseased," "criminal," and "enemy" aliens
in times of national emergency—especially during wartime intensifications
of racism, nativism, and political intolerance—the essay locates the rights of
noncitizens on a shifting juridical terrain, in which the legal rights of immigrants are vulnerable to the often racialized contexts of national security
crises.

The examination demonstrates that the legal and social structures and "undue processes" that legitimate and facilitate immigrant detention have historically been tactical policies exercised by the state to criminalize and punish
noncitizens, in turn creating new categories of lesser citizenship and sustaining inequalities already entrenched in the United States through mechanisms

of social control. Lesser citizens are subject to a course of action that I call "undue process," which refers to the suspension, curtailment, and otherwise differential legal protections to which certain immigrants are subject. As such, "undue process" carries the opposite meaning of due process, the judicial guidelines and procedural rights that protect individuals from unfair treatment under the law.[2] In sum, the construction of these political "others," by effecting a systematic denial of due process, reflects the shifting racial prejudices which shape the episodic development of immigrant detention. Considering both well-known and lesser known historical episodes, this essay demonstrates how legal antecedents and patterns in detention history anticipate and explain contemporary national security concerns in the wake of 9/11.

My central thesis is that contemporary detention policies emerge from the historical dialectic between immigrant detention and the racialized "othering" of noncitizens. The essay thus brings together a variety of historical examples in order to highlight their racial patterns. I examine, for instance, the fear of contagion in response to Chinese immigration in the late nineteenth century that contributed to their prolonged detention at Angel Island Immigration Station. Other examples include the racial justification that led to the expulsion, internment, dispersal, and in some cases, deportation of Japanese Americans during World War II, or, the Cold War inflected refugee policies in the 1980s that led to the mass detention of thousands of Cubans, Haitians, and Central Americans seeking asylum in the United States. Using these examples I argue that the consistent nature of detention practices and policies functions as a form of institutionalized racism and discrimination against noncitizens. By examining the genealogy of the expansions and contractions in the detention infrastructure I show how the conditions, legal strategies, and social contexts surrounding detention episodes reveal a racially marked pattern, further animated by the use of "war" rhetoric in the construction of national crises.

Blanket racial policies directed at noncitizens and the categorical denial of due process protections position detainees outside the justice system and codify the lesser status of immigrants in U.S. society. Therefore, the episodes examined here demonstrate how the *confluence* of immigration and national security crises lead to future policy changes and further cast immigrants as the enemy within. It is this confluence that, in basic terms, leaves an immigrant in federal custody with fewer protections than an accused criminal. Furthermore, whereas the majority of immigration scholarship rightfully recognizes the Immigration and Nationality Act of 1965 as marking the end of race-based national quotas for newly arriving immigrants, this essay contends that racialized detention policies advance episodically a more subtle and effective criminalization system that maintains blanket racial strategies against various classes of "undesirables" within the interior of the nation. Race is a salient factor in detention policy when we consider immigration history against periods of national crises—periods which have an indelible effect on the detention of immigrants.

9/11 AND THE "WAR ON TERROR"

Clearly, 9/11 is the most recent and powerful example that brings to the attention of the nation and the world the troubling coordinates of race, national origin, security enforcement, and foreign threat that I argue form the ideological foundation for the racialization and criminalization of immigrants. The destruction wrought by the hijackers breached domestic security and triggered significant modifications to domestic and international policies and bureaucracies. Besides the abrupt suspension of adjudications of refugee status and the derailment of a potential amnesty for undocumented laborers, 9/11 most notably catalyzed an immediate practice of racial profiling of persons perceived to be of Middle Eastern origin, which among popular and official observers amounts to a conflated population of Arabs, Muslims, and South Asians.

The "take no chances" stance of the government facilitated in the greater public the routine distrust of perceived-to-be Middle Easterners and widespread acceptance of their presumed terrorist affiliations. Indeed, three years after 9/11 the *Washington Post* reported that "one in four Americans holds a negative stereotype of Muslims, and almost one-third responds with a negative image when they hear the word 'Muslim.'"[3] For instance, a survey conducted at Cornell University found that about 44 percent believed that "some curtailment of civil liberties is necessary for Muslim Americans" (Friedlander 2004). Moreover, institutionalized racial profiling of presumed "suspected terrorists" was accompanied by vigilante acts of violence and the official divestment of civil and, in some cases, human rights for citizens and noncitizens. While government policies singled out Muslim men for "interviews" or noncitizen Muslims for "special registration," widespread vigilante action included burned mosques, racist speech and assaults, and in some cases, murder. For instance, the Council of American Islamic Relations registered over 1,400 hate crimes against Arabs and Muslims and the National Asian Pacific American Legal Consortium documented 250 bias-motivated crimes targeting Asian Americans, mostly South Asians, in the three months following 9/11 (Kochar 2002). Outside this context of anti-Muslim violence has been the widespread detention and deportation of Muslims thought to be connected to designated terrorist organizations.

The "war on terror" served the federal government as a blank check to intimidate and detain any person deemed suspect. Furthermore, evidence against detained individuals remained secret and undisclosed to the public. In nationwide sweeps in the months following 9/11, over 1,200 persons of presumed Middle Eastern origin were detained without charges or direct links to the terrorist attacks. As well, over 40,000 male immigrants between the ages of sixteen and twenty-five from predominantly Muslim nations were required to take part in a "special registration" program. The program led to over 5,400 deportations and between 1,700 and 2,700 detentions, although none were linked to the terrorist attacks (Cusac 2003; Dow 2004). The Absconder Apprehension Initiative, designed to apprehend and deport persons with existing deportation orders, prioritized deportations to Muslim nations and has also detained at least 1,100 persons since 9/11, bringing the overall total of 9/11 detainees to over 5,000 persons—none of them linked to terrorism (Dow 2004; Cole 2004). Moreover, federal authorities maintained the exceptional and continuous national security threat to the United States in order to rhetorically justify the widespread use of secrecy, in effect both concealing and confirming the criminalization of detainees.[4]

In response, immigrant advocates, civil libertarians, and the Justice Department's Inspector General have documented numerous abuses of detainees by federal officials in the courts and detention centers. Reacting to such charges and reports of abuses of authority from human rights organizations and from within the Department of Justice, former Attorney General John Ashcroft steadfastly refused to apologize or admit error,[5] and infamously attacked his critics for "aid[ing] terrorists" and "diminishing our resolve."[6] Criticism and dissent in the democratic tradition, in other words, approximate treason in the context of the "war on terror." Ashcroft also stated, "I don't apologize for a system that can ensure the security of the United States by detaining individuals who were in violation of the law, pending the outcome of their adjudication" (Duffy and Ragavan 2004: 33). The attorney general's methods of ensuring security, however, were promulgated without transparency or checks and balances from other branches of government.

The Bush administration has stonewalled efforts at providing relevant information to Congress, to persons suing under the Freedom of Information Act, and to the general public. According to the Information Security Oversight Office, for example, the 2003 fiscal year witnessed a 25 percent increase in classified documents, and a ten-year low in the number of pages declassified (Eggen, Aug. 2004). In a federal "national security" case about the government's post-9/11 procedures, New York District Judge Victor Marrero wrote, "Democracy abhors undue secrecy. . . . An unlimited government warrant to conceal . . . has no place in our open society" (Eggen, Sept. 2004: A16). Despite this censure, the government's strategy of secrecy pertaining to immigrant detentions has largely been enacted as a blanket policy, and not a

practice based on individual review of facts and circumstances related to terrorism. As with other episodes of detention expansion, political expediency
and the need to construct a record of security efforts collide with legitimate
fears generated by national crises, resulting in categorical determinations and
policies about racialized noncitizens and the minimal prioritization of the
rights as individuals of detainees, immigrants, and citizens.

PRECURSORS TO THE 9/11 DETENTION EPISODE

9/11 and the ensuing expansion of immigrant detention briefly surveyed
above are only one part of a broad pattern of noncitizen incarceration that
reaches beyond the "war on terror"—to the "war on drugs," to the Cold War,
and to declared military conflicts, the primary sites this essay examines. For
instance, immigration control and its changing mandates can be traced bu-
reaucratically through the location of immigrant enforcement in the government structure revealing its evolving attitude toward immigrants. In particular, the Immigration and Naturalization Service (INS) or its precursors moved
from the Department of the Treasury (1891–1903) to the Department of
Commerce and Labor (1903–1913), then to the Department of Labor
(1913–1940), followed by the Department of Justice (1940–2003) and now,
to the Department of Homeland Security (spring 2003–present). Immigration's bureaucratic history is more or less split into two halves—the first
forty-nine years in Treasury, Commerce, and Labor, and the last sixty-six at
Justice and Homeland Security. This movement reveals a continuing shift in
the government's position toward immigration enforcement and control, most
dramatically by viewing predominantly white European immigrants at the
turn of the century through the outset of World War II in terms of their contributions to economic development and their role, sometimes through radical political action, in the labor market. After 1940, the bureaucratic location
at the Department of Justice coincides with Japanese internment, large scale
Mexican migrations, both sanctioned and unsanctioned, and increased
refugee streams stemming from the Cold War. No longer associating immigrants with economic incorporation and contributions, but with criminality
and national security, the INS's long tenure at the Department of Justice and
recent transfer to the Department of Homeland Security coincides with radi-
cally changing immigration flows, from European to predominantly Latino
and Asian migrants, after the removal of racist immigration barriers in 1965.

   In order to illuminate the racial features of immigrant detention and provide the context for understanding immigrant incarceration as a historical
process, I present key historical moments that reflect the confluence of

immigration and national security crises that produce, through a systematic undue process, lesser citizens. Immigrants have been detained for numerous reasons and under various political and historical conditions throughout the twentieth century. The episodes of detention expansion on which this essay focuses include the quarantine of "diseased aliens" at ports of entry such as Angel and Ellis Islands, the domestic detention of "enemy aliens" and foreign nationals during wartime, most notably found in the example of Japanese American internment. Also included are Cold War detainees, the mass detention of refugees resulting from 1980s Latin American foreign and economic policies, as well as what are termed "criminal aliens" due to the "war on drugs," immigration legislation in 1996, and anti-terrorism efforts in the 1990s.

The continuity and expansion of immigrant detention and incarceration are related to the expansion of executive power which exploits the ruse of national security. "Wars" against various classes of enemies (e.g., World Wars I and II), domestic social problems (e.g., the "wars" on poverty and drugs), or global dynamics without end (e.g., the Cold War and the "war on terror") resonate with the public and garner significant political currency for elected officials. "Even at its most metaphorical, martial rhetoric gives presidents a chance to invoke their mystique as commander in chief," says Yale law professor Bruce Ackerman (2004: 40). Historically, the availability of war rhetoric finds greater acceptance when exercised against already unpopular immigrants and citizens. Legal scholar Kevin Johnson (2004: 3) explains further that "because of the unpopularity of—even hatred toward—foreigners among the general population in times of crisis and social unrest, a meaningful political check on the unfair treatment of immigrants does not exist. As a result, both Congress and the president have the ability to direct the most extreme action toward noncitizens with little fear of provoking a judicial response." As the Bush administration invokes an unending national security crisis in order to rewrite the laws of citizenship and personhood, of torture, and of war, it is critical that we consider the genealogy of immigrant detention in order to better understand the racial and systemic inequalities surrounding detention episodes.

In the following sections, I compare these episodes through a historical analysis of U.S. racial formation as well as an examination of legal processes governing and defining noncitizens. Illustrating Omi and Winant's definition of racial formation as "the sociohistorical process by which racial categories are created, inhabited, transformed, and destroyed" (1994: 55), I analyze how immigration laws and detention practices encode race and periodically expand the borders between citizenship and noncitizenship.

EXCEPTIONALISM

It is often stated that the September 11, 2001, terrorist attacks on the United States "changed everything" and denoted a "loss of innocence" in the nation's beliefs about safety and security. New concerns about national security and the supposed exceptionalism of 9/11 have ushered in what Ashcroft has termed "a new era in America's fight against terrorism" (Eggen, 2001: A20). However, the attorney general's "new era" of anti-terrorism strategies only echoes tactics introduced eighty years prior during the Red Scare, when noncitizenship also served as the government's "prosecutorial advantage." The national security trump card and the reduced and lesser status of immigrants thus work hand in hand, and are deliberate aspects of federal strategies of immigration control.

Under the guise of a carefully framed national security crisis, the Department of Justice under Ashcroft broadened its prosecutorial and investigative powers, using minor immigration charges, material witness statutes, invented legal categories, and unprecedented secrecy to sweep up and detain noncitizens at great cost to nonwhite immigrants and their families and communities. Indeed, the ACLU's executive director Anthony Romero has remarked, "Clearly the actions, policies, and laws he's [Ashcroft] promulgated show a fundamental lack of concern for enforcing civil liberties and civil rights" (Ragavan 2004: 36). With criticism of the Department of Justice's handling of post–9/11 detainees emanating from civil libertarians, from the Department of Justice's Inspector General, and from the commission investigating 9/11 (see Janofsky 2004), contemporary detention policy functions similarly to how political scientist Peter Andreas (2003: 2) characterizes border control policies—as "politically successful policy failures." They are valued more for their political symbolism and high visibility than for their practical achievements in deterring immigration. The "war on terror," likewise, creates a culture of fear, while merely loudly pronouncing an atmosphere of security.

The detention of immigrants, of course, is not a new story, rather another face of the criminalization of immigrants in the United States. This pattern underscores the structural persistence of the legal and social hierarchy to which subsequent immigrant groups are incorporated. As law professor Bill Ong Hing (2004: 3) writes, "we are a nation of immigrants. However, the simplicity of that statement conceals the nation's consistent history of tension over whom we collectively regard as 'real Americans' and, therefore, who we would allow into our community." The shocking tragedy of 9/11, the executive declaration of an indeterminate "war on terror," the Bush administration's restoration of national security as the definitive trump card against civil liberties and governmental checks and balances, and the criminalization of dissent asserted by the attorney general serve together to obfuscate and discount the historical underpinnings of contemporary detention policies and the devaluation of due process protections for noncitizens at the center of national security enforcement.

In examining the pre–9/11 episodes of immigrant detention, my goal is to challenge the rhetoric professing the "unprecedented" nature of the "war on terror." Such framing not only furthers a long history of violation against immigrants in the United States, but 9/11's exceptionalism seeks to achieve a status of incomparability, contributing to the suppression of the United States' systematic treatment of noncitizens. The logic entailed in exceptionalist rhetoric would imply that it is virtually impossible to analyze the historical precursors to the diminished rights of immigrants, and particularly, immigrants marked by race, religion, or other negative cultural stereotypes, because the historical moment framing the abuse of immigrants is regarded as having no precedent. The advent of 9/11 and the federal government's global and domestic reaction supposedly changed everything, from presumptions about national security, to attitudes about the United States abroad and indeed about immigrants and refugees. Speaking directly to immigrant incarceration, law professor Teresa Miller (2002: 233) concludes, "one could argue that the one thing that remained unchanged by the events of September 11 was the United States' system of immigrant detention." Whereas Attorney General John Ashcroft declared "a new era in America's fight against terrorism" (Eggen 2001: A20), the ahistorical frame applied to contemporary national security concerns conceals important legal antecedents and long-standing patterns in detention history.

A critical historical analysis of immigrant detention is necessary because the so-called exceptional character of 9/11 requires a recontextualization in order to reveal its complexity and trace its preexisting infrastructure. In order to see through the carefully constructed historical amnesia that surrounds 9/11, I suspend the rhetoric of exceptionalism and show the relationship between immigrant detention and race in other moments of national emergency. Indeed, the patterns in U.S. immigrant detention history do offer us clear precedents to the "war on terror." Its so-called unprecedented nature is employed merely as a rhetorical diversion and to rationalize the reduction and eradication of constitutionally protected freedoms purged by the government.

A nearsighted analysis of Ashcroft's "new era" in anti-terrorism techniques, for example, does not explain why the number of immigrant detainees increased dramatically by 300 percent during the late 1990s nor does it reflect the deep historical roots and intensified periods of detention since the early 1900s.[7] Most often, such episodes are viewed as individualized events—

disconnected from the history of government policies and judicial rulings that enable them—in which the federal government responds to distinct national security crises utilizing a temporary strategy of incarcerating noncitizens, and thus protecting the nation and "homeland" from enemies within its borders. According to law professor David Cole (2002: 20), "administration supporters argue that the magnitude of the new threat requires a new paradigm. But so far we have seen only a repetition of a very old paradigm—broad incursions on liberties, largely targeted at unpopular noncitizens and minorities, in the name of fighting a war." Therefore, we might more accurately view the contemporary response to 9/11 under the catch-all "anti-terrorism" as the expansion of an infrastructure of immigrant detention that had already witnessed many episodes of expansion, including a dramatic escalation in the 1990s.

IMMIGRANT DETENTION

The detention of noncitizens is linked to the racialization of immigrants. The capacity for increased detentions of nonwhite immigrants is made possible by the history of detention expansion during national crises and the consistent legal vulnerabilities of noncitizens. Occurring episodically over the last one hundred years, the federal government's expansive authority to detain and deny due process to noncitizens during national crises legitimates the increasing criminal scrutiny of all segments of the U.S. population. Noncitizens who are vulnerable to unequal social relations or specifically categorized en masse as undesirables or enemies of the state are particularly susceptible.

Dehumanizing conditions for noncitizens in immigrant detention centers continues to parallel and often exceed the conditions for inmates within the United States' penitentiary system. Indeed, almost two million people—two-thirds of whom are nonwhites—are currently locked up in U.S. prisons and jails, representing a tripling of this population since 1980. The number of immigrants in INS detention has also tripled in the last decade (see Solomon 1999). While the severity of conditions within what Angela Davis terms the "punishment industry" is being rightfully questioned, the criminalization and detention of immigrants has not yet been satisfactorily addressed in the emerging discourse on the "prison-industrial complex." Because immigrant detainees are incarcerated under a different system of punishment than the criminal courts, the conditions of their confinement remain obscured and legally ambiguous.

In general terms, detention is the practice of incarcerating immigrants— undocumented migrants, legal permanent residents, and in some cases, citizens—who are apprehended at ports of entry or in the nation's interior and maintained in custody until they are released, paroled, or deported from the United States. Formerly run by the INS, custody of detainees is managed by Immigration and Customs Enforcement (ICE). Today, immigrant detention is facilitated by a three-part system of captivity: permanent federal detention centers, privately contracted "micro prisons," and local public facilities renting bed space for immigrant detainees. The differing detention sites, with varying standards and conditions, result in an unequal execution of federal detention policy. Where an immigrant is detained can determine the immigrant's and his or her family's detention experience by way of the length of stay, the ability to post bond, and eventual legal proceedings. Because in the immigration courts detainees do not have a right to a lawyer, or in many cases, to post bond, it is estimated that less than 11 percent of immigrant detainees have legal counsel in the immigration courts (see Miller 2002).

The varying conditions of detention facilities propel much of the advocacy for improvement or abolition of federal detention policy. Today, allegations of gross mistreatment—from overcrowding, to denial of medical attention, to sexual abuse and other forms of torture—make up the bulk of human interest reporting on detention and long precede the secrecy and allegations of torture being associated with 9/11 detainees. These countless individual stories reveal particular blind spots in immigration law, as well as widespread structural unfairness and racism. While these allegations and patterns of incidents plague all three types of facilities, privately contracted detention facilities and local jails, which together hold almost two thirds of all detainees, have received the most criticism, and indicate a severe lack of monitoring and evaluation.[8]

In keeping with the bureaucratic shifts of the INS from an economic context to a national security context, the study of immigrant detention also reveals a unique relationship between immigrants and the federal prison system, in which immigrant status intersects with sentencing guidelines and the reclassification of crimes for noncitizens. For example, excluding the over 5,000 9/11 detainees and the emerging international detention infrastructure at Guantánamo Naval Base and in the Middle East, there are over 23,000 immigrants being detained today within the United States, and over 230,000 immigrants are detained each year. Yet, the Federal Bureau of Prisons reports that almost 50,000, or 29 percent, of its inmates are also noncitizens. Nearly 40,000 of them are Latino immigrants.[9] Not only do these immigrants represent more than double the daily detainee population, but nearly all of them are *future* detainees, having committed deportable offenses which take effect upon being released from federal prison. This means that upon serving the mandated sentence for criminal offenses, immigrants, including legal permanent residents, are rearrested and placed in immigrant detention until their permanent removal or release upon successful appeal. In addition, recent changes in immigration law in the 1990s have resulted in the reclassification of crimes for noncitizens, which results in dissimilar penalties for immigrants and citizens convicted of crimes with the same elements. As a result, from 1990 to 2000, the number of offenders in federal prisons on immigration violations increased eightfold, and the average length of time served increased by over 600 percent.[10] As such, immigrants and their families are caught between two systems of punishment, the immigration courts and the criminal courts, in which their lesser citizenship status has a multiplier effect on their criminalization.

LESSER CITIZENSHIP

Lesser citizens are produced when the rights of citizenship and legal personhood are abrogated by various levels of government as well as by private members of society. Lesser citizenship is a condition of negativity that is unstable and dependent on social, political, and legal factors. While it shares a kinship with the notion of being a "second-class citizen," I choose to use lesser citizenship because it emphasizes more flexibility and the contingency of such persons' access to rights within society. This lesser status is not in opposition to other citizenship or racial statuses, but it is constituted by them.

Lesser citizens consist of both immigrants—who are supposed to be entitled to the protections of the Constitution—and what historian Mae Ngai calls "alien citizens"—that is, "persons who are American citizens by virtue of their birth in the United States but who are presumed to be foreign by the mainstream of American culture and, at times, by the state" (Ngai 2004: 2). Contributing to the proliferation of lesser citizenship are "legal neologisms" (Schell 2004: 7), such as the terms "enemy combatant" or "suspected terrorist," that are asserted in order to confound national and international law concerning the civil and human rights of persons, and to impress upon the media and general public, new criminalized identities. Such invented categories of legal personhood not only redefine the boundaries of U.S. citizenship, but in creating lesser classes of noncitizens and citizens, these new blanket categories of persons—steeped in race, ideology, country of origin, and other subjectivities—sanction legal and social practices which punish lesser citizens and their families and communities.

While national borders represent in the public imagination the central focus of immigration policy, the crucial border to be examined in the discussion of immigrant detention is not the militarized border between the United States and its North American neighbors, but the social and structural divisions

between citizens and noncitizens. The racial context of this unequal relationship has been explored by many scholars, firmly documenting the racist construction, categorization, and treatment of nonwhite immigrants and citizens.
The racial understanding of U.S. citizenship has always been a contested
process in which noncitizens serve to shape what racially and hierarchically
constitutes America. For example, Ian Haney López (1996) analyzes what are
known as the "prerequisite cases," in which various persons from the Civil
War through the 1920s made appeals in the Supreme Court to their "whiteness" and thus fitness for naturalization as U.S. citizens. Haney López's analysis explains how the courts upheld whiteness as the precondition for citizenship, defining various categories of people as nonwhites before the law. The
legal machinations during this period which equate citizenship with whiteness
signify "the perfection of racial doctrine in citizenship law," according to Ngai
(2004: 37). Race and citizenship share an intimate and mutually constitutive
relationship in which each gives meaning and legitimacy to the other.

It is at the intersection of racial and noncitizen subjectivities that the practice of immigrant detention and the reduction of due process find their common thread, even under different racial and political contexts. In a legal borderland characterized by immigrants' and citizens' divergent relationships to
the state, statutory and juridical parameters divide citizens and noncitizens
through the codification of difference. According to political scientist Thomas
Biersteker (2003: 161), "state jurisdictional claims of authority define the op-
erational meaning of the border, both how hard or how soft it is, and precisely
where (in legal, not physical space) the authority is exercised." Citizenship
and immigration law, in other words, serve to manage legal categories of human populations within the nation's physical borders. Historically, these populations have been juridically constituted as lesser citizens through a conflation of race, national origin, religion, and ideology, thus reinforcing various
axes of inequality. Further, U.S. detention policy, in particular, often signals
an end to individual review in the courtroom and other due process guarantees in favor of categorically determined rights bound by social and political
constructions of "alienage." The unequal application of federal laws that define citizenship and personhood in addition to the denial of due process protections for immigrants thus reveal an institutionalized, unequal, and often
racialized arrangement of citizens and noncitizens. Further, ideological prejudice and the construction of political "others" complement the racialization
of immigrants and are often motivating factors in immigrant detention and
denials of due process.

Well before September 11, 2001, U.S. immigration policy had been routinely framed by what Saskia Sassen (1996) terms a "control crisis," in which
legislative initiatives historically sought to stem the flow of immigration, and

legal and administrative methods mandated the management, restraint, and deportation of undesirable noncitizens. Such a perspective has resulted in myopically conceived government strategies that attempt to address the restriction of immigration through various forms of deterrence. The regime of regulatory legislation and enforcement, most often with a focus on borders and ports of entry, narrowly addresses, according to Sassen (1999: 20), "a complex, deeply embedded and transnational process that it can only partly address or regulate through immigration policy as conventionally understood." Similarly, federal detention practices, bolstered by the widespread criminalization of immigrants, rely on categorical and blanket presumptions about detainees, often steeped in racial conjecture that can at the extreme, conflate beliefs about noncitizens and citizens. According to Evelyn Nakano Glenn (2002: 236), "citizenship shifted from a restrictive definition of membership that categorically excluded major classes of people, including nonwhites, women, and those without property, to one that was inclusive, but assigned differential rights and obligations to different categories of people." Simultaneously, blanket categorization of particular immigrant groups (e.g., Japanese, Muslims, Haitians, socialists, etc.) not only produces inequality among immigrant groups, but it also facilitates the negation of individual protections such as due process rights meant to protect persons from unlawful criminalization. The codification of difference into citizenship law, and administered through detention practices, thus constructs new embodiments of "nonpersonhood" and lesser citizenship.

If, as political philosopher Joy James (1996: 34) argues, "American prisons constitute an 'outside' in U.S. political life," then what about those immigrants who are *outside* of this outside? Living externally to the boundaries of citizenship and in the legal vacuum of detention contributes to the lesser citizenship of immigrant detainees and their families and communities. For example, Vice President Dick Cheney asserted that the statutory inequality between citizens and noncitizens determines who are availed constitutional rights and protections. With regard to foreign nationals and the use of military tribunals as a substitute for criminal courts, Cheney has stated divisively, "They don't deserve the same guarantees and safeguards that would be used for an American citizen going through the normal judicial process" (Slevin and Lardner 2001: A28). The Bush administration's exploitation of noncitizenship as a pretext for administering differential rights runs counter to judicial precedents, which have explicitly denied to noncitizens only the right to vote, to hold certain public offices, and the right to enter and reside in the country. As legal scholar Gerald Neuman (1996: 4) argues, "the Supreme Court has also held for more than a century that aliens within the United States are persons entitled to constitutional protection. That includes aliens who are unlawfully present." The constitutionality of immigrants' legal personhood has been challenged by the government, successfully so, especially in times of national emergency. The statutory authority over the creation and administration of immigration policy—in which immigrant detainees historically hang in the balance—is thus a contest impacted by the judicial, executive, and legislative branches of government, and one vulnerable to unprecedented accumulation of power in the name of "national security." The denial of due process rights for immigrant detainees is the most direct means to reinforce the inequality between citizens and noncitizens. In removing the judicial safeguards protecting immigrants from unchallenged criminalization, the system of checks and balances is obstructed and noncitizens and their families are rendered what Neuman (1996) calls "strangers to the Constitution."

RACE AND DETENTION OF "ALIENS"

Presumptions of criminal foreignness, racial profiling, and denials of due process are familiar occurrences for U.S. immigrant communities. As Roberto Martínez (Serrano 2002: A8) of the American Friends Service Committee told the *Los Angeles Times* six months after 9/11, "Muslim detainees are complaining in New York, and that's nothing new for us. They are going through the fear factor that Mexicans have undergone for years." Martínez's comment links anti-terrorist security measures to U.S.-Mexico border enforcement and highlights the racialized experience of noncitizenship. The social construction of race, of course, has changed historically, especially as it pertains to immigrants. Jews and Southern and Eastern Europeans, for example, were once located on or outside the boundaries of white citizenship, and then over time were included in the superordinate racial category of whiteness. Asian and Latino immigrants, on the other hand, despite social and legal struggles to achieve first-class citizenship have been regarded consistently as nonwhites despite being in the United States for over a century. "Race is a palimpsest," says Matthew Frye Jacobson (1998: 142), "a tablet whose most recent inscriptions only imperfectly cover those that have come before, and whose inscriptions can never be regarded as final." But unlike the transitory experience of white immigrants whose racial inscription was temporary, the immigration process for nonwhite immigrants—Latinos and Asians, for example—continues to serve as the initial site of racialization which maintains their racialized foreignness before the law and society, much like the permanent nonwhite status of Native Americans and African Americans. From nonwhite immigrants' initial reception, through naturalization, and in the event of detention and deportation, the immigration process reads, categorizes and marks these persons, articulating the limits of their citizenship.

Immigrant detainees are so-called aliens apprehended by immigration authorities and held in custody until their conditional or permanent release or deportation. Apprehension may occur at ports of entry or in the interior of the country, and unless paroled temporarily, detainees remain in custody throughout the adjudication of their cases until removed (that is, deported) or admitted under a recognized status. Episodes of expansive immigrant detention reflect a construction of citizenship consistent with racialized immigrant histories, in which emerging citizenship statuses are constructed and experienced as racial markers. For example, aliens ineligible for citizenship, guest workers, and "illegals" intimate racial meaning. Moreover, new categories of criminal personhood such as "person of interest" or "suspected terrorist," or old labels such as "enemy alien," are infused with racial significance and become codified by government statistics and the media. These invented categories function as euphemisms for racialized subjects and contribute to the circulation of racial stereotypes of immigrants in public discourse. Immigrant detention serves as an instrument for such processes, leading to a race-based and citizenship-based inequality imposed on immigrants of various national origins. In the following subsections, I connect the racial character of U.S. immigrant history to detention expansion. I explore the blanket categorization of various types of immigrant detainees, such as diseased aliens, enemy aliens, refugees, and criminal aliens during national crises.

Health and Detention

One of the motivating factors in immigrant detention at the turn of the twentieth century surrounded emerging questions of public health, which often times pivoted on racialized presumptions about "troublesome diseases" that were believed to inhabit the bodies, indeed the cultures, of arriving migrants. In many ways, fear of disease served as the ideal ideological justification for the exclusion or segregation of non- and lesser-white migrants who Americans feared would contaminate the slowly consolidating sense of whiteness of the nation. According to the Commissioner of Immigration at Ellis Island in New York Harbor, such contagion was believed to be "prevalent in the countries of eastern and southern Europe, and due to low vitality and filthy surroundings" (Sargent 1903: 68). On the West Coast, such "loathsome" diseases were overwhelmingly presumed to be endemic of Asian migrants, and moreover, this belief justified double standards for nonwhite immigrants in medical examinations and resulting detentions of "diseased aliens." According to the Commissioner-General of Immigration in 1903, "The diseases which endanger the health of the American people through alien immigration are distinctively oriental in origin, and the transportation lines bringing aliens from eastern Europe and from Asia are the ones to be most carefully scanned" (Sargent 1903: 42). The port of entry to the United States, aided by an emerging bureaucracy of fees, regulations, and fines which were imposed on would-be immigrants and those transporting them, served as the nation's first line of defense and a key site for the detention of immigrants.

Marked by countless descriptions of disease and filth, Asian immigrants, before disembarking in San Francisco, were first detained at Angel Island Quarantine Station, which predated the western port's immigration and detention station at the same site by two decades (see Shah 2001). Quarantine, a centuries-old safeguard against the plague, was originally applied by the United States as protection from mortal diseases, but after the development of federal exclusion policies, it was also applied to nondeadly chronic illnesses. As Neuman (1996: 31) explains, "Indeed, the emphasis on *nonfatal* chronic diseases at the turn of the century reflected a desire to be more selective in the choice of immigrants, not merely the need to protect the resident population from infection." While at the quarantine station and later the immigration station, Asian migrants' petitions for entry were scrutinized for validity while their bodies underwent medical examination.

The conditions and spatial attributes of Angel Island Immigration Station, or the "Ellis Island of the west"—located on an island in the middle of the San Francisco Bay—were initially designed in order to isolate Chinese detainees from the Chinese and larger San Francisco community in order to prevent both communication and the arrival of communicable diseases presumed to originate from Asian migrants.[11] Later, the immigration station would be bemoaned because its "remoteness" was a "source of annoyance" (Caminetti 1919: 58–59). The station's spatial attributes, once regarded as especially suited for Chinese migrants, rendered practical difficulties after the Immigration Act of 1917 codified the "Asiatic barred zone," drawing a line of exclusion around Asia. Nonetheless, during its existence as an immigration and detention center, Angel Island, according to Erika Lee (2003: 75–76), "embodied . . . racist immigration policies" because the port of entry served primarily as a detention station relative to Ellis Island's focus on processing and receiving European immigrants. Unlike the European migrants who passed through Ellis Island, most of the migrants that were processed on Angel Island—migrants who were primarily Chinese—were detained in some cases for up to two years. During the Chinese exclusion era, when only family members of existing citizens or particular merchants were eligible for entry, migrants were required to undergo intensive interrogation to prove kinship in addition to racially biased health screening. Detention, then, served to both contain fears of disease, but also to separate and stunt the reception and growth of the Chinese community.

Along the U.S.-Mexico border, the Bureau of Immigration and U.S. Public Health Service stepped up efforts to transform its "disinfection plant" into a station capable of an "'iron-clad quarantine' against every body entering the United States from Mexico'" (Stern 1999: 41–42). Despite the fact that most communicable diseases were imported from Europe—and that these diseases were responsible for the decimation of indigenous populations throughout the Americas—the rhetoric surrounding health was used as a major ideological tool to prevent, scrutinize, and advance nativist fears about undesirable, nonwhite migrants. In the south, Mexicans, and migrants arriving through Mexico, were also detained and medically examined for contagious diseases. As with arriving Asian immigrants, race linked Mexican immigrants to disease. As one Public Health Service doctor wrote in the 1920s, "all persons coming to El Paso from Mexico" were "considered as likely to be vermin infested." For Mexican border crossers, then, medical detention thus included additional processes such as being stripped naked, deloused, vaccinated, bathed with "a mixture of soap, kerosene, and water," and having their clothes and baggage sterilized.[12]

The policies and practices directed at "diseased aliens" influenced racial policies in the United States, shifting the black-white paradigm of race and citizenship into an intersection that included nativistic fears of nonwhite immigrants and groups of persons at the uncertain borders of whiteness. Race and national origin, aspects which carried with them numerous pejorative stereotypes pertaining to intelligence, political aptitude, and loyalty, were further burdened by irrational fears of presumed contagion, potentially leading to quarantine, detention, and deportation. The health and physical condition of migrants were thus linked to the health, purity, and well-being of the nation. At a time where there was no military threat or crisis in which to rationalize the scapegoating of nonwhite migrants, the government captured the fears of the nation by projecting the threat of disease as imminent, particularly with the introduction of nonwhite, dirty, uncivilized populations from south of the border and across the Pacific Ocean.

Detention of Enemy Aliens

While national security emergencies can originate from alleged crises in public health, the national economy, and natural catastrophes, wartime emergencies most clearly legitimate the expanded powers of the federal branches of government. Positioned as threats to national security during times of war, foreign nationals from countries locked in military conflict with the United States are deemed "enemy aliens," and are subject to the emergency war powers of the executive branch, which have resulted in military tribunals as well as individual and mass incarcerations.

Before 9/11, the most notorious occurrence of the executive application of emergency war powers was the wartime relocation and incarceration of Japanese and Japanese American citizens from December 7, 1941, through September 29, 1947, also known as Japanese internment. According to the Commission on Wartime Relocation and Internment of Civilians, appointed in the early 1980s to review the "facts and circumstances" surrounding Japanese internment, "the broad historical causes which shaped these decisions were race prejudice, war hysteria and a failure of political leadership."[13] It is important to note that so-called enemy aliens from Italy and Germany were also detained—almost 3,000 in 1942—but they did not include large numbers of citizens and they were not held in proportion to their numbers listed on the federal "alien registration" lists, which outnumbered Japanese immigrants threefold (for Italians) and sixfold (for Germans). Moreover, these persons received individual review of their cases resulting in parole, which the Japanese did not (see Schofield 1942). The racial construction of "enemy aliens," tragically illustrated by the Japanese internment, blurs the distinctions between citizens and noncitizens—while underscoring racial distinctions between whiteness and nonwhiteness—using an "alienage" model that is extended to co-ethnic citizens, and in turn, used to conflate and reduce these groups to racialized political "others." As Cole (2003: 97) explains, "the close interrelationship between anti-Asian racism and anti-immigrant sentiment made the transition from enemy alien to enemy race disturbingly smooth."

Refugee Detentions

Whereas prior to World War II domestic security policies grounded in the ideological opposition to communism permitted the detention and deportation of aliens who were enemies of the state, post–World War II Cold War policies of containment of communist governments in addition facilitated the arrival and official acceptance of refugees fleeing communist governments. In general refugee policies are meant to provide asylum for persons with "well-founded fears" of persecution on a variety of grounds in their home countries. However, the passage of the Refugee Act of 1980 in combination with the 1980s Cold War foreign policies of the Reagan-Bush administrations led to a massive expansion of detention facilities specifically suited for detaining and discouraging refugees displaced by U.S. involvement in Central America and in the Caribbean.

The central features of the 1980 Refugee Act, according to the Bureau of Citizen and Immigration Services, conformed the U.S. definition of refugees to the international standards of the 1967 United Nations Protocol on Refugees and provided "the first permanent and systematic procedure for the admission and effective resettlement of refugees of special humanitarian concern to the United States."[14] Limited by Cold War politics, however, the new act suffered from a severe inequality in its application, with expansive effects on detention policy. Whereas the United States readily accepted as legal permanent residents and swiftly processed refugees fleeing communist governments, the opposite was true for refugees fleeing governments which the United States supported. The latter group of refugees was criminalized by the government and deemed inadmissible, thus increasing the need for detention space for those refugees fighting deportation or circumventing the asylum process altogether.

The 1980s, in particular, witnessed large-scale detentions of Cuban refugees and Central Americans fleeing U.S.-supported civil wars, as well as so-called Haitian boat people, who had been arriving in large numbers since the early 1970s. In 1980, for instance, 120,000 Cuban "marielitos" fled Cuba, some through the Cuban port of Mariel. The refugee exodus from the Caribbean and Central America fueled racial panic about black and Latino, criminal, and diseased refugee streams. For example, fearing a criminal class of Cuban immigrants among the mostly young and male refugees, some of whom had been in prison as criminal or political prisoners in Cuba, the United States broke with its former policy of proactive acceptance and several thousand Cubans were detained en masse in the early 1980s in order to individually determine the extent of their suspected criminal histories, leading to severe overcrowding and riots at detention centers in Georgia and Louisiana (see Kahn 1996; Hamm 1995). Despite these large scale detentions—which represented only a small percentage of the entire Mariel boatlift—the majority of Cuban asylum seekers still receive individual review and special treatment as preferred Cold War refugees. Haitian refugees, on the other hand, were treated in aggregate and were collectively denied political asylum, routinely intercepted at sea, detained, and deported.

Heightened Cold War foreign policy in Latin America dovetailed with new refugee policies to aggravate the "crisis" in detention in the 1980s. As Robert Kahn (1996: 16) explains, "the crisis in U.S. immigration prisons began in 1981, when Attorney General William French Smith decreed that undocumented people who applied for political asylum under the 1980 Refugee Act should be detained until a decision was made in their case." As noted above, while the Refugee Act of 1980 seemed to invite asylum seekers, the application of detention policy by the INS fueled an escalation in the detention infrastructure. For example, during this period the Port Isabel immigration prison in South Texas expanded its bed capacity from 425 to 10,000 beds, mostly through tent construction. The 1980s episode of expansion followed the near-doubling of daily immigrant detainees, from 2,370 to 4,062, that

developed in the 1970s. As well, there was an expansion of contracted facilities all along the U.S.-Mexico border, and a reopening of a federal facility
once used to intern Japanese Americans (see Kahn 1996; Dow 2004). The
newly expanded detention system was encumbered with pervasive allegations
of human rights abuses, ranging from beatings to sexual abuse and torture.
Further, unequal treatment of refugees of various national origins corre-
sponded to the U.S. Cold War foreign policy stance toward their countries of
origin. While the asylum applications of Salvadorans and Guatemalans fleeing U.S.-backed administrations were rejected 97–99 percent of the time,
Nicaraguans fleeing a socialist government which the U.S. opposed were
granted either asylum (at a rate of 84 percent in 1987) or a suspended deportation, leading to release from detention (see Kahn 1996).

One of the notable effects of detention policy during this period of expansion
was the origination of legal and popular citizenship statuses directly related to
detention. For example, stemming from the deportation cases against Cubans in
the 1980s and 1990s, the government has applied the legal term "excludable" to
immigrants—of which the majority are Cuban refugees. This government-cre-
ated status is used to deny due process and habeas corpus protections to persons
paroled into the United States by INS officials, but never formally admitted. This
lack of technical "admission," even though it was administered by government
officials, means that for certain immigrants already within the United States,
they are treated legally as if they had never entered the country. One Cuban detainee at York County Prison, Pennsylvania, on never being formally admitted to
the United States and "in the eyes of the law . . . not really here," asserts, "On
paper, we're still on a boat. If they say I'm still on a boat, then put me on a boat,
and I'll find my way back to Cuba" (Bahadur 2004: A12).

If an excludable migrant is convicted of a deportable offense, but cannot be
deported to his or her home country—a not uncommon occurrence for
refugees—then the excludable will remain in detention indefinitely. Over
two-thirds of excludables in United States detention are Cubans who cannot
be deported to Cuba and thus are in indefinite detention, even though some
have not committed crimes while in the United States. Numbering roughly
1,000, including 300 detainees from countries other than Cuba (see Werlin
2004), such detainees are more commonly referred to by a different popular
term, which is "lifers." Of the roughly 1,000 "lifers" in permanent detention,
over 150 have been in detention for ten years or longer (see Bahadur 2004;
Welch 2002; Hamm 1995).

As exemplified by the legal fiction of "excludables," the 1980s episode of
detention expansion flows from a familiar pattern in detention history: racialized xenophobia and the production of new classes of "aliens" via "wars" that
broadly construct, yet deliberately target, the objects of national security anx-

ieties. The Cold War in particular, with its ideological bias toward promoting capitalism—by readily accepting refugees from communist regimes—is imbedded in the structure of refugee policy, privileging only those asylum seekers who can strengthen U.S. global power. Haitians, Salvadorans, Guatemalans, and "lifers," on the other hand, during the decade of the 1980s represent the racial and political other, revealing the subtleties in the racial logic of refugee policy, seemingly contradicting its stated purpose.

Criminal Aliens and Detention

While refugees were being detained en masse at ports of entry in the 1980s, *domestic* criminalization and detention policy initiatives focused on "criminal aliens" inside the nation during the "war on drugs." Increased policing, supported by the reclassification and expansion of deportable crimes such as drug or gun trafficking coupled with mandatory drug sentencing made noncitizen immigrant drug offenders subject to detention and deportation. For instance, the Anti-Drug Abuse Act of 1988 directly affected immigration law and policy by introducing a special class of deportable offenses called "aggravated felonies," which prompted the detention and deportation of noncitizens, including legal permanent residents (see Chea 1999). The increased detention of "criminal aliens" constituted what border expert Timothy Dunn (1996: 73) called a "historic change in INS detention practices." What was so dramatic about these new drug policies was that they seemed to target racial minorities with such transparency. The "war on drugs" fueled an expansion of the mission and resources made available to the INS and its efforts to apprehend undesirable nonwhite migrants. The large populations of Central American and Haitian detainees shifted to Mexican detainees, who were held less frequently in the early 1980s because of their easier, sometimes voluntary, removal. This focus resulted in "60 percent of the agency's detention space [being] devoted to criminal aliens" by 1992, double that of the previous year, and it anticipated a radical expansion in immigrant detention throughout the 1990s (Dunn 1996: 73).

Well under way prior to 9/11, the expansion of the detention infrastructure has been in a growth spurt in the last decade, outpacing prison growth nationwide. In fact, bed space tripled in the late 1990s alone, facilitating the detention of 23,000 persons every day, and over 230,000 annually. Length of stay ranges from days to years. Detainees are imprisoned at one of a total of eight detention centers run by the federal authorities, seven contract detention facilities managed for profit by private prison operators, or one of over nine hundred state, county, and municipal jails made available through intergovernmental contracts (see Welch 2002). Spending for detention and removal has also increased fivefold since 1993 to one billion dollars. Staff more than doubled from 1,600 to 3,500 personnel. By 2001, increased expenditures on detention and removal amounted to "one third of all INS enforcement spending, or nearly as much as the agency's entire budget just seven years ago" (Tangeman 2002: 26). As a major precursor to the detentions stemming from the "war on terror," the penultimate episode in detention growth in the 1990s resulted from a combination of new legislation that targeted immigrants by reducing their due process rights, and the reintroduction and codification of "national security" in the wake of foreign and domestic terrorism in the mid-1990s.

The domestic "war on terrorism" catalyzed by the September 11, 2001, terrorist attacks generated the newest episode of expansion in the long pattern of immigrant detention in the United States. The growth of immigrant detention resulting from this expansion—approximately 5,000 new detainees—merges with the rapid expansion of detention bed space for housing "criminal aliens," especially those netted in the "war on drugs" and as a result of the 1996 immigration legislation. Of these laws, the Illegal Immigration Reform and Immigrant Responsibility Act (IIRIRA) most elaborately facilitated detention through a sweeping and regressive denial of due process to noncitizens. By ushering in "mandatory detentions" for immigrants facing removal and removing judicial relief, IIRIRA contributes to the categorically sweeping nature of immigration law and order—tactics that have led to numerous other abuses of human rights and incursions on due process.

IIRIRA extended the divide between citizens and immigrants in criminal justice by redefining and widening the parameters of an "aggravated felony" to include minor nonviolent crimes such as burglary, illegal gambling, and tax evasion for noncitizens, including legal permanent residents. This change, effective retroactively, initiates the deportation process which mandates detention for offenses that were not deportable when they were committed. According to Miller (2002: 220–21), "the retroactivity of the mandatory detention provisions combined with the vastly expanded categories of offenses which subject non-U.S. citizens to deportation are primarily responsible for the threefold increase in the numbers of non-U.S. citizens in federal immigration detention." In other words, immigrant detention swelled in the late 1990s as noncitizens and lawful permanent residents who committed crimes and served their terms, even prior to the passage of IIRIRA, were subject to detention and deportation proceedings, regardless of their tenure in the United States, their knowledge of or affinities to the countries to where they were being deported, or their lack of criminal activity since the original criminal offense.

Creating a severe legal inequality between citizens and noncitizens, IIRIRA establishes that immigrants and non-immigrants committing crimes with the same elements are punished differentially—first punished by the criminal court system and then by the immigration system, which in many cases leads to post-sentence detention and deportation. On the surface, this may appear to be an odd form of double jeopardy, but in the logic and structure of immigration law, the single criminal act that is also a deportable offense is simultaneously subject to two court systems, one criminal and one administrative. Importantly, deportation and detention are not considered punishment before the law, but instead "administrative proceedings." Such proceedings are a euphemism for the practice of incarcerating immigrants who themselves view detention and deportation as punitive rather than simply administrative. Although criminal aliens find themselves in the same cells as persons convicted in the criminal courts and are criminalized before society, they are distinguished by their lack of due process protections as administrative detainees.

The reason that the 1996 legislation is so significant in the history of immigrant detention and central to understanding the obfuscations of post–9/11 immigrant enforcement policies is that it amassed the juridical, administrative, and infrastructural foundation for a large scale, intergovernmentally coordinated expansion of detention capacity which previously was not possible. This means that while all immigrants saw an expansion in the legal rationale for their detention and deportation, and detainees experienced a reduction in due process, the immigration courts received strict mandates reducing the possibility of parole for detainees and the INS was rewarded with a massive expansion of infrastructural funding for detention and interior enforcement. Furthermore, by removing the procedural rights of immigrants and the discretionary power of immigration judges, the 1996 legislation made permanent, mandatory, and retroactive the undesirability and criminality of legal permanent residents, refugees, and undocumented immigrants. Grouping virtually all noncitizens together, the 1996 immigration legislation and public sentiment shifted the spotlight from the U.S.-Mexico border and the legal and social divisions between so-called legal and illegal immigrants, to the juridical and cultural borders between all citizens and noncitizens. Without question, 9/11 generates a new episode of detention expansion that builds upon this division. But the domestic "war on terror" is also consistent with patterns in detention history that predate the terrorist attacks and the ensuing detention expansion by over one hundred years.

CONCLUSION

In view of the government's various productions and detentions of "aliens" outlined in this essay, I have attempted to provide an overview of key episodes of immigrant detention that reflect the confluence of noncitizen statuses and national security crises which produce racial patterns that are absorbed into the structure of immigration policy. The essay has also attempted to challenge the rhetoric of exceptionalism surrounding the current "war on terror" by emphasizing its historical genealogy. The Japanese and Japanese American internment, as merely one example, is not solely a black mark on U.S. history, but part of a pattern of black marks built into immigration policy.

It is clear that the current administration's "war on terror" revives many of the statutes, strategies, and suspicions embedded in the history of immigrant detention. In a chilling reminder of the collusion between enforcement and nonenforcement divisions of the government, the Census Bureau was recently criticized for sharing with the Department of Homeland Security information that identified concentrations of Arab American populations by cities and zip codes.[15] Although technically legal, this policy replicates the policy of the Census Bureau in the 1940s that facilitated the identification and round-up of Japanese and Japanese Americans during World War II—a practice which led to a formal apology by the Census Bureau in 2000. Certainly, the logic of internment is still highly regarded in many sectors of our government—in Congress, at the Department of Justice, and among pundits—justifying the practice of racial profiling.

Despite the increased attention to the "war on terror" and the thousands of detentions of Arab, Muslim, and South Asian immigrants which have resulted in the enlargement of the detention infrastructure, "criminal aliens" and absconders who flee after their final orders to leave the country still represent the lion's share of immigrant detainees and are the primary reason for the expansion of immigrant detention today. For example, the 2005 intelligence reform bill stemming from the federal commission analyzing 9/11 and the "war on terrorism" carries a provision that expands the daily domestic detainee capacity by 8,000 beds per year, for 5 years (see Llorente 2005). This increase, under the auspices of promoting "homeland" security in the domestic "war on terror," will triple the detention infrastructure for the second decade in a row, even though the majority of detainees—criminal aliens—have nothing to do with terrorism. From this vantage point, the "war on terror" is indeed a war without end, requiring an enduring mobilization, internationally and at home. For some time to come, then, detainees and noncitizens will continue to be conflated with terrorists in our new domestic "war."

NOTES

1. From this point forward, I will use 9/11 to refer to the terrorist attacks on the United States on September 11, 2001.

2. The due process clause of the Fourteenth Amendment to the U.S. Constitution states, ". . . nor shall any State deprive any person of life, liberty, or property, without due process of law." See caselaw.lp.findlaw.com/data/constitution/amendment14 (accessed February 28, 2006).

3. Based on a national poll by Genesis Research Associates commissioned by the Council on American-Islamic Relations. See Carlyle Murphy (2002).

4. There have been numerous court challenges to the use of secrecy in 9/11 cases. In one case, the Supreme Court refused to hear an appeal challenging the secrecy of 9/11 detentions. Kate Martin, director of the Center for National Security Studies, decried this decision, stating, "There is no accountability for the abuses, and secrecy allowed abuses. That's always been the objection to secrecy." See Charles Lane (2004).

5. After Attorney General Ashcroft violated a gag order during what was at the time the government's single successful prosecution (which was later overturned for negligence on the part of the government's prosecution) a federal judge in Detroit admonished Ashcroft, who, in an unusual move, issued a written apology.

6. Testimony of Attorney General John Ashcroft, December 6, 2001, Senate Judiciary Committee Hearing on Anti-Terrorism Policy, 106th Congress.

7. See U.S. Department of Justice, Bureau of Justice Statistics, Prisoners in 2001, Bulletin NCJ 195189, p. 10, table 12, 2002; Bulletin NCJ 200248, p. 8, table 10. Washington, DC: U.S. Department of Justice. Available online at Sourcebook of Criminal Justice Statistics Online, www.albany.edu/sourcebook/1995/pdf/t654.pdf.

8. According to Anthony Tangeman, Director of the Office of Detention and Removal at the newly created Bureau of Immigration and Customs Enforcement, local jails and private facilities "provide us with half of our detention capacity." See Tangeman (2002: 27).

9. See Federal Bureau of Prisons, August 2003, "Quick Facts and Statistics." Available at www.bop.gov/.

10. See Bureau of Justice Statistics, August 2002, Immigration Offenders in the Federal Criminal Justice System, 2000, Special Report NCJ 191745. Washington, DC: U.S. Department of Justice.

11. For example, the Commissioner-General of Immigration "urgently" pressed the Treasury Department for a $200,000 appropriation for the construction of an immigration station in San Francisco harbor, where "isolation from the mainland [was] deemed of special importance" to prevent the arrival of communicable diseases presumed to originate from Asian migrants, and also "to prevent . . . attempts to communicate with the detained aliens" by "the most resourceful of alien peoples—the Chinese" (Sargent 1903: 42–43).

12. See C. C. Pierce, "Combating Typhus Fever on the Mexican Border," Public Health Reports 32 (March 1917): 426–29. Cited in Stern (1999: 45–46).

13. See Commission on Wartime Relocation and Internment of Civilians, Personal Justice Denied (Seattle: Civil Liberties Public Education Fund and University of Washington Press, 1997), 459. Originally published by the U.S. Government Printing Office, 1982 and 1983.

14. Available online at the Bureau of Immigration and Citizenship Services, uscis.gov/graphics/shared/aboutus/statistics/legishist/553.htm.

15. See Lipton (2004), Clemetson (2004), and Holmes (2000).

REFERENCES

Ackerman, Bruce. 2004, September. "States of Emergency." *The American Prospect*.

Andreas, Peter. 2003. "A Tale of Two Borders: The U.S.-Canada and U.S.-Mexico Lines after 9-11." Pp. 1–23 in *The Rebordering of North America: Integration and Exclusion in a New Security Context*, ed. Peter Andreas and Thomas J. Biersteker. New York: Routledge.

Bahadur, Gaiutra. 2004, October 10. "Boat-lift Refugees Fighting Limbo." *Philadelphia Inquirer*: A1, A12.

Biersteker, Thomas, J. 2003. "The Rebordering of North America? Implications for Conceptualizing Borders after September 11." Pp. 153–65 in *The Rebordering of North America: Integration and Exclusion in a New Security Context*, ed. Peter Andreas and Thomas J. Biersteker. New York: Routledge.

Brinkley, Alan. 2003. "A Familiar Story: Lessons from Past Assaults on Freedoms." Pp. 23–46 in *The War on Our Freedoms: Civil Liberties in an Age of Terrorism*, ed. Richard C. Leone and Greg Anrig Jr. New York: Century Foundation.

Caminetti, Anthony J. 1919. *Annual Report of the Commissioner-General of Immigration*. Washington, DC: Government Printing Office.

Chea, Socheat. 1999. "The Evolving Definition of an Aggravated Felony." Institute of Continuing Legal Education of Georgia. www.rogerathi.com/felony.doc (accessed February 28, 2006).

Clemetson, Lynette. 2004, July 30. "Homeland Security Given Data on Arab-Americans." *New York Times*. www.notinourname.net/detentions/data-30jul04.htm (accessed February 18, 2006).

Cole, David. 2002, September 23. "Enemy Aliens and American Freedoms." *The Nation*.

———. 2003. *Enemy Aliens: Double Standards and Constitutional Freedoms in the War on Terrorism*. New York: New Press.

———. 2004, October 4. "Ashcroft: 0 for 5,000." *The Nation*.

Cusac, Anne-Marie. 2003, May. "No Lawyers beyond This Point." *The Progressive*.

Dow, Mark. 2004. *American Gulag: Inside U.S. Immigration Prisons*. Berkeley: University of California Press.

Duffy, Brian, and Chiltra Ragavan. 2004, January 26. "Respecting the Client, with Clarity." *U.S. News and World Report*.

Dunn, Timothy J. 1996. *The Militarization of the U.S.-Mexico Border, 1978–1992: Low Intensity Conflict Doctrine Comes Home*. Austin, TX: Center for Mexican American Studies.

Eggen, Dan. 2001, October 26. "Tough Anti-Terror Campaign Pledged." *Washington Post*: A1, A20.

———. 2004, August 20. "U.S. Uses Secret Evidence in Secrecy Fight with ACLU." *Washington Post*: A17.

———. 2004, September 30. "Key Part of Patriot Act Rule Unconstitutional." *Washington Post*: A16.

Friedlander, Blaine P., Jr. 2004, December 17. "Fear Factor: 44 Percent of Americans Queried in Cornell National Poll Favor Curtailing Some Liberties for Muslim Americans." Ithaca, NY: Cornell University. www.news.cornell.edu/releases/Dec04/Muslim.Poll.bpf.html (accessed February 28, 2006).

Glenn, Evelyn Nakano. 2002. *Unequal Freedom: How Race and Gender Shaped American Citizenship and Labor*. Cambridge, MA: Harvard University Press.

Hamm, Mark S. 1995. *The Abandoned Ones: The Imprisonment of the Mariel Boat People*. Boston: Northeastern University Press.

Haney López, Ian F. 1996. *White by Law: The Legal Construction of Race*. New York: New York University Press.

Hing, Bill Ong. 2004. *Defining America through Immigration Policy*. Philadelphia: Temple University Press.

Holmes, Steven A. 2000, March 17. "Census Blamed in Internment of Japanese." *New York Times*. seattlepi.nwsource.com/national/cens17.shtml (accessed February 18, 2006).

Jacobson, Matthew Frye. 1998. *Whiteness of a Different Color: European Immigrants and the Alchemy of Race*. Cambridge, MA: Harvard University Press.

James, Joy. 1996. *Resisting State Violence: Radicalism, Gender, and Race in U.S. Culture*. Minneapolis: University of Minnesota Press.

Janofsky, Michael. 2004, April 17. "9/11 Panel Calls Policies on Immigration Ineffective." *New York Times*: A8.

Johnson, Kevin R. 2004. *The "Huddled Masses" Myth: Immigration and Civil Rights*. Philadelphia: Temple University Press.

Kahn, Robert. 1996. *Other People's Blood: U.S. Immigration Prisons in the Reagan Decade*. Boulder, CO: Westview Press.

Kochar, Jasmit Singh. 2002. "Hate Crimes and Discrimination." Pp. 5–12 in *Justice for ALL: The Aftermath of September 11th, Report from the Public Hearing, September 21, 2002*. Seattle, WA: Hate Free Zone Campaign of Washington.

Lane, Charles. 2004, January 13. "Terror-Arrest Data to Stay Secret." *San Francisco Chronicle*: A1, A10.

Lee, Erika. 2003. *At America's Gates: Chinese Immigration during the Exclusion Era, 1882–1943*. Chapel Hill: University of North Carolina Press.

Lipton, Eric. 2004, November 10. "Panel Says Census Move on Arab-Americans Recalls World War II Internments." *New York Times*: A7.

Llorente, Elizabeth. 2005, January 18. "Reform Plan Will Escalate Detention of Immigrants." *The Bergen Record*. www.bergen.com (accessed January 20, 2005).

Miller, Teresa A. 2002. "The Impact of Mass Incarceration on Immigration Policy." Pp. 214–38 in *Invisible Punishment: The Collateral Consequences of Mass Imprisonment*, ed. Marc Mauer and Meda Chesney-Lind. New York: New Press.

Murphy, Carlyle. 2002, October 5. "Distrust of Muslims Common in U.S., Poll Finds." *Washington Post*: A2.

Neuman, Gerald L. 1996. *Strangers to the Constitution: Immigrants, Borders and Fundamental Law*. Princeton, NJ: Princeton University Press.

Ngai, Mae. 2004. *Impossible Subjects: Illegal Aliens and the Making of Modern America*. Princeton, NJ: Princeton University Press.

Omi, Michael, and Howard Winant. 1994. *Racial Formation in the United States from the 1960s to the 1990s*. New York: Routledge.

Ragavan, Chitra. 2004, January 26. "Ashcroft's Way." *U.S. News & World Report*.

Sargent, F. P. 1903. *Annual Report of the Commissioner-General of Immigration*. Washington, DC: Government Printing Office.

Sassen, Saskia. 1996. *Losing Control? Sovereignty in an Age of Globalization*. New York: Columbia University Press.

———. 1999. "Beyond Sovereignty: Immigration Policy Making Today." Pp. 15–26 in *Immigration: A Civil Rights Issue for the Americas*, ed. Susanne Jonas and Susie Dodd Thomas. Wilmington, DE: Scholarly Resources, Inc.

Schell, Jonathan. 2004, May 31. "Empire without Law." *The Nation*.

Schofield, Lemuel F. 1942. *Annual Report of the Special Assistant to the Attorney General in Charge of the Immigration and Naturalization Service*. Washington, DC: Government Printing Office.

Serrano, Richard, A. 2002, March 2. "Arrests on Border Fall after 9/11." *Los Angeles Times*: A1, A8.

Shah, Nyan. 2001. *Contagious Divides: Epidemics and Race in San Francisco's Chinatown*. Berkeley: University of California Press.

Slevin, Peter, and George Lardner Jr. 2001, November 15. "Bush Plan for Terrorism Trials Defended." *Washington Post*: A28.

Solomon, Alisa. 1999, March 24–30. "A Dream Detained: Why Immigrants Have Become America's Fastest-Growing Jail Population." *Village Voice*.

Stern, Alexandra Minna. 1999, February. "Buildings, Boundaries, and Blood: Medicalization and Nation-Building on the U.S.-Mexico Border, 1910–1930." *Hispanic American Historical Review* 79: 41–81.

Tangeman, Anthony. 2002. "Immigration Detention: The Fastest Growing Incarceration System in the United States." Pp. 25–30 in *In Defense of the Alien: Proceedings of the 2001 Annual National Legal Conference on Immigration and Refugee Policy*. New York: Center for Migration Studies.

Welch, Michael. 2002. *Detained: Immigration Laws and the Expanding INS Jail Complex*. Philadelphia: Temple University Press.

Werlin, Beth. 2004, October. *Legal Fiction Denies Due Process to Immigrants*. Washington, DC: American Immigration Law Foundation. www.ailf.org/ipc/legalfictionprint.asp (accessed February 28, 2006).

II

RACE, ETHNICITY, AND INTERGROUP RELATIONS

Introduction to Part II

The four chapters in this section emphasize the relational aspects of identity—how people define themselves in relation to others. In every chapter the issue of race is central to the analysis. Each author engages in comparisons between groups that share certain characteristics—be it language, religion, color, class, undocumented status, geographic locale—but that are also different from one another in some ways. Each author addresses whether what is shared results in the penetration of the boundaries that might otherwise distinguish them or whether the differences become the foundation for the construction of new boundaries between them. Some authors additionally address how the society at large deals with the similarities and differences and what this means for incorporation. Each author writes about borderlands of interaction—residential areas, workplaces, religious institutions or organization, universities, sites of leisure such as a nightclub, or the political arena. In addition, collectively these chapters remind us of the importance of exploring the nature of the city or region where immigrants are settling. This question of context has recently drawn new attention (Brettell 2003; Mollenkopf 1999; Reitz 2003; Rodriguez 1996). Receiving areas present distinct dynamics as well as distinct opportunities and constraints for immigrant populations, and these differences influence social interaction and processes of incorporation.

Drawing on data from her research among Dominican and Mexican women in New York, Norma Fuentes demonstrates how race and ethnicity lead to different residential and employment outcomes for these two Latina populations. Mexican immigrants have only recently entered the complex ethnic cauldron of New York City, an urban context where other Spanish-speaking populations have been residing for much longer. Between 1990 and

2000 the Mexican population in New York grew by 275 percent, second only to the growth rate of Bangladeshis (by 393 percent). Dominicans in 2000 constituted the largest foreign-born population (at just over 369,000) but their growth rate during the decade of the 1990s was only 64 percent, putting them in eighth place among the ten fastest growing foreign-born populations in the city. Fuentes asks if Mexicans, as the "new kid on the block," enter at the bottom of the pecking order (the residential and employment markets), or is their experience different from the Puerto Ricans and Dominicans who preceded them? The data reveal that despite the human capital and legal advantages of Dominican women, they have not moved as fast out of inner city neighborhoods as have Mexican women. Fuentes attributes the less rapid social and economic incorporation of Dominican women to their blackness. Color creates an impenetrable boundary for them. Although the Dominicans she studied, like other Caribbean blacks, tend to resist being identified as black, they are confronted by residential segregation that can limit their opportunities (see also Kasinitz and Vickerman 2001).

Fuentes is equally conscious of the significance of gender in analyses of the immigrant experience. She describes for example, differences in the gendered networks that Mexican and Dominican women call on as a resource both for immigration and for housing and employment once abroad. She also discusses how employers sort out workers not only according to race and ethnicity, but also according to gender. Although scholarly interest in migration as a gendered process has expanded in recent years (see, for example, Brettell and DeBerjeois 1992; Gabaccia 1994; Hondagneu-Sotelo 2003; Mahler 1999; Pedraza 1991; Pessar 1999, 2003), what has not been addressed as rigorously is how gender and race or gender and ethnicity operate together to shape outcomes for immigrants.[1] Fuentes contributes to this discussion, arguing that the Mexican male labors in the front-stage position in New York City while both Dominican and Mexican women work in back stage positions. However, Dominican women are more isolated by class and racial factors than are Mexican women. Although Johanna Shih also explores the intersection of gender, race, and ethnicity in her chapter in the third section of this book, it is certainly a topic that merits much more attention from researchers.

In her chapter Jamillah Karim examines how the Islamic faith speaks to race divides in the United States. American Muslims include a range of ethnic groups yet see themselves as sharing a common community, or *ummah*. The ummah ideal in Islam exhorts Muslims to "come to know one another" (Qur'an, 49:13), thereby crossing the borders that divide them and overcoming color lines. Karim analyzes the extent to which African American and immigrant (South Asian and Arab) Muslims do or do not achieve this ideal. She finds that while the historical black-white racial divide influences relations between ethnic Muslim groups, color lines among American Muslims also reflect differences in class, ethnic history, and faith perspective (the interpretation of Islam), placing African American and immigrant Muslims in strikingly different communities. Nonetheless, shared faith and Islamic ideals of social justice create instances where members of these two groups, especially but not solely members of the younger generation of American Muslims, cross boundaries to interact and do collective community work. Karim thus contributes to the growing literature on the second-generation, a topic also addressed by several other authors in this volume (Hackshaw, Zeltzer-Zubida, Feliciano).

While Karim tackles religious unity, Alana Hackshaw asks whether perceptions of ethnic difference pose a barrier to political unity between Caribbean Blacks and African Americans in the United States. She examines the content and salience of common fate perceptions for Caribbean Blacks and African Americans to assess the ways both groups exhibit a shared politicized identity about race. In doing so, she captures what some scholars have labeled the "cross-pressures" of race and ethnicity (Vickerman 2001). Hackshaw finds that second-generation Caribbean Blacks and African Americans tend to articulate a vision of panracial solidarity that emphasizes a connection with the experiences of Blacks in the United States. The salience of this vision, however, is much more variable for first-generation Caribbean Blacks whose ideas of racial group membership and racial solidarity are heavily influenced by knowledge and memories of their former homelands in the Caribbean. They display what some scholars (see, for example, Kibria 2002) have labeled an ethnonational rather than a racial identity in order to resist incorporation into the hierarchical racial structure that characterizes the United States. Hackshaw's conclusions are well in line with what other researchers have found about the complex relationships between immigrants from the Caribbean and African Americans, as well as between the immigrant generation and their children. As sociologist Mary Waters (1999: 241) has suggested, Caribbean parents "grew up in a situation where blacks were in the majority" and hence do not want "to be racial in the United States." On the other hand, their teenaged children "experience racism and discrimination constantly and develop perceptions of the overwhelming influence of race on their lives."

Finally, Mariel Rose takes up the very intriguing phenomenon of immigration into the "new" South by exploring the interactions among Mexicans, Blacks, and Indians in western North Carolina. North Carolina has experienced rapid growth (by 274 percent) in its foreign-born population between 1990 and 2000. This compares with a 57.4 percent growth rate at the national level.[2] In 2000 the foreign-born represented 5 percent of the state's population as compared with 1.7 percent in 1990 and compared with 11.1 percent nationwide. Of these, 62 percent entered between 1990 and 2000 and the majority (55.8 percent) were from Latin America with the next largest group being Asians (21.7 percent). The top three groups in the state were Mexicans (40 percent of the foreign-born), Indians (3.8 percent), and Germans (3.8 percent). Of the total foreign-born in North Carolina, 40.7 percent reported their race as white alone, 6.7 percent as black or African American alone, 0.5 percent as American Indian, 18.6 percent as Asian alone, 28 percent of some other race alone, and 5.3 percent reported two or more races. Fifty-three percent reported that they were of Hispanic origin. These newcomers must find their place in a social order divided by race.

Rose explores the shifting racial and ethnic boundaries that characterize this new territory of immigration through an analysis of the cultural boundary crossings that occur at a country and western dance hall (a type of borderland in the Appalachian Mountains) in the small town of Waynesville, North Carolina on Saturday nights. She argues that while class and gender are operative in distinct ways in these new alliances across barriers of culture and economic competition, race is paramount. African Americans, though generally left out of the picture, are ever-present in a black/white social polarity, into the middle range of which Mexicans easily fit alongside the "white Indians" who have long occupied this in-between space.

NOTES

1. But see, for example, Kurien (2003) and Lopez (2003).
2. Statistical data is drawn from Migration Information Source, www.migrationinformation.org/USFocus.

REFERENCES

Brettell, Caroline B. 2003. "Bringing the City Back In: Cities as Contexts for Immigrant Incorporation," in *American Arrivals: Anthropology Engages the New Immigration*, Nancy Foner, ed., pp. 163-196. Santa Fe: School of American Research.

Brettell, Caroline B. and Patricia A. deBerjeois. 1992. "Anthropology and the Study of Immigrant Women," in Donna Gabaccia, ed., *Seeking Common Ground: Multidisciplinary Studies of Immigrant Women in the United States*, pp. 41-63. Westport, CT: Greenwood Press.

Gabaccia, Donna. 1994. *From the Other Side: Women, Gender, & Immigrant Life in the U.S. 1820-1990*. Bloomington, IN: Indiana University Press.

Hondagneu-Sotelo, Pierrette (ed). 2003. *Gender and U.S. Migration: Contemporary Trends*. Berkeley: University of California Press.

Kasinitz, Philip and Milton Vickerman. 2001. "Ethnic Niches and Racial Traps: Jamaicans in the New York Regional Economy," in *Migration, Transnationalization, and Race in a Changing New York,* Hector R. Cordero-Guzman, Robert C. Smith, and Ramon Grosfoguel, eds., pp. 191-211. Philadelphia: Temple University Press.

Kibria, Nazli. 2002. *Becoming Asian-American: Second-Generation Chinese and Korean American Identities.* Baltimore: Johns Hopkins University Press.

Kurien, Prima. 2003. "Gendered Ethnicity: Creating a Hindu Indian Identity in the United States," in *Gender and U.S. Migration: Contemporary Trends*, Pierrette Hondagneu-Sotelo, ed., pp. 151-173. Berkeley: University of California Press.

Lopez, Nancy. 2003. "Disentangling Race-Gender Work Experiences: Second-Generation Caribbean Young Adults in New York City," in *Gender and U.S. Migration: Contemporary Trends*, Pierrette Hondagneu-Sotelo, ed., pp. 174-193. Berkeley: University of California Press

Mahler, Sarah J. 1999. "Engendering Transnational Migration: A Case of Salvadorans," *American Behavioral Scientist* 42:690-719.

Mollenkopf, John H. 1999. "Urban Political Conflicts and Alliances: New York and Los Angeles Compared," in *The Handbook of International Migration: The American Experience.* Charles Hirschman, Philip Kasinitz, and Josh DeWind, eds., pp. 412-422. New York: Russell Sage Foundation.

Pedraza, Silvia. 1991. "Women and Migration: The Social Consequences of Gender," *Annual Review of Sociology* 17:303-325.

Pessar, Patricia R. 1999. "Engendering Migration Studies: The Case of New Immigrants to the United States," *American Behavioral Scientist* 42:577-600.

———. 2003. Anthropology and the Engendering of Migration Studies," in *American Arrivals: Anthropology Engages the New Immigration*, Nancy Foner, ed., pp. 75-98. Santa Fe, NM: School of American Research.

Reitz, Jeffrey, ed. 2003. *Host Societies and the Reception of Immigrants.* San Diego: Center for Comparative Immigration Studies.

Rodriguez, Nestor. 1996. "U.S. Immigration and Intergroup Relations in the Late 20th Century: African Americans and Latinos," *Social Justice* 23:111-124.

Vickerman, Milton. 2001. "Jamaicans: Balancing Race and Ethnicity," in *New Immigrants in New York*, Nancy Foner, ed., pp. 201-228. New York: Columbia University Press.

Waters, Mary. 1999. *Black Identities: West Indian Immigrant Dreams and American Realities.* Cambridge, MA: Harvard University Press.

3

The Immigrant Experiences of Dominican and Mexican Women in the 1990s

Crossing Class, Racial, and Gender Boundaries or Temporary Work Spaces in New York City

Norma Fuentes

On an average day in New York City, more unemployed Dominican males are observed on street corners today than ten years ago. Mexican males, on the other hand, ostensibly vulnerable as new arrivals, are visible at work. This comparison offers a more positive picture than the one observed among the women. In New York City, Mexican and Dominican women are largely invisible, working in the shadows of servitude. A decade ago, by contrast, many women worked in manufacturing, with spouses and other males, including other ethnic and native groups. These differences raise questions about the significance of class, race, and gender in the integration and segregation of new immigrant groups within the service labor market of New York City.

In this essay I explore these differences, focusing in particular on the process of work integration among Dominican and Mexican women who arrived in New York City during the 1990s. I examine the role of networks in the immigration, settlement, and work integration of these two groups, as well as the mediating effects of gender and household structures, both before immigration and upon arrival in New York City. I argue that the relocation of numerous immigrant Dominican families into segregated work and housing structures has increased their marginalization and racialization within New York City, with more negative consequences for the women. By contrast, the widespread and rapid integration of Mexicans within the service sector contributes to the perception of Mexicans as a "hard working," preferred, and "ethnicized" group. This characterization that contrasts with the past, racialized work integration experience of Mexicans in other parts of the United States, particularly the Southwest (Montejano 1997).[1] More precisely, I suggest that immigration type, race, and ethnic networks as well as household structures differentially affect the resources available to the women upon arrival. Changes in service sector jobs and in the racial and ethnic composition of employers in New York City during the past decade combine to affect the type of integration immigrant women experience today as well as the *problematized* and *racialized* perception of the group in the 1990s.

In the first section of this essay, I compare the pre-migration experiences of Dominican and Mexican women, with attention to differences in class and gender structures that mediate the immigration, settlement, and work integration process. In the second section, I analyze the Dominican and Mexican settlement patterns and their implications for the type of work opportunities and racial and/or ethnic relations the women experience in New York City. In the third section, I explore the impact of employers on the general integration of the two groups and the role of gender and race in the selection of workers. Throughout the essay, I emphasize the factors and processes affecting the *racialization* or *ethnicization* of these two immigrant groups.

This essay is informed by and contributes to the literature on the immigrant adjustment experience of post-1965, Latino groups in New York City, specifically among members of the third cohort of Dominican and Mexican nationals arriving during the 1990s. It offers insight on the working conditions immigrant groups now confront within the changing service labor markets, especially in sectors attracting mostly women (Sassen 1984, 1991, 2003; Fernandez-Kelly and Garcia 1997; Hondagneu-Sotelo 1994, 2001, 2003; Menjivar 2003). It also contributes to the literature on the role of gender, ethnicity, and network structures among Latino immigrants (Hondagneu-Sotelo 1994, 2001, 2003; Waldinger 1986, 2001; Smith 2002); as well as to the nascent and limited literature on the role of race, ethnicity and identity formation among Latino and Caribbean groups in New York City (Rodriguez 1991, 2000; Cordero-Guzman, Grosfoguel and Smith 2001).

Data were gathered during the fall of 1999 and summer of 2002, using both ethnographic and survey methods, in four different neighborhoods of New York City where many Dominican and Mexican immigrant families have settled in the past ten years. Semi-structured, in-depth interviews were conducted with a sample of eighty-six women selected according to years of residence in the United States, family composition, and previous work experience in the service sector. Additional information was gathered among thirty key informants, including employers and housing officials, drawn retroactively from a representative list of housing and employment sites identified by women participating in the study. Information on the women's spouses/partners was gathered mainly from the women's narratives but also from a number of male informants and from the spouse/partners.

PRE-MIGRATION FACTORS AFFECTING THE IMMIGRATION AND INITIAL INTEGRATION OF THE WOMEN IN NEW YORK CITY

Three major factors influence the immigration of Mexican and Dominican women to New York City: the economic conditions within the household in the country of origin; the transnational networks and the social and material capital they offer; and, the gender relations they sustain *before* emigrating. Dominican and Mexican women often describe their immigration as a desperate response to both economic and emotional constraints within their households. But their responses also illustrate how class shapes their decisions and expectations about the migration to New York City, as the following narratives indicate:

> I came to New York not just for material needs. I thought, here one can move up, save money, realize one's dream! In the spring of 1993, German was unemployed. I noticed the economic situation was getting worse. My husband was not an educated man, but I loved him. I told him, wait until I get my feet in NYC, German, just wait and see how we get out of this. . . . I told him that if my sisters and brothers had done well there, why not me with a CPA [Certified Public Accountant] degree? I remember seeing people, in return, in my neighborhood filled with jewels . . . looking good. I remember my sisters sending us money to buy the house where I used to live with my mother. . . . I'd figured with a degree I can even go further. . . . My sister has always looked out for us; she helped me come to NYC with an arranged marriage with a Puerto Rican man. (42-year-old Dominican woman, ex-professional)

> He was irresponsible. My mother advised me to come to NYC so we could work and pay the bills that he owed. I was afraid if he came alone that he would abandon us. (30-year-old Mexican woman, pink-collar worker)

> I think I came here with very favorable conditions. Other persons, Mexicans as well as others, have a lot more difficulties. I think the young Mexican kids have the greatest problems here. . . . But, some of the Dominican kids I see in school, their fathers are in jail. (31-year-old Mexican woman, au pair worker)

These three women's different class backgrounds and pre-existing gender relations conditioned the perceptions and expectations of their migration and the level of agency exercised in the decision to emigrate. Tables 3.1 and 3.2, which present the pre-migration household and class composition for all the women, illustrate that more Mexican than Dominican women lived with a spouse or partner prior to their migration and also had lower levels of education. Dominican women also had smaller families. Seven percent had no

Table 3.1. Pre-Migratory Demographics

	Dominicans N=45 %	Mexicans N=41 %	Total Sample N=86 %
Age			
18 to 28	31.8	55.0	44.1
29 or older	68.2	45.0	55.9
Household Structure			
Lived spouse/partner	54.5	78.0	65.9
Lived alone	45.5	22.0	34.1
Number of Children			
0	7.1	0	4.0
1–2	45.2	48.2	46.7
3–4	38.1	39.4	38.7
5 or more	9.6	12.1	10.6
Level of Education			
None	4.5	12.8	8.4
K–8	15.9	51.3	32.5
9–12	52.3	23.1	38.6
12 or more	27.3	12.8	20.5

Source: N. Fuentes's dissertation data, New York survey, 1999–2002.

children in the household and only 9.6 percent had five or more children, compared with 12.1 percent of Mexican women. Significantly, more Mexican than Dominican women said that their spouse or partner was the one who decided that they should migrate to the United States while significantly more Dominican than Mexican women cited family pressures, or their own decisions, as the main reason for migration. Women with more education and work experience frequently decided to emigrate despite family responsibilities and spouses/partners' mandates. Indeed, declining gender relations were often the catalyst for the departure of women in both groups, irrespective of who took the decision or arranged the migration.

Table 3.2. Who Decided to Migrate to the United States

	Dominicans N=45 %	Mexicans N=41 %	Total Sample N=86 %
Respondent	48.9	43.9	46.5
Spouse/Partner	28.9	46.3	37.2
Family	22.2	9.8	16.3

Source: N. Fuentes's dissertation data, New York survey, 1999–2002.

Beyond household and gender structures, class differences also shaped the women's divergent *gendered* networks facilitating immigration. This is partly illustrated in the different geographic locations of these networks (see table 3.3) and analysis of the qualitative data. Forty-six percent of Dominican women relied on female-based links for help with the immigration, while 63 percent of Mexican women came to New York City aided by a spouse/partner, or his connections. These pre-migration differences affected the type of settlement as well as different access to work information upon arrival to New York City.

Another pre-migration difference between these two groups is found in the racial and class composition of the women.[2] Two-thirds of Dominican women came from urban centers, and from a diversified laboring class. Similarly, seven out of ten Dominican women in the sample exhibited distinctive Afro-Caribbean phenotypes. This contrasts with the class and racial composition of earlier waves of Dominican migrants who were mostly *criollos or* Cibaeños, composed of nonurban entrepreneurs, landed elites, and politically displaced individuals (Grasmuck and Pessar 1991; personal reports of community representatives from earlier cohorts). By contrast, more than half of the Mexican women came from the agricultural sectors of the *Mixteca Baja*, composed of three contiguous Mexican states, Puebla, Oaxaca, and Guerrero (see also Smith 2001, 2006). These groups have distinctively visible Mesoamerican, or indigenous phenotypes. These racial and class differences have implications for the type of work and racial or ethnic integration both groups of women experience in New York City. In particular, these differences help employers and housing officials draw clear distinctions between the two groups in the selection of workers and tenants.

SETTLEMENT PATTERNS: HOUSEHOLD STRUCTURES AND NETWORK LINKS

Rather than following the immigrant settlement trajectories predicted by the Chicago school of sociology (Gordon 1964), Dominicans and Mexicans who arrived in New York City in the 1990s have by-passed ethnic enclaves to settle in residential and racialized areas amidst other majority and minority groups. However, as discussed above, the settlement patterns for both groups have been fueled by different family and gender structures, as well as divergent network links.

Table 3.3 and further analysis of both the survey and the qualitative data illuminate the different locations and breadth of the network links that help both groups of women with immigration and settlement within New York

Table 3.3.   Immigrant Network Links of Dominican and Mexican Women

	Dominicans N=46 %	Mexicans N=30 %	Total Sample N=76 %
Washington Heights	30	13	23
East Bronx	39	23	33
East/West Harlem	20	27	23
Queens	0	26	10
PR/Mexico	11	3	8
Other	0	8	3

Source: N. Fuentes' dissertation data, New York survey, 1999–2002.

City. While the network links of Dominican women consist of mostly females, concentrated in the East Bronx (39 percent), Washington Heights (30
percent) and East or West Harlem (20 percent), Mexican women relied
mainly on spouses/partners and male relatives. The majority of these links are
located in Queens (26 percent), East or West Harlem (27 percent) and "other
locations" or suburban areas (10 percent). In addition, further analysis of the
network data indicates that the locations of "receiving" networks among
Mexican groups in the 1990s has affected the more scattered housing integration paths of Mexican than Dominican women.

Finally, the data also suggest that although the networks of both groups included mostly co-ethnics with low levels of education and social capital,
Mexican women found work more quickly than Dominican women, often
within a month after arrival.[3] This may be attributed to the different class
backgrounds of the women and to the spread of spouses/partners' networks,
with greater access to jobs in different service sectors of the city. Another
finding of the housing data is that Mexicans tend to move faster than Dominicans from inner-city and "group-living" arrangements. In addition,
group-living arrangements among Mexican women increased network size
and wider access to different work opportunities. Co-ethnic group-living
arrangements also seem to help buffer the risks of poverty during the first
years of settlement, or while living within areas that are economically and/or
racially isolated.

In sum, the more scattered settlement experience of Mexican women contrasts with that of Dominicans due to both structural and group characteristics
that have influenced the integration of both ethnic groups since the previous
decade. For example, before the 1990s, most Dominican immigrants resided
in Washington Heights and West Harlem, alongside diversified racial and
class groups, including entrepreneurs, merchants, and private residents. In addition, during the 1980s, the main source of work integration for the group

was within the garment district of lower Manhattan. Similarly, before the 1990s Mexican immigrants were not in New York City in significant numbers and their settlement was scattered and shaped by the needs of a mostly male immigrant population (see Smith 2001). Both the type of settlement and the type of work integration experienced before the 1990s kept Dominicans culturally and economically insulated from impoverished and racialized groups. However, both labor market and demographic changes in the city have altered the group's settlement trajectories as well as network structures, affecting more the racial and class isolation of the working poor, increasingly consisting of single, head of household women living in public or government subsidized housing.

Figures 3.1 and 3.2 illustrate interrelated changes in the immigration and residence patterns of Dominican and Mexican groups in New York City between 1990 and 2000. Interestingly, the number of Dominicans settling in New York City declined at the same time that the number of Mexicans increased. More significantly, rather than the newly arriving immigrants settling directly within traditional ethnic communities, a growing number of Dominicans in the 1990s directly arrived or relocated within areas in New York City with close to 70 percent minority concentration (Logan 2002). By contrast, the number of Mexicans settling in areas previously settled by the most

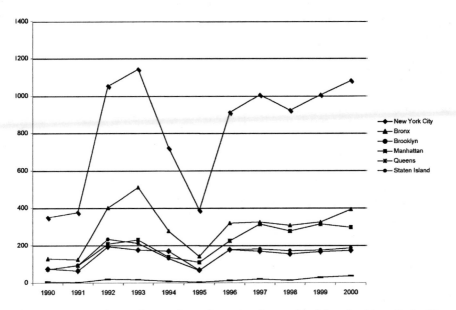

Figure 3.1. Total Numbers of Mexican Immigrants Arriving in New York City, 1990–2000
Source: Computed by author, using data from the U.S. Bureau of Census, through Columbia University's Info-Share data set for New York City.

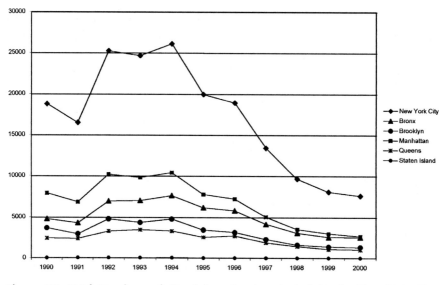

Figure 3.2. Total Numbers of Dominican Immigrants Arriving in New York City, 1990–2000.
Source: Computed by author, using data from the U.S. Bureau of Census, through Columbia University's Info-Share data set for New York City.

successful Dominicans (such as in Manhattan and Queens) has increased from 137 to 400 percent. Analysis of the 2000 Census housing data further illustrate that in the 1990s Dominicans faced the highest index of neighborhood segregation, with an isolation score of 73.7 percent. The index of segregation for Mexicans and other immigrant Latinos, by contrast, was 45.5 percent (Logan 2002).[4] This corroborates with my finding on the divergent integration paths that Dominican and Mexican women experienced in the 1990s in New York City as a result of larger changes at the structural and the group level.

Another factor contributing to the segregated settlement experience of Dominican women is related to changes in the gender composition of the Dominican and Mexican immigrant groups. For example, during the last three decades, women have comprised the majority among Dominican immigrants to the United States (Castro and Boswell 2002), especially within traditional destination centers like New York. Furthermore, the parallel immigration boom in Manhattan of Latinos, Caribbean Blacks, Asians, and European groups affected housing market rates within immigrant settlements. Many of these new non-immigrant groups have settled and competed for housing within traditional immigrant and minority communities (Miyares and Gowen 1998; Rosenbaum and Friedman 2001).

A significant indicator of the different integration experiences of Mexican and Dominican immigrant women appears in the group's pattern of racial segregation in housing. Although two-thirds of all respondents (66 percent) rent apartments from white landlords, Mexicans are more widely integrated as 53 percent rent from whites, 19 percent from Asians, and 25 percent from Latino landlords. While 80 percent of Dominican women rent from white landlords, only 2.4 percent rent from Asians and 16.7 percent from other Latinos. However, their overrepresentation among white landlords gives a distorted picture, as most of their dwellings are located in areas with the highest racial and class segregation (Logan 2002), where most buildings are owned and operated by "absent" landlords. This reduces the likelihood of Dominicans to develop contacts or networks with white landlords. Overall, and consistent with earlier research (Massey and Denton 1993; Rosenbaum and Friedman 2001), landlords prefer renting to immigrant, Latino groups than to African Americans and Puerto Ricans. However, my research indicates that single women with children are the least desirable tenants, given their association with welfare and/or lower incomes. Overall, the preference among landlords is for Mexican single males or nuclear families. Conversations with a number of superintendents and real estate agents confirm a preference for Mexican tenants in neighborhoods traditionally occupied by immigrants and minority groups in the city:

> Landlords or people in this neighborhood do not want to rent to Dominicans because they are loud; always on the streets; . . . sell drugs. . . . The women are too aggressive and problematic for landlords; they complain and call on you [the housing department] for most things. (Puerto Rican superintendent, East Harlem, Manhattan)

Even within the traditional Dominican community of Washington Heights, some landlords have contracted real estate agents to find tenants from specific class and racial backgrounds. Their view is that bringing in "outsiders" as tenants is necessary to resurrect the "old" quality of the neighborhood. Dominicans and other middle-class Latinos from previous immigrant cohorts, like Cubans who owned apartments in the area for the past thirty years, have also devised strategies to rent rooms within their apartments to meet increased rental fees and hold on to their apartments. One of these strategies has been to openly reserve rentals for Mexicans and Ecuadorians, but also increasingly for white, middle-, and upper-class professionals, including students affiliated with hospitals and universities in the vicinity.

> The problem is that the people that used to live here before used to bring their families, and their friends, and before you know the whole place was vandalized. The management has changed everything. . . . You have nothing to worry

[about]. The place is now secured . . . and drugs have never been an issue in this building. I am glad you [referring to a professor friend that accompanied me during the interview] work with the hospital [she meant the university]. . . . They have . . . um, good jobs. (Dominican superintendent, 1970s cohort, Washington Heights, Manhattan)

The *problematized* perception of recent waves of Dominicans by members of earlier cohorts is illustrated in the previous narratives. However, conversation with supers and building managers indicate that this perception extends to the larger majority and is also affirmed by the presence of different tenants, like Mexicans and Yuppies, from inversely related class and racial backgrounds but who are willing to pay the higher rental fees. As a consequence, Mexicans are preferred tenants for room rentals and middle-class whites for apartment leases. Mexicans too are viewed as nonthreatening, *absent* and *silent tenants*, despite complaints about their shared-living arrangements and violation of occupancy codes. Many of the Latino superintendents joked about the "people in this country living more like Mexicans," which is a sardonic yet compassionate expression for the "overworked" Mexican male.

Beyond the problematized perception of Dominicans held by some landlords and informants, Dominican women more than Mexicans face the brunt of gender and class discrimination in housing as a result of contrasting living arrangements and family structures between the two groups in the 1990s. For example, analysis of household and family structures reveals that while 63 percent of Mexican households included three or more working adults, 75 percent of Dominican women live in households usually alone. Unlike the majority of Mexican women who can count on a spouse/partner or his links of support to find and rent an apartment/room, three-quarters of Dominican women rent apartments on their own, usually with the help of a female family/friend or broker/agencies, but many times as a result of public assistance eligibility. Although Mexican women tend to experience harsher living conditions due mainly to "group living arrangements" and crowding, these arrangements increase the web of job links and also pool resources from the group within the home and tend to deter poverty or homelessness.

Group-living arrangements were mainly prevalent among Mexican households, especially among the undocumented and/or the recently arrived. Paradoxically, despite the benefits of group living arrangements for deterring poverty and social isolation, crowded conditions tend to negatively affect gender relations and family structures. As the following narrative illustrates, many times these arrangements increase the risk of abuse for women and children:

We arrived at 112th Street, on the West Side. We lived with eight other men! In the floor, we all used to sleep at night; even the bathtub was occupied. I remember holding myself until the morning, with pain and all, but I could not ask to go to the bathroom. This year was the most horrible experience. Two of the men used to make me feel really uncomfortable [being the only woman there]. This man was scarier; he was related to my husband. . . . He was the one that tried to molest me. I told my husband and, he told me there was nothing he could do for now. We needed to save money and get out. I suffered a lot.

Group living and "over crowding" arrangements provide both benefits and liabilities for both Mexican and Dominican immigrant groups with undocumented immigrant status.[5] The restructuring of affordable and public housing in New York City (Rosenbaum and Friedman 2001) also affects immigrants, and the living arrangements and housing choices of the poor. Equally, undocumented status results in more deplorable living conditions and increases the risk of exploitation by landlords and employers among both groups of women.

Further analysis of the housing data reveals that close to 30 percent of Dominicans, compared with 22 percent of Mexican women, had experienced some form of housing instability, including homelessness. Among single heads of household, twice as many Dominicans as Mexicans had exchanged sex for a place to live or spend the night. More troubling, the single head of household and the undocumented tend to share similar economic and housing risks, but undocumented and isolated women have the greatest risks of experiencing poverty, homelessness, and abuse. Overall, Dominican women experience higher levels of housing instability and racial and class segregation than do Mexican women, as Dominicans on public assistance are many times forced to relocate into cheaper public and government subsidized housing within racially and class-isolated areas. These housing changes also affect the women's future life chances and the integration and public perception of the group in general in New York City.

THE PROCESSES OF WORK INTEGRATION

Divergent household structures and housing locations also impact the networks and work possibilities of Dominican and Mexican women in New York City. Analysis of the survey and the women's narrative data compare the origins of the links that both groups of women used to find work in the 1990s. The data show that Dominican women are, from the start, at a greater disadvantage than Mexican women in the process of work integration upon arrival to New York City since most of their network links consist of women and other individuals with lower levels of education or work experience in the lower rungs of the economy, usually within co-ethnic groups. The following narratives illustrate a pattern of women-centered network origins found more among Dominicans than among Mexican women:

> My grandmother used to live in NYC. She sent me the money for the ticket. She had a Section 8 apartment and, you know, she needed someone to help with the bills in the house; but she helped me; she used to save her "centavitos" [pennies]. . . . I grew up with my grandmother. . . . I used to work in D.R. in a factory, en Zona Franca [duty free industrial zone]. I worked eight hours a day. I used to make 300 [DR] pesos a week. I left because I was coming to New York. Before this I used to work in a pawn shop; I was the cashier, doing the bookkeeping and some paperwork. (29-year-old Dominican woman, domestic worker)

> I came because I did not make enough money and knew I would get a job in New York. My sister had a beauty salon in the Bronx. She helped me with the money for the trip. I worked for her for a while but things did not work out for us. I ended up working in a discotheque in New Jersey for almost a year. I used to work in the bathroom from 4 p.m. to closing hours, which could be between 2, 3, [or] 6 a.m. I used to fight the sleep. I worked in the bathroom assisting women, but in reality I had to check people did not smoke, you know, drugs. . . . The owner was Puerto Rican. (36-year-old Dominican woman, ex-university student, restaurant worker)

These accounts can be contrasted with the experiences of Mexican women who relied mostly on spouses/partners or their links to help with the immigration, the initial settlement and work integration.[6] This is illustrated in the following narratives:

> Here we all work. . . . My husband came first. He arranged everything for me and the kids to come. He got me a job in the same factory where he works, packing telephone cables in New Jersey. He came first, and then he sent for me. It has not been easy. We had to pay $2,000 for the "cross-over," so we both needed to work. (26-year-old Mexican woman, factory worker)

> My husband got a job in a restaurant. My brother in-law helped the two of us to get work in this restaurant in the Bronx. He washed dishes, I cleaned shrimps all day! Now that I have my little daughter, he doesn't want me to work. . . . I came with my husband, my aunt and my kids to New York. My husband had to sell his [goat] herd and borrow $6,000 from his brothers in the U.S. to pay the crossing fees of the coyotes. (21-year-old Mexican woman, ex-restaurant worker)

The wider reach of Mexicans' spouse/partner networks in New York City, both within minority and majority neighborhoods, increases the probability for better economic integration for the women. However, the immigrant work integration story needs to be understood in the context of broader changes in the labor market and its impact on the two immigrant groups. For example, in the past decade the pattern of niche formation and work concentration among Mexicans has expanded while the economic integration of most post-1965 immigrants has lagged behind those from earlier cohorts. (Logan 2002; Waldinger 2001). Since the 1980s, the pattern of work integration for Dominicans changed from concentration in manufacturing and the apparel industries to nonunionized, seasonal jobs in the lower rungs of the service economy (Sassen 1984, 1991, 2003; Waldinger 2001). Paradoxically, my data suggest that while the number of more educated and skilled Dominican women has increased among immigrants in New York City, a greater number of Dominicans is concentrated in the service sector, with a change from 34 to 62 percent.[7] Despite higher education and prior, pre-migration, work experiences they face declining work and housing opportunities. This corroborates Saskia Sassen's (1991, 2003) observation that as immigration increases, the "concentrated" pool of laborers available for cheaper wages increases the proletarization and feminization of the service sector. My findings point to the inclusion of ex-skilled and ex-professional women among the new immigrant proletariat. Consequently, many of the professional and previously skilled Dominican and Mexican women in my study have experienced downward occupational mobility.

The work integration of males reveals a more interesting story and points to a troubling economic and racial isolation gap observed more between the genders than between the groups. The Mexican male story, in particular, helps validate the *more ethnicized* integration that the group in general experiences in New York City compared to that of *problematized* Dominicans. Analysis of census data on the labor market distribution of both groups reveals that in the 1990s, 57 percent of Mexicans (versus 62 percent of Dominicans) concentrated in the service sector. The data also illustrate that Mexican males hold better-paying jobs than Dominicans, as 30 percent work as "operators, fabricators and handlers," jobs with higher skills, compared with only 22 percent of Dominicans in similar positions. Only within professional and managerial jobs do Dominicans rank just above 2 percent. However, the census data include both past and new cohorts of immigrants, making it difficult to determine whether the Dominicans doing better in professional jobs arrived in New York City during the 1990s. Waldinger (1996, 2001) has compared the niche concentration of immigrant groups, including Dominicans and Mexicans, between the 1970s and the 1990s. Although census data is missing for the niche concentration of Mexicans in New York City during the 1970s and 1980s, Waldinger's findings provide a picture of the higher levels of niche concentration and work integration of the group in the 1990s. His data further reveal a niche concentration of 70 percent for Mexicans compared with less than 50 percent for Dominicans, predominantly in manufacturing and the garment sector.[8]

Beyond these structural changes, *gendered* network structures in the 1990s have increased women's work and class segregation. Table 3.4 summarizes the initial jobs the two groups of women obtained in New York City. The first job in New York City for Mexican women tends to be either in a factory (53 percent) or the domestic sector (20 percent). Although Dominicans tend to be more widely distributed in jobs within domestic service (11 percent), restaurants (22 percent), or other services (24 percent), these are usually concentrated within co-ethnic businesses or within businesses catering mostly to co-ethnics or native-born racial minorities. As table 3.4 illustrates, both groups of women tend to work in jobs within the lower rungs of the service sector. For example, while no Mexican woman is listed in the job category for "other services," close to one-third of Dominican women work in these jobs, usually older women who have lived in New York City for five or more years. Most "other services" jobs included women as home-attendants and beauticians, caring either for the infirm and/or seniors, mainly in Spanish- speaking homes in the city or catering to a mostly minority clientele, including mostly racialized groups.

JOB TYPES AND WORKING CONDITIONS

Unlike the highly visible Mexican male worker who can be found in restaurants, construction sites, or green-grocery shops, the shadowed locations and

Table 3.4.   Migrant Women's First Job Found

	Dominicans N=43 %	Mexicans N=41 %	Total Sample N=84 %
Type of Work Found			
No Job	2.2	12.5	7.1
Domestic	11.1	20.0	15.3
Restaurant	22.2	2.5	12.9
Factory	22.2	52.5	36.5
Other Services	24.4	0	12.9
Self-employed	17.9	12.5	15.3

Source: N. Fuentes's dissertation data, New York survey, 1999–2002.

poorer work conditions of Dominican and Mexican women is mediated by the nature of the jobs available to them. Among these, the worst form of work and racial segregation is experienced by women working as home-care or home-health attendants and domestics. One thirty-six-year-old, Dominican single mother confided that the isolation she felt working in the bathroom of a discotheque in New Jersey checking for the use of drugs was preferable to the isolation felt working as a home attendant, where her only social interaction within a twenty-four-hour, six-days-a-week shift was with the infirmed or physically challenged Latina or African American persons in her care.

In addition, analysis of the women's weekly wages illustrates that both Dominican and Mexican women earn the lowest of salaries among the gender groups. This pattern is evident in table 3.5. The top part of the table illustrates that most Dominican and Mexican women concentrate in jobs with wages between $100 and $200 per week. However, although not statistically significant, there is an apparent pattern of more Mexican women than Dominicans earning higher wages as salaries increase from $300 to $500 per week. Ironically, the jobs that offer Dominican women weekly wages comparable to the better paid jobs of Mexican women are found either in home health-care or within beauty parlors. These jobs usually cater exclusively to clients consisting of co-ethnics, or native minority, mostly African American and immigrant, Caribbean Black women. These jobs expose Dominican women only to the culture of racialized minority groups, while the integration of Mexican women within family-owned, business

Table 3.5.   Weekly Wages for the Women and Spouses/Partners

	Dominicans N=45 %	*Mexicans* N=41 %	*Total Sample* N=86 %
Women's Wages			
$100–$200	62.2	67.6	64.6
$200–$300	24.4	20.6	22.8
$300–$400	8.9	5.9	7.6
$400–$500	2.2	5.9	3.8
$500+	2.2	0.0	1.3
Husbands/Partner Wages			
$100–$200	0	9.8	4.7
$200–$300	22.2	17.1	19.8
$300–$400	8.9	17.1	12.8
$400–$500	6.7	14.6	10.5
$500+	6.7	12.2	9.3

Source: N. Fuentes's dissertation data, New York survey, 1999–2002.

establishments in the cities or suburbs exposes them to other ethnics and whites, including a growing number of Asians. Although these jobs offer poor working conditions, they expose Mexican women to majority groups, or the middle class (see Menjivar 2003 for related findings in Los Angeles).

The survey data equally reveal that the first jobs obtained by Mexican males are concentrated in restaurants (22 percent), factories (12.2 percent), and in other services (7.3 percent). Unlike Mexican women, a growing percent of Mexican males work in "other services," in such jobs as sub-chefs, bartenders, meat cutters, and carpentry, or in private and public-sponsored construction projects. These jobs provide opportunity for training and for access to a wider web of links. Analysis of interviews among employers reveals that Mexican males, more than the women, work in establishments where they get "perks" as well as opportunities to learn the language and legal sponsorship by employers for them and/or their families.

Another difference in the working conditions of men and women is found at the bottom part of table 3.5. The data illustrate that more Dominican males than Mexicans are unemployed or are reported without weekly wages. Also, although initially more Mexican males earn lower weekly wages than Dominican males, usually in the $100–200 wage category, years of residence seem to increase average weekly wages more among Mexicans than Dominicans. For example, 17.1 percent of Mexicans earn $300 a week compared with only 8.9 percent of Dominicans. As the wages increase, the pattern is more consistent. Twice as many Mexican males earn weekly wages of $400–500 and above than do Dominican males, 14.6 and 6.7 percent, respectively. Most notably, three times as many Mexican than Dominican males earn weekly wages of $400–500. Interestingly, gender differences become more significant, the higher the wages.

Finally, the different work trajectories of both ethnic groups in New York City is affected by the racial and ethnic ideologies that employers have of both groups, as the following narrative indicates:

The Mexican labor force can be identified from other groups. For me, the difference is as stark as Irish from Chinese. . . . In the Southwest Mexicans are as noticeable as the elephant in the living room! Within the restaurant industry, Asians, like the Chinese, and even Polish workers, are preferred, just like Mexicans. These groups are perceived as motivated. . . . Dominicans and Puerto Ricans have been here for generations, this makes it more complicated. It seems that these groups have an edge with the main culture, one which has also been fueled by the media. (restaurant owner and ex-graduate student, West Village, Manhattan)

As this narrative and discussion with employers illustrate, employers' awareness of the past history of Mexican migrant labor in other parts of the United States increases the desirability of these workers within specific work sectors, such as in restaurant and construction sectors. Building on research by Smith (2002) and Chin (1998), I explore the process of worker selection among employers and the role of race, ethnicity, and gender. The findings suggest that employers assign separate tasks to male and female workers, but that ethnicity and race play a crucial role in their selection. I asked an employer in Queens whether he had ever helped or sponsored workers.

> Yeah, some of them, they ask me for money. I can't help all of them. I gave one [Mexican worker] $10,000 to help him buy a house, and then he gave it back to me little by little. And, let me tell you something: Some workers, they deserve it, some of them, they don't deserve it. Some of these I tell you 'cause I have a lot of experience. . . . See people who helped me in the past, I see them like a God. People I help, they see me like God too. . . . You need people to trust you and you need to keep a clear face [meaning, you must be honest and truthful to the friendship]. (Greek, restaurant owner, Queens)

The segregation of women within different work sectors in the service economy is affected by preferences for male workers by employers, many of whom are immigrants of working-class backgrounds with rigid attitudes about the functions and inclusion of women at work. The following factory owner, the son of Asian immigrants in New York City, feels that women's physical characteristics limit their inclusion in certain "male" jobs, even within the service sector.

> In this job we need guys to do the lifting and the women to do the arrangements, so they don't work together. The women do the sorting, organize the merchandise from the boxes and help prepare boxes with orders . . . you know, this requires women's hands. The men, they are quick and strong, I need men to handle the boxes and the trucks, the deliveries. These guys are diligent, honest. (Chinese-American employer, garment district, Manhattan)

A restaurant owner, the son of immigrants, has reassessed his views about the hiring of women and their effectiveness to work in his restaurant, as his business has grown from a family-run establishment to a mid-sized, fast-paced establishment.

> His sister is a very good cook. She was the backbone [strength] of the floor when I first started. But now my business is too large. We don't work here like you see on TV . . . we are really fast, this is a really fast establishment. These jobs are not for women. I [have kept] only Edwin's mother, who is a porter. She cleans and supervises that everything is in its place. (Restaurant owner, Bronx)

These *gendered* ideologies further the segregation of immigrant men and women within the service, labor markets and limit the integration of women within jobs with potentials for higher wages, social mobility and access to wider network links. Despite these gendered labor market segregation, the only workers present in the Asian establishments I visited, were Mexicans and Asian immigrants, including women. There were no visible Dominican workers within Asian establishments, especially among green grocers.

Another significant factor contributing to the *ethnic* integration of Mexicans as opposed to the more *racialized* experience of Dominicans is illustrated by employers' preference for hiring workers, irrespective of gender, from outside the neighborhood. My interview with another restaurant owner in the southeast Bronx illustrates the emphasis on "trust" in the selection of workers as well as the tendency to see workers as different from himself. His views also indicate the poorer images of Latino workers in general.

> Q. You have to watch them [workers] for a little while?
> Well, I like to test them. I give them an opportunity to either hang or choke themselves. It's very easy in this industry. And, also, another important quality, this one that they can't have, is alcoholism. . . . The Latinos love to drink, especially Mexicans. . . . They have a problem drinking. Every single one of them. Don't let anybody tell you different. Every single one. They're terrible. (restaurant owner, second-generation ethnic white)

Another restaurant employer, also the son of ethnic white immigrants, who runs a butcher shop in the east/south Bronx in a neighborhood that is 70 percent minority, had this to say about "trust":

> Yes. . . . I tend to hire through recommendations. Rarely have I hired someone in seventeen years who has come by looking for a job. . . . I also hold into higher consideration if the worker doing the recommendation is one of my good workers. . . . Workers are hard to recruit for this business because not everyone is suited for this job. Not all my workers can handle the machines.

This employer as well as the majority of others I spoke with admitted to never having hired an African American, Puerto Rican, or Dominican, despite the fact that his clientele is largely Spanish-speaking and his business is situated in a mostly Puerto Rican, African American, Dominican, and Italian neighborhood. Mexicans comprise the majority of his seventeen employees; the rest are Italian immigrants. It is possible to suggest that the closer employers are to poor and racialized groups, the more they construct spatial and ideological boundaries to remove themselves from them, by hiring "outsiders." They justify their actions as a result of having to accommodate their clients' needs; but, I find that the justification employers use in the selection and sorting of manual workers in New York City is guided by racial and class biases ingrained in the American culture of race relations. These ideologies, I believe, serve to continue to reproduce the class and racial divides that America has experienced since its inception and that now is being reproduced among newer immigrant groups, with greater negative consequences for non-white, immigrant women.

CONCLUSION

The data in this essay address three growing bodies of knowledge about immigration and racial formation. The first is encapsulated in the context of the reception/immigrant adjustment model (Portes 1996; Salinger 2001). This model suggests that class and ethnicity, as well as the opportunities provided by the context of reception, determine the integration of immigrant groups. It assumes that ethnic groups will help each other to obtain jobs through a process of ethnic *solidarity* and *re-enforceable trust* between workers and employers (Portes and Sensenbrenner 1993). The restructuring of the economy in New York presents an opportunity to see under what circumstances ethnic "niches" are created or become obsolete, especially in relation to the gender and skill-level of new immigrant workers. My data reveal that race, household, and gender structures significantly affect the process of work integration among Latino groups. Analysis of census data as well as the existing literature also reveals that the restructuring of the economy has negatively affected more Dominican than Mexican workers. These changes have serious consequences for the type of network and work sectors where immigrant women find employment. Data from my study further reveal the poorer conditions and the class and gender segregation that Dominican immigrant women face at work today compared to the experiences of previous cohorts (Grasmuck and Pessar 1991; Carnegie 1997–2000). Finally, different work integration trajectories contribute to higher class and racial isolation among Dominican than among Mexican women.

The second theoretical framework is the concept of spatial assimilation or integration of immigrant groups, first outlined by the Chicago School and extended recently by Alba and Nee (2003). This model predicts that immigrants follow a spatial trajectory: first-generation waves concentrate in the inner city within an ethnic community while successive generations, or the offspring of the immigrants, will gradually integrate within suburban and middle-class neighborhoods. My data show that Mexican immigrants in the 1990s are by-passing the classical predictions of spatial integration among the first gener-ation. They arrived directly into diversified city-wide and suburban neigh-borhoods, crossing racial and class boundaries not open to other minority, racial groups. By contrast, Dominicans in the 1990s experience a more ac-celerated form of spatial integration, but unlike Mexicans or previous cohorts, this now takes place within marginalized and racialized communities of the inner city. Their experience is similar to that experienced by impoverished and racialized African American and Puerto Rican women in New York City. Economic and housing market restructuring makes it impossible for Domini-can women to compete for market-rate apartments within traditional areas of reception or ethnic enclaves. This new form I call *racialized, spatial integra-tion* is an adaptation of the model of segmented assimilation advanced by both Portes (1996) and Wilson (1996) in relation to the fate of the second gen-eration and racialized, minority groups. However, these new forms of *racial-ized* integration have consequences for the type of work opportunities and racial integration of the first and future waves of immigrant groups within the host society.

A third body of knowledge addressed by this study is rooted in racial for-mation theories (Rodriguez 1991, 2000; Montejano 1997; Omi and Winant 1994). My data reveal that racial and class factors affected by segregated net-work structures explain the more marginalized and racialized immigrant ex-perience of Dominicans, especially for working poor women. The 2000 Cen-sus portrays close to one million Latinos who identify as black (Logan 2002). The socioeconomic profile of these individuals is similar to that of inner-city minorities. The data from this study confirm that Dominicans who tend to identify as black usually live next to racialized and marginalized groups and experience not only higher poverty but also racial and class isolation from other Dominicans.

This essay argues that gender structures and relations also contribute to the type of racial or ethnic integration Latino immigrants may experience. Within public housing, it is harder for women and families to reconstruct their gen-der relations and family structures, as the nature of public housing and wel-fare dictates that families remain poor in order to continue to qualify for rent subsidies or public help. This affects Dominican women, who are forced to remain as single mothers and/or as "public charges," carrying more of the racial and poverty stigma than males.

Finally, the class-spatial model developed by Wilson (1987, 1996) suggests that the disappearance of jobs and the concentration of poor and marginalized Dominican women within inner-city structures will further separate Dominicans from society. This will result in the formation of another, *racialized,* Latino underclass in New York City who will be forced to assimilate to the culture of isolated and racialized minority groups. By contrast, Mexicans, with their distinctive, non-black, "in-between" racial characteristics and their more vulnerable immigrant and class position will continue to experience preferential treatment by employers. Despite the exploitation of Mexicans, their experience points to their possible integration as an allied *ethnicized* hard-working minority and should have more positive effects on the fate of the second generation. These findings attest to the fluid aspect of race and ethnicity and the significant role of the new service economy in the making and reproduction of racial and class divides in New York City.

NOTES

1. I refer to *marginalization* as the gradual economic and social decline, usually accompanied by economic stagnation, experienced by immigrants due to a combination of structural and individual causes. See for example Rodriguez (1991) and Mahler (1995). Similarly, *racialization* conveys the multiple confounding effects of marginalization, racial and class isolation, and public problematization that poor, African Americans and Puerto Ricans experienced in Chicago during the 1980s, as a direct consequence of larger structural and demographic changes in the service economy (see Wilson's work [1987, 1996]). Finally, I use *ethnicization* to describe a process where the immigrant group's imported social capital, including entrepreneurial experience, and in some instances, whiteness, or non-black physiognomy, contributes to the groups' access and acceptance within majority sectors that facilitate the gradual and successful integration of immigrants, even if segmented, into allied, ethnic, minority groups. See Portes (1996), Waldinger (2001), Alba and Nee (2003), and Montejano (1997).

2. The questionnaire was designed with a racial classification checklist, where women were classified as having either Afro-Caribbean or *criollo* phenotypes. Criollo phenotypes included individuals with the racial intermixing of Europeans and native, Indigenous, or Meso-American groups.

3. Social capital, as applied by Portes (1996), refers to the ability of a group to gain access to certain resources by having access or membership in a social network or larger social structures. (See Waldinger 2001: 313.)

4. Logan's model of segregation at the census tract level can be obtained at the Lewis Mumford Center website: mumford1.dyndns.org/cen2000/data.html. The index ranges from 0 to 100. A value of 60 or above is very high. Among Dominicans, it means that 73.7 percent will have to move out of the tracts where they live in order to be more evenly distributed among majority groups; or, conversely, an equal number of non-Dominicans will have to move within the Dominican settlement tracts.

5. However, in the 1990s, new research demonstrates that home-sharing or "group-living" appears to be more prevalent among natives, including middle-class groups, than it was assumed (Ahrentzen 2003).

6. The marital status and family structures are strikingly different, with close to 50 percent of Dominican women living in households as single mothers while only 25 percent of Mexicans live as single mothers.

7. The national figure for Dominicans in the service sectors is half of that found among New Yorkers, with 33.2 versus 62 percent. This may reflect the larger percentage and concentration of Dominicans in NYC. See Castro and Boswell (2002) for national data analysis.

8. I rely here on Grasmuck and Pessar (1991) and Roger Waldinger's (1986) cogent survey data among Dominican workers in the NYC labor market. My own information gathering efforts for this and earlier cohorts among Dominicans is limited since the U.S. Census clustered them under "other Hispanics" prior to the 1990s.

REFERENCES

Alba, Richard, and Victor Nee. 2003. *Remaking the American Mainstream: Assimilation and Contemporary Immigration.* Cambridge, MA: Harvard University Press.

Ahrentzen, Sherry. 2003. "Double Indemnity or Double Delight? The Health Consequences of Shared Housing and Doubling Up." *Journal of Social Issues* 59, no. 3.

Camarillo, A. 1996. *Chicanos in a Changing Society: From Mexican Pueblos to American Barrios in Santa Barbara and Southern California, 1848–1930.* Cambridge, MA: Harvard University Press.

Castro, Max, and Thomas Boswell. 2002. *The Dominican Diaspora Revisited: Dominicans and Dominican-Americans in a New Century.* North South Center, Miami, FL: University of Miami Press.

Carnegie Endowment for International Peace. 1997–2000. *New York-based Immigration and Welfare Reform's Longitudinal Research Project (1997–2000).* Washington, DC.

Chin, Margaret. 1998. "Sewing Women: Immigrants and the New York City Garment Industry." Ph.D. dissertation. New York: Columbia University Press.

Cordero-Guzmán, Hector, Robert Smith, and Ramon Grosfoguel (eds.). 2001. *Migration, Transnationalization, and Race in a Changing New York.* Philadelphia: Temple University Press.

Fernandez-Kelly, M. Patricia, and Anna M. Garcia. 1997. "Power Surrendered, Power Restored: The Politics of Work and Family among Hispanic Garment Workers in California and Florida." Pp. 215–28 in *Challenging Fronteras: Structuring Latina and Latino Lives in the U.S.*, ed. Mary Romero, Pierrette Hondagneu-Sotelo, and Vilma Ortiz. New York: Routledge.

Franklin, Raymond S. 1991. *Shadows of Race and Class.* Minneapolis: University of Minnesota Press.

Foner, Nancy (ed.). 2001. *New Immigrants in New York.* New York: Columbia University Press.

Fuentes, Norma. 1997. "Immigration and Health: Mental Health Stressors among Dominican Immigrants in New York City." Paper presented at the Annual Conference of the American Sociological Association, Toronto, Canada.

———. 2005. *Gender, Racialization and the Incorporation to Work among Dominican and Mexican Women in New York City*. Ph.D. dissertation. New York: Columbia University Press.

Gans, Herbert J. 1979. "Symbolic Ethnicity: The Future of Ethnic Groups and Cultures in America." *Ethnic and Racial Studies* 2, no. 1: 1–19.

———. 1992. "Second Generation Decline: Scenarios for the Economic and Ethnic Futures of Post-1965 American Immigrants." *Ethnic and Racial Studies* 15, no. 1: 1–19.

Georges, Eugena. 1990. *The Making of a Transnational Community: Migration, Development and Cultural Change in the Dominican Republic*. New York: Columbia University Press.

Gilbertson, Greta, and Douglas T. Gurak. 1993. "Broadening the Enclave Debate: The Labor Market Experiences of Dominican and Colombian Men in New York City." *Sociological Forum* 8, no. 2: 205–19.

Gordon, Milton. 1964. *Assimilation in American Life*. New York: Oxford University Press.

Grasmuck, Sherri, and Patricia Pessar. 1991. *Between Two Islands: Dominican International Migration*. Los Angeles: University of California Press

Grosfoguel, Ramón, and Chloé Georas. 1996. "The Racialization of Latino Caribbean Migrants in the New York Metropolitan Area." *CENTRO: Journal of the Center for Puerto Rican Studies* 8, nos. 1–2.

Hernandez, Ramona, and Silvio Torres-Saillant. 1998. *The Dominican Americans*. New York: City University of New York Press.

Hondagneu-Sotelo, Pierrette. 1994. *Gendered Transitions: Mexican Experiences of Immigrations*. Berkeley: University of California Press.

———. (ed.). 2003. *Gender and U.S. Immigration: Contemporary Trends*. Berkeley: University of California Press.

Kasinitz, Philip. 1992. *Caribbean New York: Black Immigrants and Politics of Race*. Ithaca, NY: Cornell University Press.

Levitt, Peggy. 2001. *The Transnational Villagers*. Berkeley: University of California Press.

Logan, John R. 2002. "Separate and Unequal: The Neighborhood Gap for Blacks and Hispanics in Metropolitan America." Report prepared by the Lewis Mumford Center for Comparative Urban and Regional Research, University of Albany. mumford1.dyndns.org/cen2000/SepUneq/SURxeport/SURepPage1.htm (accessed December 1, 2002).

Mahler, Sarah J. 1995. *America Dreaming: Immigrant Life on the Margins*. Princeton, NJ: Princeton University Press.

Massey, Douglas S., and Nancy A. Denton. 1993. *American Apartheid: Segregation and the Making of the Underclass*. Cambridge, MA: Harvard University Press.

Massey, Douglas S., Jorge Durand, and Nolan J. Malone. 2002. *Beyond Smoke and Mirrors: Mexican Immigration in an Era of Economic Integration*. New York: Russell Sage Foundation.

Menjivar, Cecilia. 2003. "The Intersection of Work and Gender: Central American Immigrant Women and Employment in California." Pp. 101–25 in *Gender and U.S.*

Immigration: Contemporary Trends, ed. Pierrette Hondagneu-Sotelo. Berkeley: California Press.

Miyares, Ines M., and Kenneth J. Gowen. 1998. "Re-creating Borders? The Geography of Latin Americans in New York City." *Conference of Latin American Geographers Yearbook* 24 (1998): 31–43.

Montejano, D. 1997. *Anglos and Mexicans in the Making of Texas, 1836–1986*. Austin: University of Texas Press.

Omi, Michael, and Howard Winant. 1994. *Racial Formation in the United States: From the 1960s to the 1990s*. New York: Routledge.

Pedraza, Silvia. 1991. "Women and Migration: The Social Consequences of Gender." *Annual Review of Sociology* 17: 303–25.

Portes, Alejandro. 1988. "Social Capital: Its Origins and Applications in Modern Sociology," *Annual Review of Sociology* 24: 1–24.

———. 1996. *The Economic Sociology of Immigration: Essays on Networks, Ethnicity, and Entrepreneurship*. New York: Russell Sage Foundation.

Portes, Alejandro, and Robert L. Bach. 1985. *Latin Journey: Cuban and Mexican Immigrants in the United States*. Berkeley: University of California Press.

Portes, Alejandro, and Julia Sensenbrenner. 1993. "Embeddedness and Immigration: Notes on the Social Determinants of Economic Action." *American Journal of Sociology* 98: 1320–50.

Portes, Alejandro, and Min Zhou. 1993. "The New Second Generation: Segmented Assimilation and Its Variants among Post-1965 Immigrant Youth." *Annals of the American Academy of Political and Social Science* 530 (November): 74–96.

Rivera-Batiz, Francisco, and Ramona Hernandez. 1994. "Dominicans in New York: Fast Growth, Low Income." Report prepared by the Institute for Urban Minorities, Teachers College, Columbia University.

Rodriguez, Clara. 1991. *Puerto Ricans: Born in the U.S.A.* Boulder, CO: Westview Press.

———. 2000. *Changing Race: Latinos, the Census, and the History of Ethnicity in the United States*. New York: New York University Press.

Rosenbaum, Emily, and Samantha Friedman. 2001. "Mobility Incidence and Turnover as Components of Neighborhood Racial and Ethnic Change in New York City, 1991–1996." *Journal of Housing Research* 12, no. 1: 27–54.

Ruiz, Vicki L. 1998. *From Out of the Shadows: Mexican Women in Twentieth-Century America*. New York: Oxford University Press.

Sassen, Saskia. 1984. "Notes on the Incorporation of Third World Women into Wage Labor through Offshore Production." *International Migration Review* 18, no. 4: 1144–67.

———. 1991. *The Global City: New York, London, Tokyo*. Princeton, NJ: Princeton University Press.

———. 2003. "Strategic Instantiations of Gendering in the Global Economy." Pp. 43–60 in *Gender and U.S. Immigration: Contemporary Trends*, ed. Pierrette Hondagneu-Sotelo. Berkeley: University of California Press.

Smith, Robert C. 2001. *Migration, Transnationalism and Race in a Changing New York*, ed. H. R. Cordero-Guzman, R. C. Smith, and R. Grosfoguel. Philadelphia. Temple University Press.

———. 2002. "Gender, Ethnicity and Race in School Outcomes of Second Generation Mexican Americans." Pp. 110–25 in *Latinos in the Twenty-first Century*, ed. Marcelo Suarez-Orozco and Mariela Paez. Berkeley: University of California Press.

———. 2006. *Mexican New York: Transnational Lives of New Immigrants*. Berkeley: University of California Press.

Suarez-Orozco, Marcelo. 1998. *Crossings: Mexican Immigration in Interdisciplinary Perspectives*. Cambridge, MA: Harvard University Press.

Waldinger, Roger. 1986. *Through the Eye of the Needle: Immigrants and Enterprise in New York's Garment Trades*. New York: University Press.

———. 1996. *Still the Promised City? African-Americans and New Immigrants in Postindustrial New York*. Cambridge, MA: Harvard University Press.

———. 2001. *Strangers at the Gates: New Immigrants in Urban America*. Berkeley: University of California Press.

Wilson, William Julius. 1987. *The Truly Disadvantaged: The Inner City, the Underclass, and Public Policy*. Chicago: University of Chicago Press.

———. 1996. *When Work Disappears: The World of the New Urban Poor*. New York: Random House.

4

Ethnic Borders in American Muslim Communities

Jamillah Karim

Herein lie buried many things which if read with patience may show the strange meaning of being black here in the dawning of the Twentieth Century. This meaning is not without interest to you, Gentle Reader; for the problem of the Twentieth Century is the problem of the color-line. (W. E. B. Du Bois 1903)

A century after W. E. B. Du Bois wrote about the color line, black-white racial boundaries persist throughout American culture. They extend into America's newest communities, including American Muslim communities. However, race and ethnic relations between American Muslims transcend the simple binary of *black and white* given that the majority of American Muslims are nonwhite. Predominantly African American and immigrant, American Muslims reflect a complex array of ethnic borders. In this chapter, I explore the question of how shared faith identity forges relations across borders: between African American Muslims and immigrant Muslims. As recent studies on immigration show, analysis of interaction between "newcomer immigrants and established residents" provides a critical window into understanding the ways in which race and ethnic boundaries in the United States continue to get constructed but also crossed (Stepick et al. 2003).

Connected through the *ummah*, Muslims imagine themselves crossing ethnic borders. An Arabic word, ummah literally means "community." The Qur'an states, "You are the best community [*ummah*] raised for humanity, enjoining what is right and forbidding what is wrong and having faith in God" (3:110). Notwithstanding the vast cultural and political differences among the world's Muslims, Muslims take this Qur'anic verse to mean that they represent a single community. I call this concept the *ummah ideal*: a global community of Muslims united across race, ethnicity, culture, language, gender, and class. The ummah ideal acknowledges human variation but encourages Muslims to connect across differences: "O Humanity! We created you from a single [pair] of a male and a female, and made you into nations and tribes, that you may come to know each other" (Qur'an, 49:13).

American Muslims include a range of ethnic groups including African American, Anglo American, and Hispanic/Latino converts as well as South Asian (Pakistani, Indian, Bangladeshi), Arab, African (Sub-Saharan), European (Bosnian, Tartar, Kosovar, etc.), Southeast Asian (Malaysian, Indonesian, Filipino), Caribbean, Turkish, and Iranian Muslim immigrants.[1] I call this cross-section of the global ummah the *American ummah*. The sheer diversity of the American ummah underscores the complexity of color lines in the United States. American Muslims represent distinct cultural identities, distinct histories in the United States, and distinct historical experiences in Islam. Therefore, boundaries between American Muslims reflect differences not only in race but also differences in class, ethnic history, and faith perspective (interpretation of Islam), placing African American and immigrant Muslims in strikingly different communities. Nonetheless, shared faith and Islamic ideals of social justice, particularly economic justice, create instances where members of these two groups encounter, exchange ideas, and cross borders to do collective community work.

I address multiple themes in this chapter. I show how the historical color line, the boundary between blacks and whites, is significant to the construction of ethnic identity not only among African American Muslims but also among immigrant Muslims. My first section analyzes how race and class intersect, constructing the historical color line as a significant boundary within the American ummah. The study of immigrant groups, however, expands notions of borders beyond black and white and renders multiple ways of understanding how color lines are constructed and crossed. In my second section, I show how distinct ethnic histories and struggles outside the United States frame the distinct ways in which ethnic Muslims respond to power structures within the United States. There, I also explore multiple ethnic expressions of Islam, particularly in American mosques. In my third section, I further consider how the different ways of becoming part of an American ummah, either through conversion or immigration, impact interethnic relations in a common American faith community.

In my fourth section, I begin to move toward an analysis of how American Muslims cross borders, particularly through a common Islamic commitment to justice. Although American Muslims fulfill this commitment in different ways, therefore reinforcing boundaries, young Muslims committed to social justice increasingly create alliances across ethnic borders. I explore the second generation in my fifth section: how young Muslims search for the American Muslim identity, negotiating color lines in the process. I show both African Americans and the children of immigrants aspiring toward the Qur'anic ideal of justice, resisting the inequalities of racial, ethnic, and class borders.

With increased focus on border crossing between established residents and immigrants, the American ummah emerges as an ideal frame for the analysis of U.S. ethnic relations. African Americans, South Asians, and Arabs constitute the largest ethnic groups in the American ummah. A 2000 study breaks down ethnic representation across American mosques as follows: African American 30 percent, South Asian 33 percent, and Arab 25 percent (Bagby, Perl, and Froehle 2001). Among America's old faiths (Christianity and Judaism) and new faiths (Islam, Buddhism, Hinduism, etc.), Islam reflects a unique ethnic makeup: the majority (two-thirds) of Islam's adherents are either African American or South Asian immigrants, both groups having almost equal representation.[2] Therefore a study of the American ummah translates as a study of relations between native-born Americans and immigrants, both nonwhite. While other studies explore relations between African Americans and immigrants on the basis of shared experience as nonwhites, for example, phenotype or common African ancestry, I link African Americans and immigrants on the basis of shared faith. While most studies on relations between native-born Americans and immigrants show color lines (or boundaries) contested in the shared spaces of residence and commercial market, my analysis considers color lines contested in a shared community of faith, one that asserts the ummah ideal of united community.

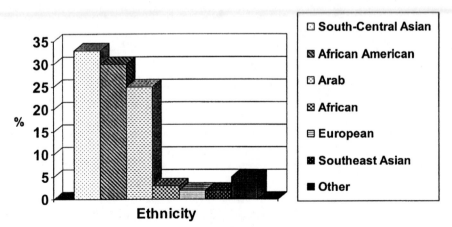

Figure 4.1.   Ethnicity of American Muslims.[3]

My study considers the extent to which American Muslims do or do not achieve this Islamic ideal. Islam can be understood as inward devotion *or* community practice, that is, as a personal commitment to Qur'anic guidance *or* as a collective expression of the Qur'anic spirit in a specific social context (Hodgson 1974). As a collective expression of Islam, American Muslim communities reflect both Qur'anic ideals and the realities of the larger U.S. context. In other words, Muslims fully participate in American life at large, and their experiences as Americans are reflected in how they imagine, interpret, and live Islam. Thus, as we consider the Islamic faith vis-à-vis U.S. color lines, we would expect that the American Muslim community embodies both the Qur'anic ideal of different ethnic communities united as one, but also the realities of its larger American context. Rooted in a world of color lines, the American ummah claims a faith that ideally unites across race but is realistically challenged by race.

As immigration scholars argue, immigrants respond to existing social structures in the United States through processes of acculturation but also through processes of ethnic awareness and reaffirmation; therefore, through both accommodation and resistance to the status quo (Portes and Rumbaut 2001). Similarly, how members of the American ummah respond to historical race borders varies. Alex Stepick and others emphasize *context* in analyzing how newcomer immigrants respond and relate to established ethnic groups. "Instead of reflecting individual immigrants' beliefs and actions," they argue that "the quality and form of interaction depends upon the relative power of groups within a particular context" (Stepick et al. 2003: 26).

Analyzing ummah boundary crossing in context, I focus my study on Muslims residing in Chicago. Chicago's high rate of racial segregation makes it suitable grounds on which to test the ability of the ummah ideal to overcome America's race divides.[4] I also chose Chicago because, as the home base for a number of American Muslim institutions and organizations, it stands as the capital of the American ummah. Every Labor Day, thousands of American Muslims converge on Chicago to attend two distinct yet concurrent national Islamic conventions, one predominantly African American and the other predominantly immigrant.[5] Chicago has over 60 mosques serving an estimated 285,000 Muslims, and the South Asian Muslim community there is one of the most influential in the nation.[6] Between March and September 2002, I carried out participant observation in Chicago mosques, Islamic social organizations, student groups and Muslim homes. I researched majority African American and South Asian Muslim communities but also Arab communities. I conducted 60 formal interviews with Muslim women and men across 2 generations. I incorporate informal, spontaneous conversations in my research as well as public speeches and lectures.

DIFFERENT NEIGHBORHOODS: RACE AND CLASS IN THE UMMAH

Separate and disparate residential communities most vividly illustrate color lines in a society in which whiteness grants privilege. Through most of the twentieth century, whites managed through both direct and subtle political maneuvers to keep blacks out of their neighborhoods. When these maneuvers failed, as in the case of major urban population growth that inescapably pushed blacks across invisible borders, whites fled to the suburbs, creating newer and whiter neighborhoods (Cohen and Taylor 2000). Inevitably whites enjoyed better resources that made for higher-quality living communities. As twentieth century civil rights battles helped to create a culture in which integrated living communities became more valued as an American ideal, class emerged as a critical dimension of privilege. Wealth and education gave blacks access into middle- and upper-middle-class white neighborhoods. This form of class leverage indicates "an unspoken U.S. hierarchical social order" that positions rich whites at the top and poor blacks at the bottom (Lawrence 2002: 10). Based on this hierarchy, whiteness, high income, and quality education (which includes the ability to speak standard English) grant greater resources and continue to create tensions between blacks and whites.

In multiracial America, racialized residential patterns indicate color lines not only between blacks and whites, but among various ethnic immigrants. However, the racial composition of neighborhoods populated by immigrants often reflects historical black-white race divides. The majority of South Asian Muslim immigrants in Chicago, for example, live in predominantly white suburbs far away from black neighborhoods. In fact, "Asian Indians are the least residentially clustered (that is, the least segregated from whites) in several studies (for example, Allen and Turner 1997: 231)" (Leonard 2003: 14). This trend can be attributed to the ability of South Asians to position themselves closer to Anglos on the spectrum of white privilege: "Latinos join Asians and Native Americans as subgroups less privileged than Anglo Americans, though not as underprivileged as African Americans. It is this contest for middle ground that links both Latinos and Asian Americans in an ongoing struggle for recognition" (Lawrence 2002: 39).

South Asians have achieved this recognition:

Despite the setback in 1923 (when the U.S. Supreme Court classified them as nonwhite and ineligible for citizenship, a ruling that would not be reversed until passage of the Luce-Celler Act of 1946), South Asians in the United States today are often perceived as white (unlike South Asians in the United Kingdom and Canada). There is disagreement about this, and many South Asians claim nonwhite status or feel that others perceive them as nonwhite, yet it is undeniable that some are often treated or classified as white. (Leonard 2003: 14)

Their contested white status is partly attributed to their position on the higher end of wealth distribution in the United States. Asians have the highest median household income ($64,000) compared to African Americans ($33,500), Hispanics ($37,600), and whites ($52,000), according to a State University of New York at Albany report. Therefore, high income places Asian immigrants in white neighborhoods.

However, while high income also affords African Americans privilege, they continue to be disadvantaged on account of race. The same SUNY-Albany report "found that black families with incomes of more than $60,000 tended to live in communities with higher poverty rates than white families with income of less than $30,000."[7] Hence, "black and white" continues to frame color lines even in a multiracial class-driven society, as indicated in the words of Dr. Yusuf Sharif, a middle-aged South Asian immigrant Muslim who directs Al-Qalam, an influential publishing house in Chicago. Explaining the separation between African American and South Asian immigrant Muslims in Chicago, he stated, "The issue is the American issue. African Americans live in separate neighborhoods; the whites live in separate neighborhoods. The schools, the standard of life, the security do not compare between the inner city and the white neighborhoods." For this reason, South Asian Muslims prefer living in white neighborhoods, "and compared to African Americans," Dr. Sharif explained, "South Asians do not have a problem in terms of acceptance in these [white] neighborhoods."[8] The disparate ways in which nonwhite groups, for example, blacks and Asian immigrants, find acceptance among whites indicate layers of privilege based on whiteness; the ways in which nonblack groups, for example, whites and Asian immigrants, do not seek acceptance among blacks indicate cultural notions linking low social status with blacks.

A degree of social distancing between African Americans and Asian immigrants emerges very clearly in American mosque communities, according to the 2000 American mosque study. "Sixty-four percent of mosques have one dominant ethnic group. In most cases, this one group is either African American or South Asian" (Bagby, Perl, and Froehle 2001: 19). This finding indicates that the two largest ethnic Muslim groups tend to worship separately from each other. Both of these groups also tend to worship separately from Arabs, the third largest ethnic Muslim group. However, African American mosque communities are the most separate and independent among the three ethnic groups based on the following findings:

1. "Thirty-one percent of mosques have two dominant ethnic groups, with the most frequent combination being South Asian and Arab," and

2. A quarter of mosques have "90 percent of one ethnic group" and 7 percent have "only one ethnic group"; "in both cases most of these
mosques are African American" (Bagby, Perl, and Froehle 2001:19).[9]

Therefore, the study indicates a substantial percentage of integration between
different immigrant Muslim groups yet a substantial degree of segregation
between African Americans and immigrants.

This higher percentage of integration across immigrant lines mirrors socioeconomic differences: South Asian and Arab immigrants share an income
bracket significantly higher than that of African American Muslims. In 1994
American Muslims had an "average household income of $53,000. The aver-
age Arab Muslim family income is the highest at $69,000, while African-
American Muslim families earn the least at $32,000 per year."[10] Historical
black and white racial divides shape color lines in the American ummah as
this income difference places ethnic Muslims in strikingly different neighborhoods. The majority of African American Muslims live in predominantly
black neighborhoods, and immigrant Muslims in predominantly white suburban neighborhoods. Although a number of immigrant mosques are located in
the city,[11] and a few African American mosques in the suburbs, the mosque
study shows residential patterns increasingly affecting mosque location, and
therefore, increasingly separating American Muslims.

The survey breaks down mosque growth by ethnicity, showing immigrant
mosques experiencing more growth than African American mosques, 80 percent and 70 percent respectively. Alongside these figures, the study also represents mosque growth by location, showing suburban mosques experiencing
more growth than inner-city mosques, 87 percent and 67 percent respectively
(Bagby, Perl, and Froehle 2001: 14).[12] Thus, greater growth in immigrant
mosques correlates with greater growth in suburban mosques, which means
that immigrant Muslims increasingly build mosques in their suburban neighborhoods.[13] Describing "the Muslim community in Chicago," Noni, an
African American Muslim woman in her late twenties, vividly captures the
relationship between ethnic geography and borders in the American ummah:

In the South Side of Chicago, the majority of Muslims are African American.
Going towards Midway Avenue, there is a south suburb called Bridgeview with
mostly Palestinians. On the North Side, you find various nationalities, but
everyone stays in their own individual precinct. For example, there is the
Chicago Islamic Center, which is supposed to be a center for all Muslims, but
the people who run it are Pakistani, and most of the people who go there are
Pakistani.[14]

DIFFERENT ETHNIC HISTORIES:
U.S. RACISM VS. EUROPEAN COLONIALISM

Borders in the American ummah not only reflect historical race hierarchies. They also reflect distinct ethnic histories: South Asian and Arab immigrants have become part of the American ummah primarily through immigration to the United States, and African Americans primarily through conversion (however, both groups include growing numbers of second, third, and fourth generation American Muslims, born and raised Muslim in America). A shared Muslim-immigrant experience, a subset of American culture, accounts for greater integration between Arabs and South Asians while a distinct Muslim-convert, African American subculture accounts for greater isolation of African American Muslims. However, even their different cultural experiences are linked to race; that is, their cultural expressions are often shaped by their relations with whites, especially in the case of African Americans whose ethnic history has roots in slavery. These distinct (often racialized) ethnic histories contribute to segregated mosques since American mosques serve not only as sacred spheres but also ethnic and political spheres, similar to the multiple social function of the black church.[15]

An ethnic history of race oppression countered with black religious nationalism gave birth to a Black Power movement that attracted thousands of African Americans to Islam: the Nation of Islam (NOI). Largely a social movement, the NOI taught African Americans to acquire economic resources and build community independent of whites. However, a religious creed anchored the NOI's political objectives: the black man is god and the white man is the devil. By proclaiming a black liberation version of Islam, Elijah Muhammad established an American Muslim community independent of immigrant Muslims. Immigrants rejected the race theology of the NOI because it contradicted global Islamic teachings. Elijah Muhammad, however, played down global Islamic teachings as they would undermine the racial, political objectives of the NOI (Clegg 1997: 133–34). As C. Eric Lincoln states, Muhammad resisted "the possibility of his black nation losing its identity in the vast configurations of international Islam" and went even further, boldly stating that black Muslims would establish "a New Islam" surpassing "the Old Islam" led by "white people, white Muslims," meaning Arab and South Asian Muslims (Lincoln 1994: 211, 212).

When Elijah Muhammad died in 1975, his son Imam W. D. Mohammed succeeded him as leader of the NOI but abandoned his father's race theology. He taught the NOI following the teachings of global Islam, thereby joining thousands of African American Muslims with millions of Muslims around the world, including South Asians and Arabs in the United States. However, as Imam W. D. Mohammed turned NOI temples into mosques, they remained predominantly African American. Former NOI ministers became *imams* (prayer leaders). They struggled to recite Arabic, but they continued to deliver their English sermons with the same eloquent cadence of black preachers.[16] Now professing belief in One God and the Prophet Muhammad and performing the five daily prayers, the month of fasting, almsgiving, and pilgrimage to Mecca, African American Muslims acquired new ways of expressing personal faith, but they continued to envision Islam as a means to building stronger families and communities, hoping to attain quality living and resources lacking in black communities. As the new Black Muslims remained active in African American communities, they brought African American culture, experience, and issues to American mosques.

At the same time, a decade after the 1965 Immigration Act, South Asian and Arab immigrants continued to proliferate in the American ummah. Although assimilating into America, they maintained ties to their ethnic cultures, developing small social networks of immigrant family and friends who shared a common background. Their small social gatherings also served as prayer gatherings, and eventually mosques emerged from these ethnic networks. Like African Americans, immigrants have also brought their cultural experiences to American mosques, often reflecting norms and practices in their native cultures. Friday lectures are delivered in English accents, and in some cases, in Arabic or Urdu followed by an English translation. Men and women often wear South Asian and Arab cultural dress. Immigrants remain apprised of problems facing their native countries as *imams* urge mosque members to pray for and send aid to Muslims suffering in Palestine, Kashmir, Afghanistan, and Gujarat.

For immigrant Muslims, these present-day struggles hark back to European colonialism. Marking the beginnings of global racism, colonialism adversely affected Muslims as Anglo hegemony prevailed across Asia and Africa. Thus, like African American Muslims, immigrants also carry ethnic histories of race oppression that create difference in the American ummah; that is, immigrant mosques focus heavily on the injustices in their native countries while African American mosques focus more on U.S. issues. The critical words of a major American Muslim leader, Shaykh Hamza Yusuf, present another dimension to how colonialism affects color lines among American Muslims:

> The Muslims haven't gotten over colonization. We all still want to become just like the white European. That's what the Muslim goal is now. "Let's get degrees from the university in technology so we can build like they build."[17]

His statement underscores how Muslim immigrants largely represent the educated elites who benefited most from European presence in Muslim lands and now, in the United States, maintain that privilege. A thirty-year-old African American Muslim in Chicago commented on how this privilege creates a disconnect between affluent immigrants and African Americans:

> The people buying into the American dream don't realize that the American nightmare is working right under it. The beauty of America is built on the horror underneath. I don't think a lot of them [immigrants] understand this concept. Most of them don't even know our history.[18]

Therefore, while both African Americans and immigrants experienced centuries of economic exploitation by whites, the first Black Muslims largely resisted the white status quo in America while the majority of immigrant Muslims accommodated it.

DIFFERENT FAITH PERSPECTIVES: MULTIGENERATION MUSLIM VS. AMERICAN CONVERT

In their interactions with South Asians and Arabs, African American Muslims often perceive immigrants as having assumed both the lifestyle and outlook of prejudiced white Americans. The following diatribe by a popular African American imam, Imam Faheem Shuaibe, reveals this perception:

> And some [immigrants] are just as racist as some of the racists that we are trying to deal with right here in America. That's a fact. There *are* racists—racist Arabs, racist Egyptians, racist Pakistanis, racist Indians. . . . They come all the way over here, many of them, with the same attitude that the British gave them, status conscious, the same attitude that the mass media from the West gave them, race conscious, and they don't think that an African American Muslim is a real Muslim—the ones I'm thinking about. They ask, "Are you Muslim?" "Yes, I'm Muslim." "Do you pray?" "Yes, I pray." You want to say, "What do you mean do I pray? I just told you that I was a Muslim. Is my Islam different from your Islam? Or is my Islam somehow less because of the color of my skin. No, you are a racist too. You're a racist right in the Islamic *ummah*."[19]

Many African American Muslims would agree that immigrants do not regard them as "real" Muslims. Most black Muslims attribute this disregard to race prejudice, yet it can also be attributed to another critical difference between African American and immigrant Muslims. South Asian and Arab immigrants come from countries with Muslim populations dating back to over a thousand years. Therefore, they associate authentic Muslim identity with their native countries. On the contrary, they associate American culture with non-Muslim identity. As a result, consciously or not, some immigrants tend to perceive *American* converts as less authentic Muslims. A young African American Muslim woman raised in a predominantly Palestinian community describes immigrants' perceptions of black Muslims:

> They have this attitude of, "They are not really Muslims. They are not practicing the way they are supposed to. . . . They are just American. They are not the real thing."[20]

As alluded to in the comment above, immigrants often reject African American practice of Islam. Immigrants also have distinct cultural practices of Islam, often creating divides among Arab and South Asian immigrants. Despite these divides, different ethnic immigrants tend to recognize and accept that traditional Muslim cultures have always varied. African American Muslims, however, find that immigrants are less likely to recognize African American practice of Islam as another authentic cultural expression of Islam. Rather, they find immigrants assuming that they have less knowledge since they are converts. If their practice differs from immigrants, many take it upon themselves to teach African American Muslims immigrant cultural practices; that is, what immigrants consider "the correct practice" of Islam.

But African American Muslims are not ignorant about their religion. Indeed, African American Muslims have developed an independent intellectual tradition in Islam, rendering their own interpretation of the Islamic sacred sources. In particular, Imam W. D. Mohammed, who has the largest following of African American Muslims, promotes an Islamic faith perspective that accommodates American identity and cultural norms. For example, he does not endorse forms of gender segregation common in immigrant mosques. Rather, he teaches Muslims to respect Islamic guidelines for gender interaction while maintaining the general ethos of gender mixing in American society. The aspect of Imam Mohammed's faith perspective most emblematic of an American approach is his emphasis on interfaith alliance and religious pluralism. He regularly participates in international ecumenical conferences, showing solidarity with other religious leaders. "The mission of the major religions—Judaism, Christianity, Islam—is very much the same on this Earth: obedience to God, an ethical and moral society, sacrifice for others," Imam Mohammed states. "Our differences can be accepted and appreciated if we also understand our oneness. Our oneness is that we are all human beings, people of faith believing in one God."[21]

While most immigrants do not necessarily reject Imam Mohammed's practice and interpretation, they often find it unfamiliar or culturally irrelevant. Immigrant religious leadership, however, tends to be more critical of Imam

Mohammed given that many immigrant imams have been influenced by twentieth-century Islamic reform movements that taught that Western values undermine and oppose Islam. Therefore, many have considered any accommodation of American norms as compromising the faith. Rather than building alliances with Americans of other faith traditions, these religious leaders have paid more attention to preserving Muslim cultural values while living in a non-Muslim society.[22]

While Imam Mohammed tends to focus on commonalities with other faith traditions, many immigrant leaders tend to focus on their differences. Imam W. D. Mohammed resists this approach:

> To the rest of the Islamic world, he [W. D. Mohammed] tries to convey a sense of Islam's historic openness and peacefulness, traits he believes were badly eroded by the Crusades and Christian-Muslim tensions in the centuries that followed. "Some leaders have a view that Islam is to conquer all other religions. That's what those bad instances in our history breed," he said. "But that's what's causing some Muslims to miss the real beauty of Islam, which is its universality."[23]

On the other hand, immigrant religious leaders like the Kuwaiti American author Imam Feisal Abdul Rauf have also encouraged interfaith alliances (Abdul Rauf 2004). Despite religious leadership that does not emphasize interfaith dialogue, most immigrant and African American Muslims have formed relations with non-Muslims in their daily interactions, that is, with coworkers and neighbors. Since 9/11, American Muslims across ethnic borders realize the need for religious leadership to actively endorse interfaith dialogue and understanding.

Having established independent religious authority, Muslims under the leadership of Imam W. D. Mohammed (WDM Muslims)[24] reflect a strong sense of group autonomy and therefore demonstrate very little interaction with immigrant Muslims. African American Muslims outside his leadership (non-WDM Muslims), however, tend to have greater interaction. Their faith perspective reflects greater immigrant influence. They are more likely to wear immigrant cultural dress. They attend immigrant mosques or they attend mosques that are predominantly African American but immigrant in outlook, for instance, mosques that encourage gender segregation. Most of their leaders have studied Islam from Arabs and South Asians abroad, particularly in Saudi Arabia. Some, though certainly not all non-WDM African American Muslims, demonstrate aspects of *Salafi* doctrine, Saudi-based fundamentalist teachings that deem anything outside "pure Islamic culture" as unacceptable. Salafis tend to reject American identity and dismiss interfaith dialogue. However, Salafis represent a minority of the American Muslim population, and while their doctrine has influenced some African American Muslims, fewer have embraced Salafi teachings wholeheartedly. Rather, in their zeal to leave behind their non-Muslim lifestyle, new converts are easily attracted to the Salafis or other communities with origins abroad because they appear to embody true Islam, carrying centuries of Islamic cultural traditions from Asia and Africa.[25]

JUSTICE IN ISLAM, JUSTICE IN AMERICA

While some African American Muslims inherit their faith perspective from immigrant Muslims, they still seek religious leadership that addresses issues in African American communities, particularly issues of race and class equality. Muslims consider justice a cornerstone of the Islamic faith. Economic justice particularly emerges as central to Qur'anic guidance. One verse commands Muslims to "stand out firmly for justice" regardless of whether it exposes "the poor or the rich: for God can best protect both" (4:135). Thus, the Qur'an accounts for the rights of both the poor and the rich; however, it repeatedly reminds the wealthy of their financial obligation to kin, orphans, the needy, and wayfarers. In the context of one verse, the Qur'an states that the purpose of this obligation is to prevent material acquisition from merely "making a circuit between the wealthy among you" (59:7). Thus, while the Qur'an does not challenge wealth and income differences as part of human existence, it does command a sense of balance and equity that grants the poor protection and welfare. This financial obligation (*zakat*) is for *all* Muslims who have savings. They must give 2.5 percent of what remains of their income after expenses.

However, African American and immigrant Muslims respond differently to this Islamic duty. Living in black communities, African American Muslims dedicate much of their resources to creating social and economic equality for blacks. Living in affluent white suburbs, immigrants are far less connected to communities of poor in America. However, they are connected to the poor in their native countries. Yet immigrant funds do often reach poor Americans. Many immigrants, perhaps the majority, pay their zakat to their local mosque, trusting mosque officials to distribute the zakat to needy Muslims. In one immigrant mosque in Chicago, 85 percent of the zakat is distributed to needy African American Muslims. Despite this financial assistance, issues in black communities are not readily addressed by immigrant religious leaders.[26]

African American Muslims, particularly non-WDM, take offense at how immigrants dismiss African American race-class struggles. Immigrants attribute black poverty to laziness, according to Fatima, a young black Muslim woman:

> They [immigrant Muslims] come here as doctors and engineers and then look down on us: "You guys been here for I don't know how long and what have you done? Nothing. And you still got your hand out. Quit whining. This is America." They have this attitude that if you just work hard and go to school, you'll have it, and you won't have to ask for it.

Fatima feels that in order to heal divides in the American ummah,

> foreign Muslim brothers need to really understand the dynamics of being an African American—the factors that really work against us, because they unfortunately do not believe that there are any factors that work against us.[27]

Others, like Fatima, feel that immigrant Muslims do not understand the full implications of the legacy of American slavery. They believe that wealthy Americans who continue to benefit from the historical exploitation of blacks share the responsibility to redress race-based inequalities.

Some African American Muslims hold wealthy immigrant Muslims especially accountable since their religion teaches them to fight injustice. Hakim Ra'uf, an African American who studied several years in Saudi Arabia and now lectures in both black and immigrant mosque communities in Chicago, believes immigrants have this responsibility due to the mere fact that they are Muslim, and by being Muslim, they hold the solution to any form of injustice in America:

> The immigrants should be putting forth more of an effort to utilize their resources towards the upliftment of the African American community. . . . The objective of every Muslim should be to see to it that Allah's *din* [religion] is established throughout the land. The most prominent spots to establish Allah's *din* are those places where injustices and poverty exist.[28]

Thus, Imam Hakim envisions the end of race and class injustice by establishing Islam "throughout the land," and, therefore, calls all Muslims, including immigrants, to establish Islamic-based service organizations in black communities.

Imam W. D. Mohammed articulates a more inclusive approach, envisioning justice as the mission of all faith communities:

> This is the country of people of faith. In my opinion, it is only possible for us to really purge ourselves of the poison of racial prejudices if we become spiritually healthy. . . . The government can't get rid of the ugly problem of racism, but the religious people can indirectly bring about an end to this racism.[29]

His ecumenical approach is based on a Qur'anic verse enjoining all of the different faith communities to "compete with one another in good works."[30] Based on this same Qur'anic principle of competition, WDM leaders believe that all communities, religious or ethnic, must be equally capable of establishing and sustaining the welfare of their community. Thus, they tend to stress African American self-sufficiency over immigrant accountability. One WDM leader in Chicago stated,

> The imam [Imam W. D. Mohammed] has said that he wants us to be competitive. We cannot use other folks' feet to stand on, not the White man's feet, or Pakistanis' or others', to escape doing a job that we as men gotta do for ourselves. This is not [a] racial, radical [position], but [a stance] for individual dignity.[31]

Non-WDM African American leaders in Chicago also advocate African American responsibility; however, they tend to criticize immigrants more than do WDM Muslims due to the mere fact that they have more encounters with immigrants. Despite differences in outlook and emphasis between WDM and non-WDM African American Muslims, both see racial justice as a religious responsibility. And both ultimately recognize that the underprivileged cannot do it alone, but need the resources of the collective, religious and ethnic.[32]

YOUNG MUSLIMS: THE FUTURE OF THE AMERICAN UMMAH

Imam Hakim Ra'uf finds some immigrant Muslims responding positively to his speeches calling for more immigrant presence in the inner city. He finds sincere individuals who actively live up to Qur'anic ideals of unity and economic justice. In my field research, I also found instances where Muslims crossed color lines. I encountered African Americans attending a predominantly South Asian mosque or South Asians attending a predominantly African American mosque. Often the pursuit of Islamic knowledge or the convenience of mosque location brought African American and immigrant Muslims together. If an African American woman wanted to attend an Arabic class offered only at an immigrant mosque, she would attend there instead of an African American mosque, her usual preference. Or if she lived in a predominantly white suburb, she attended the nearest mosque, an immigrant mosque. An Arab man with a job in the inner city might attend an African American mosque. In some cases, a "downtown mosque" would attract both African Americans and immigrants with jobs in the city. Breaking from their work, they would go to the mosque to pray the afternoon prayer. In some cases, though rarer, individual Muslims would visit different mosques with the sole purpose of getting to know other ethnic Muslims. Such visits were often made during the Ramadan season, when Muslims try harder to live up to religious ideals. I discovered interethnic encounter among both first and second-generation American Muslims,[33] yet more frequently among the second generation. In what follows, I analyze intergroup relations among second-generation Muslims, as they provide a frame from which to assess the future of American Muslim communities.

Second-generation South Asians and Arabs are the children of immigrants. They speak Arabic and Urdu, don their parents' cultural dress at home, at the mosque, or at a traditional wedding ceremony, keep up with the latest Arab and Desi music and cinema, and prefer their parents' ethnic food. But they are also the children of America. They speak English without an accent, listen to hip hop, shop at The Gap, and follow Will Smith in his ventures from *Independence Day* to the *Wild Wild West*. Raised in an era marked by "multiculturalism" and urban cosmopolitanism, they resist parents' expectations that they marry within the same ethnic, class, or language group. They attend public and private schools, predominantly white yet integrated with ethnic minorities. At school (and the mosque) they develop relationships with other ethnic Muslims. Discovering variation in Muslim practice, they realize that much of their parents' practice of Islam is cultural and not essential to the faith (or impractical given their experiences as young Americans). They resist, often seeking a "pure" Islamic identity, transracial and inclusive.[34] But surrendering culture becomes difficult since Islam, like any other faith tradition, always takes on the cultural expression of the people who practice it. Therefore, they struggle to define their Muslim identity, carrying on remnants of their parents' cultural practice at the same time that they create new practices that reflect their American context. For example, many second-generation women follow traditional South Asian engagement protocol, that is, minimum interaction with a fiancé, but at the same time challenge strict gender segregation in the mosque.

Second-generation African American Muslims also live new experiences that set them off from their parents' generation. Most of them born after the assassination of Malcolm X and Dr. Martin Luther King, they do not have to engage the same race and class struggles as their parents. They read Alice Walker, Langston Hughes, and Toni Morrison, imagining black despair and cries for Black Power, but they live far better lives than earlier generations, full of opportunities and resources. Hence, they understand, even celebrate, their parents' black nationalist roots in Islam, yet they do not share their connection to the NOI or indebtedness to Elijah Muhammad and W. D. Mohammed. Among the architects of hip hop, they form the bedrock of a pop culture that celebrates ethnic mixing. Therefore, while linked to African

American mosques, they value friendships with Pakistanis or Egyptians outside the mosque. Many of them have been born Muslim. They have learned Arabic, Qur'an, and Prophetic traditions since childhood, thereby surpassing their parents in Islamic knowledge. They travel abroad to Cairo, Damascus, and Medina to learn more, gaining a better understanding of other Muslim cultures. Some of them also struggle with how to project their Muslim identity as they learn other possibilities for Muslim practice and perspective. They reflect these multiple options; for example, a second-generation African American woman who wears African American Muslim dress yet learns traditional styles of Qur'anic recitation from Egyptian peers.

While these trends appear promising, intergroup relations among second-generation Muslims remain limited. Raised in white suburbs, the majority of Asian and Arab Americans know very little about the experiences of African Americans. And while African American youth have more opportunities, most of them still live in predominantly black communities. Only in a shared context can the ummah ideal fully blossom among the dynamic hip-hop generation of American Muslims. More than any other shared context, the university setting fosters this possibility. "College campuses expose young Indian-Americans to wide-ranging discussions about class and gender as well as new forms of ethnic organizing," Johanna Lessinger writes, commenting about young Indian Americans, Muslim and non-Muslim, in New York. They interact with other ethnic groups on campus and develop "cross-ethnic coalitions" (Lessinger 1995: 138).

College campuses similarly signify potential for interethnic alliance among second-generation Muslims in Chicago. On college campuses, second-generation Muslims from distant neighborhoods come together. They live next door to each other in first-year dormitories, share meals in upper-class dining halls, exchange ideas in their Islamic history class, and pray together in the "prayer room" designated for Muslim students. Often away from home, Muslim students seek a sense of community and family among fellow Muslims, often forming Muslim student organizations. Although they still encounter differences, American Muslim students share activities such as preparations for "Islamic Awareness Week," creating bonds from which to respectfully engage their differences.

However, the university context has its limits. The African American Muslim students who attend college with second-generation South Asians and Arabs generally come from educated, middle-class families. This leaves behind a substantial number of African American Muslims who cannot afford to attend the same universities or did not grow up with the educational resources that would qualify them admission to these universities. And while the African American Muslim middle-class is large and growing, therefore still indicating promise for young African Americans to share experiences with privileged South Asian and Arab Muslims, many black Muslims choose to attend historically black colleges. For this reason, the children of immigrants dominate the Muslim student organizations of most predominantly white schools.

What Muslim students do beyond the four to five years of college indicates another limit to the university context in transcending color lines in the ummah. Often Muslim students do not carry their intercultural exchanges into the real world. This limitation Sunaina Maira discovered among young South Asian Americans in New York. While many South Asian American college students reflect an "Indian remix subculture" marked by an appropriation of "urban African American style," this identification is often transient and "superficial," as indicated by the remarks of a young South Asian woman describing the outlook of her peers: "'at the back of their minds [they] are thinking, this is not long term . . . you know [the identification] is only up to a certain point, there are big, distinct differences'" (Maira 1999: 40). Along similar lines, Lessinger found that "just like their parents," many of the children of Indian immigrants "are deeply committed to earning money, success, flashy possessions, a well-paid professional job and a house and family in the suburbs" (Lessinger 1995: 133).

Lessinger's and Maira's findings resonate with trends among Chicago Muslims. After graduation, most South Asian American Muslims move back to the suburbs. Most African American Muslim students, on the other hand, desire the familiarity of their black communities, often committed to giving back. Members of both communities maintain ties to the ethnic mosque communities of their childhood; therefore, they make the same choices as their parents. However, to underestimate signs of promise would misrepresent these communities. In the remainder of the chapter, I illustrate ways in which second-generation Muslims show signs of boundary crossing. I show how the university in particular serves as a space of new possibilities and how young Chicago Muslims particularly rally around movements of justice, not only for America's poor but also justice for Muslims profiled after 9/11. However, I also show the challenges that they face as they strive to do collective work.

In the early nineties, a group of Muslim friends at DePaul formed the organization UMMA, United Muslims Moving Ahead. They desired a forum in which Muslim students could achieve greater visibility and activism on their college campus. While their activism reflects a common commitment to a Muslim identity that advocates social justice (Schmidt 2002), it also reflects larger trends on college campuses, like those Lessinger discovered among non-Muslim Indian American students who "formed coalitions with black and Hispanic groups over particular issues—often issues of racial discrimination" (Lessinger 1995: 138). Immediately UMMA became involved with black and Latino student organizations, engaged in issues of institutionalized racism on campus. Rami Nashashibi, a second-generation Palestinian active in UMMA, recalls, "We realized that it was important to not just be active on campus but to take that spirit outside. As Muslims, we should be doing things in society inspired by the models for us, particularly those communities of color that have struggled in this country."[35] The students joined with other groups doing work in Chicago's inner city, and discovered a number of Muslim families in the South and Southwest sides, mostly Palestinian and African American. They organized with members of the community, creating outreach programs, and within two years, established a non-profit organization: IMAN, the Inner-City Muslim Action Network. "Driven by the Islamic ethic of serving humanity, IMAN has initiated an array of programs and projects that seek to effect real and positive social change. In order to achieve its goals and keep its vision relevant, IMAN has developed a diverse membership and staff, which includes community residents, youth, professionals, and students."[36] Originally a student organization, IMAN continues to draw most of its volunteers from Muslim students at universities including DePaul, the University of Chicago, and the University of Illinois at Chicago. Bringing second-generation South Asians to inner-city neighborhoods, IMAN is the only organization in Chicago that consistently provides interaction between diverse ethnic and class groups in the ummah. IMAN's volunteer activities include an after-school tutoring program, a health clinic, high school workshops, prison outreach, career development, and computer training.

IMAN actively seeks participation from immigrant communities and has been quite successful. As IMAN grows, Rami would like to see affluent immigrant Muslims investing in businesses and property in the inner city, redeveloping neglected neighborhoods. The group Muslim Youth of Chicago sponsored an event in an immigrant mosque and invited Rami to speak: "This is your ummah. It is one ummah. Never underestimate a concept that unites beyond ethnicity, class, and race. . . . It is a lofty ideal but Muslims have championed this concept for 1,400 years."[37] He told the predominantly immigrant audience not to forget the underprivileged Muslims and non-Muslims in their city, urging them to give a share of their wealth to communities of poor in America. He followed this plea with a reminder of how the Prophet Muhammad is reported to have said that the way to gain the love of God and the love of people is by preventing your hearts from becoming attached to worldly possessions. Through his speeches, Rami influences many South Asian and Arab youths to volunteer at IMAN. Rami notes, "I find them thirsty for the type of diversity that they had been somewhat denied as children growing up in primarily white suburbs on the North Side."[38]

Nailah, a South Asian American student at DePaul, began volunteering at IMAN her sophomore year. At first, her parents would not permit her to participate in the after-school program because they considered it dangerous for her to travel in black neighborhoods. Finally Nailah convinced them:

> I started volunteering, and I got really attached to a lot of the kids. They all called us mommy and daddy, and it was very heartbreaking to see that because [it comments on how] they come from a social structure that wasn't very nurturing for them. Basically, they didn't have the opportunities that other students their age had.

Because of the negative stereotypes about African Americans common among South Asian Muslims, she wishes that more of them would work with IMAN:

> In the Indo-Pak community you hear a lot of, "Why don't they [blacks] just do this or do that?" There's this attitude that if we are foreigners in this country and we didn't even speak English properly, and we were able to establish ourselves and our community, why can't they do the same?

Not only does she hear this among her parents' generation, but also, Nailah states, "I actually hear it from my peers." Nailah, on the other hand, holds a different perspective:

> We have so much wealth in this country yet impoverished people in the inner cities are still not able to access it. They are kind of trapped in a system, a cycle that is really hard to break. So I think that it is very unfair to say, "Oh why don't they just get a job?"

She condemns the attitude that poor African Americans are somehow responsible for their poverty. She believes that, while poverty should be addressed, it is ultimately God's way of testing the wealthy and the poor:

> In every society, God has designed for there to be wealthy and poor people so that those who are wealthy can be purified by sharing their wealth and those who are not wealthy can be purified by accepting what Allah has given them. Now if someone who has wealth doesn't fulfill his rights to his brothers who are not as fortunate as he is, it would be a disservice to the larger community.[39]

Khadija, an African American woman, also volunteered for IMAN in college. Khadija converted to Islam after attending a series of programs sponsored by the Muslim Students Association (MSA) at the University of Illinois at Chicago. Only one of a handful of African American Muslim women attending the university, Khadija spent most of her time with second-generation

South Asians and Arabs, an experience very different from her childhood in a predominantly black and Latino neighborhood. Having always desired to finish school and spend her resources to help build black communities, Khadija continued full-time work with IMAN after college. IMAN offers a rare opportunity because it allows Khadija to maintain ties with the black community as well as interaction with South Asian and Arab Muslims. However, Khadija admits that interaction with second-generation immigrants can be challenging. She finds particularly annoying the way that they use the word ghetto, especially since "they have never seen the ghetto in their lives," remarks Khadija.

> At ISNA [a Muslim conference], I was in a room with eleven sisters, ten Pakistanis and then me. It was so offensive that weekend because everything was ghetto. Everything bad that I would not want to have associated with me was ghetto. They would say, "Oh my God, look at my shoes! They are so ghetto."

Eventually Khadija told them not to make "ghetto remarks" around her. However, a few continue to do so as a joke. "But it's just a really overplayed unfunny joke," states Khadija. "Like at my shower I got a jazz CD set even though I don't really listen to that. But like the joke was that you all like jazz." She says that "things like that" irritate her to the point where she prefers not to hang out with them on a social level.[40]

However, Khadija, who eagerly studies Islam, has no problem attending religious classes with them. Both Khadija and Nailah participate in classes sponsored by the Nawawi Foundation, a Chicago-based non-profit educational institution that offers academic courses in Islam. Nawawi seeks to teach American Muslims how to apply Islamic traditions in ways relevant and suitable to their twenty-first century American context. Nawawi's scholar-in-residence, Dr. Umar Faruq Abd-Allah, an Anglo convert, has offered a number of classes on "Islam in America." The classes take place in the evenings on college campuses around Chicago and are attended mostly by second-generation immigrants. He encourages American Muslims to cultivate an American Islamic culture to which other Americans, non-Muslim, can relate. He encourages individual Muslims to actively participate in non-Muslim organizations and for Muslim organizations to provide services to non-Muslims, establishing positive relations with their neighbors and correcting negative images of Islam and Muslims in the media.

Khadija notes how in several of his lectures, he has stated how African American Muslims have already achieved this type of reception in non-Muslim African American communities, encouraging immigrants to learn from African American Muslims. Khadija had hoped that Dr. Umar's words would inspire second-generation immigrants to see African American

Muslims as models in the American ummah and therefore seek ties with them, but she hardly sees them showing increased interest in African American Muslims. Nailah explains why:

> When most people [immigrants] hear Dr. Umar, they are thinking about how they can be more American and how they can interact better with Americans. They are more interested in developing their cultural identity of being Indo American or Paki American or Arab American than [they are in] having an all-inclusive Muslim community.

Particularly after 9/11, second-generation Muslims have thought about how they can better relate to *white* Americans. This has especially frustrated young African American Muslim males who work with IMAN. Many of them imagined that the racial profiling that immigrants experienced after 9/11 would cause them to have greater sympathy for African Americans who have experienced racial profiling for years. They thought that immigrant Muslims would seek them out for solidarity. When they did not, but instead vigorously waved their American flags, many young African American Muslim men (non-WDM) decided that immigrants were still more concerned to show solidarity with whites than to establish ties with African Americans in their same religion. They felt especially alienated by local Arab Muslims when they hired Chicago police to patrol their mosque against non-Muslim neighbors who terrorized the Arab community in the days following 9/11. They were disappointed that the immigrants did not ask them to serve as bodyguards, but rather sought help outside the ummah.

Although immigrant Muslim responses to 9/11 created some initial tensions in the American ummah, over time they are more likely to create opportunities for greater dialogue and collective work between African American and immigrant Muslims. Even if immigrants' amplified outreach is directed mostly toward white communities, it allows immigrants to more effectively engage U.S. issues, particularly the struggle for civil liberties that has ensued since 9/11. Targeted as threats to homeland security, Muslim immigrants fear that domestic policies post–9/11 will increasingly undermine their civil rights. With this battle, they cannot ignore the civil rights struggle of African Americans. But more importantly, as they further engage what it means to be an American Muslim, they will continue to develop a faith perspective more accommodating to an American lifestyle, positioning them closer to African American Muslims, especially in the WDM community. With second-generation Arabs and South Asians born and raised in the United States, a shared sense of American Muslim identity has already begun to take form. But also, as current events highlighted in the U.S. media continue to turn the attention of the American public to Muslims outside the United

States, especially in Iraq and Palestine, African American Muslims will also relate more to the experiences of immigrant Muslims. As encounters and tensions in the American ummah cause African American Muslims to grow more conscious of issues abroad and immigrant Muslims to grow more conscious of issues here in the United States, the struggle to overcome color lines in the American ummah reflects a unique opportunity: standing for racial and economic justice at home and abroad.

CONCLUSION

Rooted in a world of color lines, the American ummah claims a faith that ideally unites across race but is realistically challenged by race. Race and ethnic relations in the American ummah mirror relations between established residents and immigrants in the broader society. As race and class intersect to locate African Americans at the lower end of U.S. race-class hierarchies, immigrants often distance themselves from African Americans in their quest for economic and cultural citizenship. At the same time, however, dynamics in the American ummah emphasize the need to theorize other models of how ethnic boundaries get constructed but also crossed in the American ummah. The notion of a common American faith community functions as one important model. Instead of restricting interethnic analysis to ways of acquiring acceptance in the larger American society, my study explores the question of mutual and equal membership in the American ummah, a highly critical location of acceptance for American Muslims. The different ways of becoming part of the American ummah, one through conversion, the other through immigration, construct boundaries between African American and immigrant Muslims. Immigrant Muslims imagine themselves superior to convert Muslims. At the same time, African American Muslims imagine their American Muslim identity less vulnerable to 9/11 religious profiling, which often translates as an imagined position of privilege and power within the American ummah.

Similarly, different cultural expressions of Islam within American mosques and different ways of rendering ummah ideals shaped by distinct ethnic histories and struggles create boundaries among American Muslims. These differences point to the need for ethnic preservation and reaffirmation, but also for moments of interethnic exchange. In other words, the American ummah must emerge as a community of ethnic borders yet border crossing at the same time. Ethnic mosques and "minority specific activities are essential" but "must be complemented with broader activities that bring all groups together" (Stepick et al. 2003: 154). More than their parents, second-generation Muslims indicate a growing possibility for boundary crossing. Indications of ethnic affirmation and income difference persist in the second-generation; however, young Muslims find spaces, especially the college campus, to cultivate ethnic exchange. And while college space has its limits, as young Muslims, African American and the children of immigrants, continue to experience racial and religious profiling in increasingly overlapping ways, they will constantly be challenged to cultivate common ground. As the new generation of American Muslims, they must both tackle common questions: How can groups on different levels of the racial hierarchy work together to overcome race and class inequalities? How can African Americans benefit from self-help programs but also the resources of others? To what extent are privileged South Asian and Arab immigrants accountable to poor communities in America? Can African Americans learn lessons in community building from immigrants? Can immigrants learn from African Americans how to create a political voice and gain the political leverage to change America's domestic and foreign policy? How can shared faith function to bring different racial groups together, not only for worship, but for community accountability, economic growth and civil liberties at home and abroad?

NOTES

For supporting her research, the author is grateful to the Social Science Research Council, the Fund for Theological Education, the Woodrow Wilson National Fellowship Foundation, the Fadel Educational Foundation, and the Carter G. Woodson Institute at the University of Virginia.

1. Although Latinos are immigrants, I group them with African Americans and Anglo Americans because the majority of them converted to Islam. This distinction bears importance because when African American Muslims refer to their relations with immigrant Muslims, they mean Muslims who come from traditionally Muslim countries.

2. These figures reflect American Muslim population based on mosque participation. Other demographic models produce different numbers. A 1999 study put South Asians at 29.3 percent, Arabs at 32.7 percent, and African Americans at 29.9 percent (Ba-Yanus andd Siddiqui 1999). A 1992 study put African Americans at 42 percent, Arabs at 12.4 percent, and South Asians at 24.4 percent (Nu'man 1992).

3. From the Council on American-Islamic Relations (CAIR) website, www.cair -net.org/mosquereport/. Permission to print granted by CAIR.

4. According to an Associated Press analysis of 2000 Census data, Chicago is the most racially segregated city in the United States: "about 90 percent of black Chicagoans would have to move for the city to be integrated" (Cohen and Taylor 2000: 11).

5. With the exception of 2002, Chicago has been the home of two separate annual national Islamic conventions since 1999. An article in the Associated Press reported on the 2003 conventions: "American blacks and immigrant Muslims are holding separate conventions just three miles apart—underscoring the divide between the two groups that Muslim leaders have been struggling to bridge for years" (*The Herald Sun* [Durham], August 28, 2003; "Two Conventions, Two Worlds, One Divide," soundvision.com/info/muslims/2conferences.asp, September 2003).

6. Population estimate taken from Schmidt (2004: 10).

7. *Washington Post* (Washington, DC), March 9, 2003.

8. Yusuf Sharif (pseudonym), interview with author, August 26, 2002, Morton Grove, Illinois.

9. "About one in twenty mosques (5 percent) is composed of numerous ethnic groups, none having a significant percentage" (Bagby, Perl, and Froehle 2001: 19).

10. Abdul Malik Mujahid, "Muslims in America: Profile 2001," www.soundvision.com/info/yearinreview/2001/profile.asp, 2001.

11. Many of the first immigrant mosques were built in urban areas as early immigrants first settled in the city before moving to the suburbs. The 2000 mosque report states, "Approximately 40 percent of mosque participants travel more than 15 minutes from their home to get to the mosque" (Bagby, Perl, and Froehle 2001: 16). This finding reflects how immigrants often travel from the suburbs to attend a major immigrant mosque in the city.

12. The increase in suburban mosques also reflects growth in African American mosques in predominantly black suburbs.

13. The greater increase in suburban, immigrant mosques also indicates immigration as the primary factor of growth among American Muslims. Conversion constitutes the other major growth factor, with African Americans as the largest ethnic group converting to Islam (Lampman 2001).

14. Interview with author, July 9, 2002, Chicago.

15. The concept of the "ethnic mosque" was theorized in a seminal work in the field of American Muslim studies (Haddad and Lummis 1987).

16. Arabic is the language in which the Qur'an was revealed. Muslims must recite portions of the Qur'an in Arabic in their five daily prayers.

17. Hamza Yusuf Hanson, "What Are We Doing Here?" Alhambra Productions, cassette.

18. Interview with author, July 10, 2002, Chicago.

19. Faheem Shuaibe, "The Declaration of Our Islamic Independence," July 4, 1996, cassette.

20. Interview with author, August 22, 2002, Chicago.

21. *Chicago Tribune* (Chicago), June 12, 1998.

22. This emphasis is not unique to Muslim immigrants: Indian parents frequently feel that within their families they must defend India and Indian culture by preventing the corrupting influences of American society from affecting their children. Yet a certain degree of Americanization is inevitable. Children frequently find that their parents pose all questions of right and wrong in terms of Indian versus American culture. (Lessinger 1995: 98)

23. *Chicago Tribune* (Chicago), June 12, 1998.

24. I invented the acronym WDM to designate the community and followers of Imam W. D. Mohammed. During the span of my research in 2002, his community was named the Muslim American Society (MAS). In the fall of 2002, Imam W. D. Mohammed changed the name from Muslim American Society because an immigrant group also used this name, and Imam Mohammed wanted to distinguish his community. He replaced MAS with ASM, the American Society of Muslims. In September 2003, Imam Mohammed resigned from the ASM to commit to other service and business projects and founded TMC, The Mosque Cares, based in Chicago. Because of the constant name changes and the unclear status of the ASM and its relationship with TMC, I refer to communities and Muslims who affiliate with Imam Mohammed as WDM for consistency. Also, African American Muslims both under and outside of his leadership often refer to his following as Imam Warith Deen Muslims.

25. For more on Salafis, see El Fadl (2003).

26. This high percentage of assistance to poor black Muslims occurs as a result of their going to immigrant mosques to ask for help, not as a result of immigrants going into black communities and distributing funds.

27. Fatima (pseudonym), interview with author, July 23, 2002, Chicago.

28. Hakim Ra'uf (pseudonym), interview with author, May 29, 2002, Chicago.

29. Paola Santostefano, "From the Interview of *Living City* to Imam W. D. Mohammed," www.focolare.org/En/sif/2000/20001114e_e.html, November 2000.

30. From the Qur'an:

And to you [O Muhammad!] We have sent down the Book in truth as a confirmor of the Books [i.e., all revelations] that have come before it and as a protector over them. . . . For every one of you [Jews, Christians, Muslims], We have appointed a path and a way. If God had willed, He would have made you but one community; but that [He has not done in order that] He may try you in what has come to you. So compete with one another in good works; unto God shall you return all together; and He will tell you of that whereon you were at variance. (Qur'an, 5:48; translation from Sachedina 2001: 38)

31. Interview with author, September 6, 2002, Chicago.

32. In the following speech by Imam W. D. Mohammed, he addresses both the poor and the rich:

God says, "Use what I have made available to you to get to the Hereafter, the Latter, the Destiny, the End that I have planned for you. But don't forget your share of the material world." G-d is speaking to the wealthy man. He rose upon the poor and weak; he got rich upon them. But in his wealth was a share for them, if he were just. . . . The poor upon whom he had built his wealth have a share in his wealth. So have a charitable heart and remember those who you abused in the process [of acquiring wealth] have a share in it, too. At the same time, G-d is speaking to the poor. He is saying to the poor man, "Yes, you are entitled to your share of wealth, too. I made the material world not only for these rich people, I made this world for all of you." G-d is saying, "I have created every individual for honor, dignity and great works, [but] some will be held down and confused and their minds overcome by the deceit of those who want to exploit their resources and keep them as a company of workers or a company of slaves or a company of consumers. But I will not tolerate that. I am a just G-d. I will awaken in them an awareness of their great worth, their equal dignity, and they will begin to rise. And one day, I on their side will bring them into great wealth and great prosperity." (*Muslim Journal* [Chicago], June 6, 2003)

33. The majority of immigrants and African American Muslims account for only two generations of Muslims in the United States. The majority of immigrants came to the United States after 1965 and the majority of the first African American converts came to Islam around 1965. Second-generation Muslims refer to young Muslims born after the baby boomer generation.

34. This notion marks the influence of Salafi doctrine asserting that the fall of Islam against European hegemony has to do with the cultural corruption of Islam.

35. Rami Nashashibi, interview with author, July 18, 2002, Chicago.

36. www.imancentral.org.

37. Author's notes, April 6, 2002.

38. Nashashibi, interview with author.

39. Nailah (pseudonym), interview with author, August 20, 2002, Chicago.

40. Khadija (pseudonym), interview with author, May 14, 2002, Chicago.

REFERENCES

Abdul Rauf, Imam Feisal. 2004. *What's Right with Islam: A New Vision for Muslims and the West*. New York: Harper San Francisco.

Allen, James P., and Eugene Turner. 1997. *The Ethnic Quilt: Population Diversity in Southern California*. Northridge: California State University.

Bagby, Ihsan, Paul M. Perl, and Bryan T. Froehle. 2001. *The Mosque in America: A National Portrait, A Report from the Mosque Study Project*. Washington, DC: Council on American-Islamic Relations.

Ba-Yanus, Ilyas, and Moin Siddiqui. 1999. *A Report on the Muslim Population in the United States*. New York: Center for American Muslim Research and Information.

Clegg, Claude. 1997. *An Original Man: The Life and Times of Elijah Muhammad*. New York: St. Martin's Press.

Cohen, Adam, and Elizabeth Taylor. 2000. *American Pharaoh, Mayor Richard J. Daley: His Battle for Chicago and the Nation*. Boston, New York, and London: Little, Brown and Company.

Du Bois, W. E. B. 1903. *The Souls of Black Folk*. Chicago: A. C. McClurg & Company. Reprint, New York: Penguin Books, 1989.

El Fadl, Khaled Abou. 2003. "The Ugly Modern and the Modern Ugly: Reclaiming the Beautiful in Islam." Pp. 33–77 in *Progressive Muslims: On Justice, Gender, and Pluralism*, ed. Omid Safi. Oxford: Oneworld Publications.

Haddad, Yvonne Yazbeck, and Adair T. Lummis. 1987. *Islamic Values in the United States: A Comparative Study*. New York and Oxford: Oxford University Press.

Hanson, Hamza Yusuf. "What Are We Doing Here?" Alhambra Productions. Cassette.

Hodgson, Marshall G. S. 1974. *The Venture of Islam: Conscience and History in a World Civilization.* Vol. 1, *The Classical Age of Islam.* Chicago and London: University of Chicago Press.

Lampman, Jane. 2001. "A New American Piety." search.csmonitor.com/durable/2001/05/31/p11s1.htm.

Lawrence, Bruce. 2002. *New Faiths, Old Fears: Muslims and Other Asian Immigrants in American Religious Life.* New York: Columbia University Press.

Leonard, Karen. 2003. *Muslims in the United States: The State of Research.* New York: Russell Sage Foundation.

Lessinger, Johanna. 1995. *From the Ganges to the Hudson: Indian Immigrants in New York City.* Boston: Allyn and Bacon.

Lincoln, C. Eric. 1994. *The Black Muslims in America*, 3rd ed. Grand Rapids: William B. Eerdmans Publishing Company and Trenton: Africa World Press, Inc.

Maira, Sunaina. 1999. "Identity Dub: The Paradoxes of an Indian American Youth Subculture (New York Mix)." *Cultural Anthropology* 14, no. 1: 29–60.

Mujahid, Abdul Malik. 2001. "Muslims in America: Profile 2001." www.soundvision.com/info/yearinreview/2001/profile.asp.

Nu'man, Fareed. 1992. *The Muslim Population in the United States: A Brief Statement.* Washington, DC: American Muslim Council.

Portes, Alejandro, and Rubén G. Rumbaut. 2001. *Legacies: The Story of the Immigrant Second Generation.* Berkeley: University of California Press and New York: Russell Sage Foundation.

Sachedina, Abdulaziz. 2001. *The Islamic Roots of Democratic Pluralism.* Oxford and New York: Oxford University Press.

Santostefano, Paola. 2000. "From the Interview of *Living City* to Imam W. D. Mohammed." www.focolare.org/En/sif/2000/20001114e_e.html.

Schmidt, Garbi. 2002. "The Complexity of Belonging." Pp. 107–23 in *Muslim Minorities in the West: Visible and Invisible*, ed. Yvonne Yazbeck Haddad and Jane I. Smith. Walnut Creek: Altamira Press.

———. 2004. *Islam in Urban America: Sunni Muslims in Chicago.* Philadelphia: Temple University Press.

Shuaibe, Faheem. 1996, July 4. "The Declaration of Our Islamic Independence." Cassette.

Stepick, Alex, Guillermo Grenier, Max Castro, and Marvin Dunn. 2003. *This Land Is Our Land: Immigrants and Power in Miami.* Berkeley: University of California Press.

5

Black Ethnicity and Racial Community

African-Americans and West Indian Immigrants in the United States

Alana C. Hackshaw

In recent decades, there has been a significant shift in the demographics of American immigration. Historically, European immigrants defined the image of new Americans, but today, people from countries in Central and Latin America, Asia, and Africa comprise the majority of immigrants coming to the United States (Alba and Nee 1999). Consequently, a prominent topic of academic inquiry is how these nonwhite or "new" immigrants are being incorporated into U.S. society.

Competing models in the social science literature offer different explanations for the incorporation experience of immigrants in U.S. society. Some theories suggest that these communities are following a path of incorporation similar to European immigrants of the late nineteenth and early twentieth centuries (Dahl 1961; Gordon 1964), while others argue that their experiences mirror those of historically excluded minority groups in the United States (i.e., African-Americans) (Denton and Massey 1989; Hero 1992; Alba and Nee 1999; Waters 1999; Neckerman, Carter, and Lee 1999). The case of European immigrants presents the quintessential example of inclusion into society, while the experience of African-Americans represents the primary model of exclusion (or incomplete incorporation) in U.S. society. The former paradigm suggests that race poses few barriers to full membership in U.S. society, while the other paradigm proposes that race remains a serious obstacle to complete assimilation for nonwhite groups. Still more recent theories propose that perhaps neither the experience of African-Americans nor those of European immigrants fully explains the patterns of assimilation among today's immigrants (Rogers 2001).

Theories of assimilation offer a useful framework to evaluate specific dimensions of incorporation (e.g., social, economic, and political) and the broader project of assimilation of immigrant groups as well as native-born groups on the whole. In this discussion, I focus on one aspect of political incorporation, specifically, the values, attitudes, and beliefs about race that inform perceptions of racial community or group interest.[1] I am interested in how perceptions of racial inclusion and racial exclusion connect to politicized racial identities among contemporary immigrant groups and U.S.-born racial minorities.

To understand how narratives of racial exclusion shape group cohesiveness, I examine notions of racial community between Black West Indians (an immigrant group) and African-Americans (a U.S.-born group). I engage in this unique comparison of attitudes between U.S.-born and foreign-born Blacks to situate the Black community within the context of the immigrant experience, and further, to consider how the migration experience complicates traditional representations of Black political identity. Identifying the connections and distinctions in perspectives among African-Americans and West Indians presents an opportunity to reevaluate traditional explanations about the roots of political unity within the broader Black community. Are immigrant Blacks rejecting or claiming the African-American narrative of racial exclusion, a narrative that emphasizes a politicized group identity?

Using focus group data of African-Americans and first- and second-generation West Indians living in New York City and Washington, D.C., I assess the language, ideas, and stories that define racial community for the two groups. I investigate the possibilities of community and cooperation by locating shared perspectives about race between the two groups and I identify attitudes that potentially shape the seeds of conflict between the two groups.

BACKGROUND: REEXAMINING THE ROOTS OF RACIAL COMMUNITY AMONG BLACKS

Social identity theory posits that self-identification within a group is informed by the meaning an individual attaches to abstract social categories (Tajfel and Turner 1979). In the case of U.S.-born Blacks, racial group identification is associated with a "psychological attachment to a social category based on race, skin color or a common history of oppression and discrimination attributable to race" (Sanders Thompson 1999). Thus, racial group identification has been linked to distinct political views for African-Americans (Conover 1984). Scholars argue that concerns about racial group status distinctly inform the political orientations of African-Americans in particular (Walton 1985; Allen, Dawson, and Brown 1989; Tate 1993; Dawson 1994, 2001).

Dawson (1994) states that African-Americans have cultivated a distinct political identity in response to systematic social, economic, and political exclusion in the United States. This distinct identity of African-Americans incorporates a shared perspective that the status of the racial group is inextricably intertwined with one's individual interests. Consequently, a shared sense of racial interdependence, defines the roots of racial community and political solidarity for African-Americans. Thus, racial group concerns have a significant impact on political interests for African-Americans.

The African-American political experience is an essential point of reference to evaluate how group concerns shape contemporary political perspectives among Blacks. However, if we consider differences in birthplace a relevant distinction among Blacks in the United States (i.e., having U.S. origins versus non-U.S. origins), it is questionable whether the political incorporation experiences of immigrant Blacks can be understood solely through the experience of African-Americans. West Indian immigrants have experienced diverse contexts of colonization, independence, and incorporation within their respective Caribbean societies that overlap with but do not mirror the experiences of African-Americans. Consequently, distinctions in racial attitudes between African-Americans and West Indians may be linked to different cultural norms about the meaning of racial identity and racial status (Bashi and McDaniel 1997). Further, the beliefs that politicize race and group status for U.S.-born Blacks may not have the same significance for immigrant Blacks. Thus, an important question is whether or not race is politicized for immigrant Blacks as it is for African- Americans. If we consider the case of West Indians, the largest immigrant Black group in the United States, the historical and institutional relationships that inform perceptions of interdependence among African-Americans may not have a similar scope or relevance for this group.

RACIAL COMMUNITY AND IMMIGRANT BLACKS

The majority of West Indians in the United States come from the English-speaking islands of the Caribbean and comprise one of the largest immigrant communities in New York City. They constitute approximately 8 percent of New York City's population, a number that increases when the American-born children are included in these demographics (Kasinitz 2001). In addition, sizeable West Indian communities exist in other areas along the Eastern coast of the United States, including Florida, New Jersey, Massachusetts, Connecticut, Maryland, and Washington, D.C.[2] West Indians have a long history of migration to the United States and have played an important role in political leadership and political mobilization in local contexts, particularly in New York City (Kasinitz 1992).

Scholars argue that racial attitudes among West Indian immigrants in the United States reflect diverse experiences of racial socialization within their respective Caribbean societies (Bryce-Laporte 1972; Vickerman 1999). The knowledge of distinct social norms in the Caribbean influences how West Indians make sense of what it means to be Black in the context of U.S. society. Some will find that the diverse social and racial contexts of Caribbean society present a drastic contrast to that of U.S. society; specifically, they must grapple with what it means to have minority status—a relatively unfamiliar status in the context of Caribbean society. Furthermore, racial group status, discrimination, and opportunity may be experienced and interpreted differently for members of this group relative to African-Americans. Thus, for West Indians, unique values and practices that define them as Black and West Indian reinforce a sense of distinctiveness from other groups including African-Americans.

Rogers (2001) argues that first-generation West Indians do not express a "highly cultivated" sense of racial group consciousness, and links this phenomenon to expressions of ambivalence about the contemporary relevance of slavery for Blacks in the United States, and criticisms of African-Americans for being overly concerned with issues of race. Other scholars have found that many West Indians object to being categorized as African-American and prefer to be identified by their national origin group in the Caribbean (Vickerman 1999; Waters 1999).

While the attitudes of first-generation West Indians complicate traditional representations of Black political identity and Black political culture, the political incorporation of the West Indian community cannot be understood solely through the experience of the first generation. The experiences of the second generation are equally relevant to this discussion if we want a understanding the assimilation experience of the West Indian community. While racial categorization profoundly impacts the lives of immigrant Blacks in the United States (Kasinitz 1992; Alba and Nee 1999; Model 2001; Crowder and Tedrow 2001), this experience may translate differently between the first generation and the second generation. The response West Indians cultivate to experiences of discrimination offers important clues about how race and racial group membership become (or do not become) politicized for this group.

While an "immigrant perspective" characterizes the first generation, scholarship suggests that their experience does not fully explain the viewpoint of second-generation West Indians, whose perspectives will likely center on problems they experience as racial minorities in U.S. society (Waters 1999). Thus, identifying how immigrant identity and racial identity are defined within the West Indian community may explain relevant differences in perspectives between first-generation and second-generation West Indians. To the extent that first-generation and second-generation West Indian perceptions about race and community converge with those of African-Americans, this will have great implications for explaining the relationship between race and full incorporation in U.S. society, specifically for immigrant Blacks, and communities of color more generally.

Despite the distinctions in attitudes that scholars believe separate the experiences of African-Americans and West Indians, the perspectives of both groups have yet to be directly contrasted with one another. Evidence of ethnic distinctiveness among West Indians is not necessarily an indication that West Indians do not recognize racism or that they do not feel a sense of racial community with Blacks. Further, it is unclear whether African-Americans will exhibit attitudes of ethnic distinctiveness toward West Indians or claim racial community when asked to evaluate ethnic diversity within the Black community. Thus, in this discussion, I assess whether awareness of ethnic difference among African-Americans as well as West Indians presents a barrier to mobilization around common problems of race in the context of the United States.

METHOD

This analysis examines the meaning of racial community for African-Americans and first-generation and second-generation West Indians using focus group data collected in the New York and Washington, D.C. metropolitan areas. In this discussion, I examine the following questions about racial community:

1. Do African-Americans and West Indians share a similar sense of racial community with each other?
2. What ideas, values, and practices link or distinguish the perspectives of first-generation West Indians and second-generation West Indians and African-Americans?

Twenty-two focus group discussions of first-generation West Indians and second-generation West Indians and African-Americans provide the data for these analyses. All of the focus groups were conducted between December 2002 and December 2003. Participants were drawn from a snowball sample recruited from churches and universities, as well as social and community organizations, in order to include a variety of perspectives in focus group discussions. In addition, the use of individual referrals and personal networks were also part of the recruitment efforts in order to minimize organizational

bias among participants. Most of the African-American focus group participants were placed in groups with different age cohorts (i.e., eighteen to thirty-
five years and thirty-six years and older). First-generation and second-generation West Indians also participated in separate focus group discussions.[3]

The literature on West Indians tends to focus primarily on their experiences
in New York (Green and Wilson 1989; Kasinitz 1992, 2001; Model 2001, Waters 1999; Rogers 2001). Incorporating the experiences of West Indians from
a different social context (like the Washington, D.C. area) serves as a useful
comparison for evaluating the validity of research findings in scholarship that
focus on New York. In general, there are relatively few notable differences
between the attitudes of focus group participants in New York and in Washington, D.C. [4]

The focus group discussions were beneficial for exploring a range of
perspectives about race and group membership between first- and second-
generation West Indians. The strength of focus groups is that group interaction between participants facilitates discussion (Morgan 1987; Krueger
2000). Nevertheless, focus group methodology that separates participants
by background requires that multiple group discussions of the same group
be conducted. This technique helps minimize the likelihood of documenting homogeneity in responses that may not exist outside of the focus group
context. To incorporate as many diverse perspectives as possible, I conducted at least two focus group discussions of each group separately in
both the New York and Washington, D.C., areas.[5]

Within this sample of focus group participants, I find that African-
American focus group participants subscribe to a vision of community that
emphasizes individual obligations to the Black community as a whole. In
contrast, first-generation West Indian focus group participants are more likely
to articulate a sense of community through individualistic values and individual interests rather than through a sense of racial obligation or loyalty. The
second-generation emphasizes a perspective that reflects the perspectives of
both African-Americans and first-generation West Indians.

This discussion does not generalize about the content of racial community
for the entire universe of African-Americans and first- and second-generation
West Indians in the United States. However, I do rely upon the content of focus groups to identify relevant ideas and attitudes that provide us with a richer
understanding about what racial community looks like for these groups. In the
next section, I present a discussion of African-American perceptions of racial
community, followed by a discussion of first- and second-generation West Indian focus group participants.

IN SEARCH OF REDEMPTION: AFRICAN-AMERICANS' PERCEPTIONS OF RACIAL COMMUNITY

Moderator: What's the struggle?

Participant: I'll tell you what the struggle is! I know exactly what the struggle is. The struggle is trying to survive in a place that does not want you there. That's the struggle. (December 6, 2002, New York City)

African-American focus group participants describe racial exclusion as a simple matter of custom in U.S. society and a catalyst for racial community. Furthermore, shared phenotype, skin color, and culture define the basis of experiences of racial exclusion in society. African-American focus group participants relate these common factors to a negative image of "Blackness" in the wider U.S. society—a status that offers Blacks few allies except those who are similarly categorized as part of their racial group. Thus, racial community for participants is often defined through narratives of racial redemption. Participants express a shared sense that community is rooted in a common struggle to survive the destructive social and economic consequences of racial exclusion in U.S. society. These shared perceptions of exclusion are linked to expressions of common fate among African-American focus group participants—the belief that the lives of all Blacks are uniquely linked by how those outside of the community view them and treat them.

In the following dialogue participants articulate how race connects the lives of Blacks to one another.

Moderator: I'd be interested to hear from each of you what you find . . . connects Black people to each other.

Participant #3 (male): Well I guess, just, racial oppression. I mean that's the first thing that comes to my mind. I mean I don't care what part of the country you come from or what land you're from other than this country. When you set foot on this land and you're perceived to be Black—and we know they're still laws on the books—One-drop law, three-fifths law, whatever, and that sort of stuff, you're not as good, in controlling groups' eyes—we're pretty much all the same. . . . So I'd have to say that's our common thread no matter how we perceive ourselves in relation to one another.

Participant #4 (female): I agree with the struggle, oppression and discrimination as the common thread that Blacks, African-Americans experience. In some cultures people can hide their race. We cannot. People will discriminate against us because of the way we look—the color of our skin. So that is a common thread that we will all experience throughout our lives and I don't think it matters in all instances what degrees you hold, what positions you hold. There's still that common thread that exists among Black people. (May 13, 2003, Washington, D.C.)

The "common thread"emphasized by participants is the struggle to survive the damaging consequences of discrimination regardless of one's position or place in life.

Linked to these concerns of racial exclusion is the notion that racial progress is an ideal all Blacks should strive toward *together*. Participants offer similar narratives of how being American yet having African ancestry defines a distinct experience among Blacks. Thus, common fate perceptions not only incorporate recognition of how shared problems of race define the status of Blacks; these problems also make racial community an imperative for the broader Black community. Consequently, a desire to protect and preserve the community defines group cohesiveness, or unity, a compelling interest for African-American focus group participants.

Shared recognition of racial exclusion and an interest in group action represent a crucial community resource to African-American focus group participants because they form the basis of common agendas around which Blacks can mobilize together. Consequently, a common sentiment offered by African-American focus group participants is that *all* Blacks have a responsibility toward preserving community. One female focus group participant emphasizes how group cohesiveness is an untapped source of influence for Blacks:

I think being in the U.S. we really have become our own tribe even though we're not monolithic, but, we have so much in common in this country. . . . And I think that makes us a tribe and if we were smart enough, it would make us a very, very strong tribe. So, that's my feeling about that. (March 15, 2003, New York City)

These perspectives on racial community highlight not only how Blacks understand the scope of discrimination in U.S. society, but also what Blacks believe constitutes the appropriate response to racial exclusion in U.S. society. The prospect of disunity elicits great concern among focus group participants because it represents the "death knell" of redemption, or racial progress. In the following exchange, a group of African-American women frame individualism as a catalyst for community dissolution.

Participant #1: If we don't have a responsibility to each other then we will completely lose our cohesiveness and our children will learn nothing.

Participant #3: Yes, we do have a responsibility to each other. We should be our brother's and our sister's keepers.

Participant #1: That's right!

Participant #4: Absolutely.

Participant #3: But sometimes we don't want to. I'm going my way, you go your way.

Participant #1: But that's all a part of the whole individualism that's sold to us in the overall society. And we buy into that too.

Participant #2: Learn how to disagree but agree . . . you know we all have different brains and think about things. But learn how to agree when it's a majority in order to get something accomplished. We don't always have to agree.

Participant #1: We're not always going to agree.

Participant #2: We could be agreeably disagreeable.

Participant #4: Which is what we don't do. (March 15, 2003, New York City)

In the above exchange, focus group participants emphasize the significance of a shared consciousness that aligns individual interests with community interests, or what they define as authentic loyalty and obligation to the community. Thus, focus group participants emphasize consensus (or a shared awareness of the problems facing the Black community) as well as a personal investment in community as prescriptions for racial progress in the United States. Obligation to one's racial community incorporates not only a willingness to accept the burden of being a racial minority (i.e., being Black); it is also about "carrying the torch," or doing one's part to facilitate racial progress.

Perceptions of racial community among African-American focus group participants are embedded in stories and memories about past racial discrimination. The past provides a historical frame of reference that they use to interpret their present-day experiences as Blacks in society. These memories define the foundations of a unique language and shared consciousness of "the struggle." Further, a collective memory of racial inequities faced by generations of African-Americans reinforces the present imperatives of community progress for African-American focus group participants.

Focus group participants describe obligation in terms of individual responsibility to the group, yet they are aware that it is not an unproblematic approach to racial progress. At the same time, they consider it impossible not to frame the imperatives of community through this lens. Focus group participants from the Washington, D.C. area reflect upon the inherent tension of having a sense of mission toward the group and wanting to be an individual:

Participant #2: I think that's why it's so hard for Black people to feel that way—to watch other Black people in whatever situation not take that ownership because that's even more weight than I ought to carry 'cause you're not carrying your part and in essence you begin to resent that person because they're not taking ownership of it. They're refusing to see, it they're gonna live their way, live their life to see it the way they want to see it and not own it . . . that creates a sense of dissidence right there. . . . So I think that's what people have a problem with. We all have to deal with the consequences, there's no question about it, but, who's going to be proactive about making a change so that we don't have these same consequences over and over again. (May 13, 2003, Washington, D.C.)

Visions of racial redemption among African-American focus group participants incorporate a desire to protect and preserve the bonds of unity (and community) among Blacks. Thus, perceptions of group obligation among focus group participants reflect an implicit desire for conformity within the Black community around beliefs and practices that minimize the impact of discrimination and racial exclusion on the Black community as a whole.

Participants perceive that acts of obligation to the racial group promote shared consciousness and common action within the community, whereas "playing up" differences within the community is viewed as potentially divisive. Cleavages within the community are defined primarily in terms of class differences, skin color differences, and regional differences—issues participants relate specifically to the African-American population. African-American focus group participants do not typically emphasize birthplace as a significant distinction among Blacks, primarily because they expect immigrant Blacks share a similar vision of common fate and racial progress with African-Americans. Thus, from their viewpoint, immigrant background does not preclude one from sharing a sense of racial community with other Blacks.

AFRICAN-AMERICANS' PERCEPTIONS OF WEST INDIANS

African-American focus group participants rarely initiated discussions of birthplace and origin differences among American-born and foreign-born Blacks; however, many participants expressed well-formed opinions about their relationship with West Indians when asked to share their thoughts. Participants noted seemingly obvious cultural differences in terms of music, food, and accent between West Indians and African-Americans; nevertheless, these distinctions were viewed as minuscule relative to the greater goal of racial progress. Thus, African-American focus group participants' perspectives emphasize that African-Americans hold the same expectations about group cohesiveness and community obligation of West Indians that they do of U.S.-born Blacks.

Overall, focus group participants view the African-American community as more concerned about the problems of racial exclusion relative to the West Indian community. In the exchange below, focus group participants capture a common sentiment that the West Indian community did not share a similar sense of racial community with African-Americans, and were more likely to focus on birthplace differences as a serious social cleavage among Blacks.

Participant #1 (female): No. I feel more like [West Indians] than they feel like me.

Participant #2 (female): Right! Because they don't feel anything like us.

Participant #1: No! I don't think they feel for me what I feel for them.

Participant #2: Right.

Participant #1: Because we understand the ancestral contact that happened to us in coming over here. We remember how we came over here. We were taught very strongly about that. . . . We are more alike than we are different.

Participant #3 (female): No matter where you're from, it's all the same animal. (March 15, 2003, New York City)

The exchange between the women suggests that some African-Americans view racial community in panethnic terms; specifically, problems of race represent a unique bond between Blacks regardless of background differences. Embedded in the comment about African-Americans' understanding of the "ancestral contact" is a value judgment about those who minimize the significance of racial commonalities among Blacks. Expressions of frustration and disappointment are directed toward West Indians whom they perceive as indifferent about the goals of racial progress and racial community. Further, these expressions of disappointment among participants are connected to the belief that West Indians also carry the burden of racial exclusion as members of U.S. society. One focus group participant captures the frustration and disappointment of African-American focus group participants as he describes why he believes West Indians' distancing attitudes toward African-Americans violate the norm of obligation within the Black community:

When I lived down here—I guess it was after high school and I didn't have any contact with folks from the Caribbean. But when I went to school in New York, college, that's when I got my exposure. I was up there about ten or twelve or thirteen years or so and I had some problems initially with folks from the Caribbean thinkin' they're better than Black folks here in this country. I had a real problem with that. I thought it was arrogant on their part to think that way, especially, you know you're here because we had to struggle you know. We're the ones that had to knock down the doors and put our bodies on the line out there to make these policies so that everybody could come here. You could come here to think you're better than me.

I don't buy that line about your pain is greater than mine or your poverty is worse than mine in this country. Bottom line is you're right here in this country and you better understand that as far as white people are concerned in this country, you're just like us. You may speak with a different accent, you may have a different shade, your hair texture may be different. . . . When you see a brother gettin' beat down here in this country by the police—don't think it can't happen to you . . . you're in the same boat that we are. (May 13, 2003, Washington, D.C.)

The focus group participant perceives that the implications of racial exclusion ought to be common knowledge to West Indians—the implication being that the larger society makes no distinctions between U.S.-born and immigrant Blacks. Thus, distancing attitudes among West Indians elicits intense criticism from African-American focus group participants. Another focus group participant draws upon widely publicized cases of racially motivated violence against Black immigrants in New York as symbolic of how ethnic differences among Blacks are irrelevant to the broader society:

I think having lost Amadou Diallo from Africa and having lost Dorismond from Haiti that it has certainly put a spotlight on what can happen to you in this country as a Black person no matter where you're from. And if you can't take those examples and use them to make yourself a more cohesive group of people and share your experiences, rather than focus on your differences then we are in trouble and we will be in trouble for a long time. (March 15, 2003)

This participant's criticisms are connected to concerns that disunity among Blacks portends greater obstacles to racial progress and promotes community dissolution.

Most African-American focus group participants noted that tensions between the African-American and West Indian communities are related to distancing behavior among West Indians; however, some admit that distancing attitudes and stereotyping among African-Americans also reinforce divisions between the two communities:

Participant #1 (male): There's a big divide where "I'm from here, so I don't like you" or . . . "I'm from this island so I don't like you," "I'm from America and you're from the Caribbean and I don't like you." So there's a big separate divide already from the beginning and that's the biggest problem to me right there—that we buy into the separate—'cause you're Caribbean . . . perpetuate it with stereotypes and everything else.

Participant #4 (male): There are some stereotypes that we have on both sides. And some of them are nasty stereotypes. I am not Caribbean and I have heard some of the Caribbean criticisms and I have some of the people on our side say things like, it's not fair or nice. . . . A lot of American Blacks think Caribbeans automatically think they are better than American Blacks when they come here. . . . (March 29, 2003, New York City)

Some focus group participants acknowledged that as much as some African-Americans promote an inclusive notion of racial community, not all members of this group extend the same sense of community to West Indians that they extend to other African-Americans. Rather, the imperatives of racial progress do not always incorporate the ability to overlook mutual stereotypes and cultural differences between the two communities. Thus, focus group participants argue that African-Americans also contribute to problems of organization in the Black community when they reify cultural differences between themselves and immigrant Blacks.

The data suggest that African-Americans draw upon notions of race and community rooted in their culture and history in the United States to articulate the boundaries of community and cohesion between themselves and other Blacks. This knowledge informs a set of norms that they draw upon to evaluate their relationship to others within the Black community, including immigrant blacks. The perception that West Indians' distancing attitudes breach community norms connects to expectations that immigrant Blacks understand and define the "Black experience" in similar terms to African-Americans.

The perspectives of African-American focus group participants suggest that racial common fate incorporates more than an awareness of group discrimination among U.S.-born Blacks. Perceptions of common fate reinforce the importance of one's obligation to the racial group and shapes expectations of conformity around the common goal of racial progress. Participants frame the Black experience through common narratives of racial inequality — a narrative that they perceive applies equally to all Blacks regardless of social cleavages that may exist within the group. Consequently, conformity for the sake of group interest incorporates recognition and acceptance of shared racial problems within the Black community, and an interest in taking action to improve the status of the group. Thus, expectations of conformity among African-Americans incorporate the view that racial commonality among Blacks demands a shared perspective around problems of racial discrimination, and further, support for a shared racial agenda. Unfortunately, the expectation that Blacks "recognize problems of race" and "act in unison" potentially conflicts with how first-generation West Indians believe their history and culture from the Caribbean inform their experiences as Blacks in the United States.

In sum, for African-American focus group participants, the bonds of community are defined through group values, (i.e., group concerns and group expectations about race). But, how do the perspectives of West Indians fit within this particular narrative of community? The next section examines the values that define community for West Indians and how they articulate their connection with African-Americans.

VISIONS OF ACHIEVEMENT: FIRST-GENERATION WEST INDIANS' PERCEPTIONS OF RACIAL COMMUNITY

I cannot truthfully say I can identify with what's going on with all the Blacks in the United States. . . . Not me! I am Barbadian by birth and by background I'm Black. I suit the profile of the United States in that I'm Black. I was a law-abiding citizen in Barbados and I'm hopefully still a law-abiding citizen while I'm in the United States and that's what we were taught from the ground up. So, I don't see myself as the regular, run-of-the-mill Black. . . . My color is run-of-the-mill, but in thinking, I'm not run-of-the-mill. . . . (November 22, 2003, New York City)

The ability to identify with their country of origin is important to how first-generation West Indians identify themselves as members of U.S. society. Within the focus group discussions, participants describe themselves as "proud" and "hardworking" and use these adjectives to characterize West Indians more generally. However, when participants describe their race, they often emphasize skin color, physical features, and African ancestry. In the following exchange, a group of West Indians living in the United States for over thirty years artfully distinguishes between what it means to be "Black" and what it means to be "African-American."

Moderator: A couple of terms that are pretty often applied to people of African descent living in the United States are "Black" or "African-American." . . . Do you identify with any of those terms? Is being Black the same thing as being African-American?

Participant #1 (male): I'm Barbadian!

Participant #2 (male): I'm Black . . .

Participant #1: I know that I'm Black. I've no problem over that. I live by that. No more . . .

Participant #4 (female): Yeah, I'm comfortable with Black, but I don't see myself as an American . . .

Moderator: So how about African-American? Do you identify with that term?

Participant #2: Not really.

Moderator: So who is African-American?

Participant #1: The black people who were born here. . . . If you were born here, then you probably should identify as Black/African-American. (November 23, 2003, New York City)

In the above passage, participants emphasize that birthplace distinguishes West Indians and African-Americans. Focus group participants know that they are Black, yet this knowledge is not particularly remarkable to them because in their respective societies in the Caribbean, race is not the primary marker of status that it is in the United States. Further, race defines their physical characteristics and ancestry, but not their culture. The attitudes of focus group participants suggest that they do not rely on American racial categories to define themselves; rather, they use a different reference point—one shaped by their experiences in the Caribbean.

First-generation focus group participants emphasize values and attitudes that they believe reflect a unique mind-set about racial identity and achievement in the United States. Drawing from knowledge of their respective societies in the Caribbean, focus group participants rely upon the norms of their home cultures in the Caribbean to make sense of their Black identities in the context of U.S. society. Thus, their perceptions of distinctions between African-Americans and West Indians center on the belief that their strategies for confronting issues of race in U.S. society do not coincide with the strategies employed by African-Americans.

Many first-generation focus group participants view themselves as having a different Black identity relative to African-Americans. In the following exchange, a group of students explain how their Caribbean "heritage" informs different identities and different perspectives about racism among West Indians and African-Americans.

Participant #1 (male): I can't claim the experience of being African-American because I wasn't born in this country and my ancestors didn't go through the same thing the African-Americans' ancestors went through. So it would be unfair of me to claim the same heritage as African-Americans, just as it would be kind of unfair for them to claim my heritage, in a way. I mean, when you look at it, the bottom line is we're all African, we come from one, you know, from the same continent. But more specifically, on this continent, in this country— you know the civil rights from the Harlem Renaissance and everything else that African-Americans have done for the United States. I, of course, cannot claim

that, just as someone—they can't, claim everything that's West Indian or An-
guillan to me. So that's the way I look at it.

Participant #2 (male): Basically, we walk, talk and act—

Participant #1: —differently. (May 1, 2003, Washington, D.C.)

These first-generation focus group participants emphasize that they use
different norms to evaluate and navigate society compared to African-
Americans because of where they come from. Further, they believe that
these values and beliefs lead to different responses to racial discrimination
among West Indians.

Many first-generation focus group participants seem particularly wary
about interpreting the world through a "racial lens," or what they define as
blaming one's problems on race. They perceive that African-Americans live
with expectations of discrimination while West Indians do not. In the exchange below, Jamaican and Trinidadian male participants explain why attitudes about discrimination distinguish them from African-Americans.

Participant #1: What do you have in common with Black Americans?

Participant #2: I should say besides color, I can't say anything else.

Participant #1: Honestly . . . the only thing we have in common is color—that
is it . . . I never understand how come everything here has to do with the Black
man being held down by someone else. I never understand if you don't get
something that you want, first thing comes to you it has to be racial. If I don't
get something I want . . . I'm checking myself first. Maybe I did something
wrong, maybe I could have done something differently and I say it was because
of my own shortcomings and never because I was Black. . . . (December 8,
2002, New York City)

As the above passage suggests, the suspicion first-generation West Indians
display toward using a "racial lens" is often connected to how they interpret
the context of opportunity within the United States. Once again, knowledge
of the contexts of opportunity in the Caribbean colors how they make sense
of their achievements and failures in the United States. Specifically, first-generation West Indian participants tend to evaluate personal success as a fruit of
their individual efforts.

Unlike their African-American focus group counterparts, first-generation
West Indians often describe progress in terms of individual economic accomplishments or through improvements in the well-being and achievements of
family members. Thus, for this group, progress is often framed through indi-

vidualistic ideas and experiences, not group goals and group concerns. Consequently, focusing on personal successes (e.g., educational, financial, and social) is one common strategy first-generation West Indians believe helps them to confront and circumvent discrimination in U.S. society. Further, many perceive that focusing on "past wrongs" presents a potentially self-imposed barrier to progress in U.S. society. This sentiment is reflected in the following comments by a group of students in Washington, D.C.:

Participant #1 (male): . . . the few times we get in conversations with African-Americans, they start to talk about the struggle, they start to talk about, you know, opportunities, opportunities, opportunities.

Participant #2 (male): Right. Opportunities are available for whites and they're not available for us, etc., blah, blah, blah. And I mean, I understand that and to a certain extent, I agree with what the other guy was saying earlier, that we haven't lived the experience, etc.

Participant #3 (male): Right.

Participant #1: But my question is, at what point do you stop making excuses and start doing something? I mean, are you going to for millennium after millennium, just saying, "Well, we suffered and this was done to us," etc., blah, blah, blah, rah, rah, rah! " (May 1, 2003, Washington, D.C.)

The three males in the above exchange exemplify how some first-generation West Indians believe they have a different perspective about the possibilities of opportunity and achievement in U.S. society compared to African-Americans. Although they sympathize with the experience of African-Americans, they criticize the narrative of denied opportunity as beyond the scope of their own experience. To focus on past inequities is to miss existing opportunities—a fundamental difference between themselves and African-Americans.

Shared values, beliefs, and practices reinforce a sense of community among West Indians and, at the same time, reinforce a sense of distinctiveness from African-Americans. Focus group participants reveal that experiences of discrimination within the West Indian community are not always related to race. For first-generation West Indian focus group participants, a sense of cohesiveness with other West Indian immigrants is reinforced by how other groups respond to their immigrant background. Focus group participants perceive that they are often subject to mistreatment from others (including African-Americans) not only because of their race, but also because they are immigrants. Participants describe being treated as interlopers who have come to "take away what belongs" to African-Americans, or who think that they are "above" African-Americans.

. . . We are constantly reminded by African-Americans that "you're not one of us," that you are an outsider. . . . I think that the fact that we try to make a concerted effort to reach out and . . . realize that it's not helping . . . you're feeling . . . worse because at the same time you're making that effort, you're recognized as just being a West Indian or St. Lucian national and that's about it. (December 12, 2003, New York City)

Thus, experiences of conflict and exclusion with U.S.-born Blacks reinforce a sense that racial commonalities do not always supersede ethnic differences between immigrant Blacks and African-Americans for first-generation West Indians. Rather, ethnic differences can undermine the possibilities of cooperation and harmony between the two communities.

Definitions of race and opportunity reify a sense of difference among first-generation focus group participants. However, they simultaneously hold the opinion that they are not always able to circumvent discrimination. Although many first-generation focus group participants do not articulate the language of racial community and group obligation offered by African-American focus group participants, they do recognize that discrimination can happen to them.

As much as perceptions of distinctiveness inform notions of identity and racial community for first-generation West Indians, the focus groups reveal that first-generation West Indians confront and negotiate contradictions between what race and ethnicity represent in the Caribbean and what race and ethnicity mean in the context of U.S. society. First-generation focus group participants perceive that West Indian background is not readily apparent to those outside of their community, who may simply evaluate them based on their physical appearance; thus, focus group participants commonly express the view that they are not exempt from being negatively stereotyped like African-Americans.

Moderator: In this country, do you feel that what happens to other Blacks will impact you?

Participant #1 (male): Most definitely! They don't see us as Caribbean . . .

Moderator: Who's "they"?

Participant #2 (male): Society.

Participant #1: Society. White America.

Participant #3 (male): Yeah. They're not going to see us as Caribbean, even African. . . . And the thing that they go on, society's based solely on a first impression. First impressions [are] usually as [a] visual form. They see the color of our skin; we are labeled like everybody else who's Black. So whatever happens to the Blacks that live—that are native Americans, will adversely affect us solely because of the color of our skin. (May 1, 2003, Washington, D.C.)

The passage above captures how first-generation West Indians are sensitive to how the larger society responds to negative images of Blacks, and that they experience the burden of stereotyping and racial discrimination similar to African-Americans.

Despite feeling different from African-Americans, some first-generation focus group participants acquire a new understanding about the significance of race in the United States. They question whether their ideology about race in the Caribbean truly fits with the reality they experience in U.S. society. For some, race denotes more than a reflection of their ancestry; it has come to signify status, an identity that defines their place as members of society.

A student in the Washington, D.C. area equates this consciousness with an understanding of what it means to be a racial minority in the United States. He notes the oddity of having to think about issues surrounding skin color and race in the United States because these were not issues he had to think about in his homeland of Anguilla.

In most West Indian countries—not to say "most," all West Indian countries, you have a Black prime minister, a Black—you've got to have a Black person. Your mom went to a Black lawyer. You know, you went to a school with many Black people. So there was never a question as to "Am I Black, am I minority?" You know, the first time you realize that you're actually a minority is when you come to the States because you're like, oh! You go to Virginia and you're like, wow! You know. I'm actually a minority here. But you don't even think about it. (May 1, 2003, Washington, D.C.)

Some first-generation West Indians describe coming to terms with a dissonance between racial norms in the Caribbean and their racial realities in the United States as a process. Part of this negotiation process involves developing greater sensitivity to how discrimination shapes their experiences and the experiences of others within the Black community. A Jamaican focus group participant living in the United States for over thirty years describes how exposure to American racial attitudes and American racism completely changed her perspective about the significance of differences between African-Americans and West Indians.

When I came here just with my knowledge about African-Americans, I was told that African-Americans were lazy . . . that they were all on welfare and that we as Jamaicans were better. . . . I have to be honest, I held these thoughts, but, after I began to read about the civil rights movement and I saw what they went through and what they did for us—they made it possible for me to come to this country and to go to school and get a job. . . . I read about the lynchings and the protests and what they went through. . . . I am grateful for them because they have done much for us. And other Blacks are usually in the forefront whether it is apartheid, Haiti, the issues in the Caribbean. They are usually out there for other Blacks. . . . Diallo was not African-American and [but] they are in the forefront of the struggle . . . so I think we have more in common and I think it's the White people who help to make, who want to make this division by telling us, "oh you work harder," and then we prove them right and go and work harder 'cause we want to show these African-Americans that they are lazy. (February 1, 2003, New York City)

This focus group participant contrasts her prior attitudes about race with those she cultivates as a member of U.S. society, attributing the shift in her attitudes to personal lessons learned from the experience of U.S.-born Blacks. She draws upon the African-American experience to suggest that the politics of distinctions distract West Indians from focusing on the more significant problem of racism. Her comments suggest that the African-American experience provides a relevant frame for understanding race as West Indians acculturate to U.S. society.

First-generation focus group participants express diverse and, at times, contrary perspectives about the meanings of race, opportunity, and community in U.S. society. The narrative that emerges from the group discussions corroborate findings in the literature that a different reference point informs West Indians' attitudes about race, community, and opportunity in the context of U.S. society. Thus, an attempt to identify a language of racial community among first-generation West Indians becomes a fragmented endeavor at best. First-generation West Indians' ideas about race do not fit neatly within American paradigms of race and Black identity. They have their own interpretations about what it means to be Black in the United States—a perspective that often puts them at odds with African-Americans. The ideas and experiences revealed by first-generation West Indian participants uncovers a flawed assumption that racial commonality begets racial community. For West Indians, an awareness of discrimination informs their perspectives of what it means to be Black in the United States, yet, the language of community (when articulated) is often connected to values, practices, and experiences they have in common with other immigrants, specifically other Blacks from the Caribbean.

Despite the salience of distinctiveness among first-generation West Indians, perspectives on racial community within the West Indian community are not solely defined by the views of first-generation West Indians. To connect the question of racial community to patterns of incorporation within this group requires that we also examine the experiences and perspectives of second-generation West Indians. The viewpoint of the second generation allows us to examine the continued salience of ethnic distinctiveness and, more broadly, how racial attitudes are evolving within the West Indian community. The following section explores perceptions of racial community among second-generation West Indians.

SECOND-GENERATION WEST INDIANS' PERCEPTIONS OF RACIAL COMMUNITY

I remember growing up as a kid the older generation . . . would always tease us and say you are the American 'cause we were the first generation here, and so they saw us as Americans and yet I don't think, it sounds like we didn't necessarily feel like Americans 'cause their values were what [was] taught to us and their values are not American, so it was weird . . . being told you were an American but being raised as a West Indian. (December 7, 2003, New York City)

A defining characteristic of the second generation is that they are both U.S.-born and the children of immigrants. Thus, their experiences as a group are not easily categorized because they reflect an "in-between" status as neither fully immigrant, nor fully American. Scholars argue that "racialization" and "class formation" in the context of U.S. society (Neckerman et al. 1999) have a more significant impact on the adaptation possibilities of second-generation individuals relative to the first generation. Specifically, the ways in which the second generation negotiates experiences of racial categorization are likely to be influenced by their knowledge of U.S. racial categories and U.S racial norms.

As native-born Americans and the children of immigrants, second-generation West Indian focus group participants possess unique attitudes about racial community. Their perspectives about community reflect a duality that incorporates both a sense of distinctiveness from other groups as members of an immigrant community and, at the same time, sensitivity to the problems of discrimination and minority status for the Black community. Thus, they draw upon norms from both the African-American community and the West Indian community to define their place as Blacks in U.S. society. The discussion examines how this duality informs perceptions of community among second-generation West Indians.

Second-generation focus group participants express a range of opinions about what it means to be Black and American in the United States. When participants describe their ethnic background, they often refer to themselves as "hyphenated" Americans. Specifically, they see themselves as "Caribbean-American," "West Indian–American," or connected to a specific national origin group in the Caribbean (i.e., Jamaican, Trinidadian, or Barbadian). Further, the majority of focus group participants in New York and Washington, D.C., perceive a distinction between referring to themselves as Black and referring to themselves as African-American. Participants frequently refer to "African-American" as a "geographically specific" or "culturally distinct" identity that describes U.S.-born Blacks who identify their ancestry within the United States. These comments highlight that for some second-generation West Indians, identifying as "Black" is specifically about not being defined as "African-American." Thus, a preference to be called Black is connected to a desire to claim their race, culture, and Caribbean heritage simultaneously without having to identify as "African-American." This common sentiment is captured in the following statement by a young woman living in the Washington, D.C., area.

> For me just the word African-American it means . . . United States American . . . I say you can't be African-American unless you feel that your culture is American and you are Black . . . [the term] Black is broader. (May 12, 2003, Washington, D.C.)

Thus, as Black Americans of West Indian descent, second-generation focus group participants perceive that they occupy a unique niche within the Black community. Some do not see themselves as fitting within traditional norms that define an American identity; while others do not see themselves as typically African-American.

Beyond talk of identity preference, perceptions of ethnic distinctiveness emerge through second-generation West Indians' comparisons of American culture and "West Indian" culture. Participants in New York and Washington, D.C., offer similar anecdotes that emphasize how their "West Indian" identities are cultivated and reinforced within the context of the immigrant family. Being "raised West Indian" informs a sense that although they are American by birthright, as the children of West Indian immigrants, they do not fit traditional stereotypes of what it means to be American. One participant from New York elaborates upon this distinction in the following manner.

> **Participant (female):** In my household . . . [it] is very negative to be American even though I myself am American and my parents are American citizens now . . . they also make distinctions between American and non-American. They think that Americans in general are very lazy and they don't really value education and bettering themselves and I see it myself. Most Caribbean Americans do concentrate more on hard [work] and education . . . so they can better themselves from their situations [in] their original islands. . . . (December 12, 2002, New York City)

Similarly, many second-generation participants perceive that being born in America and "being American" are not the same thing. Thus, many express the common sentiment that their U.S. origins represents a claim to citizenship with all of the rights and privileges that come with it, yet "being American" does not capture their day-to-day lived experiences within the context of the immigrant community.

> I am American by default. I was born here and I reap the benefits of being an American, but I guess if I had to "choose," I'm not sure that I would pick being American. . . . I don't think it's explicitly stated, but it's like trips to see family, staying with my father every summer. It's just that I range from being in one culture to being American at the same time. It kind of put the idea in my head that there is just something lacking about American culture that it is not fulfilling to be an American, so I try to claim my Caribbean heritage when I can. (December 12, 2002, New York City)

The sentiments expressed above encapsulate a shared perception among participants that their ties to their immigrant community negatively impact how they make sense of their identities as Americans. Thus, for some second-generation West Indians, being American does not define their culture as much as it signifies their place of birth. These attitudes are also present within the written comments of focus group participants, where some describe themselves as "American-born and raised in a West-Indian culture/environment," or in comments such as: "I am an American citizen because I was born in America. I am Trinidadian by birthright" (in written comments, June 8, 2003).

Although second-generation West Indians see themselves as Black, immigrant background represents an important distinction from other U.S.-born groups, particularly African-Americans. They reveal that these attitudes of distinctiveness are connected to witnessing the various ways that African-American identity is contrasted with West Indian identity within the immigrant community. Participants draw upon simple habits and practices that govern their most basic interactions with others to explain what makes West Indians different from African-Americans. In the following exchange, a group of students from Maryland emphasize "cultural differences" to highlight what separates West Indians from African-Americans:

Participant #1 (female): Most of my friends are African-American and there is a big difference I would say in African-Americans — they don't necessarily have a culture to embrace . . . like traditional values, morals, family tales that some Caribbean people have.

Participant #2 (male): My parents would tell me don't follow those African-Americans. So that was a clear distinction growing up. Growing up here you will pick up some of the culture, but when your parents make an effort. . . .

Participant #3 (female): My father is American, and I feel closer to my Mom's family than I do my father's family and it's weird. I don't know if this is just a Caribbean thing, but, when I was younger I just started to feel it was a different way of being raised. You know the whole thing of when you walk into the room you have to say "good morning," good afternoon, good evening. Growing up I had to get used to my father's side of the family—they don't do that. They come in the house and my mother will be playing her reggae and stuff and they make comments about that and comments about food. . . . There is a difference in terms of respect, how you talk to your elders. My culture is Guyanese-American, but, because I have been here so long, I am very American. Just to still see that comparison, I know that somebody who's lived in another country and come here it's just got to be really different if I see the difference then. (May 12, 2003, Washington, D.C.)

Thus, one way in which participants express a sense of distinctiveness from African-Americans incorporates making value judgments that frame West Indian culture in a positive light and paint African-American culture negatively.

Across group discussions in both cities, participants routinely cite disparities in attitudes toward achievement and work ethic as distinguishing factors among West Indians and African-Americans. Whether or not they actually subscribe to this perspective, they perceive that there is a widespread belief within the immigrant community that "West Indians" are better prepared to succeed in the United States. In the following dialogue, a group of students from New York highlights how this perspective is articulated within the immigrant family and how it has shaped their own views about achievement and entitlement in the context of U.S. society.

Participant #1 (female): Well personally, on my block there's definitely a dichotomy. Within the West Indian community, I see there's definitely a notion that Black Americans are "those Blacks," "those people" and they tend to be the negative reflection of everything that is. If something is going on, it's probably a Black American that's doing it on the block or you don't want to act like "those Black Americans."

Participant# 2 (female): My mother's thing is Black people in America are waiting for someone to owe them something whereas Black people from the Diaspora or wherever, come to the U.S., find opportunities and kind of make do with whatever they have, but, because there's the social welfare system the government can help you out. She is like "They just need to get off that and do something for themselves instead of waiting for somebody to hand out something. . . ."

Participant #3 (male): I feel that one of the biggest issues that I face is work ethic and just growing up and just seeing what my parents do with me in comparison to some of my other friends and school. Like my father, he used to sit me down—he had a blackboard and a pointer in my house. He made sure before I went to school I knew everything, so it was just like me doing it again and I know just in terms of competitive drive, I find with a lot of Black people from the U.S. in general—competition, the want, the drive to be first, to be the best in your class, I feel like that was instilled in me and looking at my other friends of Caribbean or West Indian descent I see that much more than some of my other friends. (December 12, 2002, New York City)

The immigrant community is one context where second-generation West Indians observe competing definitions of Black identity. They see African-Americans depicted as lazy and ill-behaved, while West Indians are represented as hard-working and achievement-oriented. Although some focus group participants agree with these characterizations of African-Americans and West Indians, others do not. However, regardless of where they stand on this issue, their exposure to these attitudes is well reflected in how they easily articulate differences between the two groups.

Racial and ethnic identity choice reveal intersecting and diverse experiences around race and ethnicity that have implications for how we understand their perceptions of racial community for second-generation West Indians. Beyond talk of relationships within the immigrant community and cultural differences between immigrant Blacks and U.S.-born Blacks, talk of race and community takes on a different tone for second-generation focus group participants. Based on their perceptions of distinctiveness one might expect that second-generation West Indians share similar perspectives with first-generation West Indians on the question of common fate and racial community. What I find instead is a noticeable shift in perspectives between the two generations of West Indians. As second-generation focus group participants describe their perceptions of how they are viewed by the larger society, discussions of distinctiveness from other Blacks becomes a conversation about racial community with other Blacks.

SECOND-GENERATION WEST INDIANS' PERCEPTIONS OF RACIAL COMMUNITY WITH AFRICAN-AMERICANS

Although many second-generation West Indians unequivocally see themselves as culturally distinct from African-Americans, they also perceive that those outside of their community (including African-Americans) do not distinguish ethnic differences (or differences in national origin) among Blacks.

Thus, the second-generation perceive that they are "just Black" in the larger society. Being "just Black" incorporates the sense that all Blacks share a common experience of being lumped into a generic category despite their differences.

Two participants from Maryland capture these sentiments in the following exchange:

> **Participant #1 (male):** The society looks at us as just black. That's it. . . . So what applies for African-Americans will apply to Caribbean Americans and sometimes Latinos too. . . . When they are looking at you they are not going to decipher all that—you are black.

> **Participant #2 (female):** If you are a minority, you will pretty much be affected if it's black or African-American. If you are African-American or a minority you will be classified like that.

> **Moderator:** So how do you know this?

> **Participant #1:** They don't distinguish between African-American this or Caribbean that. When I meet with West Indians they start asking what country are you from? There is an instant bond. Other people ask me, I'll be like my parents are from Jamaica and there will be no more conversation. I just get the impression. They don't make distinctions. We do. (May 12, 2003, Washington, D.C.)

Many second-generation West Indians express a shared sense that their lives and the lives of most Blacks in the United States are shaped by a common negative group image in U.S. society. The above dialogue reflects a shared perception among second-generation West Indian participants that their Caribbean identities are all but "invisible" to others. The perception that the wider U.S. society will categorize them based on their racial characteristics defines the meaning of minority status in U.S. society for second-generation West Indians. They describe the "consequences" of minority status through shared perceptions of racial inequality.

Talk of common fate among second-generation West Indians is connected to concerns about existing racial stereotypes about "Blackness," and further, how these stereotypes define them in the eyes of others. A Guyanese-American college student from Long Island uses this language to demonstrate how unfounded assumptions about his race shape his daily experiences:

> **Participant:** The minute I sit down, I walk in the class, before I say a word, they see I'm Black . . . they already have these preconceived notions about me. And

that's something I have to just face every time I walk into a room, every time I meet somebody . . . because I'm Black there's things . . . you think you know about me. . . . Whenever I meet you, you're going to have this perception of me. . . . You're going to see stuff on TV, hear something on the radio . . . and it has nothing to do with me. But because it's about Black people and I'm Black, from that I step right into that, whether I want to or not. (December 8, 2002, New York City)

This participant captures a shared sentiment among focus group participants that despite how they view themselves as Blacks, they have little control over how others view them (e.g., as West Indian or African-American). Further, they perceive that they are limited in their options to circumvent situations where they are the target of negative societal stereotypes about Blacks.

A Jamaican-American male offers a simple yet powerful example of how he understands the relationship between negative stereotypes of Blacks and experiences of racial exclusion in the following comment: "You're pulled over at two in the morning in Alabama or you're pulled over on the streets of Brooklyn at 4:30 in the morning, you have dark skin—doesn't matter if you're African, doesn't matter if you're Caribbean, doesn't matter if you were born in Washington, D.C., you're Black. . . ." (February 15, 2003, New York City). He highlights the problem of racial profiling to illustrate how common experiences of mistreatment shape an individual's experiences so long as they are perceived as Black by others in the United States. Further, his comment brings home the point that the second generation is acutely aware that ethnicity (or being culturally different) from African-Americans offers no protection from the injury of discrimination.

The sense of denial that second-generation Blacks associate with the belief that ethnic identity is either ignored or minimized for people of African descent in the United States, may reinforce the idea that being perceived as "just Black" will singularly define their experiences as members of society. As second-generation Asians and Latinos are found to exhibit "reactive ethnicities" in response to racial categorization and racial discrimination from the wider society, second-generation West Indians seem to be engaging in a parallel process with respect to race. Although second-generation West Indians define themselves as "Black" to distinguish themselves from African-Americans, their identification as Black also incorporates the recognition of a shared experience of race with other Blacks outside the Caribbean community.

Second-generation West Indians articulate their perceptions of racial community differently from those of first-generation West Indians. In contrast, discrimination represents a deeply entrenched societal problem for the second-generation rather than an individual instance of negative behavior by whites, as it is sometimes characterized by the first-generation. Thus, the contexts of opportunities for Blacks are inextricably linked to contexts of racial inequality for the second-generation:

> **Participant #1 (male):** I do believe that . . . overall the majority . . . of the government run by white people they feel that there's something . . . you know, they have against Black people. Just a simple thing like being bothered in a grocery store or shopping. I think it is a common feeling . . . that . . . that . . . there's a type of discrimination or some type of racism.
>
> **Moderator:** What do you guys think about that?
>
> **Participant #2 (female):** I agree.
>
> **Participant #3 (female):** I think black people on the whole, deal with the struggle. . . . Everything is a struggle. Nothing is really given to you. Even if you do have money and you're up there, whatever, you still struggle to compete. The majority of black people, we all have to struggle whether we're poor or rich. (January 25, 2003, New York City)

Similar to the participants above, second-generation focus group participants perceive that experiences of racism cut across experiences for all Blacks, regardless of background differences. Thus, "struggle" incorporates the expectation that they must work twice as hard or that they prove themselves to others so that they may enjoy a moderate level of economic and social progress in society. Focus group participants perceive that opportunities are widely available for all Americans, yet they also believe that the paths to success are thornier for Blacks compared to other racial and ethnic groups, particularly whites. Further, they are completely frustrated that their experiences are mainly defined by expectations of blocked mobility.

Through talk of common fate, the second-generation West Indians claim a unique bond with Blacks that distinguishes them from first-generation West Indians. The attitudes of focus group participants suggest that common experiences of injustice bring them closer to other Blacks rather than creating a distance from them. This is distinctly reflected in how they use the African-American experience to frame their understandings of race and minority status for Blacks in the United States.

The African-American experience in the United States is a primary reference for second-generation focus group participants' assessments about the implications of discrimination for Blacks, and the appropriate strategies for responding to discrimination within the Black community. The following dialogue by focus group participants in Maryland typifies how second-generation focus group participants draw from their African-American experience to make sense of their own:

Moderator: Do you feel that the history of African-Americans is also your history? Do you feel close to it?

Participant #1 (male): Yeah, me personally, I identify with it as much as my Jamaican culture. I can't say that one wins out more than the other.

Participant #2 (female): Me too.

Participant #3 (male): Reading history textbooks, and how black people were being lynched and Jim Crow laws, I got mad. I'm not really African-American, but just to be Black and to say that, I feel what they went through, I still feel it.

Participant #4 (male): I think we feel it so much because we feel its effects . . . but yeah like we said you can still walk into a store and get watched. You can still feel its effects, so that ties the past to the future together whether you want to deny it or not.

Participant #2: I want to say that I definitely feel a closeness to you know, the lynching and all that, all the oppression that African-Americans have faced in America. One thing—if you look at people who suffered you say that could have been me—that person looks like me. If I was here earlier, that could have been me. You feel closeness to that. (May 12, 2003, Washington, D.C.)

For second-generation West Indians, African-American history reinforces the belief that shared race is connected to a set of parallel experiences among people in the West Indian community and the African-American community despite their cultural differences. Thus, the African-American experience represents a heuristic for understanding contexts of racial inequality and personal experiences of discrimination. The language that the second generation uses to articulate their identification with the African-American experience distinguishes them from the first generation whose ideas and language appear to be more heavily mediated by their experiences in the Caribbean. For second-generation West Indians, experiences of racial exclusion for Blacks are not "culturally specific" or unique to African-Americans; rather, they represent a shared experience among people of African ancestry in the United States.

"Racial progress" represents the central outcome of collective solutions and group action for second-generation West Indian focus group participants. To address problems of racial exclusion, they emphasize minimizing community divisions to advance a common agenda around shared interests. Similar to their African-American counterparts, second-generation West Indian focus group participants also believe in "individual responsibility" and "obligation" to the racial group. This sentiment is captured in the following comment by a Jamaican-American woman:

> I just believe that we are in charge of turning around our communities. If you don't like what your community is today, well fine! Do something about it . . . contribute something. Even if it's just playing a bigger part in a child's life, it should come down to the fact that we are the minority, that we are in the struggle, and we should identify with each other. . . . That's the obligation . . . to make life easier for somebody else. (January 25, 2003, New York City)

Other focus group participants express visions of racial unity through more extreme examples of group action within the Black community. A Jamaican-American male draws upon notions of Black self-reliance, to articulate his vision of racial community and racial progress for Blacks in the United States:

> **Participant:** In a perfect world race shouldn't matter . . . but unfortunately in this world everyone has taken a side and they're generally siding with their own, and as Black people we cannot go out to play a team sport individually. We have to be on our own team, if we are going to get somewhere. The whites are with the whites and then you have Black people who just want to scatter. It doesn't make sense and it's not going to get you anywhere. . . . My sense of it [unity] is supporting Black business, living in the Black community. The Black community will not get anywhere if as soon as you get a job, [you] go to the suburbs." (February 15, 2003, New York City)

Participants express a desire for racial group cohesiveness with different levels of intensity, yet most subscribe to the idea that racial unity among Blacks is necessary to the protection of rights and opportunities for Blacks in the larger society. These ideas reveal how second-generation West Indians are invested in what happens to them in the context of U.S. society; and further, they believe that they have an important stake in what happens to Blacks in the wider society.

The attitudes of focus group participants suggest that second-generation West Indians do not find the first-generation emphasis on individual accomplishments a sufficient strategy for confronting problems of race in U.S. society. Some directly distance themselves from this idea through critiques of the first-generation's ideology about race and opportunity in U.S. society. This ideological conflict between the second generation and the first generation is captured by a Dominican[6] woman's discussion of why she and her mother have taken different sides on the issue of affirmative action:

I try to separate myself from the things that my parents do. One thing that my mother is against is affirmative action and I am for it and I could completely understand why she is against it, but, she comes from a predominantly Black country where everyone is on the same playing level. When she came here for college, I know she did not take African-American history and they surely did not teach it where she is from so she doesn't really know what the experience . . . the hardships [of] people that were living in America. . . . That's why she probably sees it as people being lazy and affirmative action being some handout. We have long conversations about me trying to explain to her that it's not the fact that people are lazy; it's just the fact that people weren't given the advantages that other people in America were given and that they do need to help. I don't think I'll ever win that battle with my mother, I don't think she'll ever believe that affirmative action is the way to go, but that I think that's one thing I can take from me being American and living here. . . . (December 12, 2002, New York City)

This participant readily emphasizes her American reference point to distinguish her position from her mother's position on affirmative action. As someone born in the United States, she perceives that she has a unique understanding of the legacy of racial discrimination in the United States that informs her support for affirmative action. In contrast, she perceives that her mother's Caribbean reference point poses a barrier to understanding how problems of race shape the lives of Blacks in the United States.

For second-generation West Indians, ethnic distinctions are likely to be minimized outside the internal dynamics of the Black community. Second-generation focus group participants exhibit a collective wisdom that within contexts of mainstream society, race is defined by the idea that all Blacks confront a common problem of racial inequality in society; furthermore, this problem creates a bond that is stronger than the cultural differences that exist between West Indians and African-Americans.

The duality of the second-generation perspective is reflected in how they navigate the contexts of immigrant community and mainstream society. Although West Indian culture defines a unique experience and distinct membership within an immigrant community, a sense of personal obligation toward the progress of Blacks defines their sense of community with other Blacks despite their West Indian heritage. Consequently, the relationship that exists between group cohesiveness and Black social and economic progress defines the roots of a politicized Black identity for second-generation focus group participants.

Although many second-generation focus group participants do not identify as African-Americans, their opinions suggest that they identify strongly with the experiences of African-Americans. The perspectives of second-generation

West Indians suggest that although they maintain a unique sense of identity within the context of the immigrant community, their racial concerns and beliefs are situated primarily within the American context and, furthermore, are shaped by their knowledge of the African-American experience. The African-American narrative of racial inequality represents a useful frame for understanding their experience as Blacks in U.S. society.

CONCLUSION

Understanding processes of political incorporation within a community requires that we not only examine specific acts of participation, but that we also understand the values and beliefs that shape the political perspectives of a group. The African-American and West Indian focus group participants provide powerful narratives about how they think racial inclusion and racial exclusion define the status of Blacks in U.S. society. Their perspectives also reveal that shared experiences and shared knowledge about race are the foundations of community between immigrant Blacks and U.S.-born Blacks.

African-American focus group participants and first-generation and second-generation West Indian focus group participants have diverse opinions about what it means to be Black in the context of U.S. society. One idea common to all three groups is that ancestry and shared phenotype define race—a relevant connection among all Blacks. Although African-American, first-generation West Indian, and second-generation West Indian participants also associate race with minority status and a common (often negative) group identity in the context of U.S. society, this knowledge is of varying significance for each group. When focus group participants consider race and minority status in relation to community, competing values and attitudes about racial inclusion and racial exclusion emerge. African-American and second-generation West Indian focus group participants tend to exhibit greater consensus about the meaning of racial community, relative to first-generation West Indian focus group participants.

African-American and second-generation West Indian focus group participants espouse similar narratives of racial community. For African-American and second-generation participants, race and minority status define a common experience of racial exclusion at the individual level and at the group level as well. Both African-Americans and second-generation West Indians articulate community through aspirations of racial progress and individual obligations to the group (or Black community). Furthermore, African-American and second-generation participants offer shared solutions for challenging inequality through group action and group cohesion, exhibiting a "collectivist orientation" toward race.

Although African-American and second-generation focus group participants readily acknowledge the presence of cultural and ethnic tensions between African-Americans and West Indians, these differences are secondary
to the imperative of racial progress in mainstream society. African-American
and second-generation focus group participants' ideas about racial community present a distinct response to how they perceive that others categorize
them. Participants' perspectives suggest that they think Blacks are (or should
be) each other's closest allies (i.e., "without each other we have no one else")
as it relates specifically to the problem of discrimination in U.S. society. On
the question of racial community, there is a convergence of perspectives between African-American and second-generation focus group participants.
Both groups acknowledge there are shared aspects about being Black in the
United States that cultural difference cannot minimize or negate.

By contrast, first-generation West Indian focus group participants express
diverse and contradictory ideas about racial community in comparison to
African-American and second-generation focus group participants. The
"Caribbean" experience remains a relevant reference point for first-
generation focus group participants. Some first-generation focus group participants draw heavily upon prior experiences, cultural practices, and beliefs from back home to make meaning of race and community within U.S.
society. These participants often derive a sense of community through fa-
milial bonds or common beliefs, values, and practices present within the
immigrant community that distinguish them from other groups, particularly
African-Americans. Conversely, others draw upon the experience of minority groups (specifically, African-Americans) to explain race and community
in the context of U.S. society. Thus, first-generation focus group participants exhibit different opinions about what constitutes racial inclusion and
racial exclusion, revealing that within the first-generation community itself;
there are competing ideas about the meanings of race, identity, and community.

Arguably, the perspectives of second-generation West Indians and African-
Americans present a compelling case that they perceive their experience in
U.S. society will be defined by racial exclusion. The connection between the
perspectives of second-generation West Indians and African-Americans suggests that race continues to negatively impact the incorporation experience of
immigrant Blacks. This certainly has implications for explaining the fates of
nonwhite immigrants and, more generally, racial minorities in U.S. society.
However, the complex and often contradictory ideas about race and community espoused by the first generation suggest that incorporation for immigrant
Blacks is not fully explained by the model of U.S.-born minority groups. To
explain processes of political incorporation more fully, future research must
distinguish the impact of important factors such as education, class, length of

residency, and gender on the creation and maintenance of racialized perspectives and shared narratives of race within the Black community.

NOTES

1. Assessing levels of participatory action in society is the traditional approach to understanding political incorporation of groups. However, to evaluate political incorporation, in this discussion, I focus on the ideas and opinions that shape predispositions for activity, or the ideas and opinions that define one's orientation toward politics.

2. This is based on analysis of the reported ancestry question from the 2000 Census.

3. Among first-generation Caribbean and African-American recruits there were no eligibility limits. However, among second-generation Caribbean individuals there were two criteria for eligibility: (1) individuals had to be of African descent, born in the United States, and having at least one parent in their household from the Caribbean; or, (2) individuals could be born outside of the United States but had to have spent their formative years growing up in the United States. Of the participants born outside of the United States that participated in second-generation discussions, most came to the United States between the ages of five and fourteen.

4. Some participants in New York however, were more likely to believe that other racial and ethnic groups, particularly whites, did make distinctions between West Indians and African-Americans.

5. Using a semistructured protocol, participants were able to share their perspectives on the topic of racial community in their own words. Questions were coded, as were the entire interview transcripts, for language and references that might indicate evidence of common fate. The following discussion is based on coding of focus group transcripts that reveal common trends and themes which emerged among focus group participants.

6. My description of this young woman as Dominican refers to her background in the Commonwealth of Dominica, a small island in the West Indies. Dominica is not part of the Dominican Republic.

REFERENCES

Alba, Richard, and Victor Nee. 1999. "Rethinking Assimilation Theory for a New Era of Immigration." Pp. 137–60 in *The Handbook of International Migration: The American Experience*, ed. Charles Hirschmann, Josh DeWind, and Philip Kasinitz. New York: Russell Sage.

Allen, Richard L., Michael Dawson, and Ronald Brown. 1989. "Modeling an African American Racial Belief System." *American Political Science Review* 83: 421–41.

Bashi Bobb, Vilna F., and Antonio McDaniel. 1997. "A Theory of Immigration and Racial Stratification." *Journal of Black Studies* 27: 668–82.

Bryce-Laporte, Roy S. 1972. "Black Immigration: The Experience of Invisibility and Inequality." *Journal of Black Studies* 3: 26–56.

Conover, Pamela. 1984. "The Influence of Group Identification on Political Perceptions and Education." *Journal of Politics* 46: 760–85.

Crowder, Kyle D., and Lucky Tedrow. 2001. "West Indians and the Residential Landscape of New York." Pp. 81–114 in *Islands in the City: West Indian Migration to New York*, ed. Nancy Foner. Los Angeles: University of California Press.

Dahl, Robert. 1961. *Who Governs? Democracy and Power in an American City*. New Haven, CT: Yale University Press.

Dawson, Michael. 1994. *Behind the Mule: Race and Class in African-American Politics*. Princeton, NJ: Princeton University Press.

———. 2001. *Black Visions: The Roots of Contemporary African-American Political Ideologies*. Chicago: University of Chicago Press.

Denton, Nancy A., and Douglas Massey. 1989. "Racial Identity among Caribbean Hispanics: The Effect of Double Minority Status on Residential Segregation." *American Sociological Review* 54: 790–808.

Gordon, Milton. 1964. *Assimilation in American Life*. New York: Oxford University Press.

Green, Charles, and Basil Wilson. 1989. *The Struggle for Black Empowerment in New York City: Beyond the Politics of Pigmentation*. New York: Praeger.

Hero, Rodney. 1992. *Latinos and the U.S. Political System: Two-tiered Pluralism*. Philadelphia: Temple University Press.

Kasinitz, Philip. 1992. *Caribbean New York: Black Immigrants and the Politics of Race*. Ithaca, NY: Cornell University Press.

———. 2001. "Invisible No More? West Indians in the Social Scientific Imagination." Pp. 257–76 in *Islands in the City: West Indian Migration to New York*, ed. Nancy Foner. Los Angeles: University of California Press.

Krueger, Richard A. 2000. *Focus Groups: A Practical Guide for Applied Research*. Thousand Oaks, CA: Sage Publications.

Miller, Arthur H., Patricia Gurin, Gerald Gurin, and Oksana Malanchuk. 1981. "Group Consciousness and Political Participation." *American Journal of Political Science* 25: 494–511.

Model, Suzanne. 2001. "Where New York's West Indians Work." Pp. 52–80 in *Islands in the City: West Indian Migration to New York*, ed. Nancy Foner. Los Angeles: University of California Press.

Morgan, David. 1997. *Focus Groups As Qualitative Research*. Thousand Oaks, CA: Sage Publications.

Neckerman, Kathryn, Prudence Carter, and Jennifer Lee. 1999. "Segmented Assimilation and Minority Cultures of Mobility." *Ethnic and Racial Studies* 22: 945–65.

Rogers, Reuel. 2001. "Black Like Who? Afro-Caribbean Immigrants, African Americans, and the Politics of Group Identity." Pp. 162–92 in *Islands in the City: West Indian Migration to New York*, ed. Nancy Foner. Los Angeles: University of California Press.

Sanders-Thompson, Vetta. 1999. "Variables Affecting Racial Identity Salience among African Americans." *Journal of Social Psychology* 139: 748–61.

Tajfel, H., and J. C. Turner. 1979. "An Integrative Theory of Intergroup Conflict." Pp. 33–47 in *The Social Psychology of Intergroup Relations*, ed. W. G. Austin and S. Worchel. Monterey, CA: Brooks/Cole.

Tate, Katherine. 1993. *From Protest to Politics: The New Black Voters in American Elections*. New York: Russell Sage.

Vickerman, Milton. 1999. *Crosscurrents: West Indian Immigrants and Race*. New York: Oxford University Press.

Walton, Hanes. 1985. *Invisible Politics*: *Black Political Behavior*. Albany: State University Press of New York.

Waters, Mary. 1999. *Black Identities: West Indian Immigrant Dreams and American Realities*. New York: Russell Sage.

6

Appalachian *Mestizaje*

Race and Latino Immigration in Western North Carolina

Mariel Rose

ZZ's[1] is a nightclub in the small town of Waynesville, North Carolina, a short drive from the Smoky Mountains National Park and the Reservation of the Eastern Band of Cherokee Indians. It is also an illuminating site of cultural boundary crossing in this corner of the Southern Appalachians, a region undergoing rapid demographic and economic change in the age of neoliberal capitalism. A country-western establishment in the past, the club has in recent years converted to a Mexican dance hall, featuring live bands and the slow rhythms of *polka norteña, cumbia,* and Jaliscan *jarabe*. The Saturday night crowd here is overwhelmingly young, male, heterosexual, and Mexican. A few Mexican women are present with their husbands or boyfriends, from whose sides they rarely stray during the evening. Most of the small, much-in-demand female contingent, however, are native-born white and Cherokee Indian women from the ranks of the working poor, many of whom are divorced or single mothers and generally older than the Mexican men they come here regularly to meet. With precision, they follow the men in the steps and swirls of *bailes mexicanos* they have obviously been practicing at home. Notably, certain segments of the local population are not represented on the dance floor. The only white men present are bouncers or managers. The few Cherokee men who make rare appearances do so in small family groups with mothers, aunts, or sisters, and usually sit out the dancing. African Americans of both sexes are completely absent, although they constitute a small but long-standing community in this mountain town.

This essay addresses questions posed by this intriguing Saturday night scene of cultural, ethnic, and racial boundary crossing: What do the liaisons—and the occasional long-term relationships and marriages—formed

on the dance floor of ZZ's tell us about the integration of new immigrant arrivals into existing social constructs of race and ethnicity in the Mountain
South? How do historical relations among blacks, whites, and Indians in the
region color the encounter of immigrant newcomers and native-born residents? What is the significance of the skewed gender mix we find here? And,
how does socioeconomic class enter into the picture?

In tackling these questions, I evoke a metaphor that is both potent and
loaded in Latin America: *mestizaje*. Though sometimes translated simply as
"race mixing," the term encapsulates an often painful history of European
conquest, subjugation of indigenous peoples, and sexual domination of the
conquered in which the conquered nonetheless triumphed through the rise of
la Raza Cósmica, the Cosmic Race. While José Vasconcelos's (1966 [1925])
concept of *la Raza Cósmica* celebrated the blend of all the world's races in
the Americas, the notion of the ascendance of a European/Amerindian mix
has been embraced with an especially nationalistic fervor in Mexico. Although in titling this essay "Appalachian *Mestizaje*" I use the term only in the
sense of "race mixing," my findings underscore the fact that crossing the
boundaries of such a formidable social construct as race is never devoid of
implications of power and privilege.

This essay draws upon two years of ethnographic fieldwork in the region.[2]
The research focuses on the cultural effects of rapid industrial decline and increasing Latino immigration, predominantly from Mexico, in seven mountain
counties in close proximity to Asheville, North Carolina. The epicenter of this
research was Haywood County, where I lived and volunteered as an ESL tu-
tor for the duration of the fieldwork, although I followed the path of inter-
locking social networks into surrounding counties in arranging interviews and
attending various community meetings and events. The political-economic
dimensions of this research meant that the one hundred unstructured interviews that I conducted were predominantly with factory workers, past and
present, among both native-born and immigrant residents. Other interviewees
were community leaders, service agency workers, industrial personnel officials, and labor and social activists. These interviews were conducted in either English or Spanish, at the participant's preference.

The responses of various informants, as well as information gleaned in
participating/observing in local daily life, led me to explore the ethnograph-
ically rich site of ZZ's, and to pursue the topic of racial/ethnic boundary
crossing at the level of intimate relationships and marriage. In this regard,
the qualitative methods that I employ are of particular value, as these relationships occur in small numbers that more quantitatively inclined researchers would likely dismiss as statistically unimportant. Despite their
minimal occurrence, however, these relationships tell us much about how

existing racial and ethnic boundaries are shifting to accommodate the new demographic realities of the region.

I come to this research as both insider (as a white woman native-born to the Southern Appalachians) and outsider to the Latino, African American, and Cherokee Indian communities; and, inevitably, as an academic from a Northern university, an outsider at times to all local residents in the area of my research. Having grown up in East Tennessee and having spent most of my adult life in Western North Carolina, I have been sometimes amused and sometimes offended by portrayals of mountain people in the national media, in popular culture, and in academia. This life experience will, I hope, help me write with respect about the people of Western North Carolina and the immigrant newcomers who have chosen to settle among them.

NEW SOUTHERN DEMOGRAPHICS

The racial and ethnic boundary crossings that are the subject of this essay take place in what Leon Fink and others have dubbed "the *nuevo* New South" (Fink 2003). The 2000 Census awoke the nation to a reality that Southerners had gradually grown accustomed to for several decades: the Southeastern United States has become a new target location for Latino immigrant settlement. The Latino population, which had been slowly and steadily increasing in the region since the early 1970s, mushroomed across the South during the 1990s.[3] New demographics validate Richard Alba and Victor Nee's (1999) prediction that continued rapid immigration growth, especially for Hispanics, would result in a spatial dispersion of settlement away from traditional areas of geographic concentration such as California, Florida, Texas, and New York. Table 6.1, which ranks the top fifteen states in numeric Latino population growth for the decade of the 1990s, shows that these states still top the nation as destinations of choice for Latino immigrants. The most rapid growth rates, however, occurred in Southern states other than Texas and Florida. Table 6.2, which ranks the top fifteen states according to the percent change in the Latino population for the decade, shows North Carolina, Arkansas, Georgia, and Tennessee heading a list that includes four other states from the region. North Carolina led the nation with an explosive growth rate of 393.9 percent. New Latino cultural centers are now taking shape across the South, especially in metropolitan areas such as Atlanta and Raleigh/Durham.

In the seven counties of Western North Carolina that were the focus of my research, Latino population growth was equally dramatic for the decade of the 1990s. Table 6.3 shows that the total Latino population for these counties grew from 2,703 in 1990 to 12,992 in 2000, an increase of 380.7 percent. As

Table 6.1. Top Fifteen States in Latino Population Growth, Ranked by Numeric Change

Numeric Change Rank	Entity	4/1/2000	4/1/1990	Numeric Change	Percentage Change	Percentage Change Rank
	United States	35,305,818	22,354,059	12,951,759	57.9	
1	California	10,966,556	7,687,938	3,278,618	42.6	44
2	Texas	6,669,666	4,339,905	2,329,761	53.7	36
3	Florida	2,682,715	1,574,143	1,108,572	70.4	30
4	New York	2,867,583	2,214,026	653,557	29.5	48
5	Illinois	1,530,262	904,446	625,816	69.2	32
6	Arizona	1,295,617	688,338	607,279	88.2	26
7	New Jersey	1,117,191	739,861	377,330	51.0	37
8	Georgia	435,227	108,922	326,305	299.6	3
9	Colorado	735,601	424,302	311,299	73.4	29
10	North Carolina	378,963	76,726	302,237	393.9	1
11	Nevada	393,970	124,419	269,551	216.6	5
12	Washington	441,509	214,570	226,939	105.8	20
13	New Mexico	765,386	579,224	186,162	32.1	47
14	Virginia	329,540	160,288	169,252	105.6	21
15	Oregon	275,314	112,707	162,607	144.3	13

Source: Census data for 1990 and 2000 compiled by the Inter-University Program for Latino Research at the University of Notre Dame, file 2: Region/State, table 2.2, "Population Change for Hispanics from 1990 to 2000 by State," Latino Population Counts: 1990–2000, www.nd.edu/~iuplr/cic/data_files.html (accessed Oct. 9, 2003).

Table 6.2. Top Fifteen States in Latino Population Growth, Ranked by Percentage Change

Percentage Change Rank	Entity	4/1/2000	4/1/1990	Numeric Change	Percentage Change	Numeric Change Rank
	United States	35,305,818	22,354,059	12,951,759	57.9	
1	North Carolina	378,963	76,726	302,237	393.9	10
2	Arkansas	86,866	19,876	66,990	337.0	29
3	Georgia	435,227	108,922	326,305	299.6	8
4	Tennessee	123,838	32,741	91,097	278.2	26
5	Nevada	393,970	124,419	269,551	216.6	11
6	South Carolina	95,076	30,551	64,525	211.2	30
7	Alabama	75,830	24,629	51,201	207.9	33
8	Kentucky	59,939	21,984	37,955	172.6	37
9	Minnesota	143,382	53,884	89,498	166.1	27
10	Nebraska	94,425	36,969	57,456	155.4	31
11	Iowa	82,473	32,647	49,826	152.6	34
12	Mississippi	39,569	15,931	23,638	148.4	38
13	Oregon	275,314	112,707	162,607	144.3	15
14	Utah	201,559	84,597	116,962	138.3	19
15	Delaware	37,277	15,820	21,457	135.6	39

Source: Census data for 1990 and 2000 compiled by the Inter-University Program for Latino Research at the University of Notre Dame, file 2: Region/State, table 2.2, "Population Change for Hispanics from 1990 to 2000 by State," *Latino Population Counts: 1990–2000*, www.nd.edu/~iuplr/cic/data_files.html (accessed Oct. 9, 2003).

Table 6.3. Latino Population Growth in Seven Western North Carolina Counties, 1970–2000

County	1970 Census Population of "Spanish Origin"	1980 Census Population of "Spanish Origin"	1980 Census Percentage Change from 1970	1990 Census Hispanic Population	1990 Census Percentage Change from 1980	2000 Census Hispanic Population	2000 Census Percentage Change from 1990
Buncombe	541	883	63.2	1,173	32.8	5,730	388.5
Haywood	93	261	180.6	240	-8.0	763	217.9
Henderson	238	337	41.6	846	151.0	4,880	476.8
Jackson	76	718	844.7	155	-78.4	577	272.3
Madison	97	18	-81.4	86	377.8	266	209.3
Transylvania	124	85	-31.5	154	81.2	298	93.5
Yancey	—	39	—	49	25.6	478	875.5
Total	1,169	2,341	100.3	2,703	15.5	12,992	380.7

Sources: U.S. Department of Commerce, Bureau of the Census, table 119, "Social Characteristics for Counties: 1970," *1970 Census of Population, Volume 1: Characteristics of the Population, North Carolina* (Washington, D.C.: Bureau of the Census, 1973), 381–89; table 59, "Persons by Spanish Origin, Race, and Sex: 1980," *1980 Census of Population, North Carolina: General Social and Economic Characteristics* (Washington, D.C.: Bureau of the Census, 1983), 41–44; census data for 1990 and 2000 compiled by the Inter-University Program for Latino Research at the University of Notre Dame, file 4, State/County, table 3.2., "Population Change for Hispanics from 1990 to 2000 by County, Sorted by State," *Latino Population Counts: 1990–2000,* www.nd.edu/~iuplr/cic/data_files.html (accessed Oct. 9, 2003).

the table includes Latino population totals for 1970 and 1980, it also indicates that for at least thirty-five years Latinos have been a small but growing presence in the region, even in rural areas and small towns like those that dominate the landscape of these mountain counties.

The roots of the current explosion of Latino population in North Carolina are agricultural. Since the early 1970s, Mexican migrant crews have harvested tobacco in the Piedmont and tomatoes, squash, and apples in the mountain counties near Asheville. The crews that come through this part of western North Carolina often work a circuit from Florida oranges to Georgia peaches, and, after the harvest here, on through the mountains to Christmas trees in the northwestern counties of the state. These crews have always been predominantly male, although women and children have traveled the circuit in increasing numbers over the years. From the beginning, a few migrants settled down to year-round work at various points along the circuit—a pioneering endeavor in North Carolina, a state with very little history of Latino immigration and few Spanish-speaking residents. These early settlers often became the anchor points in transnational networks of family and friends, expanding rapidly in recent years, that brought other year-round Mexican residents to the region.

Several states in central Mexico—Michoacán, Guanajuato, Querétaro, Hidalgo, Guerrero, and Veracruz—are best represented in the current population of the area, although during the course of my fieldwork I encountered people from all regions of the country, except for the far reaches of the Yucatán Peninsula and Baja California. While the majority of Latinos here are Mexicans, they are joined by Caribbean, Central, and South Americans, who mostly reside in the city of Asheville, in Buncombe County, but are also scattered in small numbers throughout the other six counties. During my research, I met people from Cuba, Puerto Rico, Guatemala, Honduras, Nicaragua, El Salvador, Ecuador, Colombia, Bolivia, Chile, and Argentina.

INTIMATE ACCOMMODATIONS

The scene that one encounters at the nightclub ZZ's on a Saturday night, however, is a distinctly Mexican social space. When I visited the place with a male Colombian friend, we looked sufficiently out-of-place that an Anglo employee at the door warned us that "we only have Spanish music here." Apparently he equated "Spanish" with the Mexican foreignness now so familiar in local life. On special occasions live bands come all the way from Mexico to perform, and on those nights *mexicanos* sometimes drive from as far away as Atlanta, a three-hour trip from the Southwest over winding mountain roads. On most Saturday nights, however, the club draws its Mexican clientele from the immigrant networks that extend throughout the hollows and coves of surrounding counties and into upstate South Carolina.

Like soccer matches in Henderson County on Saturday afternoons and certain flea markets on Sundays, ZZ's serves as a site of community for kin and friends who live and work in far-flung locations. My key informant on the club was Amy Suarez, a woman of mixed Cherokee and white descent who met her Mexican husband there twelve years ago. As she informed me,

> For awhile we went, just pretty steady. . . . My husband does not drink. He don't drink anything. We drink sodas, but we would go there because we live in Canton, [and] his cousins, his friends live, like, [in] Mars Hill [and] South Carolina. No matter where they worked, a long time ago it was the only place to go. So they would all kind of go there on Saturday night, and not necessarily to drink or to dance. Just, they knew their family, their friends, everybody was going to be there. It was just kind of like a gathering place, where no matter where they lived in this area, they would be there on Saturday night.[4]

In addition to being a community gathering place, the club also serves as a singles bar, where—despite the drinking habits of Amy and her husband—beer and pick-up lines flow freely. As Amy laughingly told me, even men with very limited English ability have no trouble with certain sentences at ZZ's: "Do you have a husband?" "Do you have a boyfriend?" "Do you want one?" And, of course, "What is your phone number?" and "I love you."[5] In these circumstances, the linguistic motivation for these men is not difficult to decipher. Despite increasing numbers of women and children among Mexican immigrants in the area, males still outnumber females in this population. For example, in Haywood County the 2000 Census counted 230 males and 180 females among Hispanics over the age of sixteen.[6] The actual gender disparity is probably much greater. In addition to a likely undercount of the total Latino population due to the obvious incentive for the undocumented to avoid interaction with the U.S. government, the census tally probably disproportionately included family groups with stable residence patterns and missed many of the single male Latino workers who live more transient lifestyles. It is men of the latter group who often come to ZZ's in search of scarce female companionship. And, in an alien environment where they cannot always be sure of a welcome, it is less threatening to let willing American women cross the boundary of this Mexican social space, rather than to pursue them on their own ground.

But what motivates the white and Cherokee women who come here to meet Mexican men? News of the club has spread by word of mouth among them, with women inviting friends to accompany them for an experience outside the norm. As Amy Suarez remembered, "I have a friend, her husband is Mexican, and she asked me to go with her. She said, 'I know you like different things. I know you'll probably love the music.'"[7] Charlotte Simpson, a white woman now expecting a baby with her Mexican boyfriend, described her initial reluctance to go to the club: "My friend, she's dated a lot of Hispanic people. She said, 'Why don't you come with me?' And I said, 'I don't know.' 'Cause I'd never dated anybody Hispanic and I was like, I don't know about this, you know. Well, we went, and [after that] we'd go like every Saturday. It was kind of addicting, like once you go, you want to go back again."[8]

Like Amy and Charlotte, most of the women who frequent ZZ's have been divorced at least once, and many are working single mothers who find it difficult to compete for male companionship in the local mainstream. In addition to the lure of a "different" experience, Amy Suarez described another appeal of the club,

> Mexican people accept people the way they are, sometimes. It's just easier. You go to a club in Asheville, the American men are looking for the most beautiful, well-dressed [woman]. And you can go up to ZZ's and you can wear your sweatpants, you can wear your shorts, you can wear anything you want. And there's always way more guys than there is girls, and you will dance all night, if that's what you want to do. And if you want to go home with somebody, somebody will take you home. It's sad to say, but it's an easier place to find somebody. Nobody cares what you're dressed like, everybody will ask you to dance. No matter what your size, no matter your color, no matter how you're dressed.[9]

Marriages and long-term relationships are not uncommon among men and women who meet at ZZ's, although most liaisons are of a shorter duration.

Immigrant/citizen couples also meet on factory production lines, in restaurant kitchens, in trailer parks, and flea markets. Others are introduced to their partners through friends and family who are themselves involved in such relationships. For example, Sherry Ramirez, a woman of Cherokee descent, met her Mexican husband at a trailer park where they both lived. Her marriage caused a deep rift with her father, who did not speak to her for six years, but her mother extended kindness and acceptance to her new son-in-law from the beginning. The four children born of the marriage eventually softened their grandfather's heart to the relationship. Her two sisters are now also married to Mexican men, and their husbands' acceptance into the family has been eased by Sherry's marriage. One sister met her husband at a restaurant where she waited tables and he washed dishes, and the other found romance while accompanying Sherry and her husband to a soccer match in a neighboring county.[10]

Intermarriage is often cited as a factor in immigration studies. Robert Park's (1950) classic race relations cycle model sets out four progressive stages through which immigrants, through successive generations, pass in the transformation from alien newcomers to fully integrated members of their adopted country. After initial contact and a period of competition with the native-born population, relations reach a stage of accommodation in which immigrants find a stable niche within existing—and usually unequal—relations of power and privilege, before they eventually become fully assimilated. Park and other theorists point to intermarriage with the mainstream population as a key indicator of assimilation (Alba and Golden 1986; Lieberson and Waters 1988; Park 1950). The applicability of Park's model to today's immigrant streams has been widely discounted because it focused solely on the experience of white Europeans and did not take into account factors of economic structural change. Further, it predated technological advances that now facilitate transnational ties of family and community. While acknowledging these limitations, Richard Alba and Victor Nee (1999) argue convincingly that assimilation theory is still viable, with modification to account for new realities of immigration. They cite group convergence as an alternative to the notion of a new population's eventual disappearance into a cultural melting pot. Rather, acculturation is a mutual process as newcomers adapt, the mainstream evolves, and new cultural hybridities emerge. Applying Park's model, Alba and Nee assess the current rapid influx of new immigration in the United States at the initial stages of contact and competition. Especially for Latinos, they predict a "ratcheting forward," or speeding up, of assimilation as newcomers move into new areas of the country, far from the cultural comfort of well-established immigrant communities.

This mountain region of Western North Carolina, at the geographic center of the "*nuevo* New South," is such a new ground for immigration. Following Alba and Nee in applying Park's model, I characterize the cultural negotiations that take place within immigrant/native-born marriages as a form of intimate accommodation. Certainly, the predominantly male composition of the new Latino population adds impetus to their crossing racial/ethnic boundaries to find female companionship. When marriages and long-term relationships occur, even in small numbers, and especially when children are born of these unions, families and communities are forced to make adjustments in attitude, in cultural practices, and in the sharing of resources. Thus, acculturation and accommodation on both sides are "ratcheted forward."

These relationships seem to arouse a great deal of social anxiety. During the course of my research, I heard gossip and comments attributing ulterior motives to both the men and women in such unions. Mexican men were supposedly after annual casino profit shares—about $6,000 per tribal member in 2003—when they pursued Cherokee women. Green cards were often mentioned as an incentive for these men to marry American citizens, although current immigration law makes it extremely difficult for the undocumented to legalize their status in this manner. As for the women involved, Amy Suarez cast aspersions on their motives, as well:

> Plus—this is only my opinion, and it bothers me sometimes—you see some of these Mexican boys that are just so cute and just so smart, and they're working so hard. And they just end up with—now, this sounds awful—some really awful people. People that don't want to work, and they just want somebody to take care of them. It sounds horrible to say, and I'm sorry to say, but sometimes they end up in relationships that is not to their benefit. These girls, a lot of them, are just looking for somebody so they have money, a place to stay. It's really sad sometimes.[11]

While marriage and long-term relationships always involve material considerations, the exaggerated suspicions of malice cast on the parties involved are symptoms of the social anxieties surrounding these unions.

Social anxieties come to bear within the relationships as well, and the parties involved sometimes attribute these tensions to cultural difference. Pedro Zarate of Veracruz, for example, identifies his wife's fondness for credit cards and her lack of money-saving habits as American traits.[12] And Tomás Quiñones of Puebla cited cultural differences as the reason for the failure of his marriage to a white woman from the town of Hendersonville:

> What happens is that we have problems with her friends. It's because we are from different cultures. I told her that when I go to work, she should respond by having dinner ready for me. At first she did well and things were fine with us, but her friends would ask her why she cooked for me. At times they would say to her, "Let's go dancing," and she would say, "No." And we had problems like that. They kept on pulling and pulling at her. Because of that, we separated.[13]

Charlotte Simpson, a white woman who was expecting a baby girl with a Mexican partner, expressed her anxieties about the situation in terms of a comparison between white and Mexican men:

> White guys, from my experience, they are more better about taking care of, like if they have a baby with a girl, they're more apt to take care of it. Like, they don't just get you pregnant and leave, skip off across the country. . . . But Hispanic people, they treat you a lot better than white people. I notice a lot of white people, really, you might say they want perfect people. And Hispanic people don't. Like, if you're a little bit overweight, they're fine with that. . . . They treat you really nice. . . . But they are a lot different, even like their family life and stuff. Like if you was to marry a Hispanic person, they want you to be like the girls in Mexico. A lot of women here are less into cooking and more into school

or working and stuff. And they don't like that. They like you to be at home and them do all the working. They like it more traditional.[14]

Charlotte also expressed worry that in the future her daughter and her boyfriend would "team up" on her, speaking Spanish that she would not understand. She said, "I told him, she can be my translator. When I don't know what none of them says, she'll translate for me."

Despite tensions and cultural hurdles, many couples adjust and relationships survive. In the process, couples make various social accommodations according to the particular circumstances of the relationship. Among my informants, a few of the women have gone to Mexico with their husbands for a few months, in order to secure entrance visas for their husbands and to begin the long legalization process when they returned to the United States. For instance, Sherry Ramirez spent three months with her husband at his parents' home in a village in Guanajuato. While there, she began to learn Spanish, participated in her sister-in-law's wedding, washed clothes on an outdoor washboard, learned to make tortillas for the family at daybreak each morning, and answered many questions about what it is like to be an Indian in North Carolina. She forged lasting bonds with her in-laws and now has weekly phone conversations with them. In other cases, the couple communicates only in English and the husband enters the social world of his wife and her family in North Carolina, while he separately maintains ties with kin and friends here and in Mexico. Other couples form flexible arrangements like those of Amy Suarez and her husband, who enjoy a wide circle of friends among Mexicans in Haywood and surrounding counties. Yet he goes alone, every few years, to visit his parents near Mexico City, and she goes without him to celebrate holidays with her family. All the couples maintain close relationships with friends in similarly mixed marriages in the area.

As with Sherry Ramirez's six-year rift with her father after her marriage, the wives of Mexican men often encounter staunch resistance from family members. Fortunately, my informants reported that the relationships eventually healed. Their Mexican in-laws, in contrast, usually welcomed them into the family warmly and immediately. Interestingly, my informants also unanimously reported that the wife's father was far more resistant to the relationship than was her mother, leading one woman to speculate that males in the area are more racist than females. She may be right, but I am more inclined to suspect that the reason for this phenomenon lies in the particular gender mix of immigration in the region. More Mexican men than Mexican women are in the local workforce. Because many jobs continue to be segregated by gender, the men experience a more direct economic competition with native-born men than with native-born women, which may engender more ill-will between them. Another factor may be that marriages between Mexican women and American men are very uncommon in the area, as most women immigrate within family groups, and young Mexican girls tend to be guarded protectively by kin and family friends. As more one-and-a-half and second-generation girls enter local high schools and begin dating classmates, such marriages may become more common. It is possible that family dynamics could change when a son rather than a daughter brings home a Mexican spouse.

Although Western North Carolina is not a particularly unfriendly place for immigrants, newcomers report occasional slights and unfair treatment in schools, supermarkets, health clinics, restaurants, and other public situations. The women involved in mixed immigrant/citizen relationships—wives, girlfriends, and grandmothers of children born to the unions—often become vociferous advocates and defenders of Mexican immigrants in their home communities.

HISTORICALLY LOADED QUESTIONS OF COLOR

When I first met Amy Suarez, my key informant on the Saturday night scene at ZZ's, she was behind the counter of the small *taquería* that she operates with her husband. I mistook her as Mexican, not only because of the setting but also because of her appearance, and spoke to her in Spanish. She responded in English, with ready laughter and an accent unmistakably native to the Southern Mountains. Her grandfather on her mother's side was Cherokee, she explained, although he was not officially "on the books." His sister has traced the genealogy, and they know which tribal members they are related to, although they have always lived off the reservation and have never applied for official tribal membership. Amy bears a strong phenotypic resemblance to many who are "on the books" of the Eastern Band of Cherokee Indians, although she regrets that her skin is not as dark as her mother's and her grandfather's. It happens frequently that people think she is Mexican.

Such cases of mistaken ethnic identity occur throughout the region. Alberto Gonzalez, a factory worker whom I interviewed in the neighboring county of Henderson, talked about approaching a young woman at work whom he described as dark-skinned, pretty, and seemingly Mexican. However, when he spoke to her in Spanish and got a surprised reaction in English, he realized, "*¡No es mexicana, es india!*"[15] Sherry Ramirez, a Cherokee woman who has four bilingual children with her Mexican husband, told me that the health department has tagged her file with "Speaks English" in large block letters across the top.[16] Ironically, the staff treats her as a newcomer in this land of her ancestors.[17]

It is not surprising, then, that the two groups sometimes recognize each other's *indigenismo*. As Alberto Gonzalez expressed it, "We Mexicans are Indians. The Cherokees know that we are indigenous and they are too, so it could be that we are the same race."[18] Amy Suarez pointed out common physical features between the two groups when she explained the appeal of ZZ's and Mexican men for many Cherokee women,

> I don't know, in my eyes Mexican people are just handsome. A lot of them are just handsome and beautiful, the girls are beautiful. But like I say, I love the brown skin, the dark eyes. I wish I had that from my mom and my grandpa. I guess if you were an Indian you would think dark skin, dark hair, dark eyes is handsome and beautiful.[19]

Despite a far-distant shared ancestry and some common physical traits, however, the two groups are separated by wide gulfs of history. And I should mention here that a great number of Cherokees on the official tribal rolls are phenotypically indistinguishable from local whites.

The Cherokees have, for millennia, been a constant presence in these mountains. Their vast territory of 40,000 square miles originally stretched through portions of the present-day states of Virginia, West Virginia, Kentucky, Tennessee, Georgia, Alabama, North Carolina, and South Carolina (King 1979a: ix). From the earliest days of European penetration into their territories, they dealt with French, Spanish, and English imperial interests in the complex borderland relations of trade, intercultural mixing, military alliance, and conflict that Jeremy Adelman and Stephen Aron (1999) describe among indigenous peoples across North America. The Cherokees and other tribes quickly became ensnared, as both victims and perpetrators, into the driving capitalist venture at the core of European expansion on all fronts: the slave trade. Many Cherokees were enslaved alongside Africans, even as their fellow tribe members altered traditional patterns of warfare and hostage-taking to allow exploitation of the lucrative market in human beings from neighboring tribes. Appalachian *mestizaje* began very early in the colonial period, as children were born of mixed African and Cherokee parentage in slave quarters, and of mixed European and Cherokee parentage in pairings with early white traders and soldiers. While in social organization, belief systems, and cultural practice the tribe had far more in common with the Africans they encountered in bondage, many Cherokees recognized the advantage of casting their lot with the powerful white conquerors. In the process of becoming "civilized" in the early nineteenth century a small, elite class of Cherokee plantation owners and slaveholders emerged, having adopted European systems of ownership and inheritance. "White Indian" prosperity flourished, especially in the low, rolling terrain of upper Georgia, Alabama, and South Carolina (Dunaway 2003; King 1979b; Perdue 1979).

Throughout the Mountain South, social, political, and economic relations were often a matter of geography. Those who claimed large tracts of fertile, level soil along river and creek valleys often garnered prosperity to be passed on to heirs, while the less fortunate eked out sparse livings on steep, hardscrabble soil. This was true among the "civilized" Cherokee as well as among the Scotch Irish and German settlers that rapidly displaced the tribe in Western North Carolina, pushing them westward toward the high peaks of the Great Smoky Mountains (Dunaway 1996; Dykeman 1955). Ironically, when the United States forcibly removed the tribe to Oklahoma in 1838, the "white Indians" who had adopted Western lifeways and occupied the most desirable lands received the most pressure to leave, and a good number of their slaves departed with them on the Trail of Tears (Dunaway 2003; Perdue 1979).

Tribal members who resisted removal and stayed on in the high mountains of Western North Carolina were long considered to be the most traditional of the Cherokees. They continued for decades to follow the tribe's ancient matrilineal clan system of kinship. The few slave owners among them usually employed a traditional egalitarian form of bondage, in which slaves were expected to work no harder than their masters and could even be adopted into the clan—an honor also extended at times to free blacks or whites who came to live among them. These resistors and their descendants would later become the Eastern Band of Cherokee Indians. Federal recognition of the tribe and blood-quantum rules of membership would eventually act to solidify the fluid racial/ethnic boundaries surrounding the group, although intermarriage with their neighbors continued. As the peculiar history of Southern racial politics progressed through the Civil War, Reconstruction, and Jim Crow, the tribe increasingly sought to distance itself from its early African American family ties. Political struggles between traditionalist "full-bloods" and modernist "white Indians" continue today in tribal life (Neely 1991; Perdue 1979; King 1979b).

Despite the rich past of the Cherokee, however, Southern history has most often been rendered primarily in black and white—and mostly in white in the Appalachian region. Small farmers and the landless poor, whose descendants operated machines in the textile, furniture, and paper mills that prospered here during the twentieth century, made up the majority of the white population (Dunaway 1996). Some elite white farmers owned slaves in the antebellum period in these mountain counties, though not in large numbers (Dunaway 2003). The freed black men and women who chose to stay in the region in the postbellum period usually settled in the towns, working as domestics for merchants and managers or performing menial tasks in the early mills. Close-knit kinship networks and strong churches provided a buffer against the racist stings and invisibility that blacks often experienced in a predominantly white culture (Turner and Cabbell 1985). They continue to do so today.

No black women frequent the club ZZ's on Saturday nights in hopes of meeting Mexican men. And while marriages between African Americans and whites or Cherokees do occur in the area, they are far more uncommon than the intermarriages with Mexican immigrants described above.

Pablo Gutierrez of Hidalgo was astute in his observation of the relative acceptance of African Americans and Latinos among whites in the region. Equating "American" with "white," he said,

> You know that the Americans are racists, many of them, but with blacks. With Hispanics, Americans are friendlier. Always, when you see an American with a flag that has stars and a blue "X" [the Confederate battle flag], you know that they are racists. But you never see that they say to a Mexican or to a Hispanic, "You are less than I." No, that they do with blacks, but not with Hispanics. Yes, you will find, perhaps, some people who don't like Hispanics, but I have almost never run into them.[20]

Most local whites would probably dispute his assessment of racism in the area. Confederate flags are not ubiquitously on display, but they can be seen occasionally on front porches or bumper stickers. People who display them typically say that the flags signify Southern history, not racism, an interesting argument considering that these mountain counties were home to many Union sympathizers during the Civil War. Whites typically characterize the region's history of desegregation as unproblematic, making comments such as "Everybody gets along here, and they always have." Not surprisingly, African Americans share a different memory and can cite numerous examples of local racism, past and present, in both subtle and blatant forms. And I should note here that Mexicans, too, often characterize social slights and unfair treatment from local residents as *racismo*. But given the relative ease with which intimate relationships between white women and Mexican men are accepted, especially in light of the highly charged history of black male/white female relationships in the South, Pablo Gutierrez's assessment of local race relations is astute.

Harvey Miller, an African American paper mill worker, would agree. As he told me,

> I believe that Mexicans are accepted more so than black people, and I say this because I've seen it before my own eyes. Plus, I dated a white girl from Maggie Valley. She had a job working for the state. We were really close, but she was

scared that her people wouldn't accept me. And her sister started dating this Mexican guy, and I think he's a good guy. They got married, and the whole family was really happy and everything, but I didn't go to the wedding. Well, when she told them [about me], that I was black, and she wanted to have dinner at her house and for me to come over, they disowned her. And she said, "But this guy is Mexican and you all love him." Her dad said, "He's not a nigger. I won't have a child of mine dating a nigger."[21]

Throughout the South, racial dynamics are modifying to accommodate the new demographics of the region, although the status of blacks at the bottom of the social hierarchy remains, unfortunately, firmly in place. For example, Studstill and Nieto-Studstill (2001) note that blacks in southern Georgia view the occurrence of white American and Mexican intermarriage there with wariness, fully aware of the implications of their relative status. James Loewen's (1971) ethnography of the Chinese in segregated Mississippi illustrates how an immigrant presence in a population forces a renegotiation of racial boundaries, even the strict color line of the Old South, affording the Chinese an "in-between" space in the black/white binary.

Here in the Western North Carolina mountains, the Cherokees have long occupied the social space between black and white. In casual conversations with people in the area, I discovered an interesting historical precedent to the Saturday night scene at ZZ's. In the 1950s and 1960s, white high school girls from Maggie Valley would often drive the winding road across Soco Gap on Friday nights to go to dances at Cherokee High School on the reservation. And, while parents did not fully approve, the outings did not evoke anything like the social stigma that would have accompanied a trip, say, to the segregated black high school in the city of Asheville.

Fundamental contradictions prevail in local white attitudes toward the Cherokees, not surprisingly in a nation that has celebrated the cultural nobility of Native Americans even as it has systemically destroyed their traditional ways of life. Many whites in the area claim to have "a full-blooded Cherokee Indian" somewhere in their ancestry, usually in the absence of any genealogical proof. Given the extent of past intermarriage between tribal members and whites in the area, it is quite possible that some of these claims are valid. Whether their "Cherokee blood" is real or imaginary, however, whites often employ this "symbolic ethnicity" (Gans 1979; Waters 1990) as an assertion of pioneer mountain authenticity. At the same time that they champion Cherokee origins, however, some whites denigrate the current Cherokee population. As Sharlotte Neely observed in her ethnography of the Snowbird Cherokees in nearby Graham County, "Seldom openly expressed, the derogatory stereotypes picture Indians as lazy, tardy, and financially irresponsible, the latter view leading to the stereotype that Indians accept government handouts"

(Neely 1991: 51). During the Jim Crow years, Cherokee or mixed white/Indian children who lived off the reservation went to school with whites, but they often had to endure taunting by their classmates. Amy Suarez remembered, for example, that her mother hated being called "Little Beaver" in school.[22] And while intermarriage between whites and Indians is common, a survey conducted by Neely found that, in a Graham County High School, "65.8 percent of white males and 60.7 percent of white females had problems with the idea of marrying an Indian" (Neely 1991: 52).

Mexican newcomers now deal with similarly contradictory attitudes, exacerbated by their often tenuous immigration status. They are praised for their hard work but castigated for "taking our jobs," eagerly sought by employers but the first to be laid off when work slows, solicited as consumers but treated rudely by sales people. And, though families often balk at the notion when Mexicans marry among the native-born, acceptance is eventually granted. They have joined the Cherokees in the uncertain social space between black and white in the region.

MATTERS OF CLASS

Despite racial and ethnic differences, the men and women who seek each other's company on the dance floor of ZZ's each Saturday night share common ground in one important aspect: socioeconomic class. It is a decidedly working-class crowd. And other meeting places where Mexican men and native-born women form intimate relationships—factory production lines, restaurant kitchens, trailer parks, and flea markets—reflect a similar class orientation.

Interestingly, another type of immigrant/native-born intermarriage in the area exhibits a similar parity of class between partners. As Sarah Mahler (1995) noted among the Latino population in Long Island, South Americans who come to the United States are, in general, more affluent and better educated than most Mexican and Central American immigrants, because, among other reasons, more resources are required to travel the distance. That pattern holds in Western North Carolina, as well. In my research, I have met middle-class South Americans of both sexes—from Ecuador, Colombia, and Argentina—who have paired with white professional or management-class American men and women. Although these immigrants have no choice when they first arrive but to work at the same low-end factory, cleaning, and restaurant jobs as do Mexican immigrants, in personal relationships they easily fit into a class strata more familiar to them. For example, several South Americans have told me that they formed close friendships with their supervisors and

managers while working on factory production lines. An immigration special-
ist with Catholic Social Services in the city of Asheville, who has counseled
many mixed immigrant/citizen couples in the region, confirmed my observation that cross-cultural matches usually occur strictly within class boundaries.

In my research, I encountered only one immigrant/citizen relationship that
crossed the boundary of class. Alejandra Restrepo is a linguist trained at a
university in her native Colombia. After overstaying a student work exchange
visa she settled in Western North Carolina, where she took a production job
at a factory in Madison County. She worked alongside a high-school graduate who was of mixed parentage, with a white Appalachian mother and a
Mexican father. Alejandra and the young man married soon after they met and
were divorced a year later. In fluent English, she described her former in-laws
as "mountain people":

> They live in the mountains, they like staying in the mountains. They don't like
> going and traveling. And the family likes hunting a lot. What I don't like! And
> they eat a lot of meat and potatoes, sweet potatoes. They have a language, their
> language is different. They say "coon" for "raccoon," or "possum." They use
> "ain't." They say "ain't" a lot, or "you'n's." And many, many other words.
> "Taters" instead of "potatoes." It was extremely hard to change from Colombia,
> where I was, to here. It was totally different. I don't know if it's the family or
> the mountain way of thinking, but education is not so important. Education is,
> well, you can finish high school, but it's not like my family, where I am from,
> where you want to go to college, then you want your Master's degree, then you
> want your PhD. You want everything. And things are so hard for us, but we just
> want to keep growing and learning. Maybe people here are, they are fine with
> what they have. That's the vision I have from the family. I admit, I don't know
> if all the mountain people are like that. The only person in the family that is
> Mexican is his daddy, and he speaks English all the time. He has lived here for
> twenty-two years. And I think that he has lived here for so long that he's kind of
> a mountain man in his language.[23]

While Alejandra couched her discussion in terms of Appalachian versus
Colombian culture, it is easy to read her in-law problems as a clash of class
values in regard to education, food, travel, and the use of language. Notably,
her Mexican father-in-law, from a working-class background, seems to have
adjusted well to mountain life. In this volume, Jamillah Karim asserts that
class disparity acts to exacerbate the cultural divides between immigrant and
African American Muslims. Within this family, a difference of class between
Alejandra and her husband's family has been similarly divisive, while class
parity—in the case of her husband's Mexican father and his white Appalachian in-laws—has apparently eased his transformation into a "kind of a
mountain man."

In his article "The Possibility of a New Racial Hierarchy in the Twenty-first-Century United States," Herbert Gans speculates that, as white tolerance and racial intermarriage increase in this country, class homogamy—marriage among people of similar class—may become more prevalent than racial homogamy. He observes that, among college-educated youth in the United States, class is already a more important factor than race in choosing a mate. The one exception to this process that he notes, however, is of paramount importance. White tolerance is increasing, he writes, "except with respect to blacks" (Gans 1999: 384–85). Obviously, racial homogamy still prevails in the majority population in Western North Carolina. And, in the limited degree of class homogamy that exists in intermarriages between immigrants and citizens, blacks are certainly excluded. Still, the degree of class parity that exists in intimate relationships among whites, Cherokees, and Latinos in the region underscores the importance of socioeconomic class in processes of acculturation and group convergence.

CONCLUSION

As the demographics of the United States have changed rapidly in recent decades, several scholars have proposed that a new racial order is emerging to supplant the familiar black-white binary that has shaped our national history. Yet, whether the new order is seen as a multiracial hierarchy (Alba 1990), a new bimodal structure consisting of a nonblack–black dichotomy with an in-between "residual" category of shifting status (Gans 1999), or a triracial stratification of whites, honorary whites, and collective blacks (Bonilla-Silva 2004), blacks unfortunately remain at the bottom. Another common feature of all these hierarchal models is a shifting middle ground of tenuous status.

James Loewen's (1971) *Mississippi Chinese: Between Black and White* is an apt illustration of the fact that a tenuous middle category between black and white is nothing new in American life, even in the segregated South. In the rigid racial hierarchy of the Mississippi Delta, Chinese storeowners originally fell into the category of Negro by virtue of being nonwhite. Over decades, however, through economic prosperity and by creating a parallel universe of institutions that mimicked white society, they were able to attain something akin to the honorary white status often granted to Asians in American society. If honorary status can be bestowed, however, it can also be easily retracted (Bonilla-Silva 2004; Tuan 1998). The Delta Chinese never experienced full membership in Mississippi white society, just as many Asian Americans today feel excluded from full cultural citizenship in mainstream national life.

Native Americans have always confounded the logic of the black-white binary in the United States, especially in the South. For example, Karen Blu (2001) documents a shift from a not-black to a nonwhite identity among the Lumbee Indians in Eastern North Carolina, as they formed a political coalition with African Americans during the War on Poverty. On the level of intimate relationships, Native Americans have challenged the color line more so than groups like the Mississippi Chinese, as they were never subject to the antimiscegenation laws that barred African Americans and Asians from marrying whites (Moran 2001).

The Eastern Band of Cherokee Indians has, for centuries, been negotiating the middle ground between black and white in Western North Carolina. And, despite the blood quantum rules that define tribal membership, the fluid racial/ethnic boundaries of the group have always been porous enough to allow them to blend at the margins into the white population. Rather than being honorary, their status relative to local whites has often been a matter of kinship. At the same time, there have always been enormous cultural incentives—and economic incentives, due to various government programs and, now, to casino profits—to practice endogamy and to maintain strict tribal boundaries.

Today, a little Mexican *indigenismo* has been added to the mix. As I noted above, many local whites sometimes evoke a distant Indian ancestry in a casual, conversational form of symbolic ethnicity. For Mexicans, however, claiming an Indian past is a matter of participating in the cultural citizenship of their nation. Herbert Gans (1979) identifies the symbolic and situational nature of ethnicity for many Americans, arguing that an ethnic identity is often employed as a matter of personal satisfaction or as a means of community building, though usually not expressed in daily cultural practice. Mary Waters (1990) stresses the voluntary nature of expressing a symbolic ethnicity for white ethnics, while racial and ethnic identity is not a matter of choice for nonwhites and Hispanics. Mia Tuan's (1998) elaboration on the struggles of Asian Americans and other "racialized ethnics" to be accepted as fully American underscores Waters's point. Yet there is often a voluntary aspect to being Native American in the United States, especially with regard to Pan-Indian cultural expressions that have evolved through national pow-wows (Blu 2001; Coates 2002; Nagle 1996). Mexicans and Cherokees in Western North Carolina who choose to find common ground with each other in terms of a shared ancestry are practicing what might be called a voluntary racialized ethnicity, each expanding notions of *la Raza Cósmica* and the American Indian to include the other. The association, along with the long history of incorporating an "in-between" group into local society, acts to place Mexican newcomers alongside the Cherokee in the middle ground between black and white. Thus, intermarriages with whites and Cherokees are accepted with relative ease.

While I have only touched briefly on such matters in this essay, economic structures in general, and job markets in particular, are of utmost importance in racial formation, ethnic identities, and processes of immigrant assimilation (Gans 1999; Waters 1999; Portes and Zhou 1993; also, in this volume, Fuentes, Shih, and Zeltzer-Zubida). Before closing, I want to elaborate briefly on the economic upheaval that neoliberal capitalism is wreaking here, as in local settings across the globe. Industrial prosperity and the growth of union organization during the latter twentieth century created a very stratified working class in the region, with levels at the top approaching a middle-class standard of living. As low-end service work replaces factory jobs, as unions disappear, and as flimsy government safety nets of unemployment insurance and worker retraining programs expire, the strata are likely to collapse into the lowest rungs of the economic ladder. Currently, Mexican newcomers labor at the heart of the region's new economic reality that many native-born displaced factory workers adamantly resist—cleaning the homes and mowing the lawns of retirees, washing the dishes and changing the hotel beds of tourists, digging trenches and carrying the heaviest loads in construction crews. In the future, however, immigrants may experience sharper economic competition with native-born white, black, and Indian workers. In addition, the formerly disadvantaged Eastern Band of Cherokee Indians is now a major employer in the area, as the reservation's casino provides a relatively decent wage and a complete benefit package to employees, items of increasing rarity in the local economy. The unsteady ground of this shifting economic landscape will be a major determinant in the shape of future relations among area blacks, whites, Cherokees, and Latino immigrants—especially those of an intimate nature.

NOTES

1. This is a pseudonym. I also use pseudonyms for all informants cited in this essay, and I have altered some factual data related to them, such as descriptions of workplaces and the names of towns and counties of residence, to further protect their confidentiality.

2. One year of this research was funded by the Social Science Research Council's International Migration Program.

3. As illustrated, for example, by table 6.3.

4. Amy Suarez (pseud.), interview, June 6, 2003, Jonathan Creek, North Carolina.

5. Suarez, interview.

6. North Carolina State Data Center, "Employment Status by Sex, by Race, and Hispanic or Latino Origin," *NC Census Lookup: Summary File 3, P43/P150A-1,* census.state.nc.us (accessed Oct. 8, 2003).

7. Suarez, interview.

8. Charlotte Simpson (pseud.), interview, September 17, 2002, Fines Creek, North Carolina.

9. Suarez, interview.

10. Sherry Ramirez (pseud.), interview, October 1, 2002, Canton, North Carolina.

11. Suarez, interview.

12. Pedro Zarate (pseud.), interview, December 16, 2002, Hendersonville, North Carolina.

13. Author's translation from the following transcription:

Lo que pasa es que tenemos problemas por sus amigas. Es porque somos diferentes culturas. Entonces, yo le dije a ella que me respondiera cuando voy a trabajar, teniendo la comida lista. Por un tiempo ella lo hizo bien, estuvimos bien, pero sus amigas le decían que porqué me preparaba la comida. A veces le decían, "Vamos al baile." Y decía ella, "No." Y tuvimos problemas así, y la comenzaron a llevar y llevar. Así nos separamos. (Tomás Quiñones [pseud.], interview, December 23, 2002, Hendersonville, North Carolina)

14. Simpson, interview.

15. Author's translation: "She's not Mexican, she's Indian!" Alberto Gonzalez (pseud.), interview, November 26, 2002, Hendersonville, North Carolina. He described the young woman in Spanish as follows: "Es morena, es bonita, miro que parece mexicana."

16. Ramirez, interview.

17. Table 6.3, which shows Latino population figures for the period 1970 through 1980 for the seven-county region where I conducted this research, includes an anomaly that may also be a case of bureaucratic mistaken identity. Jackson, one of these counties, is the home of the tribal town of Cherokee and a portion of the reservation land known as the Qualla Boundary. The table shows that the 1980 Census recorded an astonishing count of 718 people of "Spanish Origin"—defined as "those who reported either Mexican, Puerto Rican, Cuban, or other Spanish/Hispanic origin"—in Jackson county. This figure represents a percentage growth rate of 844.7 percent over the 1970 Census total of seventy-six Hispanics in the county, far greater than the predictably explosive growth of 272.3 percent recorded for the decade 1990–2000. The growth rate for this population in the other six counties combined, from 1970 to 1980, was only 51.0 percent. Interestingly, the 1980 Census also shows that of these 718 Hispanics in Jackson County, 507 were also identified by race as "American Indian, Eskimo, and Aleut," while in the other six counties combined, only three Hispanics were so designated. In 1990, the Hispanic population count in Jackson County had dropped to a more believable figure of 155. While it is possible that a large group of indigenous migrant workers of Latin American descent were sojourning in Jackson County in April of 1980, it is very unlikely. A more plausible explanation is that the figures reflect confusion on the part of census takers sent out to find people who had not returned mail-in forms. When confronted with people of both Cherokee and Latino descent, sometimes similar in appearance, census takers quite likely recorded numerous instances of mistaken racial/ethnic identity. U.S. Dept. of Commerce, Bureau of the Census, "Definitions and Explanations of Subject Characteristics," B-4,

table 59, "Persons by Spanish Origin, Race, and Sex: 1980," in *Census of Population, North Carolina: General Social and Economic Characteristics* (Washington, D.C.: Bureau of the Census, 1983), 41–44.

18. Author's translation from the following transcription: "Nosotros los mexicanos somos indios. Los Cherokees saben que uno es indígena. Ellos también, o sea que la raza viene ser la misma raza de ellos." Gonzalez, interview.

19. Suarez, interview.

20. Author's translation from the following transcription:

Usted sabe que los norteamericanos son racistas, muchos, pero con los negros. Los americanos con los hispanos son mas amigables. Todo el tiempo cuando usted ve a un americano con la bandera que tiene las estrellas y la equis azul, usted sabe que son racistas. Pero usted nunca ve le digan a un mexicano o a un hispano, "Tu eres menor que yo." Eso lo hacen con los negros, pero no con los hispanos. Si, encontrará, tal vez, unas personas que no quieren a los hispanos, pero yo casi nunca me he topado con ellos. (Pablo Gutierrez [pseud.], interview, December 14, 2002, Leicester, North Carolina)

21. Harvey Miller (pseud.), interview, June 7, 2003, Canton, North Carolina.

22. Suarez, interview.

23. Alejandra Restrepo (pseud.), interview, October 2, 2002, Mars Hill, North Carolina.

REFERENCES

Adelman, Jeffrey, and Stephen Aron. 1999. "From Borderlands to Borders: Empires, Nation-States, and the Peoples in between in North American History." *American Historical Review* 104, no. 3: 814–41.

Alba, Richard D. 1990. *Ethnic Identity: The Transformation of White America*. New Haven, CT: Yale University Press.

Alba, Richard D., and Reid M. Golden. 1986. "Patterns of Ethnic Marriage in the U.S." *Journal of Social Forces* 65: 202–23.

Alba, Richard, and Victor Nee. 1999. "Rethinking Assimilation Theory for a New Era of Immigration." Pp. 137–60 in *The Handbook of International Migration: The American Experience*, ed. Charles Hirshman, Philip Kasinitz, and Josh DeWind. New York: Russell Sage.

Blu, Karen I. 2001 [1980]. *The Lumbee Problem: The Making of an American Indian People*. Lincoln: University of Nebraska Press.

Bonilla-Silva, Eduardo. 2004. "'We Are All Americans': The Latin Americanization of Race Relations in the United States." Pp. 149–86 in *The Changing Terrain of Race and Ethnicity*, ed. Maria Krysan and Amanda E. Lewis. New York: Russell Sage Foundation.

Coates, Julia M. 2002. "'None of Us Are Supposed to Be Here': Ethnicity, Nationality, and the Production of Cherokee Histories." PhD Dissertation, University of New Mexico, Albuquerque.

Dunaway, Wilma A. 1996. *The First American Frontier: Transition to Capitalism in Southern Appalachia, 1700–1860*. Chapel Hill: University of North Carolina Press.

———. 2003. *Slavery in the Mountain South*. Cambridge: Cambridge University Press.

Dykeman, Wilma. 1955. *The French Broad*. Newport, TN: Wakestone Books.

Fink, Leon. 2003. *The Maya of Morganton: Work and Community in the Nuevo New South*. Chapel Hill: University of North Carolina Press.

Gans, Herbert J. 1979. "Symbolic Ethnicity: The Future of Ethnic Groups and Cultures in America." *Ethnic and Racial Studies* 2: 1–20.

———. 1999. "The Possibility of a New Racial Hierarchy in the Twenty-first-Century United States." Pp. 371–90 in *The Cultural Territories of Race: Black and White Boundaries*, ed. Michèle Lamont. Chicago: University of Chicago Press.

King, Duane H. 1979a. "Introduction." Pp. ix–xix in *The Cherokee Indian Nation: A Troubled History*, ed. Duane H. King. Knoxville: University of Tennessee Press.

———. 1979b. "The Origin of the Eastern Cherokees as a Social and Political Entity." Pp. 164–80 in *The Cherokee Indian Nation: A Troubled History*, ed. Duane H. King. Knoxville: University of Tennessee Press.

Lieberson, Stanley, and Mary C. Waters. 1988. *From Many Strands: Ethnic and Racial Groups in Contemporary America*. New York: Russell Sage Foundation.

Loewen, James W. 1971. *The Mississippi Chinese: Between Black and White*. Cambridge, MA: Harvard University Press.

Mahler, Sarah. 1995. *American Dreaming: Immigrant Life on the Margins*. Princeton, NJ: Princeton University Press.

Moran, Rachel F. 2001. *Interracial Intimacy: The Regulation of Race and Romance*. Chicago: University of Chicago Press.

Nagle, Joane. 1996. *American Indian Ethnic Renewal, Red Power and the Resurgence of Identity and Culture*. New York: Oxford University Press.

Neely, Sharlotte. 1991. *Snowbird Cherokees: People of Persistence*. Athens: University of Georgia Press.

Park, Robert E. 1950. *Race and Culture*. Glencoe, IL: Free Press.

Perdue, Theda. 1979. *Slavery and the Evolution of Cherokee Society, 1540–1866*. Knoxville: University of Tennessee Press.

Portes, Alejandro, and Min Zhou. 1993. "The New Second Generation: Segmented Assimilation and Its Variants among Post-1965 Immigrant Youth." *Annals of the American Academy of Political and Social Science* 530 (November): 74–96.

Studstill, John D., and Laura Nieto-Studstill. 2001. "Hospitality and Hostility: Latin Immigrants in Southern Georgia." Pp. 68–81 in *Latino Workers in the Contemporary South*, ed. Arthur D. Murphy, Colleen Blanchard, and Jennifer A. Hill. Athens: University of Georgia Press.

Tuan, Mia. 1998. *Forever Foreigners or Honorary Whites? The Asian Ethnic Experience Today*. New Brunswick, NJ: Rutgers University Press.

Turner, William H., and Edward J. Cabbell (eds.). 1985. *Blacks in Appalachia*. Lexington: University Press of Kentucky.

Vasconcelos, José. 1966 [1925]. *La Raza Cósmica: Misión de la Raza Iberoamericana*. Madrid: Aguilar.

Waters, Mary C. 1990. *Ethnic Options: Choosing Identities in America*. Berkeley: University of California Press.

———. 1999. "Explaining the Comfort Factor: West Indian Immigrants Confront American Race Relations." Pp. 63–96 in *The Cultural Territories of Race: Black and White Boundaries*, ed. Michèle Lamont. Chicago: University of Chicago Press.

III

ETHNICITY AS A RESOURCE

Introduction to Part III

The four chapters in this section focus on how race and ethnicity shape the economic lives of immigrants. More specifically, each paper addresses the question of whether making ethnic identity salient works to the advantage of immigrants (i.e., it is used as a strategic resource) or to disadvantage them (by separating and isolating them in ethnic enclaves, for example). Broadly speaking, this section draws on and moves forward discussions of the impact of ethnic enclaves and niche markets[1] on the incorporation of immigrants (Logan, Alba and Stults 2003; Portes 1995b; Zhou 1992); the literature on immigrant entrepreneurs (Light and Bhachu 1993; Zhou 2004); the literature on the significance of social capital in the immigration process (Portes and Sensenbrenner 1993); and the literature on segmented assimilation and the second generation (Portes 1995a; Rumbaut 2004; Rumbaut and Portes 2001; Zhou 1999). As with the chapters in part II, several chapters in this final section of the book address questions of context and some of them explore further the relationship between gender and immigration. Ultimately each author is asking about the boundaries to economic incorporation—where are they located, on what basis are they constructed, how fixed or permeable are they, what agency do immigrants have in penetrating them, and are there variations in successful incorporation across nationality groups, across generations, or between men and women?

In a very original essay, Johanna Shih explores how white women and Asian men and women in the Silicon Valley draw on their social capital to change jobs when they think they are facing discrimination in the workplace. She describes two patterns of job-hopping: the first, a strategy of "shopping for bosses" with the goal of full integration into companies, and the second, a strategy of separation by moving into co-ethnic dominated firms or entre-preneurship. In both these forms of job-hopping, access to gender and ethnic-based resource-rich networks (forms of social capital) is fundamental in gar-nering information and referrals. However, Shih cautions that the existence of these networks is conditioned by historical and group specific factors that may not always be present. She also observes that in the special context of Silicon Valley Asian immigrants are increasingly able to convert social capi-tal from their homeland into valuable resources in the region's hi-tech indus-try. In other words, they reach outside the domestic structure of ethnic and race relations to access resources in a transnational context that work to their advantage and help them to become part of a "global elite."

The data for Shih's paper emerge from intensive, in-depth interviews with a snowball sample of fifty-four respondents. By contrast, Zulema Valdez draws on nonpublic 1990 U.S. Census data to investigate how ethnic concen-tration and social capital differentially affect entrepreneurial participation (self-employment) among four different populations in California. She begins by outlining a key debate in the literature on entrepreneurship, contrasting the ethnic enclave hypothesis (which states that ethnic concentration is essential to entrepreneurial success because it encourages the development of close-knit ties and ethnic solidarity) with the ethnic economy hypothesis (which states that social capital and market opportunities facilitate ethnic entrepre-neurship regardless of co-ethnic proximity). In other words, is a bounded, lo-calized community the key to success, or does an unbounded social network offer more opportunity?

Valdez explores these issues by comparing Whites, Koreans, Mexicans, and Blacks. While Koreans have been consistently identified as a group with a high degree of entrepreneurship, Blacks and Mexicans have been described as groups with weak communities and low group solidarity, and hence low rates of entrepreneurship. She operationalizes ethnic solidarity as ethnic con-centration at the census-tract level—indicative perhaps of an ethnic enclave. The proxy measure for the market opportunities associated with an ethnic economy is ethnic concentration at the county level. Analysis of the data demonstrates that for Koreans, Mexicans, and Blacks the concentrated ethnic community does not facilitate entrepreneurship. On the other hand, market opportunities in the larger economy are beneficial for all ethnic minorities. Valdez concludes that ethnic entrepreneurship thrives when the population density of a particular group is high and hence supply and demand are high—that is, that an ethnic economy perspective, rather than an ethnic enclave per-spective, better explains differential rates of entrepreneurship. What is miss-ing from this analysis is an evaluation of the impact of race which may, as Kasinitz and Vickerman (2001: 192) have suggested based on their research on Jamaicans in New York, "truncate the development of niches and limit the effectiveness of social capital."

Aviva Zeltzer-Zubida includes both race and ethnicity in her analysis of the labor market trajectories of immigrants and their children. Using data from the "Second Generation in Metropolitan New York" project and the Census Bureau's Current Population Survey, she examines patterns of ethnic and racial concentration in the local labor market, and the factors that influence and shape them, among five second-generation immigrant groups and three native-born groups of eighteen- to thirty-two-year-old New Yorkers. By applying a direct measure of co-ethnicity in the workplace, and examining how human capital, social networks, organizational characteristics, and labor market opportunity structure shape patterns of co-ethnicity in the labor market, Zeltzer-Zubida concludes that co-ethnic employment is a significant experience for second-generation immigrants as well as for their native born counterparts. She also argues that patterns of co-ethnic employment and the factors shaping them vary across groups and industries. She concludes by suggesting that race and ethnicity do and probably will continue to have an important role in shaping the economic trajectories of groups and individuals. She also suggests that the economic consequences of co-ethnicity in the workplace vary across groups, serving as a safety net for some and as a springboard for others. Zeltzer-Zubida's research seems to suggest that boundaries in the workplace and, by extension, in the social arena, are still very strong, isolating one group from another into the second generation.

Finally, Cynthia Feliciano, who, like Zeltzer-Zubida, focuses on the second generation, uses a large data set to address migrant selectivity and its impact on outcomes for the children of immigrants. She is capturing the "less tangible" forms of capital that vary from one group to another. She looks not at labor market trajectories but at educational trajectories to explore the thorny question of why some national-origin groups excel in school while others do not. Feliciano focuses on educational selectivity—that is, how immigrants differ educationally from their nonmigrant counterparts in the home country and how these differences might influence educational outcomes (average years of schooling, high school graduation, college attendance rates) among groups of immigrants' children. The more positive selection of Asian immigrants, for example, helps to explain their second generations' higher college attendance and high school graduation rates as compared to Europeans, Afro-Caribbeans, and Latinos. Feliciano argues that her findings suggest that stratification models need to be revised in the case of children with immigrant parents, because absolute measures of parental educational attainment do not adequately capture the educational resources that immigrants bring with them.

Recently sociologists Richard Alba and Victor Nee (1999) have proposed that scholars have been too hasty in rejecting the concept "assimilation." They define assimilation as "the decline, and at its endpoint the disappearance, of an ethnic and racial distinction and the cultural and social differences that express it" (Alba and Nee 1999: 159)—that is, a dissolution of boundaries. Some of the scholars represented in this volume demonstrate that boundaries are in fact maintained into the second generation—partly as a result of individual or group agency and partly as a result of structural constraints. However, Alba and Nee's call for research that involves a more objective analysis of assimilation rather than its outright abandonment is probably one worth heeding. Indeed, Edward Lazear (1999) proposes an economic theory of assimilation that includes both structure and agency. Lazear begins by posing the question of why, for example, Spanish-speaking immigrants (the largest group in the United States today) learn English at a lower rate than German-speaking immigrants (the largest group at the turn of the twentieth century) did in 1900. Does this reflect a slower rate of assimilation? Lazear suggests that we focus on the importance of learning English as a skill for economic success and on the historical and social context. He argues, for example, that when a non-English-language–speaking group is in a minority, English language skill acquisition is encouraged and pursued. In the reverse situation, the opposite is the case. Thus, "a native Pole who migrates to the Polish neighborhood in Chicago can function much better without a knowledge of English than he could were he to move to, say, San Francisco" (Lazear 1999: S119). In other words, Lazear is arguing that the assimilation of immigrants depends upon the conditions in which they find themselves. The chapters in this section suggest some of these conditions and therefore begin to offer a better understanding of processes of economic incorporation, assimilation and, hence, boundary crossing.

NOTE

1. Enclaves are geographic concentrations of immigrant or ethnic enterprises. These enterprises generally employ co-ethnics. When a particular group dominates a specific employment sector the term ethnic niche is used. People usually find their position in ethnic niches through social networks.

REFERENCES

Alba, Richard, and Victor Nee. 1999. "Rethinking Assimilation Theory for a New Era of Immigration." Pp. 137–60 in *The Handbook of International Migration: The*

American Experience, ed. Charles Hirschman, Philip Kasinitz, and Josh DeWind. New York: Russell Sage.

Kasinitz, Philip, and Milton Vickerman. 2001. "Ethnic Niches and Racial Traps: Jamaicans in the New York Regional Economy." Pp. 191–211 in *Migration, Transnationalization, and Race in a Changing New York*, ed. Hector R. Cordero Guzman, Robert C. Smith, and Ramon Grosfoguel. Philadelphia: Temple University Press.

Lazear, Edward P. 1999. "Culture and Language." *Journal of Political Economy* 107: S95–S126.

Light, Ivan, and Parminder Bhachu (eds.). 1993. *Immigration and Entrepreneurship: Culture, Capital, and Ethnic Networks*. New Brunswick, NJ: Transaction Books.

Logan, John R., Richard Alba, and Brian J. Stults. 2003. "Enclave and Entrepreneurs; Assessing the Payoff for Immigrants and Minorities." *International Migration Review* 37: 344–73.

Portes, Alejandro. 1995a. "Children of Immigrants: Segmented Assimilation and Its Determinants." Pp. 248–80 in *The Economic Sociology of Immigration; Essays on Networks, Ethnicity, and Entrepreneurship*, ed. Alejandro Portes. New York: Russell Sage.

—— (ed.). 1995b. *The Economic Sociology of Immigration: Essays on Networks, Ethnicity, and Entrepreneurship*. New York: Russell Sage.

Portes, Alejandro, and Julia Sensenbrenner. 1993. "Embeddedness and Immigration: Notes on the Social Determinants of Economic Action." *American Journal of Sociology* 98: 1320–50.

Rumbaut, Ruben G. 2004. "Ages, Life Stages, and Generational Cohorts: Decomposing the Immigrant First and Second Generations in the United States." *International Migration Review* 38: 1160–74.

Rumbaut, Ruben G., and Alejandro Portes (eds.). 2001. *Ethnicities: Children of Immigrants in America*. New York: Russell Sage.

Zhou, Min. 1992. *New York's Chinatown: The Socioeconomic Potential of an Urban Enclave*. Philadelphia: Temple University Press.

——. 1999. "Segmented Assimilation: Issues, Controversies, and Recent Research on the New Second Generation." Pp. 196–211 in *The Handbook of International Migration: The American Experience*, ed. Charles Hirschman, Philip Kasinitz, and Josh DeWind. New York: Russell Sage.

——. 2004. "Revisiting Ethnic Entrepreneurship: Convergencies, Controversies, and Conceptual Advancements." *International Migration Review* 38: 1040–74.

7

Job-Hopping

Social Networks in the Global High-Tech Industry

Johanna Shih

When Silicon Valley was still in its heyday in the late 1990s, the fifty-mile drive on Highway 101 from San Francisco down to San Jose was a cultural experience, replete with an induction into the regional ideology. As you drove out of San Francisco and onto the highway entrance ramp, a canary yellow billboard painted on the corner of Van Ness and Mission announced, "We've asked the best minds in academia to join another venerable institution. . . . It's called Capitalism." As you went past the southern portion of the city where the dot-coms had come to roost, you were greeted by another tongue-in-cheek sign that inverts some old adages about money, "Root of all evil . . . can't buy happiness . . . blah blah blah."

As you left the city and passed San Francisco airport, you were regaled with the advice "Automate or Die" and glimpsed a shiny building housing the company "Liberate." Then came Palo Alto, where Stanford and the origins of Silicon Valley lie, where you were warned to be prepared for "High-Octane Capitalism Ahead" and later, a neon pink billboard reminded you that the status quo here was "Capitalism Served Fresh Daily."

Venturing through the cities of Mountain View and Santa Clara, you were perhaps supposed to be inspired by the sign that said that Silicon Valley is where the "Glass Ceiling Meets the Glass Cutter" and finally, as you reached San Jose, the southernmost city of Silicon Valley, you might have spied a bus whose side advertised the global nature and harmony of the region, by saying ". . . Uzbeks, Nambians, Americans. . . . All speak the same language. Money. Even in countries whose names you can't pronounce, people still speak the same language. Money."

By the end of this drive, littered with high-tech billboards, you were meant to know three things: that Silicon Valley is the harbinger of the future; that it represents the triumph of free market capitalism; and that Silicon Valley's brand of capitalism is making people rich regardless of gender, class, ethnicity, or nationality. The emphasis of the billboards in many ways reflects what has and continues to be the two complementary discourses about Silicon Valley: one an emerging body of academic literature which focuses on the region's economic organization as a key to its success, the other a public discourse which casts the region as an example of the American Dream writ large.

In particular, academic research argued that the economic structure of Silicon Valley is a model of flexible specialization, which is a mode of production that is understood as a shift away from and the antithesis of the Fordist era of mass production (Castells 1996; Harvey 1989; Piore and Sabel 1984). Saxenian (1994), for instance, argued that it was this economic structure of flexible specialization that accounts for Silicon Valley's "regional advantage" in high-tech development. In this sense, the bulk of academic research compared Silicon Valley to other regional economies such as those in the "Third Italy" that were seen to represent an emerging and important form of economic organization designed to adapt to global capitalism.

At the same time, there was an apparent consensus implicit in this academic research and explicit in media reports that Silicon Valley was a meritocratic place for the highly skilled. The public was treated to repeated stories of engineers and other highly skilled workers who made it big, using "just hard work and brains." The headlines of major newspapers and magazines all came to this consensus: Business Week proclaimed that Silicon Valley is the culmination of "the American Dream" where "all that matters is intelligence and initiative," while the Economist trumpeted that "One of Silicon Valley's secret weapons is its openness to immigrants and to women." Indeed, the message about Silicon Valley seemed to take on a religious zeal, where the saving grace of free market capitalism allowed us to overcome class, gender, and ethnic/racial boundaries.

While these two discourses on flexible specialization and on meritocracy provide important contexts in which to understand or interpret Silicon Valley, the demographic context of the region is also significant. Silicon Valley has experienced rapid population growth that was fueled by the development of the high-tech industry. Table 7.1 shows the population change in Santa Clara County (the main county of what is known as Silicon Valley), which well exceeded growth in California overall.

What is particularly interesting about this population growth is that Silicon Valley has become a major receiver of Asian immigration—it has very quickly become the county with the fourth largest concentration of Asians in the U.S. Twenty-six percent of those who live in Santa Clara County are of

Table 7.1.   **Population Change in California and Santa Clara County, 1960–2000**

	1960	*2000*	*Percentage Change*
California	15,717,204	33,871,648	115.5
Santa Clara County	642,315	1,682,585	162

Source: U.S. Census Bureau, Historical Population Counts and 2000 Census.

Asian descent, compared to 11 percent in California, and 4 percent in the U.S. overall. The major Asian ethnic groups in Santa Clara are Chinese and Indian, with a rapidly growing Vietnamese population as well.[1]

The growth in the Asian population in Santa Clara County outpaced the growth of any other racial group. As table 7.3 shows, in the past decade alone, the Asian population grew by almost 65 percent. This growth is generated by the high-tech industry, both at the low-skill and high-skill levels. Asians in Silicon Valley, who are primarily foreign-born,[2] are highly concentrated in the high-tech workforce. Using 1990 Census data, Saxenian (1999:12) found that 32 percent of Silicon Valley's scientists and engineers were foreign-born, and about two-thirds of those were Asian-born. They are overrepresented in the highly skilled, high-tech labor force, since Asians represented only 11 percent of the total workforce in 1990.[3] The overrepresentation of Asians at the high-skill level is also reflected in the levels of educational attainment among Asians in the region. Thirty-three percent of those who live in the San Jose Metropolitan Area have bachelor's degrees, in comparison to 40 percent of Asians in San Jose Metropolitan Area, and the percentages for Chinese and Asian Indians in particular are even higher: almost 56 percent of Chinese in this area have bachelor's degrees, and over 66 percent of Indians have bachelor's degrees.[4] The higher educational attainment of the Asian population is even more striking when comparing advanced degrees: while 18 percent of whites in Silicon Valley attained graduate degrees, 40 percent of Chinese and 55 percent of Indians had graduate degrees (Saxenian 1999; Alarcon 1999). Thus, Silicon Valley is an important region to

Table 7.2.   **Population of California and Santa Clara County by Race, 2000**

	White	*Black*	*American Indian*	*Asian*	*Latino/ Hispanic Origin*	*Other*	*Total*
California	59.5%	6.7%	1.0%	10.9%	32.4%	21.8%	33,871,648
Santa Clara County	53.8%	2.8%	0.7%	25.6%	24.0%	17.1%	1,682,585

Source: U.S. Census Bureau, Geographic Comparison Table by Race, 2000.

Table 7.3.   Percentage Change in Racial Categories, 1990–2000

	All	White	Black	American Indian	Asian	Other*	Total in 2000
California	+13.8%	− 1.7%	+2.5%	+37.7%	+29.9%	+88%	33,871,648
Santa Clara County	+10.2%	−12%	−16%	+22.5%	+64.5%	+108%	1,682,585

*Census 2000 differs from 1990 in racial categorization. The 2000 version has additional categories of "Native Hawaiian and other Pacific Islander," "Some Other Race" and "Two or More Races." For purposes of comparison, I have combined these categories into the "Other" designation from the 1990 Census. The large percentage change in this "Other" category is almost certainly a result of this change in categorization.

Source: U.S. Census Bureau, Geographic Comparison Table by Race, and Hispanic or Latino, 2000.

watch in terms of Asian immigration and the growing transnational links with the Pacific Rim.

The gender demographics of the region are also worth noting. While it has famously beat Alaska's long claim to fame as having the highest proportion of single men to single women (Cooper 2000), Silicon Valley has at the same time a relatively large pool of science and engineering women who, though still far outweighed by their male counterparts, do comprise a "critical mass" that is absent in other science and engineering industries. For example, in 2000, women accounted for 17 percent of Silicon Valley's engineers, in comparison to 8 percent in the nation overall. They are even better represented among computer scientists and programmers, where they constitute about a quarter of the labor force.

Given these demographics, the question of meritocracy deserves careful scrutiny. How are U.S.-born women and Asian immigrants faring in the highly skilled, high-tech labor force? Are they facing the "meritocratic" conditions promised by the regional ideology? At a more analytic level, how are the mechanisms of ethnic and gender inequality in organizations (that have been so well identified in previous literature) affected by this region's particular labor market? Do the labor market characteristics of flexible specialization in Silicon Valley present more favorable conditions for these groups? In turn, what characteristics of these groups shaped their experiences in Silicon Valley? Are ethnic resources used in the same manner that has been well documented for ethnic entrepreneurship, and among less skilled ethnics?

ETHNIC AND GENDER INEQUALITY AMONG HIGH-SKILL WORKERS: A LITERATURE REVIEW

Race and gender have consistently been shown to affect the attainment of upward mobility and, concurrently, authority within organizations (Fernandez

1998; Knoke and Ishio 1998; Baldi and McBrier 1997; Collins 1997; Huffman 1995; Jaffee 1989; Mueller, Parcell, and Tanaka 1989; DiPrete and Soule 1988; Bielby and Baron 1986; Roos 1981; Wolf and Fligstein 1979; Kluegel 1978). In this literature, three main mechanisms have been highlighted as contributing to within-occupation, intra-organizational inequality. First, at the most basic level, discriminatory attitudes of employers, managers, and coworkers can affect both the ability of individuals to secure jobs commensurate with their skills, and their rate of promotion within organizations.

Second, the relegation of white women and ethnic minorities to less prestigious jobs with shortened career ladders is a significant factor in gender and ethnic inequality (Bielby and Baron 1986). This can take the form of "racialised jobs" (Collins 1997) or gendered, "mommy track" jobs (DiPrete and Soule 1988). Job-level segregation can also occur when individuals are given fewer opportunities to acquire the necessary skills and experience for career mobility, both in terms of formal training, and in terms of informal training such as being placed on "good" or high-profile projects. Lack of access to training and experience effectively "de-skills" individuals and impedes their ability to compete (Duncan and Hoffman 1979; Knoke and Ishio 1998).

Third, exclusion from important social networks and the absence of mentors poses obstacles to individuals' careers (Kanter 1977; Baldi and McBrier 1997). Through "homosocial reproduction" (Kanter 1977), white males are more likely to advance through informal means such as mentor sponsorship and social contacts, while promotions for white women and nonwhite men are more likely to be achieved through a "contest" model, that is, through formal criteria (Baldi and McBrier 1997; Mueller et al. 1989). In this manner, "old white boys' networks" result in exclusionary closure.

These findings on the key mechanisms of inequality—gender and ethnic bias, organizational and job segregation, unequal access to training, and exclusionary closure through old boy's networks and hostile work environments—have been duplicated in studies of science and engineering sectors. The findings with respect to women generally show that the glass ceiling is widespread, and significantly impacts women's earnings and managerial status.[5] A recent study of over 1,400 engineers found that women and men engineers' wages diverge significantly as years increase (Ellis 1999). The National Science Foundation's study of "Women and Minorities in Science and Engineering" also reports that while there has been an increase in women engineers, only 13 percent of women engineers reported management as primary work activity versus 31 percent of men (1991: 6).

Asian men and women face similar problems. Research consistently indicates that Asians face a "race" effect in achieving managerial status (Fernandez 1998; Tang 1993a, 1993b; U.S. GAO[6] 1989), lower returns on experience in comparison to native-born engineers (Waldinger et al. 1998), and absolute wage differentials[7] (Matloff 1997). Furthermore, in their research on highly skilled Asians in the U.S., Madamba and DeJong (1997) found that Asian Indian, Chinese and Korean men were more likely to experience job mismatch, and thus be underemployed, than their white counterparts.

Ethnographic and other qualitative studies of scientists and engineers also reveal a gender and race disadvantage. Women report that their male colleagues often have "patronizing" attitudes, treating them as they would a daughter or secretary (Carter and Kirkup 1990; Cockburn 1991) Engineering is seen as a setting where a "locker room culture" prevails (McIlwee and Robinson 1992: 116), and a discipline ". . . where patriarchy got the moon" (Hacker 1990: 109). Here, technical skill is equated with masculinity (Cockburn 1991; Hacker 1990), and the ability to master "abstract" and "hard" science is seen as men's terrain. If women in general are seen through "gendered roles," Asians, both men and women, report being typecasted as "ethnics" (Iwata 1993), viewed as technically competent but not of managerial material. In a subcommittee report on science, research, and technology, an expert witness, Dr. Suzuki argued,

> While Asian/Pacific Americans often gain access to jobs, they usually have a terrible time rising to administrative or managerial positions. In fact, some friends of mine have told me of "Asian ghettos" within some of the larger aerospace companies in California consisting of large numbers of lower echelon Asian American engineers who never get promoted. (Subcommittee on Science Research and Technology 1981: 11)

THE CASE OF SILICON VALLEY:
JOB-HOPPING AND INTER-FIRM MOBILITY

While these previous studies have identified important intra-organizational mechanisms of inequality, they have also tended to present discriminatory mechanisms as inexorable structures over which workers have little recourse, in part because organizations are treated as bounded entities where workers are, by definition, in a subordinate status and thus have little negotiating capacity. As such, workers are depicted as "trapped" or "held captive" by organizational processes, and discrimination is viewed in a rather static manner. Outside of legal means of redress or unionization, there is relatively little discussion of the ways in which workers may respond to discrimination or how they might use resources outside of an organization to resist bias.

Empirically speaking, I find that the absence of discussion about the "other side" of discrimination, that is, individuals' responses, is particularly problematic in understanding individuals' labor market experiences in Silicon Valley. This is because inter-organizational mobility, that is, the ability to move between organizations, takes a particularly prominent role in the region. I suggest that inter-organizational mobility is an important phenomenon to understand, specifically because it has the potential to mediate the mechanisms of discrimination that occur within organizations.

Two particular labor market characteristics of Silicon Valley are relevant. First, the region has been characterized as having a "high-velocity labor market" (Hyde 1997) that is reflected in the norm of job-hopping in the region[8] (Carnoy, Castells, and Benner 1997; Hyde 1997; Baron, Hannan, and Burton 2001). A high-velocity labor market reflects the relatively fluid organizational boundaries of the region, the relinquishing of corporate responsibility for workers (Harvey 1989; Kumar 1995), and the career mobility strategies of high-skill workers. From the perspective of companies and employers, flexibility is partially achieved through the ability to quickly reshape workforce size in response to market fluctuations. Subsequently, long-term employment is not guaranteed, and workers are expected to "look out for themselves" by being accountable for their own careers. From the perspective of workers, job-hopping is a means by which they can maintain marketability by acquiring a breadth of experiences and skills. In this manner, workers with sought after skills can potentially benefit from a high-velocity job market, because "flexibility represents a new form of entrepreneurship in which the individual worker markets his or her capital portfolio among various 'buyers'" (Carnoy et al. 1997: 30).

The second characteristic of note follows from the first: in order to survive in this situation of heightened instability, high-skill workers must have resources in the general community. In particular, they must maintain extensive networks that supply them with job relevant information and contacts (Piore and Sabel 1984). Membership in a wide range of networks is what ensures their livelihood. Nardi, Whittaker, and Schwarz (2000) find, for instance, that

> Rather than being nurtured by institutionalized group structures, we found that workers are increasingly thrown back on their own individual resources . . . access to labor and information comes through workers' own social networks-structures they must carefully propagate and cultivate themselves. (2000: 2)

These two characteristics are important to understanding discrimination in Silicon Valley (and more generally flexibly organized regions) because they highlight the significance of inter-organizational processes (the ability to move from firm to firm), and the factors that influence these processes (network resources) in shaping the careers of high-skill, high-tech workers. I suggest that while all employees, white and Asian, men and women, report the use of job-hopping as a general strategy of career mobility, the phenomenon of jobhopping in Silicon Valley has also become a potentially important avenue by which Asian men and women, and white women navigate intra-organizational mechanisms of discrimination. White women and Asian men and women did have perceptions of bias within organizations similar to that which had been identified in previous literature. However, they also reported being able to job-hop into firms that they found to be more egalitarian, and were able to access resource rich networks that facilitated their job-hopping. The remainder of this chapter discusses this phenomenon, examining the two types of job-hopping that emerged, and considering the group- and region-specific factors that shaped individuals' ability to use these strategies successfully.

DATA AND METHODS

This study is based on fifty-four in-depth, open-ended interviews of highly skilled, white and Asian men and women working in Silicon Valley. The interview schedule was designed to elicit information around three primary topics of interest: respondents' perceptions of mobility in Silicon Valley, respondents' networks, and the pace of work in Silicon Valley. The interviews were conducted between March 1999 and January 2001; all interviewees worked in the high-tech industry in Silicon Valley, and were in engineering jobs or jobs that require engineering background at the time of the interview. All respondents had college degrees, and half had advanced graduate degrees. Thirty-two of the respondents were women. Nineteen of the respondents were Chinese/Taiwanese, nineteen were white, thirteen were Indian, two were Filipino, and one was Vietnamese. Twenty-four of the respondents were U.S.-born (all the whites were U.S.-born); the rest were foreign-born. The average age of the respondents was 36.3, which approximates the average age of highly skilled workers in Silicon Valley.

The respondents worked (or were entrepreneurs) at thirty-nine different firms, representing both larger, well-established organizations and smaller firms or start-ups. However, the majority of the respondents had worked in the past for both established and newer firms, and almost all the respondents had worked for more than one company. The average number of years in the workforce was over eleven. Interviewees were chosen using a snowball method. Initial respondents were found in a variety of ways, ranging from my own attendance at specialized engineering society functions, solicitation of professors at major universities in Taiwan and India for referrals to graduates they sent abroad, an ad in an alumni magazine, and referrals from acquaintances. Interviews ranged from one to two hours, and occurred primarily at interviewees' workplaces. They were audiotaped, and fully transcribed.

TWO TYPES OF JOB-HOPPING

One of the questions asked of respondents early in the interviews concerned their perceptions of opportunities and mobility in the region. At the outset, almost all of women and Asian men and women I spoke with described Silicon Valley as meritocratic, and as a place that held opportunities for everyone. They said things such as, "On the East Coast, I think pedigree tends to be important, whereas out here, having the right idea, the right model; concept is what people look at"; or "There are performance evaluations only"; or "It all boils down to letting them know you are capable." Clearly, most people saw and experienced the region as race and/or gender neutral.

However, this perception was complicated when considering respondents' comments further into the interviews, where they were asked to describe the trajectory of their careers in Silicon Valley, and when they were asked explicitly whether they believed that their experiences working in the region had been shaped by their ethnicity, nativity, or gender. As it turns out, two-thirds of respondents believed that they had experienced some form of gender or ethnic bias, describing experiences within organizations such as ethnic or gender-based typecasting, hitting glass walls (job segregation) and ceilings, or being excluded from key old boys' networks. While these reports were not surprising in the sense that they are well documented in past research on gender and ethnic inequality in organizations, they are surprising in the sense that they appear to be discordant with respondents' earlier, and generally enthusiastic comments about opportunity in the region. That is, respondents' accounts were internally contradictory. They both believed that they experienced ethnic or gender-based bias within companies in Silicon Valley, and maintained that Silicon Valley as a region is meritocratic.

I suggest that the answer to this contradiction lies in the phenomenon of job-hopping, which is ubiquitous in the region, and represents a particular form of career strategy where individuals actively move from job to job in order to gain career mobility. As it turns out, the regional norm of job-hopping has a potentially disruptive effect on intra-organizational mechanisms of discrimination, because it offers the possibility of navigating around discrimination through inter-organizational mobility. Put more simply, when faced with bias within a given firm, white women and Asian men and women often find a way to move to other firms that they view as more egalitarian. This strategy seemed common among the people I interviewed. Among the respondents who reported facing ethnic or gender-based obstacles within organizations, 80 percent also reported job-hopping as a means by which they circumvented these obstacles.

There were two discernible strategies of job-hopping. The first pattern, which was reported by most of the white women, was a strategy based on a careful search for egalitarian workplace cultures and bosses. This is exemplified by the following account of Susan, a white woman who is currently a senior vice president, but describes a situation in her past company where she believed she was being excluded from the most interesting and prestigious projects because her manager was uncomfortable working with women. She said,

> The boss, and this should have been a sign to me, was a retired army colonel with eight daughters! He had spent his entire career in what at that point in time was a male dominated military, and his entire home life he was surrounded by women . . . so I was a first time manager, and he could walk and talk and say all the words and say there wasn't going to be a problem but six months later I realized that every really interesting project that would come along, he *would never give it to me,* so I went to see him again, and I gave him three more months, and then realized, this man is going to die before he gives anything to me. And that's fine, I'm not going to report him, but I'll find someone else to work for.

Susan felt that the gender bias of her boss limited her opportunities to be on the most innovative projects, and this was problematic because it would subsequently limit her ability to gain the experience, skills, and visibility she needed for career mobility. Her response is telling, because she says she won't "report him," that is, file a formal complaint which is the traditional avenue of recourse. But what she will do is simply find someone else to work for, which is characteristic of the trend of job-hopping to circumvent bias.

Another respondent, Mary, talked about how a friend's continuous job-hopping allowed her to circumvent the "glass walls" that exist in many companies. From her perspective, women face constraints to lateral mobility within companies. This subsequently impedes the acquisition of varied skills needed for higher-level positions. "While the guys move around all the time," women are "channeled," less able to move around easily. Given this situation, she notes a friend's strategy to overcome the "glass walls" within companies.

> [My friend was] moving from this company to another company, and then moving from this company to here, to broaden her scope, so she's available for this pool of executive management. She had to have experience here and here and here, and to get that she had to change companies, because she couldn't move through the walls in her company, but she could move into the arena in a different company. So then she didn't have to move through the glass walls. So her company hopping has allowed her I think to advance.

As Mary's comments illustrate, continuous job-hopping is a means by which women can circumvent glass walls, in order to gain the experience needed to move into the pool of executive management.

In a final example of this type of job-hopping, Linda, an Asian women who is a midlevel manager, job-hopped because she felt excluded by an "old boys' network" at her previous company. She said about this company's environment,

I definitely felt out of the loop. . . . I very much felt that that company was run by an old boys' network, and you had to be a certain kind of old boy, meaning not every guy was included . . . women in general were not embraced or sought after, and I saw women attempt to break through that with marginal success so everybody came to the conclusion that they had to move elsewhere.

The women at this company believed they were excluded from key circles, and consequently, many left the company, a case, I suppose, of mass job-hopping. Ironically, the company later folded, which, Linda laughs, seemed like "justice!" When she switched companies, she looked for a place that had a higher proportion of women in general and within the executive levels, and eventually ended up at a place that she had "heard" was friendly to women.

Of course one could argue that people are job-hopping from one biased situation to another, but, as I think is hinted by the examples, job-hopping is not done blindly. Rather, individuals engage in a careful scrutiny of potential companies that includes soliciting information and advice about which companies are more egalitarian, and evaluating the companies at which they interview. This conscious strategy of looking for a new company is described by Susan, the informant quoted earlier.

What I actually think is more important for a woman is shopping for a boss. And I say that, and people laugh, bosses shop for employees, but I mean that very seriously. You need to find a boss who trusts you, who you connect with, who is going to give you opportunities as they come along. . . . [So it's important] to really push that person you're interviewing, understand how comfortable they are, look around their organization, look who they are giving work to and what decisions are being made, are there women there, are they getting on good projects, are they getting promoted, because that's what's important.

These examples have illustrated a form of job-hopping whose intention is integration and mobility into mainstream companies. Another form of job-hopping that seemed increasingly common among Asian immigrants was moving from mainstream firms into co-ethnic owned ones; or alternatively, starting their own firms with co-ethnics. This could be termed as a strategy of separation to avoid ethnic or racial bias. The high rates of Chinese and Indian entrepreneurship (in 1990, 29 percent of high-tech startups in Silicon Valley were headed by Chinese or Indians [Saxenian 1999]) made this a particularly feasible strategy for Asian immigrants.[9]

Like the previous cases, those who job-hopped into such firms did so because they felt they were the subject of bias. Asian immigrants reported feeling typecasted into technical roles, as "workhorses" rather than as management material. When directly queried about whether there were glass ceilings, one typical response, for example, was,

> Yeah, of course, that is obvious . . . glass ceiling is definitely there . . . [to succeed] you need to be very, very good, if you are just marginally better, there is one Caucasian and one Chinese, and you are just a little bit better, then chances to be promoted to the position is not good.

The case of Lei exemplifies a job-hopping strategy of separation. Lei, an immigrant from China in his forties, had recently joined as a director in a co-ethnic run start-up. His previous employment had been in "mainstream" companies and he felt he had been consistently channeled into technical roles. While he did not have difficulty finding employment when his "tech hat" was on, he felt frustrated because he believed that the companies were just "looking for a bag of skill sets, they just see me as a body." In contrast, after joining a co-ethnic run start-up, he says, "I feel very excited because I can contribute on many fronts, not only on the technology side, but product management, marketing, sales. . . ."

Similarly, Lin, a Taiwanese immigrant engineer in his late thirties who had been working at an established, large chip manufacturer for a number of years, was convinced by his manager, who was also Taiwanese, to move with some of his other coworkers to a co-ethnic run start-up. When asked why he and his boss had moved to this start-up, he explained that his manager had become frustrated and decided to leave to start his own company, taking most of the Chinese engineers in their department with him because his boss felt "always kicked around by some other guy. I think somehow he felt frustrated so he thought he might as well start his own company." He further cautiously explained,

> He thinks, he thought [long pause], well in the company people play politics, and he is always the victim or something [laughs uneasily] so he asked us if we want to join him and some of us decided to.

The boss's action of leaving and taking only other Chinese engineers suggests that some of his dissatisfaction was related to his experiences as a Chinese immigrant engineer. Similarly, the fact that most of the Chinese engineers agreed to leave with him (this seems reminiscent of the case discussed earlier, when several women left a company they viewed as biased) might also suggest that they too were uncomfortable in that environment. Unlike the cases described by the women earlier, however, Asian immigrants report opting to move to co-ethnic firms, it seems in large part because they appear to have little faith that they will be able to find mainstream firms that see them outside of technical roles.

THE CONTEXT: BUILDING RESOURCE-RICH
ETHNIC- AND GENDER-BASED NETWORKS

Thus far, I have described two variants of job-hopping that were reported, and they seemed to represent an important strategy that enabled people to negotiate what they saw as discrimination in organizations. The question that now remains is how and why was this strategy possible in Silicon Valley? I do not want to suggest that job-hopping is a feasible strategy in every context, for every job market, or for any group, and in fact, it may not even be as common in Silicon Valley today, given the downturn in the economy. Rather, there were particular historical, regional, and industry-specific contexts that allowed this strategy to flourish.

Clearly, one simple part of the answer has to do with the labor shortage in the 1990s, reported at 30 to 37 percent for high-skill jobs, which was a key reason that job-hopping itself became ubiquitous in Silicon Valley for all workers (the turnover rate, at least in the later 1990s, was double the national average). The labor shortage stemming from the rapid development of the high-tech industry created an employees' market, where workers were able to have more power in terms of their relationship to employers (Carnoy et al. 1997). Another part of the answer, as I indicated earlier, is the structure of the region, that is, the more fluid boundaries of firms in flexibly organized regions that facilitate what Hyde (1997) calls a "high-velocity labor market," where workers were not sanctioned for job-hopping.

The ability to job-hop, however, cannot be taken for granted, because job-hopping in Silicon Valley typically entailed the use of networks, a fact that initially drew me to believe that ethnic and gender inequality would be exacerbated, since lack of access to networks has been so consistently identified as a problem for women and nonwhites. However, contrary to my initial belief, women and Asian immigrants were gaining access to resource-rich networks that allowed them to tap into the opportunities and referrals necessary for job-hopping. In particular, they were constructing and tapping into gender and ethnic-based networks with resources that could compete with the utility of old white boys' networks in helping members gain access to information, jobs, and entrepreneurial opportunities.

Two examples of such networks illustrate this phenomenon. The Silicon Valley chapter of the Society of Women Engineers is a gender-based network, although from observations of meetings, it appears to be composed mostly of U.S.-born white women. The chapter has a large membership, and hosts a variety of events ranging from social networking get-togethers to career-related training sessions. One member, Gail, talked about how women's networks have helped her career:

> A good example of an "old girls' network" is the Society for Women Engineers . . . if you look within the political structure of SWE, there are definitely old, established networks where no matter what was going on in a management and organization, people in the network had the information about what was going on, down to the significant amount of details, they know what's going on.

She continued by explaining the import of these "old girls' networks":

> There are women all over the valley and in every company, so these women supply information, and when they know you and what you are doing they'll think of you and what you are doing . . . when an opportunity comes up, they'll tell you informally . . . so getting to know who they are and building a relationship is important.

Women respondents testified to the utility of this type of gender-based network in helping them with career-related information and opportunities. Of course the existence of these networks cannot be taken for granted; they clearly do not exist for women in every occupation or industry. In Silicon Valley, three specific contexts facilitated the formation of these networks. First, as mentioned in the introduction, there is a critical mass of engineering and technically trained women in the region. This has not been the case in other engineering industries either in the past or present. It makes "power in numbers" possible, having women "all over the valley and in every company." Second, and relatedly, members are stratified in terms of the positions they hold in companies: there are both senior ("old girls") and junior members in these networks, and the presence of senior women is integral because they hold important resources.

Third, the presence of women at the upper levels of engineering organizations is particular to the history of Silicon Valley, and is predicated on the fact that women were able to get their "foot in the door" of the high-tech industry at its modern inception in the 1970s. The 1970s boom in personal computing coincided with the first cohorts of women graduating with engineering degrees and the growing implementation of affirmative action programs. In addition, this was an industry that had use for those with computing and mathematics backgrounds, fields in which women had always been better represented. This historical convergence in a number of trends set the stage for the entry of women on the ground floor of the high-tech industry, creating a stratum of senior-level women who have significant resources to share. The work of the more senior members established what one member described as a "beachhead effect" where the pioneers gained a foothold and brought in other members.

Consequently, women were able to form resource-rich networks that helped in their careers in general, and job-hopping in particular. In the Society for Women Engineers, for example, where everyone is exhorted that "we definitely do have the power for those who are already there to make a difference," women reported freely that they seek other members for "back stage" information about which places or people to avoid, for advice on how to deal with projects, and for concrete aid in seeking other job opportunities.

The networks of Asian immigrants were forged in a somewhat different context and were geared more toward helping to create and maintain start-ups. But some of the factors that conditioned the numbers of immigrants present were similar to those that generated gender-based networks. Specifically, the boom in high-tech industry in the 1970s, and again in the 1990s, converged with increases in the supply of Asian immigrants. In the first period changes in immigration law, notably the 1965 Hart-Cellar Act, opened the doors for Asian immigration. In the second period, the 1990 Immigration Act re-tooled immigration categories to emphasize skills-based migration, resulting in the rapid rise in the number of H-1B visas issued in the late 1990s. While this created a cohort of Asian immigrants who entered the industry at its inception, as was the case with U.S.-born women, as well as a continuous flow since then, the resources that the ethnic-based networks had to share in the 1990s were influenced by other factors. The immigrant network among alumni from the Indian Institute of Technology (IIT) offers a good example. The IIT are a string of prestigious technology institutes in India, with a very rigorous entrance exam, and their alumni have come to the U.S. in large numbers since the late 1960s. IIT-Bombay has a particularly strong record of sending their alumni abroad. One study of Bombay alumni concludes that over 60 percent of the top quartile of electrical engineering graduates of 1973–1977 immigrated. Even as India's software industry grew, IIT-Bombay continued to send alum abroad: in 1998, around 30 percent of the graduating class left for the U.S. (Rajghatta 1999). The IITs have become a well-established name in Silicon Valley, both because they are reputed to be rigorous training grounds, and, perhaps more importantly, because so many of their graduates in Silicon Valley have spawned successful start-ups.

The networks formed have yielded great advantage to their members, as illustrated by the following story of one alumnus, Anil, who came to the region in the 1980s. When he arrived he first contacted two other alumni with whom he had kept in touch, who had moved to Silicon Valley in the 1970s. They immediately sent him a long list of job opportunities, furnished by the network of IIT alumni in Silicon Valley. Anil quickly got a job at a company where another IIT alumnus worked. He and his family also easily transitioned into Silicon Valley because of the personal aid given to him by the IIT network. A few years later, as venture funding became more accessible to Indians, and to IIT alumni in general because of the growing prestige of their educational institutions, he and his friend became co-founders of their own start-up that became quite successful and which they subsequently sold. They have since started other endeavors with other alumni, sometimes as entrepreneurs, sometimes in top-level positions, and sometimes as investors in other Indian-run start-ups.

Alumni from IIT have recently begun to try actively to formalize their diffuse networks, expressing a commitment to help other younger alumni. They see themselves as mentors, saying that they are a "successful group of people who have grown in the valley and in a sense become influential in a lot of ways." "We know what it took to get there, and we realize that we need to give back." More formal networks have been institutionalized, where speakers are brought in to talk about how to find venture funding and how to start a business in particular sectors of the high-tech industry. These meetings, which are common among a number of ethnic-based networks, are also designed to match investors with entrepreneurs with highly skilled talent.

These ethnic ties, both of a professional and personal nature, are bolstered through geographic concentration. Like other immigrants before them, Asians in Silicon Valley are forming ethnic pockets and ethnic communities. For example, Asians are unevenly dispersed in Santa Clara County, accounting for 25.6 percent of the county population, but almost 52 percent of the population of Milpitas and 44.4 percent of Cupertino. Similarly, they represent 37 percent of those in Fremont and 43 percent of those in Union City, neighboring cities in the county of Alameda (where Asians comprise 20 percent of the overall population). Asian Indians follow this pattern of ethnic concentration. They account for only 4 percent of Santa Clara County, but represent 10 percent of those who live in Sunnyvale, almost 9 percent of those who live in Santa Clara and Cupertino cities, and over 10 percent of those who live in Fremont.[10]

The IIT example highlights not only the importance of senior members aiding junior members, but also the increasing resources available to these ethnic-based networks in the 1990s stemming from a change in the structure of opportunities available to immigrants. This structure of opportunities changed because of the global context of the high-tech industry, where expansion and survival are contingent upon foreign labor, foreign subcontractors, foreign consumers, and foreign investment.

This global context means that transnational ties and cultural know-how are increasingly important (Saxenian 1999), for example, in order to make subcontracting agreements with foreign companies or recruit highly skilled labor from foreign educational institutions or seek foreign investment. The software industry of India, as well as the hardware industries of Taiwan and China, have been developing rapidly in the past fifteen years, creating a stock of highly skilled laborers to draw from, and potential partners and subcontractors.

In this scenario, Asian immigrants' social capital from their homeland, as well as reconstituted ethnic ties in Silicon Valley, has become a convertible commodity. Put differently, immigrants are increasingly able to import forms of social and cultural capital from their homelands. This is different from the past when immigrants were typically unable to transport these forms of capital because it was either useless, as in the phenomenon of professionals who are now laborers in Chinatowns or those who had nontransferable medical degrees, or it was capital that had limited use, as in the case of social capital within the confines of ethnic economies.

The ties to which well-placed immigrants have access subsequently enabled them to become the heads of start-ups at increasing rates. Indeed, those I interviewed who had been in the region since the 1970s specifically talked about the changing ability of Indian and Chinese immigrants to access material capital. Immigrants are finally being seen by venture capitalists in the U.S. as potentially successful CEOs, whereas in the past a "white American CEO" was necessary. Access to start-up funds has also been facilitated by the increasing mobility of capital, and the subsequent rise in foreign investment in Silicon Valley companies, which is primarily directed toward co-ethnics in America, providing significant capital for would-be entrepreneurs in Silicon Valley. (Additionally, immigrant entrepreneurs also report easily finding highly skilled labor for their start-ups through their ethnic networks, at a time when companies identified a labor shortage as the major problem they faced.)

The increasing convertibility of transnational and co-ethnic ties, along with increased access to funding, has made job-hopping into co-ethnic owned firms or starting one's own firm a viable option that does not constrain mobility. I view this as a potentially significant consequence of the global nature of specific industries like high-tech, because it signals the ability of some Asian immigrants to reach outside the domestic structure of ethnic and race relations to access resources. Equally, it suggests that how we understand race and ethnicity for this group must take into account what Arif Dirlik (1999) calls the "globalizing space of transnational capital" as well as the local spaces of communities.[11] In this sense, what is happening in Silicon Valley is a phenomenon that is similar to the transnational enterprises of immigrants

Johanna Shih

detailed for instance by Portes (2000) and Basch, Schiller, and Blanc-Szanton (1994), although the ethnic enterprises in Silicon Valley are not bounded, but have managed to penetrate into the heart of the high-tech industry. In some cases, it also means that they have been able to transport and legitimate certain forms of cultural capital, best represented by the acceptance of the IITs as elite schools (*Business Week* for example, dedicated a cover story to the IIT graduates), and established them, as one alumnus put it, as a "brand name" in Silicon Valley similar in cache to that of Ivy League schools.

CONCLUSION

This chapter illustrates the use of job-hopping as a potentially important avenue by which individuals can navigate discrimination. Job-hopping as a form of career mobility is ubiquitous in the region (Carnoy et al. 1997) used by white men as well as women and nonwhite men. However, I suggest that it serves an additional function for white women and Asian men and women, who have used inter-firm mobility as a strategy to avoid employers and workplaces that they view as biased, and to avoid gender- or ethnic-based stereotypes, glass walls and ceilings, and exclusive old boys' networks.

Identifying this phenomenon contributes to the existing literature on inequality, because the focus of this research has primarily been on intra-organizational mechanisms of discrimination. In doing so, workers were depicted as essentially "trapped" or held captive by organizations, with little recourse save formal means of redress, which is a problematic process that is often lengthy, and subject to repercussions. What I have shown is that we must take into account the "other side" of discrimination; that is, workers' responses and the conditions that shape their effectiveness, as well as the opportunities that other organizations proffer. While it may not always be the case, white women and Asian immigrants in Silicon Valley's high-tech industry were able to tap into resource rich ethnic- and gender-based networks to turn the tables on discriminatory employers by simply walking away. The meritocracy that respondents spoke of initially should thus be understood as an achieved condition, rather than one that is inherent to the region, as is suggested by the dominant discourse about the Silicon Valley.

However, I emphasized that this is not a strategy that would be applicable in all situations. As the other authors in this volume emphasize as well (for example, Zeltzer-Zubida, in examining the labor market concentrations of the children of post-1965 immigrants, concludes that there are "multiple logics of labor incorporation" at work for different ethnic and racial groups), contexts shape the salience of ethnicity, race and gender such that attention to the historically specific situation of Silicon Valley's high-tech industry as well as the characteristics of the groups involved is necessary. The creation and maintenance of ethnic and gender networks with significant resources was not simply contingent on the increasing numbers of skilled Asian immigrants and white women, but rather their entry at the historical time period when the high-tech market also experienced rapid expansion, both domestically and internationally. In this sense, the specific case of Silicon Valley supports the argument made by Valdez in this volume—that "the importance of ethnicity lies in the market." While the focus of her research links levels of ethnic entrepreneurship to ethnic market opportunities (rather than any tangible, or intangible, effects of ethnic solidarity), the same underlying mechanism—a suddenly expanding market that opens opportunities for entrepreneurship—is at work.

Finally, let me conclude by suggesting three aspects of the case of Silicon Valley that contrast with the significant body of literature on the relationship between ethnic networks, ethnic resources, and economic action. First and most simply, the case of Silicon Valley is predicated on the immigration of a large cohort of highly skilled, middle-class workers. Second, and related, these high-tech workers were largely able to convert the social and educational capital they brought from the country of origin into valuable sources of capital within Silicon Valley. In other words, the global nature of the high-tech industry allows social capital to transcend national boundaries. This differs from the past experiences of Asian immigrants, who typically "lost" forms of social as well as cultural capital (although Feliciano's work in this volume certainly shows us that the cultural capital immigrants bring with them can translate into advantages for the 1.5 and second generation), unless they stayed within the confines of an ethnic economy. In contrast, immigrants whose homelands have well-developed high-tech industries and recognized educational institutions find that their social capital can be imported as important commodities. Third, while anecdotal, it seems that some Asian women in high-tech were able to access resources in ethnic networks, partly because many of these networks were alumni networks of educational institutions. In this sense, the emphasis of the high-tech industry on educational credentials serves to ameliorate gender bias, at least among those who are able to gain the "right" degrees. Taken together, these three points suggest that what might be happening in Silicon Valley with respect to transnational capital is the creation of a global elite, given that the Asian immigrants who have done so well for themselves in Silicon Valley largely come from privileged positions in the countries of origin.

NOTES

1. This ethnic composition is recent and the product of rapid demographic changes. More than half of the foreign-born population in Santa Clara County, as of 1990, arrived between 1980 and 1990. There has been an even greater change in the last decade. From 1990 to 2000, Santa Clara County experienced a 65 percent increase in the Asian population, in comparison to California overall, which has experienced a 30 percent increase in the numbers of those of Asian descent (U.S. Census Bureau, geographic comparison table by race, and Hispanic or Latino, 2000).

2. Saxenian notes that in 1990, 84 percent of Chinese and 98 percent of Indians in the Silicon Valley workforce were immigrants (1999: 13).

3. In the nation overall, Ellis and Lowell (1999) found that the foreign-born represent 17 percent of the core IT occupations (computer scientists, computer engineers, systems analysts, and programmers).

4. Data from 1990 Census of Population and Housing: Census Tracts and BNA's, San Jose, CA PMSA, U.S. Department of Commerce; Bureau of Census.

5. An exception to this is a study, using multicohort longitudinal data, by Morgan (1998), who suggested that what had been seen as a glass ceiling effect can be understood as a cohort effect, with younger cohorts of women engineers experiencing negligible gender disadvantage.

6. U.S. GAO report (1989). "Equal Employment Opportunity: Women and Minority Aerospace Managers and Professionals."

7. Using 1990 Census data, Matloff (1997) showed a sizable wage disadvantage for foreign-born computer professionals in Silicon Valley. For example, among those under thirty-two, the mean annual salaries of foreign computer professionals were $8,635 less than those of native-born employees.

8. Hyde (1997) estimates that the average job duration among high-tech professionals is two years, Joint Venture (2000) found that the regional turnover rate was twice the national average, and Carnoy et al. (1997) found that human resource managers in high-tech companies report annual turnover rates ranging from 15 to 25 percent.

9. While high rates of entrepreneurship may not seem surprising given the substantial sociological literature on ethnic entrepreneurship, the distinction is that ethnic entrepreneurship has typically been understood as happening in the peripherals of the economy or in the secondary sectors or within ethnic economies, whereas in Silicon Valley, entrepreneurship is happening at the heart of a growing industry, and starting one's own or joining a start-up is considered a prestigious activity. Thus, moving into one of these co-ethnic owned firms represents a viable and palatable option.

10. Percentages calculated from preliminary geographic data tables of the 2000 Census.

11. I do not mean to suggest here that the ability of some well-placed immigrants in Silicon Valley to transport forms of social capital reflects any permanent shift toward the transnationalization of social capital, as some global theorists (Castells 1997) have suggested, or that they point to the creation of a new class of elite, transnational globe trotters who straddle two nations and who resist assimilation. Rather, my

claim is far smaller: their ability to convert social capital from their homelands rests specifically on the fact that the high-tech industry is dependent on foreign labor, foreign investment, foreign partners, and foreign consumers. While this does depend, as Portes (2000) notes, on the logic of capitalist expansion, it also depends on the particular histories and policies of China, Taiwan, and India in developing high-tech industries, as well as fostering universities that train those who would be employed or become entrepreneurs in these industries.

REFERENCES

Alarcon, Rafael. 1999. "Recruitment Processes among Foreign-Born Engineers and Scientists in Silicon Valley." *American Behavioral Scientist* 42, no. 9: 1381–97.

Baldi, Stephanie, and Debra Branch McBrier. 1997. "Do the Determinants of Promotion Differ for Blacks and Whites?" *Work and Occupations* 24: 478–97.

Baron, James N., Michael T. Hannan, and M. Diane Burton. 2001. "Labor Pains: Change in Organizational Models and Employee Turnover in Young High-Tech Firms." *American Journal of Sociology* 106, no. 4: 960–1012.

Basch, Linda, Nina Glick Schiller, and Christina Blanc-Szanton. 1994. *Nations Unbound: Transnational Projects, Post-Colonial Predicaments, and De-territorialized Nation States*. Langhorne, PA: Gordon and Breach.

Bielby, William, and James Baron. 1986. "Men and Women at Work: Sex Segregation and Statistical Discrimination." *American Journal of Sociology* 91: 759–99.

Carnoy, Martin, Manuel Castells, and Chris Benner. 1997. "Labor Markets and Employment Practices in the Age of Flexibility: A Case Study of Silicon Valley." *International Labor Review* 136: 27–48.

Carter, Ruth, and Gill Kirkup. 1990. *Women in Engineering: A Good Place to Be?* London: Macmillan.

Castells, Manuel. 1996. *The Rise of the Network Society*. Oxford: Blackwells Publishers.

Cockburn, Cynthia. 1991. *In the Way of Women: Men's Resistance to Sex Equality in Organizations*. Ithaca, NY: ILR Press.

Collins, Sharon. 1997. *Black Corporate Executives*. Philadelphia: Temple University Press.

Cooper, Marianne. 2000. "Being the "Go-to Guy": Fatherhood, Masculinity, and the Organization of Work in Silicon Valley." *Qualitative Sociology* 234: 379–405.

DiPrete, Thomas, and Whitman Soule. 1988. "Gender and Promotion in Segmented Job Ladder Systems." *American Sociological Review* 53: 26–40.

Dirlik, Arif. 1999. "Asians on the Rim: Transnational Capital and the Local Community in the Making of Contemporary Asian America." Pp. 29–60 in *Across the Pacific: Asian Americans and Globalization*, ed. Evelyn Hu-DeHart. Philadelphia: Temple University Press.

DiTomaso, Nancy, and Steven Smith. 1996. "Race and Ethnic Minorities and White Women in Management: Changes and Challenges." Pp. 87–110 in *Women and Minorities in American Professions*, ed. Joyce Tang and Earl Smith. New York: State University of New York Press.

Duncan, Greg, and Saul Hoffman. 1979. "On the Job Training and Earnings Differences by Race and Sex." *Review of Economics and Statistics* 61: 594–603.

Ellis, Richard, and Lindsay Lowell. 1999. "Foreign-Origin Persons in the U.S. Information Technology Workforce." IT Workforce Data Project: Report 3.

Fernandez, Marilyn. 1998. "Asian Indian Americans in the Bay Area and the Glass Ceiling." *Sociological Perspectives* 41: 119–49.

Hacker, Sally. 1990. *Doing It the Hard Way: Investigations of Gender and Technology*. Boston: Unwin Hyman.

Harvey, David. 1989. *The Conditions of Post-Modernity*. Oxford: Basil Blackwell.

Huffman, Matt. 1995. "Organizations, Internal Labor Market Policies, and Gender Inequality in Workplace Supervisory Authority." *Sociological Perspectives* 38, no. 3: 381–97.

Hyde, Alan. 1997, August. "Employee Identity Caucuses in Silicon Valley: Can They Transcend the Boundaries of the Firm?" *Labor Law Journal*: 491–97.

Iwata, Edwards, ed. 1993. "Qualified, But . . . : A Report on Glass Ceiling Issues Facing Asian Americans in Silicon Valley." Report by Asian Americans for Community Involvement. Santa Clara, CA: Quick Silver Printing.

Jaffee, David. 1989. "Gender Inequality in Workplace Autonomy and Authority." *Social Science Quarterly* 70: 375–90.

Joint Venture. 2000. *2000 Index of Silicon Valley*. CA: Joint Venture: Silicon Valley Network.

Kanter, Rosabeth Moss. 1977. *Men and Women of the Corporation*. New York: Basic Books.

Kluegel, James. 1978. "The Causes and Consequences of Racial Exclusion from Job Authority." *American Sociological Review* 43: 285–301.

Knoke, David, and Yoshito Ishio. 1998. "The Gender Gap in Company Job Training." *Work and Occupations* 25: 141–67.

Kumar, Krishan. 1995. *From Post-Industrial to Post-Modern Society*. Oxford: Blackwell Publishers.

Madamba, Anna, and Gordon De Jong. 1997. "Job Mismatch among Asians in the United States: Ethnic Group Comparisons." *Social Science Quarterly* 78: 524–42.

Matloff, Norman. 1997, May 21. Summary by the Institute for Economic Development of talk given at Sloan Foundation Workshop of "Migration of Scientists and Engineers to the U.S."

McIlwee, Judith, and J. Gregg Robinson. 1992. *Women in Engineering: Gender, Power and Workplace Culture*. Albany: State University of New York Press.

Morgan, Laurie. 1998. "The Earnings Gap for Women Engineers, 1982 to 1989." *American Sociological Review* 63, no. 4: 479–93.

Mueller, Charles, Tony Parcel, and Kazuko Tanaka. 1989. "Particularism in Authority Outcomes of Black and White Supervisors." *Social Science Research* 18: 1–20.

Nardi, Bonnie, Steve Whittaker, and Heinrich Schwarz. 2000. "It's Not What You Know, It's Who You Know: Work in the Information Age." *First Monday* 5, no. 5: 1–37.

National Science Foundation. 1991. *Women and Minorities in Science and Engineering*. Washington, DC.

——. 2000. *Science and Engineering Indicators, 2000*. Washington, DC.

Piore, Michael, and Charles Sabel. 1984. *The Second Industrial Divide: Possibilities for Prosperity*. New York: Basic Books.

Portes, Alejandro. 2000. "Globalization from Below: The Rise of Transnational Communities." Pp. 253–70 in *The Ends of Globalization: Bringing Society Back In*, ed. D. Kalb. Lanham, MD: Rowman & Littlefield.

Rajghatta, Chidanand. 1999, December 7. "Brain Curry." *Express Xclusive*.

Roos, Patricia. 1981. "Sex Stratification in the Workplace." *Social Science Research* 10: 195–224.

Sabel, Charles. 1991. "Moebius-Strip Organizations and Open Labor Markets: Some Consequences of the Reintegration of Conception and Execution in a Volatile Economy." Pp. 23–55 in *Social Theory for a Changing Society*, ed. Pierre Bourdieu and James Coleman. New York: Westview Press and Russell Sage.

Saxenian, Annalee. 1994. *Regional Advantage*. Cambridge, MA: Harvard University Press.

——. 1999. *Silicon Valley's New Immigrant Entrepreneurs* San Francisco: Public Policy Institute of California.

Subcommittee on Science, Research and Technology. 1982. "Symposium of Minorities and Women in Science and Technology." Washington D.C., Committee on Science and Technology, U.S. House of Representatives, Ninety-seventh Congress, Second Session.

Tang, Joyce. 1993a. "The Career Attainment of Caucasian and Asian Engineers." *Sociological Quarterly* 34: 467–96.

——. 1993b. "Whites, Asians and Blacks in Science and Engineering." *Research in Social Stratification and Mobility* 12: 249–91.

Waldinger, Roger, Mehdi Bozorgmehr, Nelson Lim, and Lucila Finkel. 1998. "In Search of the Glass Ceiling: The Career Trajectories of Immigrant and Native-Born Engineers." Los Angeles: UCLA, unpublished manuscript.

U.S. GAO. 1989. "Equal Employment Opportunity: Women and Minority Aerospace Managers and Professionals."

Wolf, Wendy, and Neil Fligstein. 1979. "Sex and Authority at the Workplace." *American Sociological Review* 44: 235–52.

8

Beyond the Ethnic Enclave

The Effect of Ethnic Solidarity and Market Opportunity on White, Korean, Mexican, and Black Enterprise

Zulema Valdez

The maintenance of the ethnic community, once considered a barrier to economic integration, is now thought to create economic opportunities and support for co-ethnic members (Portes and Bach 1985; Sanders and Nee 1987, 1996; Wilson and Portes 1980; Zhou and Logan 1989; also see Shih, this volume). In particular, scholars claim that a geographically concentrated ethnic community promotes close-knit co-ethnic ties and social capital, which facilitates entrepreneurial participation among some ethnic minorities, such as Koreans (Light and Bonacich 1988). Yet, other geographically concentrated ethnic communities, such as those among Mexicans and Blacks, do not reflect increased entrepreneurial activity (Light 1972; Light and Bonacich 1988; Portes and Bach 1985; Waters and Eschbach 1995). Since ethnic communities do not always facilitate entrepreneurship among all groups, this relationship must be more complex. Hence, I ask the question, "What is the relationship between ethnic concentration and entrepreneurship, and how does this relationship vary by ethnicity?"

THE ETHNIC ENCLAVE HYPOTHESIS

The ethnic entrepreneurship literature provides two approaches that address the effects of ethnic concentration on entrepreneurship. The ethnic enclave economy hypothesis maintains that a geographically distinct ethnic community is essential for ethnic enterprise; the ethnic economy hypothesis acknowledges the importance of social capital and market opportunities, regardless of ethnic concentration.

243

The importance of ethnic concentration is nowhere more prevalent than in the ethnic enclave, since it is the geographic density of the ethnic population—whether in work, residence, or industry—that is perceived to encourage ethnic solidarity (Light and Bonacich 1988; Sanders and Nee 1987; Portes and Bach 1985; Portes and Stepick 1993; Wilson and Portes 1980; also see Zeltzer-Zubida, this volume). Ethnic solidarity, "reciprocal obligations attached to a common ethnicity" (Wilson and Portes 1980), facilitates entrepreneurship by providing economic and noneconomic support to co-ethnic members (Bonacich and Modell 1980; Light 1972; Logan, Alba, and McNulty 1994; Light and Bonacich 1988; Nee and Sanders 1985; Portes and Bach 1985; Portes and Rumbaut 1990; Portes and Zhou 1992; Sanders and Nee 1987).

Wilson and Portes (1980) first defined the ethnic enclave as a spatially concentrated ethnic business sector of co-ethnic employers, employees, and businesses that provides goods and services to co-ethnics and others (Portes and Jensen 1989; Portes and Stepick 1993; Wilson and Portes 1980). More recent research has defined the enclave using ethnic concentration in residence, work, industrial sector ("industrial clustering"), or some combination of the three in large geographic areas such as the metropolitan area or county region (Logan et al. 1994; Sanders and Nee 1987; Waters and Eschbach 1995; Zhou and Logan 1989). The many competing definitions of the enclave have given rise to a debate on its conceptual usefulness, with some arguing that the ethnic enclave is "ambiguous" (Nee, Sanders, and Sernau 1994), "a rubber yardstick" (Light et al. 1994), and "a stew, to which researchers have added so many ingredients and seasonings that it is hard to tell what is essential" (Logan et al. 1994). Yet, rather than suspending its use as some have concluded (Waldinger 1993), I identify the central feature of the ethnic enclave on which all scholars agree: ethnic concentration promotes ethnic solidarity, which contributes to ethnic entrepreneurship (Logan et al. 1994; Portes and Bach 1985; Wilson and Martin 1982).

Proponents argue that ethnic solidarity encourages the formation of a close-knit ethnic community, such as the ethnic enclave. The ethnic community provides ethnic-specific resources for would-be co-ethnic entrepreneurs. Such resources include a source of capital accumulation, a supply of low-wage or unpaid family labor, and a demand for ethnic specialty goods and services (Light and Bonacich 1988; Portes 1987; Portes and Zhou 1992; Sanders and Nee 1996; Waldinger et al. 1990).

Ethnic business owners rely on family or co-ethnic ties within the community for capital accumulation (Light and Bonacich 1988; Portes and Zhou 1992; Sanders and Nee 1996; Waldinger et al. 1990). Waldinger and colleagues give an example of the informal borrowing strategies of some groups:

> If a Pakistani needs money he can go to a relative or friend and ask him for 200 or 300 pounds. He cannot be refused, even if the friend has to borrow money in order to lend to him. . . . It is a matter of trust. (Waldinger et al. 1990: 139)

The "trust" present in a close-knit community is critical in establishing borrowing strategies among members of some ethnic groups (Sanders and Nee 1996; Waldinger et al. 1990). More formal borrowing strategies among co-ethnics include rotating credit associations in Asian communities (Light 1972; Light and Bonacich 1988). For example, Light discusses the formation of a rotating credit association (*Kye*) among Koreans immigrants (Light 1972; Light and Bonacich 1988). Ethnic membership creates trust and ensures the effectiveness of the *Kye* by clearly defining the group that can benefit from it. Such co-ethnic institutions provide a source of capital accumulation for would-be ethnic entrepreneurs.

Ethnic concentration within the enclave also provides ethnic entrepreneurs with a source of co-ethnic, low wage or unpaid family labor (Light and Bonacich 1988; Waldinger et al. 1990). Ethnic business owners often hire family or co-ethnic members, thereby "mobilizing direct connections to the ethnic community from which they emigrated" (Waldinger et al. 1990). Family members experience the "reciprocal obligation" (Wilson and Portes 1980) to work in the family business, often without pay. In a survey of Korean entrepreneurs, Light and Bonacich (1988) find that 57 percent of Korean entrepreneurs report hiring nuclear or extended kin workers and 90 percent reported the use of unpaid family labor (Light and Bonacich 1988). Beyond family or immediate kin, the ethnic community itself provides a source of low wage labor since "closely knit networks bring them into contact with other ethnics to whom they are tied by preexisting social connections" (Waldinger et al. 1990). Additionally, since the co-ethnic employer may hire the employee regardless of immigrant status or lack of English proficiency, co-ethnic employees provide a readily available, easily exploitable low-wage labor pool for the co-ethnic employer (Logan et al. 1994). Thus, a close-knit community encourages the practice of hiring family and co-ethnics as a source of low-wage or unpaid labor in ethnic business.

Finally, ethnic concentration provides structural support for entrepreneurial opportunities. Residential segregation coupled with few majority-owned businesses in areas of immigrant and ethnic settlement creates a greater supply and demand for specialty goods and services (such as ethnic foods and spices, immigration, and naturalization information) (Zhou 1992). Such factors usher in the development of ethnic businesses and entrepreneurs (Light and Bonacich 1988; Logan et al. 1994). Consequently, ethnic concentration creates a protected market for co-ethnic firms and promotes "linkages" between them that facilitate business opportunities within the community (Logan et al. 1994; Wilson and Portes 1980).

In sum, ethnic concentration facilitates ethnic solidarity and close-knit community ties, which encourages capital accumulation between co-ethnics, provides a source of low wage labor, and creates co-ethnic business opportunities within the community. However, while ethnic concentration promotes ethnic solidarity and high rates of ethnic enterprise, such as that found in the Korean enclave (Light and Bonacich 1988), marginal rates of entrepreneurship among some groups, such as Mexicans and Blacks, even in areas of high ethnic concentration, cannot be similarly explained. Instead, the negligible rates of ethnic enterprise among these groups have led to the implicit (and sometimes explicit) suggestion that these communities lack ethnic solidarity (Logan et al. 1994; Portes and Bach 1985).

THE ABSENCE OF ETHNIC ENCLAVES

The Black community is characterized as disadvantaged (Light 1972; Logan et al. 1994; Waters and Eschbach 1995; Wilson 1980 [1978]; Wilson 1987). Plagued by "violent crime, out-of-wedlock births, female-headed families, and welfare dependency" (Wilson 1987), as well as limited education and skills, few opportunities for capital accumulation within the community, and the more structural problems of discrimination and history of exclusion in the labor market, the Black community lacks the advantages of group concentration (Logan et al. 1994; Light 1972). Specifically, Light (1972) suggests that the social structure of the Black community does not promote group solidarity and close-knit community ties necessary for the development of enterprise (Light 1972; Waldinger et al. 1990). Further, Wilson and Martin (1982) argue that since Black entrepreneurship is marginal at best, it has "weak multiplier effects for the community" (Wilson and Martin 1982). In sum, Blacks lack the skills and experience that business ownership requires as well as a close-knit community, such as that found in the ethnic enclave, which would facilitate business ownership (Logan et al. 1994; Wilson and Martin 1982).

Similarly, Portes and Rumbaut (2001) suggest that economic success is beyond the reach of Mexicans, at least in part due to "weak communities that have emerged under their precarious conditions of arrival and settlement"

(2001: 278). Portes and Bach (1985: 245) argue that while the Cuban enclave promotes entrepreneurship, the lack of a Mexican enclave relegates this group to low wage, seasonal, or part-time work of limited advancement; work characteristic of the secondary sector of the general labor market. Similarly, Light and Bonacich (1988) state, "Mexicans . . . suffer from the dispersal of their ethnic enterprises" and add that the "lack of an ethnic enclave economy may explain their relatively lower rates of self-employment." Thus, even within their communities, in neighborhoods where ethnic concentration and demand for ethnic-specific goods and services are high, Blacks and Mexicans only marginally participate in enterprise.

The conclusion reached by proponents of "ethnic solidarity theories" (Sanders and Nee 1987: 746) to explain limited enterprise within Black and Mexican communities, is that ethnic solidarity is lacking. Yet, Sanders and Nee (1987: 747) question this proposition and ask, "How strong is the evidence that ethnic solidarity encourages the mobilization of economic resources such that much of the economic cost traditionally associated with immigration and segregation is avoided" (Sanders and Nee 1987: 747)? They suggest that studies may only favor the contributions of ethnic solidarity when they omit a comparison between the ethnically concentrated ethnic enclave, and ethnic entrepreneurship that occurs "outside" the enclave (Sanders and Nee 1987).

THE ETHNIC ECONOMY

Moving beyond ethnic solidarity approaches, as suggested by Sanders and Nee, the ethnic economy approach provides a more general concept of ethnic entrepreneurship (Light et al. 1994; Waldinger 1993). The ethnic economy is defined simply, as "the self-employed and their co-ethnic employees" and "is ethnic simply because the personnel (owners and employees) are co-ethnics" (Light et al. 1994).

> In contrast to the ethnic enclave hypothesis, the ethnic economy requires no locational clustering [i.e., concentration] of ethnic firms, nor does it require that ethnic firms service members of their ethnic group as customers or buy from co-ethnic suppliers . . . [the ethnic economy] does not require an ethnic *cultural ambience* within the firm or among buyers and sellers. Finally, ethnic entrepreneurs are in the ethnic economy even if they employ non-ethnic workers or have no paid employees at all (italics mine) (Light and Bonacich 1988: xi).

Importantly, the ethnic economy does not require ethnic solidarity, the "presumed source of the distinctive enclave effect" (Bailey and Waldinger

1991). Instead, it includes many different entrepreneurial scenarios, and can be used without the need to "squeeze an ethnic economy into an ethnic enclave economy definition" (Light et al. 1994: 78). Hence, the ethnic economy moves away from the centrality of ethnic solidarity and close-knit, community ties. Yet, the ethnic economy still acknowledges the importance of group membership in aiding business:

> Group members may have unique access to a particular supply of raw materials or finished goods, they may have unusual skills that are in demand, or a special willingness to operate a certain type of business . . . it is presumed that they enjoy a favorable competitive position in some niche of the economy. (Logan et al. 1994: 694)

Moreover, a high concentration of co-ethnics in a population will presumably increase the demand for ethnic goods and services, the supply of co-ethnic labor available, and the presence of impersonal and economic co-ethnic contact, and thus, may increase opportunities for ethnic entrepreneurship. Such market considerations may increase opportunities for ethnic entrepreneurship, as suggested by the ethnic economy argument.

Thus, the ethnic enclave hypothesis and the ethnic economy argument offer two conceptually distinct approaches to the relationship between ethnic concentration and ethnic entrepreneurship. The ethnic enclave hypothesis suggests that ethnic concentration fosters ethnic solidarity; the ethnic economy perspective suggests that ethnic density creates market opportunity. In this chapter, I examine the separate effects of the close-knit community and ethnic solidarity on the one hand, from market concerns of an increasing ethnic market on the other hand, to inform the theoretical debate.

RESEARCH QUESTIONS

To accomplish this task, I measure the effects of two types of ethnic concentration on the likelihood of entrepreneurial participation. The first measure distinguishes ethnic concentration conditioned on ethnic solidarity in a close-knit community; the second measure captures market-based supply and demand forces associated with ethnic density in the larger economy.

To represent the close-knit ethnic community, where the likelihood of ethnic solidarity is high, I construct a variable of ethnic concentration at the geographic level of the residential tract. I argue that ethnic concentration at this level will roughly correspond to an area where co-ethnic, close-knit and personal ties based on face-to-face interaction may develop—that is, where the possibility of ethnic solidarity is likely (see table 8.1). While I do not have measures that indicate ethnic solidarity directly, I contend that tract level data will provide a higher concentration of co-ethnics in a smaller geographic area that will better capture an ethnic community than a larger geographic area, such as a county or metropolitan region. Such areas have been used in previous studies to measure ethnic enclaves explicitly, and ethnic solidarity implicitly (for examples, see Wilson and Portes 1980; Sanders and Nee 1987; Zhou and Logan 1989); however, as Zeltzer-Zubida (this volume) rightly points out, such large geographic areas may not adequately capture the ethnic group or ethnic community experience. Further, since I am interested in the presence of face-to-face interactions and personal ties that foster co-ethnic support *within* the ethnic community, I use ethnic concentration at the place of residence rather than the work site or industry. I am not interested in existing relationships between co-ethnic entrepreneurs already engaged in entrepreneurship in a specific business sector or industry.[1]

To capture the market-based concerns associated with ethnic density in the larger economy, I use ethnic concentration at the geographic area of the county. As the ethnic population increases at the county level, I argue that impersonal, market exchange relationships loosely associated with ethnic membership, such as co-ethnic supply and demand considerations, will rise. Previous studies have used the county or metropolitan area to determine the boundary of the ethnic enclave (Sanders and Nee 1987; Wilson and Portes 1980; Zhou and Logan 1989). Yet this geographic area may be too large and ethnically diverse to capture the presence of personal, close-knit community ties and ethnic solidarity. Therefore, I use the level of the county as a proxy for the substantial population and consequent market-based concerns of ethnic density, characteristic of the ethnic economy (see table 8.1).

Using the tract and county level indicators of ethnic concentration, I will investigate the validity of the ethnic enclave hypothesis and ethnic economy perspective on entrepreneurship. The research questions addressed here can be summarized as follows:

1. What is the relationship between ethnic concentration at the tract level, which represents the possibility of close-knit ties and ethnic solidarity characteristic of the ethnic enclave, and entrepreneurship? How does this relationship vary by ethnicity?
2. What is the relationship between ethnic concentration at the county-level, which represents the possibility of impersonal, supply and demand concerns of a dense ethnic population characteristic of the ethnic economy, and entrepreneurship? How does this relationship vary by ethnicity?

Table 8.1.   Distinguishing Features of Ethnic Enclave and Ethnic Economy

Level of Ethnic Concentration	Area	Characteristics
Ethnic Enclave	Tract	smaller geographic area where the possibility of close-knit, community ties and ethnic solidarity increases growth in entrepreneurship due to support from ethnic community
Ethnic Economy	County	larger geographic area where the possibility of impersonal, co-ethnic contacts increases growth in entrepreneurship due to increasingly ethnic supply and demand concerns

I compare entrepreneurship across four ethnic groups—Whites, Blacks, Koreans, and Mexicans—in California.[2] I provide an analysis that includes the following control variables: human capital to capture individual characteristics, socioeconomic attainment as a proxy for class background, and ethnic and family resources as a to proxy for social capital variables (separate from ethnic solidarity). These factors have been found to facilitate entrepreneurial participation and partially explain ethnic group differences in enterprise (Archer 1991; Bailey and Waldinger 1991; Bates 1994; Borjas 1986, 1990, 1991; Light 1972; Light and Bonacich 1988; Min 1987, 1988; Portes and Bach 1985; Portes and Rumbaut 1990; Portes and Sensenbrenner 1993; Sanders and Nee 1987, 1996; Waldinger et al. 1990; Yoon 1991; Zhou and Logan 1989). Since educational attainment is correlated with class position, previous research includes education as a human capital and class variable (Light and Bonacich 1988; Sanders and Nee 1996). Similarly, I use education as a proxy for human capital and socioeconomic attainment.

I include contextual, ethnic concentration variables at the tract and county level. The possibility of close-knit ties within an ethnic community is captured by tract level ethnic concentration, while the possibility of market-based, supply and demand considerations is captured by ethnic concentration at the county level. A census tract is a small subdivision of a county, with between 2,500 and 8,000 persons. Census tracts are county-specific, meaning that tract boundaries do not cross county lines. Hence, as ethnic concentration increases in a tract, the likelihood and development of ethnic solidarity and close-knit ties increases. In contrast, counties are large and diverse. For instance, Los Angeles County alone has ten million people living in it, with immigrants representing over twenty-five countries (Light and Bhachu 1993).

As ethnic density increases in the county, then, supply and demand concerns of a large ethnic population increase.

DATA AND METHODS

The U.S. Census Bureau collects data on population, housing, and geographic characteristics of persons living in the U.S. and produces a decennial census. From this data, 5 percent of the census is sampled and released for scientific inquiry. In addition, a long-form questionnaire, containing twenty-six housing questions and thirty-three person questions, is completed by approximately one-sixth (approximately 16.5 percent) of the U.S. population. The one-in-six long-form sample of the 1990 Census is compiled by the U.S. Census Bureau but is unavailable publicly without permission from the Bureau. The Bureau of the Census collects the one-in-six sample under IRS Title 13, and access is restricted to protect the confidentiality of survey respondents. The Center for Economic Studies at the U.S. Bureau of the Census approves access to the data, and in concert with the IRS, determines disclosure of data for public inspection to ensure confidentiality.

My subset includes White, Mexican, Korean, and Black working-age males, eighteen to sixty-five years old, residing in California. Given the large sample size of Whites (702,314), I select one in ten White respondents. Hence, the White sample decreases to 70,231 persons. In addition, 107,267 Mexicans, 9,907 Koreans, and 70,298 Blacks make up the rest of the sample for a total sample size of 257,703.

Variable Definitions

Table 8.2 presents definitions for the dependent and independent variables. The dependent variable used in this analysis is *self-employed*, a dichotomous variable constructed from the nine-category variable, *class of worker*, which includes private and government employees, the self-employed, and those working without pay or unemployed. In this analysis, a person is either classified as self-employed if "self-employed in own not incorporated business or professional practice" or "self-employed in own incorporated business or professional practice" (coded as 1) or other (coded as 0). Fundamentally, I seek to examine the impact of ethnic concentration on self-employment for each group separately. Hence, for the purposes of this study, *human capital*, *socioeconomic attainment*, and *ethnic and family resources* are included as "control" variables, and I examine the effects of ethnic concentration, net of these factors.

Table 8.2.   Variable Definitions

Dependent Variable:	
Self-employment	Self-employed in own incorporated or nonincorporated business or professional practice.
Independent Variables:	
Human Capital:	
Age	Continuous variable ranging from 18 to 65.
Education	Five dummy variables: less than high school, some high school, high school diploma, BA or AA degree, graduate or professional degree.
Socioeconomic Attainment:	
Household property value	Three dummy variables: low, medium, and high (rent, or own property valued at less than $69,999; own property valued at $70,000–174,999; own property valued at $175,000–$500,000+).
Total personal income	Four dummy variables: none, low, medium, and high (no income or loss of income; $1–$24,999; $25,000–$49,999; $50,000+).
Ethnic and Family Resources:	
Foreign-born status	Dummy variable coded "1" if foreign-born, "0" if U.S.-born.
Married status	Dummy variable coded "1" if married, "0" if other (not used; widowed; divorced; separated; never married).
English proficiency	Dummy variable among English speakers, coded "1" for those who speak English "well" or "very well," "0" for those who speak English "not well or not at all."
Ethnic Concentration	
% group in tract	The percentage of a given ethnic group in a tract, collapsed and attached to each individual respondent of that same group and tract.
% group in county	The percentage of a given ethnic group in a county, collapsed and attached to each individual respondent of that same group and county.
Available Co-ethnics	
% group not working in county	The percentage of a given ethnic group who are not working in a county, collapsed and attached to each individual respondent of that same group and county
% recent immigrant group not working in county	The percentage of recent, not-working immigrants in a county, collapsed and attached to each individual respondent of that same ethnic group and county.

Human capital variables include age and education. Age is a continuous variable that ranges from eighteen to sixty-five years old. Education is defined as a series of five dummy variables for the categories: less than high school, some high school, high school graduate, bachelor's degree, and professional/graduate degree.

Socioeconomic attainment includes "class resources" such as wealth and private property that may contribute to ethnic entrepreneurship (Light and

Bonacich 1988). *Socioeconomic attainment* is measured with two variables: household property value and total personal income. Household property value is measured with three dummy variables: low (reference group), medium, and high ($0–69,999, $70,000–174,999, and $175,000 or more, respectively). The four categories of income include none (reference), low, medium, and high ($1–24,999, $25,000–49,999, and $50,000 or more, respectively).

Ethnic and family resources include foreign-born status, marital status, and language proficiency (Light and Bonacich 1988; Sanders and Nee 1996; Waldinger et al. 1990). Married status is defined as married (coded as "1") and not married, including single, divorced, or widowed (coded as "0"). Foreign-born status is defined as foreign-born (coded as "1") and U.S.-born (coded as "0"). English proficiency is a dichotomous variable with speaks English well or very well (coded as "1") and speaks English not well or not at all (coded as "0").

I use four main contextual variables in this study. Two variables measure ethnic concentration. One is *percentage of ethnic group in tract*. It seeks to capture the presence of members of one's own ethnic group that facilitates personal interaction. *Percentage of ethnic group in a tract* is calculated at the tract level and appended to individual records. The second variable is *percentage of ethnic group in county* and is an indicator of presence of one's own ethnic group in the county that facilitates economic ties among group members. This is calculated at the county level and appended to individual records.

The other two county level variables are calculated to capture the availability of nonworking co-ethnics who may provide a source of low wage labor. One is *percentage of each group who are not working in a county* and is calculated for Whites and Blacks. The second is *percentage of recent immigrants who are not working* and is calculated for Koreans and Mexicans. For this variable, recent immigrants are those who have been in the U.S. ten years or less. Both variables are calculated at the county level and attached to each individual record in the sample.[3]

FINDINGS

Descriptive Statistics

Starting with the dependent variable, table 8.3 illustrates the striking difference in self-employment participation by ethnicity—Korean males are overwhelmingly more likely to be self-employed (29 percent) than any other group. Whites hold a distant second place to Koreans, as only 14 percent are self-employed, and Mexicans and Blacks lag far behind, (6 percent and 5 percent, respectively).

**Table 8.3. Characteristics of Working-Age Males
for Selected Ethnic Groups in California**

	White	Korean	Mexican	Black
% Self-employment	14.0%	28.7%	5.8%	4.8%
Human Capital:				
Age	39.1	37.0	33.7	36.2
Education:				
% less than high school	1.8	3.2	31.0	3.8
% some high school	9.3	7.1	24.2	17.8
% high school diploma	22.0	19.1	19.7	28.3
% BA or AA degree	55.2	57.9	22.8	45.8
% graduate or professional	11.8	12.9	2.2	4.4
Socioeconomic Attainment:				
Household Property Value:				
Rent or less than $69,999	41.0	53.2	61.2	61.4
$70,000–174,999	19.6	6.5	20.0	23.5
$175,000–500,000+	39.4	40.3	18.7	15.1
Total Personal Income:				
No income or lost income	3.6	15.4	10.0	12.8
$1–24,999	39.1	46.4	65.9	54.7
$25,000–49,999	46.5	30.9	22.6	30.4
$50,000+	10.9	7.4	1.5	2.2
Ethnic and Family Resources:				
% Foreign-Born	6.4	94.1	56.3	5.0
% Married	58.3	66.3	53.6	42.0
% Speak English "Well" or "Very Well"	99.3	72.4	69.1	99.0
Ethnic Concentration:				
Mean % Group in Tract	70.2	6.03	19.4	26.3
Mean % Group in County	58.4	1.3	10.9	8.4
Available Coethnics:				
Mean % Recent Immigrants Not Working in County	8.4	5.8	13.5	11.6
Mean % Group Not Working in County	5.1	4.8	10.5	12.6
Sample Size N (unweighted)	70,231	9,907	107,267	70,298

Note: One-in-six long-form sample of the 1990 Census, U.S. Census Bureau.

Human capital variables are included in table 8.3. The average age for White males in this sample is thirty-nine years old, the oldest group in the sample. Mexicans are the youngest group, who are on average, thirty-four years old. Koreans and Blacks fall in the middle, with an average age of thirty-seven and thirty-six, respectively. There are group differences in education. Fully 13 percent of Koreans have a graduate or professional degree and 58 percent have a college degree. Whites follow closely behind, with 12 percent and 55 percent, respectively. In contrast, Blacks and Mexicans trail behind in terms of education—only 4 percent of Blacks and a mere 2 percent of Mexican males hold a professional or graduate degree. And Blacks (46 percent) and Mexicans (23 percent) are also much less likely to hold a college degree than their White and Korean counterparts. Finally, many more Mexican males, 31 percent, have less than a high school education, compared with only 3 percent of Koreans, 4 percent of Blacks, and only 2 percent of Whites performing as poorly.

Table 8.3 reveals that there are large differences in socioeconomic attainment across the four groups, as measured by household property value and total personal income. Mexicans and Blacks are more likely than Whites or Koreans to rent or to own a home with a low property value (around 60 percent for each group), while 40 percent of Whites and Koreans fall into the highest property value range (followed by 20 percent of Mexicans and 15 percent of Blacks).

Whites have higher total personal income than the other groups. While 11 percent of Whites earn high total personal income, 7 percent of Koreans and less than 3 percent of Blacks and Mexicans fall in this category. Whites outnumber the other groups in the medium income range (47 percent), compared to 30 percent of Koreans and Mexicans, and only 23 percent of Blacks. Following this trend, Whites are less likely to face no income or lost income (4 percent) compared to 15 percent of Koreans and around 10 percent of Mexicans and Blacks.

Ethnic and family resources are the next set of variables in table 8.3. In this sample, just over half of all Mexican males are foreign-born, while only 6 percent of Whites and 5 percent of Blacks are foreign-born. Koreans are overwhelmingly more likely to be foreign-born (94 percent), and since it is well known that the foreign-born are more likely to be self-employed than the U.S.-born (Light 1972; Waldinger et al. 1990), the self-employment participation rate among this group is at least partially related to foreign-born status. Koreans are also more likely to be married (66 percent), while Blacks are the least likely of the groups to be married (42 percent). Whites and Mexicans fall in between, with 58 percent and 54 percent married, respectively. Since White and Black males in the sample are mostly U.S.-born, it is not surprising that these groups are also more likely to speak English well or very well. Given that Korean and Mexican males are more likely to be foreign-born, Korean and Mexican males speak English well or very well to a lesser degree (72 percent and 69 percent, respectively).

Table 8.3 shows mean percentages of the ethnic concentration of each group in a tract. The mean results reveal group differences in ethnic concentration at the tract level. The highest mean percentage of 70 percent occurs for Whites, compared to 26 percent for Blacks, 19 percent for Mexicans, and 6 percent for Koreans. The mean percentage varies dramatically among these groups—however, it is higher than the mean percentage of each group in a county. The higher concentration in the average tract supports the use of the tract to indicate the greater availability of co-ethnics in the local community from which to develop ethnic solidarity. Groups differ in their mean percentage for each group in a county. The higher the mean percentages for each group in a county, the greater the potential for ethnic supply and demand concerns in the market. Whites have the highest mean percentage in a county (58 percent), compared to Mexicans (11 percent), Blacks (8 percent), and Koreans (1 percent).

Two variables indicate the possible supply of co-ethnic, low wage labor. The first variable is the mean percentage of recent immigrants who are not working in a county. Mexicans have the highest mean percentage of recent immigrants who are not working in a county (14 percent). The lower mean percentage occurs for Koreans (6 percent). Whites and Blacks fall in the middle, 8 percent for Whites and 12 percent for Blacks. The second variable is the mean percentage of the group who are not working in a county. The highest mean percentage in this category is Blacks (12.6 percent) followed by Mexicans (10.5 percent) and Whites (5.1 percent). Koreans rank the lowest, with a mean percentage of 4.8 percent.

Multivariate Analysis Results

I examine how ethnic concentration affects ethnic entrepreneurship among Whites, Koreans, Mexicans, and Blacks, separately. Preliminary models added each set of control variables separately—human capital, socioeconomic attainment, and ethnic and family resources—to the independent variables in the final model (controls plus ethnic concentration). In this chapter, however, only the final model is presented. It would have been ideal to present, in addition to the full models, the separate sets of "control" variables but the disclosure process of the Bureau of the Census and IRS did not allow for this. Given the dichotomous nature of the dependent variable, logistic regression is used. The logistic regression model explains the effects of explanatory

Table 8.4. Ethnic Concentration on Self-Employment Participation among White, Korean, Mexican, and Black Males in California

	White		Korean		Mexican		Black	
Human Capital:								
Age	.025***	1.03	.030***	1.03	.027***	1.03	.034***	1.03
	(.001)		(.003)		(.001)		(.002)	
Education:								
Some high school	.127	1.14	-.028	.970	-.027	.970	.046	1.05
	(.097)		(.173)		(.041)		(.098)	
Diploma	.228*	1.26	.174	1.19	.042	1.04	-.058	.944
	(.092)		(.145)		(.045)		(.098)	
Bachelor's	.325***	1.38	.303*	1.35	.082*	1.09	.259***	1.30
	(.090)		(.139)		(.044)		(.094)	
Prof./Grad.	.477***	1.61	-.201	.820	.312***	1.37	.714***	2.04
	(.094)		(.152)		(.075)		(.109)	
Socioeconomic Attainment:								
Household property:								
$70,000–174,999	.040	1.04	.071	1.07	.178***	1.19	.006	1.01
	(.035)		(.105)		(.036)		(.048)	
$175,000–500,000+	.381***	1.46	.425***	1.53	.479***	1.61	.358***	1.43
	(.029)		(.055)		(.036)		(.050)	
Total personal income:								
$1–24,999	-.036	.960	.905***	2.47	.089	1.09	-.054	.950
	(.067)		(.102)		(.054)		(.063)	
$25,000–49,999	-.397***	.670	1.146***	3.15	.005	1.01	-.445***	.640
	(.068)		(.106)		(.061)		(.072)	
$50,000+	.568***	1.76	2.047***	7.74	1.634***	5.13	1.234***	3.43
	(.072)		(.130)		(.080)		(.092)	
Ethnic/Family Resources:								
Married	.251***	1.29	1.065***	2.90	.230***	1.26	.225***	1.25
	(.027)		(.079)		(.032)		(.041)	
Foreign-born	.457***	1.58	1.106***	3.02	.279***	1.32	.439***	1.55
	(.041)		(.166)		(.034)		(.074)	
Speaks English "well" or "very well"	.357*	1.43	-.183**	.830	.291***	1.34	-.027	.970
	(.149)		(.058)		(.038)		(.178)	

Table 8.4. *(Continued)*

	White		Korean		Mexican		Black	
Ethnic Concentration:								
% group in a tract	.007*** (.001)	1.01	-.001 (.003)	1.00	-.011*** (.001)	.990	-.001 (.001)	1.00
% group in a county	.001 (.001)	1.00	.176** (.063)	1.19	.008* (.003)	1.01	.016*** (.006)	1.02
Available Co-ethnics:								
% not working in a county	.079*** (.010)	1.08	—		—		-.001 (.006)	1.00
% recent immigrants not working in a county	—		.014 (.013)	1.01	-.005 (.003)	.990	—	
Constant:	-4.774***	(.194)	-5.508***	(.278)	-4.385***	(.092)	-4.887***	(.223)
N (unweighted)	70,231		9,907		107,267		70,298	

One-in-six long-form sample of the 1990 census, U.S. Census Bureau. Numbers in parentheses are standard errors. Two-tailed tests, *p<.05, **p<.01, ***p<.001.

variables on a dichotomous response variable. The interpretation of the odds ratio[4] is the probability of being self-employed versus the probability of not being self-employed, net of the control variables.

Whites

Table 8.4, first column, presents the odds ratios of the logistic regression for Whites. The first set of variables represents the positive effects of human capital on entrepreneurship. For each additional year of age, the odds of being self-employed increase by 3 percent (odds ratio = 1.03). With respect to education, the odds of being self-employed steadily increase for Whites with a diploma or higher, compared to Whites with some high school or less; the odds of being self-employed for Whites with a professional or graduate degree are over one and a half times greater (odds ratio = 1.61).

Socioeconomic attainment is generally associated with positive self-employment. Whites with a medium household property value are not markedly different from Whites with a low household property value

($69,999 or less); however, Whites with a high household value increase the odds of being self-employed by almost 50 percent (odds ratio = 1.46). Interestingly, total personal income reveals a curvilinear trend—low income and high income earning Whites are associated with self-employment participation at a significantly higher rate than their intermediate-level counterparts. The odds of being self-employed are negatively associated with medium-income earning Whites, while Whites with a high income ($50,000 or more) are associated with almost double the odds being self-employed, compared to their lower income counterparts.

Turning to the effects of ethnic solidarity, the odds of White self-employment increase if the respondent is married or foreign-born. The odds of being self-employed among married White males increase 30 percent (odds ratio = 1.29), compared to unmarried Whites. And among the foreign-born, the odds increase to over 50 percent, compared to U.S.-born Whites (odds ratio = 1.58). And while English proficiency may indicate a human capital resource rather than ethnic solidarity, English proficiency increases the odds of being self-employed by 40 percent.

The final set of variables in table 8.4 includes two measures of White concentration. First, as the percentage of Whites increases in a tract the odds of being self-employed increase by 1 percent. In contrast, White self-employment is not markedly different as the percentage of Whites increases in the county. Yet, with respect to an increase in the available coethnic labor pool, Whites are more likely to engage in entrepreneurship (odds ratio = 1.08).

Overall, self-employment among Whites increases with an increase in human capital attainment. The mixed result for socioeconomic attainment reveals a curvilinear relationship in total personal income, indicating that Whites may participate in "survival" and "elite" self-employment. And with respect to White concentration at the tract and county level, I find that Whites are more likely to participate in entrepreneurship when they live among more Whites in a tract. At the county level, however, increasing White concentration does not increase self-employment participation, with one exception: as the concentration of non-working Whites increases in a county, entrepreneurial participation increases.

Koreans

The first set of variables in table 8.4, second column, shows the effects of human capital on Korean entrepreneurial participation. While each additional year of age increases the odds of self-employment by 3 percent, education does not generally increase Korean self-employment. College-educated Koreans, however, increase their odds of being self-employed by 35 percent (odds ratio = 1.35), compared to those with less than a high school education.

Socioeconomic attainment is positively associated with Korean self-employment. While Koreans with a medium household property value ($70,000–174,999) are not markedly different from the reference group ($69,999 or less), the odds of being self-employed are 50 percent higher for Koreans with a high household property value (odds ratio = 1.53). And total personal income is dramatically associated with self-employment. The odds of being self-employed for Koreans with a low total personal income are two and a half times greater than those with no income (odds ratio = 2.47), Koreans with medium income are three times greater, and the odds for those who make $50,000 or more are almost eight times greater.

Ethnic solidarity is beneficial to Korean self-employment. The odds of being self-employed are three times greater for married Koreans (odds ratio = 2.90) or Koreans who are foreign-born (odds ratio = 3.02). Being English proficient decreases the odds of being self-employed by a factor of .83, holding all other variables constant.

With respect to ethnic concentration, the results vary. Being self-employed is not markedly different as Korean concentration increases in a tract. However, as Korean concentration increases by 1 percent in a county, the odds of self-employment increase by almost 20 percent (odds ratio = 1.19).

In sum, human capital variables do not generally increase Korean self-employment participation, with the exception of age and holding a bachelor's degree. Socioeconomic attainment, especially total personal income, is strongly associated with self-employment among this group. Ethnic solidarity also increases the odds of self-employment. Finally, increasing ethnic concentration in a tract does not contribute to Korean entrepreneurship, yet the presence of Koreans at the county level does—suggesting that self-employment is related to ethnic solidarity in large areas where the supply and demand needs of a large ethnic population are high.

Mexicans

The first set of variables in table 8.4, third column, shows that human capital increases the odds of being self-employed among Mexicans. While Mexicans with some high school or a diploma are not notably different from those with less education, Mexicans with a bachelor's degree improve their odds of self-employment by 10 percent (odds ratio = 1.09), and participation among graduate or professional degree holders increases by a third (odds ratio = 1.37), compared to their less educated counterparts.

Looking at socioeconomic attainment, a positive relationship is observed. Among Mexicans with a medium household property value ($70,000–174,999), the odds of being self-employed is associated with a 20 percent increase (odds ratio = 1.19), and Mexicans with a high household property value are associated with a 60 percent increase in their odds of being self-employed (odds ratio = 1.61), compared to those with a low property value. And the odds of being self-employed are five times greater for Mexicans with a high income than for those with no income.

In general, ethnic solidarity variables positively affect Mexican self-employment participation. The odds of being self-employed increase by 25 percent for Mexicans who are married, compared to their unmarried counterparts (odds ratio = 1.26). Similarly, foreign-born status increases self-employment participation by 1.32, compared to the U.S.-born. Yet, the odds of being self-employed also increase among Mexicans who are English-proficient, compared to those who are not (odds ratio = 1.34).

Finally, the effects of ethnic concentration reveal that as the percentage of Mexicans increases at the tract level, the odds of being self-employed decrease by 1 percent (odds ratio = .99). On the other hand, Mexicans are positively affected by the presence of co-ethnics at the county level. For each 1 percent increase in Mexican concentration in the county, self-employment participation also increases by 1 percent. Findings suggest that ethnic concentration at the level of local community (tract) and market (county) differentially affect entrepreneurial participation.

To recap, human capital and socioeconomic attainment are positively associated with Mexican self-employment, as is ethnic solidarity. The negative effect at the tract level, however, suggests that the odds of being self-employed decrease at the level of the community. On the other hand, as Mexican concentration increases at the county level, self-employment increases. Mixed findings suggest that ethnic agglomeration does not facilitate self-employment outcomes; however, ethnic solidarity does.

Blacks

The first set of variables in table 8.4, fourth column, considers the effect of human capital on Black entrepreneurial participation. For every year of age, the odds of being self-employed increase by 3 percent. And educational attainment increases the odds of self-employment. The odds of being self-employed is improved by a factor of .30 among Blacks with a bachelor's degree, and is doubled among Blacks with a professional degree (odds ratio = 2.04), compared to those with less than a high school education.

There is a positive association between socioeconomic attainment and Black self-employment. As household property value increases ($175,000 or greater), the odds of being self-employed increase by 43 percent, compared to those with low or no property value (odds ratio = 1.43). The relationship between self-employment and income, however, is not consistent. Among medium-income Blacks ($25,000–49,999), the odds of being self-employed are associated with a decrease of 36 percent (odds ratio = .64). Yet, as income increases ($50,000 or more), the odds of being self-employed are over three times greater (odds ratio = 3.43).

Ethnic solidarity variables generally result in increased self-employment participation among Blacks. The odds of self-employment increase by 25 percent among married Blacks, compared to unmarried Blacks. Similarly, the odds increase among foreign-born Blacks (odds ratio = 1.55). Finally, English proficiency (which better indicates human capital for this majority U.S.-born group) is not a significant predictor of self-employment.

Ethnic concentration affects Black self-employment differently. While Black self-employment participation does not increase at the tract level, self-employment participation is positively affected by increasing concentration at the county level. That is, as Black concentration increases by 1 percent in a county, the odds of self-employment increase by 2 percent.

While human capital and ethnic solidarity generally increase Black self-employment participation, the nonlinear relationship between socioeconomic attainment and self-employment participation suggests that Black entrepreneurs engage in "survival" and "elite" self-employment. Moreover, and with respect to ethnic concentration, the odds of self-employment participation increase at the county level, underscoring the importance of ethnic solidarity and strength of market forces on Black enterprise.

DISCUSSION

I investigate the effects of two measures of ethnic concentration on entrepreneurship to determine the strength of the ethnic enclave and ethnic economy approaches. I use ethnic concentration at the tract level to represent the possibility of close-knit ties and ethnic solidarity characteristic of the ethnic enclave, and ethnic concentration at the county level to represent the possibility of impersonal, market-based supply and demand features of the ethnic economy. Further, I include human capital, socioeconomic attainment, and ethnic and family resources as control variables, since previous literature indicates their importance on ethnic entrepreneurship. I briefly discuss the effect of the control variables on entrepreneurship, before turning to the concentration effects.

Previous research suggests that human capital contributes to self-employment participation, and that differential attainment partially explains intergroup variation (Archer 1991; Bailey and Waldinger 1991; Bates 1994; Light et al. 1994; Min 1988; Nee et al. 1994; Sanders and Nee 1987, 1996). Sanders and Nee (1996) show that self-employment participation among some groups, such as Mexicans, is hindered by limited human capital while groups with above-average human capital, such as Koreans, increase their likelihood of self-employment (Sanders and Nee 1996: 246). Results presented here are consistent with these findings, since I show that Koreans and Whites have on average more human capital, and are also more likely to be self-employed than their Mexican and Black counterparts (table 8.3). I also find differences in the effects of human capital by ethnicity. Specifically, Whites with a high school diploma significantly increase self-employment participation compared to their less-educated counterparts, while ethnic minorities require a college education. This may reflect Whites' attempt to increase earnings through entrepreneurial activity, given the value of their human capital in the open labor market—a strategy employed by ethnic entrepreneurs whose earnings are not commensurate with human capital (Bates 1994; Kim, Hurh, and Fernandez 1989; Sanders and Nee 1996). Further, I find that professional Koreans significantly decrease self-employment participation compared to college-educated Koreans, suggesting that highly educated Koreans may prefer employment in the labor market, similar to Asian Indians and Filipinos (Sanders and Nee 1996). Overall, findings are consistent with previous literature on the effects of human capital.

Research also indicates that socioeconomic attainment (or class background) increases self-employment, usually measured by education, income, and/or property (Bates 1994; Bates and Dunham 1993; Light and Bonacich 1988; Logan et al. 1994; Portes and Zhou 1992; Waters and Eschbach 1995; Wilson 1987; Zhou 1992). Using education as a proxy for class, Light and Roach (1996) find White and Korean self-employment to surpass rates of Mexicans or Blacks. Bates and Dunham (1993) report that Asian self-employment increases significantly among those with a household property value of over $100,000, compared to Asians with lower property values. Similarly, I find that Whites and Koreans, on average, surpass the educational and socioeconomic attainment (property and income) of Mexicans and Blacks, and are also more likely to be self-employed (table 8.3).

Moreover, a linear relationship is often described between class background and entrepreneurial outcomes (Bailey and Waldinger 1991; Light 1972; Light and Bonacich 1988; Portes and Zhou 1992; Sanders and Nee 1987, 1996; Waldinger et al. 1990; Zhou 1992). Likewise, I find that high socioeconomic attainment increases White and especially Korean entrepreneurship, while low socioeconomic attainment partially explains low rates among Mexicans and Blacks. I also, however, observe a curvilinear relationship between total personal income and self-employment among Whites and Blacks. That is, low income and high income Whites and Blacks are more likely to engage in self-employment compared to those with medium income. Light and Roach (1996) find that self-employment among Whites is used as a "means of economic self-defense," and I provide evidence for this argument here; that is, that Whites and Blacks may engage in "survival" self-employment. The presence of low-income White and Black business owners engaging in self-employment suggests that the relationship between entrepreneurial activity and socioeconomic attainment or class may not always be linear.

Finally, it is widely held that ethnic and family resources, sometimes called social capital, contribute to ethnic entrepreneurship by providing economic and noneconomic support (Archer 1991; Bailey and Waldinger 1991; Bates 1994; Borjas 1986, 1991; Light 1972; Light and Bonacich 1988; Portes and Bach 1985; Portes and Sensenbrenner 1993; Portes and Zhou 1992; Sanders and Nee 1996; Waldinger et al. 1990). For example, Sanders and Nee (1996) find that married status increases Korean and Mexican entrepreneurial participation, especially among Koreans and foreign-born entrepreneurs have been shown to surpass U.S.-born rates of self-employment (Fairlie and Meyer 1996; Light 1972; Waldinger et al. 1990). Similarly, I find being married increases entrepreneurial participation among Koreans, Mexicans, and Whites (table 8.3), and the foreign-born (especially Koreans) are more likely to engage in self-employment (table 8.3). I also show that English facilitates Mexican and White self-employment participation, but decreases Korean enterprise (table 8.4). This is also consistent with previous studies that suggest Mexican entrepreneurs are more likely to work in the mainstream economy, where English proficiency is valued (Light and Bonacich 1988; Portes and Bach 1985). In contrast, Korean entrepreneurship is characterized within a close-knit, ethnic community, where English language proficiency is not necessary (Light and Bonacich 1988; Portes and Rumbaut 1990; Zhou and Logan 1989). However, it is also possible that English-proficient Koreans are better prepared to enter the mainstream labor market.

ETHNIC CONCENTRATION

The ethnic enclave perspective argues that ethnic solidarity and a strong ethnic community in areas of high ethnic concentration (in work, residence, or industry) facilitate entrepreneurship, especially among "entrepreneurially oriented" ethnic groups (Light 1972; Light and Bonacich 1988; Logan et al. 1994; Logan and Zhou 1996; Portes and Rumbaut 1990; Sanders and Nee 1996; Waldinger et al. 1990). In contrast, the ethnic economy approach recognizes that an increase in ethnic density will increase ethnic supply and demand in the market economy, thereby creating unique and competitive entrepreneurial opportunities for co-ethnics (Light et al. 1994; Logan et al. 1994). I seek to distinguish the separate contributions of the ethnic community and the supply and demand concerns of a large ethnic population on self-employment participation.

In contrast to the ethnic enclave hypothesis, I find that ethnic concentration at the tract level, which I use to measure the possibility of close-knit community ties and ethnic solidarity, does not facilitate entrepreneurship among ethnic minorities (Koreans, Mexicans, and Blacks). In other words, findings are suggestive that a close-knit ethnic community may not facilitate ethnic entrepreneurship after all. My findings hold even among the "entrepreneurial" Koreans, characterized by a strong ethnic community and solidarity, especially within the ethnic enclave of Koreatown (Light and Bonacich 1988; Yoon 1991; Zhou 1992).

Previous studies show the presence of the Korean enclave, and the increased self-employment participation and income returns within it (Logan et al. 1994; Sanders and Nee 1987; Zhou and Logan 1989). However, these studies have used the county or metropolitan area to proxy the enclave (Logan et al. 1994; Sanders and Nee 1987; Zhou and Logan 1989). While the county or metropolitan area may accurately indicate the presence of an ethnic enclave or a concentration of ethnic entrepreneurship, I argue that the geographic area of county or metropolitan area is too large to capture the presence of close-knit community ties and personal interactions. Using tract level data, I can provide a more accurate measure of the presence of close-knit community ties and face-to-face interactions, the crucial feature scholars claim is fundamental to ethnic entrepreneurial success in the enclave. When the presence of ethnic community ties and solidarity is measured in this way, ethnic minorities are not more likely to engage in self-employment. Thus, my analysis provides evidence against the centrality of ethnic solidarity.

Surprisingly, there is a significant and positive effect of tract level concentration on White entrepreneurship. This finding suggests that Whites within their own communities increase their entrepreneurial opportunities. It is important to note that Whites, arguably the dominant cultural group in the U.S. (Lieberson 1963), incorporate into the economy differently than disadvantaged minorities, and may therefore require a different interpretation. The ethnic enclave hypothesis has not been used to explain White entrepreneurship, most probably because Whites are not considered ethnic minorities or disadvantaged in the labor market. That is, since the general labor market is available to Whites, they would not require an enclave or protected ethnic market from which to work (Aldrich and Waldinger 1990). Aldrich and Waldinger (1990) argue that entrepreneurship among White European immigrants and their descendants is on the decline, and ethnic minorities are replacing the previously White-owned businesses. However, in areas of high White concentration, the increase in White-owned business suggests that residential segregation may play a role in impeding entrepreneurial succession. Further, since ethnic minority entrepreneurs often rely on their group for competitive access to ethnic markets or ethnic labor (Aldrich and Waldinger 1990; Logan et al. 1994; Waldinger et al. 1990), establishing a business in a majority White community may limit such contributions.

I now turn to the analysis of ethnic concentration at the county level, which I argue measures the market-based concerns of a large ethnic population, such as the demand for ethnic goods and services, characteristic of the ethnic economy. As Light and his colleagues argue, the ethnic economy is "ethnic" simply because the business owner and employees (if any) are co-ethnics (Light et al. 1994). Furthermore, the ethnic economy is characterized by ethnic entrepreneurship that arises from a high concentration of co-ethnics in a population, since it increases impersonal contacts between co-ethnics, the supply of co-ethnic labor, and the demand for ethnic goods and services (Light et al. 1994; Logan et al. 1994).

My findings reveal that ethnic concentration at the county level increases the likelihood of self-employment participation among all ethnic minority groups (Koreans, Mexicans, and Blacks), but does not increase White self-employment. Evidence provides some support for the ethnic economy perspective: that a high concentration of co-ethnics at the county level increases the supply and demand needs of an ethnic population, thereby increasing ethnic entrepreneurship (Light et al. 1994; Logan et al. 1994). This phenomenon occurs not just among Koreans, but all ethnic minority groups in this sample. Hence, the evidence supports the ethnic economy perspective.

The ethnic concentration effects for Mexicans are especially illustrative. At the level of the tract, Mexican self-employment participation decreases. However, at the county level, Mexican self-employment increases. Previous research suggests that Mexicans do not have a close-knit community that supports entrepreneurship (Portes and Bach 1985). Since findings at the tract level are consistent with this claim, they seem to support the ethnic enclave hypothesis that the lack of an ethnic community leads to a decrease in Mexican entrepreneurship. However, the significant and positive effect of ethnic concentration at the county level qualifies such an interpretation. The reversal from negative effects at the tract level and positive effects at the county level for Mexicans suggests that ethnic solidarity may not be related to entrepreneurship at all, since Mexican self-employment increases in the county, regardless of the strength of the local community. The Mexican case provides strong support for the ethnic economy approach, since Mexican self-employment participation is contingent on ethnic density and consequent ethnic supply and demand concerns in the market economy.

Finally, and in contrast to the ethnic minorities considered here, White concentration in a county results in a decrease in self-employment participation. This finding suggests that the opportunity structure in the larger, general economy may be different for Whites, compared to that of the smaller White community. First, Whites are more likely to be U.S.-born and acquire U.S.-earned human capital. Since the general labor market favors U.S.-earned human capital (Bates 1994; Sanders and Nee 1996), would-be White entrepreneurs may elect to enter the general economy than the ethnic minorities. As Bates (Bates 1994) suggests, "highly capable owners . . . may exit self-employment when better opportunities arise. Second, as Light (1972), Light and Bonacich (1988), and Waldinger and colleagues (1990) have noted, immigrants are more likely to engage in self-employment than the U.S.-born. Since the majority of Koreans and Mexicans are foreign-born, and the population in a county is much more diverse than that found at the tract level, foreign-born groups may be more likely to engage in entrepreneurship than Whites within the same geographic area. Third, some scholars (Bonacich and Modell 1980; Waldinger 1993) acknowledge that ethnic entrepreneurs may work as "middleman minorities" (Bonacich and Modell 1980; Light and Bonacich 1988: 17) or in "economies of scale" (Aldrich and Waldinger 1990: 117), clustering in small business ventures of low capital and appeal, supplying goods and services to ethnic minorities in less desirable locations such as an impoverished ethnic community. Whites may "opt-out" of these less desirable self-employment opportunities, leaving ethnic minorities to fill the void (Aldrich and Waldinger 1990).

In sum, evidence provided in this study supports the ethnic economy perspective: that a high concentration of co-ethnics at the county level increases the supply and demand needs of an ethnic population, thereby increasing ethnic entrepreneurship. Support is not lent to the ethnic enclave hypothesis, since I find that ethnic concentration at the tract level, which represents the close-knit ethnic community, does not contribute to ethnic entrepreneurship. Hence, this study confirms that the ethnic economy approach may provide a more accurate conceptual interpretation of the contributions and generalizability of ethnic concentration and its relationship to ethnic entrepreneurship.

CONCLUSION

The ethnic enclave hypothesis suggests that ethnic concentration within an ethnic community encourages the development of close-knit ties and ethnic solidarity, "reciprocal obligations" between co-ethnic members (Wilson and Portes 1980). Ethnic solidarity in turn, facilitates ethnic entrepreneurship (Logan et al. 1994; Logan and Zhou 1996; Portes and Bach 1985; Portes and Zhou 1992; Wilson and Portes 1980; Zhou 1992). The presence of the ethnic enclave is used to explain the above-average rates of Korean and Cuban ethnic entrepreneurs, and the lack of entrepreneurship among Mexicans and Blacks (Portes and Bach 1985; Light and Bonacich 1988). Fundamentally, this argument suggests that Mexican and Black communities lack close-knit and personal ties between co-ethnic members that would encourage and facilitate entrepreneurship.

In a surprising twist and counter to the vast literature on the ethnic enclave (Logan et al. 1994; Logan and Zhou 1996; Portes and Bach 1985; Portes and Zhou 1992; Wilson and Portes 1980; Zhou 1992), I show that the ethnic community does not appear to contribute to entrepreneurial participation among ethnic minorities. Findings question previous literature that emphasizes the role of the ethnic community in facilitating entrepreneurship (Nee and Ingram 1998).

The ethnic economy perspective recognizes the utility of ethnic concentration, however, suggests that increasing ethnic density in the economy may promote ethnic entrepreneurship. In this conception, ethnic solidarity is not a central feature or even necessary for ethnic entrepreneurship to arise (Light et al. 1994). This approach allows for a more market-based account of entrepreneurship, and may provide an explanation for the marginal rates of entrepreneurship among Mexicans and Blacks, without the suggestion that their communities are lacking or somehow deficient (Light 1972; Light et al. 1994; Portes and Bach 1985; Wilson 1987). Findings indicate that market forces, such as the supply and demand for goods, services, and labor, encourage ethnic entrepreneurship as ethnic density increases in a population. These market exchange concerns are not without an ethnic component—ethnic membership may provide a competitive edge to particular impersonal, economic contacts between co-ethnics (Aldrich and Waldinger 1990; Logan et al. 1994; Waldinger et al. 1990). However, the "cultural ambience" (Light and Bonacich 1988) associated with the ethnic enclave is absent in the ethnic economy.

Further, one provocative finding suggests that the only group that appears to benefit from a close-knit community is Whites. However, this effect may have more to do with structural effects, such as the exclusivity of the area, and hindrances to ethnic minority business development in the area, than ethnic solidarity, per se. In other words, ethnic solidarity arguments put forth by proponents of the ethnic enclave hypothesis do not explain the effects of White segregation on White business ownership. Findings require further study on the opportunity structure of segregated communities.

The ethnic economy perspective finds support in this analysis. Findings reveal that entrepreneurial participation increases across all three ethnic minorities. Interestingly, while Mexican concentration at the community level decreases the likelihood of ethnic entrepreneurship, Mexican concentration at the level of the market facilitates entrepreneurship. This evidence suggests that ethnic solidarity within the community does not impact entrepreneurial outcomes. Rather, the importance of ethnicity lies in the market. Evidently, there are economic advantages to co-ethnic membership in the greater economy, and strategies which promote the use of these economic-ties and benefits are similar across ethnic groups.

NOTES

1. Nor is this research an attempt to construct the boundaries of the ethnic enclave, per se. I only attempt to investigate the effects of ethnic solidarity on entrepreneurial outcomes. It is interesting to note, however, that Zhou and Logan (1989) find negligible differences in entrepreneurial outcomes when the ethnic enclave is constructed by work site or residential site in a given metropolitan area.

2. Ethnicity is defined as a sense of shared history emerging from cultural, political, and economic differences between interacting sociocultural groups (Cohen 1978), yet the salience of ethnic group membership is not comparable across all individuals or groups. The ethnic entrepreneurship literature rarely includes Whites in its analyses, presumably since they cease to identify with their ancestral heritage (Lieberson 1980). Hence, Whites are important in the analysis as a "control" group, that is, a group that should show no effect of group concentration at the tract level. Further, for the purposes of this analysis, Blacks will be considered an ethnic group. While this group is often categorized as a racial group with a unique historical past, recent work on ethnic entrepreneurship includes this group as an "immigrant/ethnic" minority group, taking into account the migration and movement in large numbers, from the South to the North (Waldinger 1990).

3. While the analysis includes "clustering" of individual-level variables with group-level contextual variables, the large sample size ensures the maintenance of random effects and independence of the observations.

4. The odds ratio is expressed by raising e to the power of the logistic coefficient.

REFERENCES

Aldrich, Howard E., and Roger Waldinger. 1990. "Ethnicity and Entrepreneurship." *Annual Review of Sociology* 16: 111–35.

Archer, M. 1991. "Self-employment and Occupational Structure in an Industrializing City: Detroit 1880." *Social Science History* 15: 67–95.

Bailey, Thomas, and Roger Waldinger. 1991. "Primary, Secondary, and Enclave Labor Markets: A Training Systems Approach." *American Sociological Review* 56: 432–45.

Bates, Timothy Mason. 1994. "Social Resources Generated by Group Support Networks May Not Be Beneficial to Asian Immigrant-Owned Small Businesses." *Social Forces* 72: 671–90.

Bates, Timothy Mason, and Constance Dunham. 1993. "Asian American Success in Self Employment." *Economic Development Quarterly* 7: 199–214.

Bonacich, Edna, and John Modell. 1980. *The Economic Basis of Ethnic Solidarity: Small Business in the Japanese American Community.* Berkeley: University of California Press.

Borjas, George J. 1986. "The Self-Employment Experience of Immigrants." *Journal of Human Resources* 21: 485–506.

———. 1990. *Friends or Strangers: The Impact of Immigrants on the American Economy.* New York: Basic Books.

———. 1991. "Immigrants in the U.S. Labor Market: 1940–1980." *American Economic Review Papers and Proceedings* 81, no. 2: 287–91.

Cohen, Ronald. 1978. "Problem and Focus in Anthropology." *Annual Review of Anthropology* 7: 379–403.

Fairlie, Robert W., and Bruce D. Meyer. 1996. "Ethnic and Racial Self-Employment Differences and Possible Explanations." *Journal of Human Resources* 31: 757–91.

Kim, Kwang Chung, Woo Moo Hurh, and Marilyn Fernandez. 1989. "Intra-group Differences in Business Participation: Three Asian Immigrant Groups." *International Migration Review* 23: 73–95.

Lieberson, Stanley. 1963. *Ethnic Patterns in American Cities.* New York: Free Press.

———. 1980. *A Piece of the Pie: Black and White Immigrants Since 1880.* Berkeley: University of California Press.

Light, Ivan Hubert. 1972. *Ethnic Enterprise in America: Business and Welfare among Chinese, Japanese and Blacks.* Berkeley: University of California Press.

Light, Ivan, and Parminder Bhachu. 1993. *Immigration and Entrepreneurship: Culture, Capital, and Ethnic Networks.* New Brunswick, NJ: Transaction Publishers.

Light, Ivan, and Edna Bonacich. 1988. *Immigrant Entrepreneurs: Koreans in Los Angeles.* Los Angeles: University of California Press.

Light, Ivan, and Elizabeth Roach. 1996. "Self Employment: Mobility Ladder or Economic Lifeboat?" Pp. 193–214 in *Ethnic Los Angeles*, ed. Roger Waldinger and Mehdi Bozorgmehr. New York: Sage.

Light, Ivan, Georges Sabagh, Mehdi Bozorgmehr, and Claudia Der-Martirosian. 1994. "Beyond the Ethnic Enclave Economy." *Social Problems* 41: 65–80.

Logan, John R., Richard D. Alba, and Thomas McNulty. 1994. "Ethnic Economies in Metropolitan Regions: Miami and Beyond." *Social Forces* 72, no. 3: 691–724.

Min, Pyong Gap. 1987. "Factors Contributing to Ethnic Business: A Comprehensive Synthesis." *International Journal of Comparative Sociology* 28: 173–93.

———. 1988. "Ethnic Business Enterprise: Korean Small Business in Atlanta." Center for Migration Studies.

Nee, Victor, and Paul Ingram. 1998. Working paper presented at Comparative and Social Analysis Workshop, University of California, Los Angeles.

Nee, Victor, Jimmy Sanders, and Scott Sernau. 1994. "Job Transitions in an Immigrant Metropolis." *American Sociological Review* 59: 849–72.

Nee, Victor, and Jimmy Sanders. 1985. "The Road to Parity—Determinants of the Socioeconomic Achievements of Asian-Americans." *Ethnic and Racial Studies* 8: 75–93.

Portes, Alejandro. 1987. "The Social Origins of the Cuban Enclave Economy of Miami." *Sociological Perspectives* 30: 340–72.

Portes, Alejandro, and Robert Bach. 1985. *Latin Journey: Cuban and Mexican Immigrants in the United States*. Berkeley and Los Angeles: University of California
Press.

Portes, Alejandro, and Leif Jensen. 1989. "The Enclave and the Entrants: Patterns of
Ethnic Enterprise in Miami before and after Mariel." *American Sociological Review* 54: 929–49.

Portes, Alejandro, and Ruben G. Rumbaut. 1990. *Immigrant America: A Portrait*.
Berkeley and Los Angeles: University of California Press.

———. 2001. *Legacies: The Story of the Immigrant Second Generation*. Berkeley:
University of California Press.

Portes, Alejandro, and Alex Stepick. 1993. *City on the Edge: The Transformation of
Miami*. Berkeley: University of California Press.

Portes, Alejandro, and Julia Sensenbrenner. 1993. "Embeddedness and Immigration:
Notes on the Social Determinants of Economic Action." *American Journal of Sociology* 93: 1320–50.

Portes, Alejandro, and Min Zhou. 1992. "Gaining the Upper Hand: Economic Mobility among Domestic Minorities." *Ethnic and Racial Studies* 15: 491–522.

Sanders, Jimmy M., and Victor Nee. 1987. "Limits of Ethnic Solidarity in the Enclave
Economy." *American Sociological Review* 52: 745–73.

———. 1996. "Social Capital, Human Capital, and Immigrant Self-Employment: The
Family as Social Capital and the Value of Human Capital." *American Sociological
Review* 61: 231–49.

Waldinger, Roger. 1993. "The Ethnic Enclave Debate Revisited." *International Journal of Urban and Regional Research* 17: 444–53.

Waldinger, Roger, Howard Aldrich, Robin Ward and Associates. 1990. *Ethnic Entrepreneurs: Immigrant Business in Industrial Societies*. Newbury Park, CA: Sage.

Waters, Mary C., and Karl Eschbach. 1995. "Immigration and Ethnic and Racial Inequality in the United States." *Annual Review of Sociology* 21: 419–46.

Wilson, Kenneth, and W. A. Martin. 1982. "Ethnic Enclaves: A Comparison of Cuban
and Black Economies in Miami." *American Journal of Sociology* 88: 135–60.

Wilson, Kenneth L., and Alejandro Portes. 1980. "Immigrant Enclaves: An Analysis
of the Labor Market Experiences of Cubans in Miami." *American Journal of Sociology* 86, no. 2: 295–316.

Wilson, William J. 1980 [1978]. *The Declining Significance of Race: Blacks and
Changing American Institutions*. Chicago: University of Chicago Press.

———. 1987. *The Truly Disadvantaged*. Chicago: University of Chicago Press.

Yoon, In-Jin. 1991. *Self-Employment in Business: Chinese-, Japanese-, Korean
Americans, Blacks, and Whites*. Chicago: University of Chicago Press.

Zhou, Min. 1992. *Chinatown: The Socioeconomic Potential of an Urban Enclave*.
Philadelphia: Temple University Press.

Zhou, Min, and John R. Logan. 1989. "Returns on Human Capital in Ethnic Enclaves:
New York City's Chinatown." *American Sociological Review* 54: 809–82.

9

Separately Together

Co-Ethnic Employment among Second-Generation Immigrants in the Metropolitan New York Labor Market

Aviva Zeltzer-Zubida

Both social science and everyday observation suggest that immigrants and their descendants are not randomly distributed across the labor market; rather, they tend to congregate in particular industries and occupations. According to the assimilationist perspective, immigrants' ethnic and racial concentration in the labor market is a newcomers' phenomenon. As time from arrival elapses, the importance of ethnic and (perhaps) racial differences will decrease, and immigrants and their descendants will scatter and disperse across the labor market (Lieberson and Waters 1988; Alba 1998; Perlmann and Waldinger 1999; Farley and Alba 2002). Conversely, some scholars have argued that race and ethnicity have long-term effects on opportunities for immigrants and their offspring, thereby suggesting that the role of race and ethnicity in organizing economic life is enduring. According to this perspective various forms of ethnic and racial concentration are central characteristics of the labor markets in gateway cities such as Miami, Los Angeles, and New York, and are not likely to disappear over time (Model 1993; Waldinger 1996; Waldinger and Bozorgmehr 1996; Light and Gold 2000). Whether permanent or temporary—the centrality of race and ethnicity as organizing principles of labor market trajectories of immigrants and their children, the mechanisms that shape labor market concentration, and the effect of such concentrations on the economic mobility and social incorporation of immigrants and their children—are subjects of much debate in the immigration literature.

These debates have produced a wealth of research on the immigrant generation. Although the second generation's trajectories into the labor market have been the subject of contradictory predictions, they have rarely been systematically addressed in the literature mainly due to the lack of appropriate data.[1] By utilizing data from the "Second-Generation in Metropolitan New York" project (Kasinitz, Waters, and Mollenkopf 2002),[2] and the Census Bureau's Current Population Survey, this study examines patterns of ethnic and racial concentration in the local labor market, and the factors that influence and shape these patterns among five second-generation immigrant groups and three native-born groups of eighteen- to thirty-two-year-old New Yorkers.[3] By using a direct measure of co-ethnicity in the workplace and shifting the focus from assessing the economic consequences of labor market concentrations to examining the social processes that produce such concentrations, I investigate ethnic and racial concentration in the labor market to answer the following questions:

1. Are second-generation immigrants more likely to work in co-ethnic environments compared to the native-born groups?
2. Do patterns of co-ethnicity in the workplace vary across the different groups and across industries?
3. What factors shape and influence the likelihood of working with co-ethnics?

DESCRIBING AND MEASURING
IMMIGRANTS' LABOR MARKET CONCENTRATION

Three central concepts have been used in the literature to describe immigrant concentration in the labor market: the ethnic enclave, the ethnic niche and the ethnic economy. The ethnic enclave describes a vibrant, spatially concentrated, ethnically owned business sector that relies on a sizeable ethnic entrepreneurial class, and includes commercial, professional, and productive activities directed toward the ethnic community and the general consumer market (Portes and Bach 1985; Portes and Zhou 1992). The ethnic niche represents an industry or occupation where members of an immigrant, ethnic, or racial minority group are overrepresented relative to their proportion in the population (Model 1993; Waldinger 1996). The ethnic economy is a broad concept which encompasses every enterprise that is owned, supervised, or staffed by an immigrant, ethnic or racial minority group, thus including all immigrant, ethnic, or racial groups' self-employed, employers, and co-ethnic employees (Light and Gold 2000).

In light of these theoretical formulations, most studies of immigrants' concentrations in the labor market use one of two research strategies: some analyze quantitative measures of self-employment and ethnic overrepresentation derived from U.S. census data (for example, Logan, Alba, and McNulty 1994;

Model 1997; Logan and Alba 1999; Wilson 1999; Light and Gold 2000); and others conduct qualitative studies of specific groups, communities, or work sites (for example, Portes and Bach 1985; Bailey and Waldinger 1991; Zhou 1992; Waldinger 1996; Kwong 1997; Waters 1999a). Quantitative studies provide a wealth of descriptive information about patterns and trends, but they are based on high levels of aggregation and abstraction and are detached from the actual experiences of individuals and groups in local labor markets. Moreover, such studies are based on two logical but usually untested assumptions: first, that self-employment or ethnic overrepresentation in a particular industry or sector implies that people actually work in co-ethnic settings; and second, that overrepresentation in an industry or sector implies the existence and utilization of immigrant/ethnic social networks. The qualitative studies provide details about individuals and groups' experiences, but they do not provide basis for generalization or comparison.

The data used in this chapter provide a direct and detailed measure of co-ethnicity in the workplace. The measure I use is based on this question: "What is the race or ethnicity of most of the employees doing the kind of work you do on your job?"[4] Such a measure enables us to improve our understanding of patterns of ethnic and racial concentration among the different groups and in the various industries in the local labor market.

EXPLAINING IMMIGRANTS' LABOR MARKET CONCENTRATION

The different forms of ethnic concentration in the labor market are assumed to be a strategy that immigrants adopt in order to cope with language and skill deficiencies and with discrimination (Model 1993, 1997; Lieberson 1981; Waldinger 1996). Lieberson (1981) notes that members of ethnic groups have often congregated in similar jobs through control of labor unions, information about openings, or other privileged participation in labor recruitment. He calls these concentrations "special niches." Model (1993) and Waldinger (1996) use a slightly different term—that of the ethnic niche—to describe one of the major processes/mechanisms by which immigrants are incorporated into the labor market.[5] Groups, according to this argument, are funneled into special places in the labor market and maintain those specializations over time, with varying rates of persistence. The creation of an immigrant niche, Waldinger (1996) argues, is a two-stage process. First comes a phase of specialization in which placements are affected by skill, linguistic factors, or predispositions. After the initial placement, occupational closure quickly sets in, where networks of information and support are bounded by ethnic ties.

Model (1993) argues that in some cases immigrant groups become associated with particular occupations or industries because many of their members arrive with previous experiences in fields for which there is a demand in the host country. In other cases a group embarks upon a new economic activity because of a lack of more attractive options. Sometimes a niche develops because of changes in legislation and hiring policy, as happened with the African American niche in public sector jobs (Light and Gold 2000; Waldinger 1996; Wilson 1987). Once such an association between ethnicity and employment is initiated, however, different mechanisms operate to sustain it. The simplest sustaining mechanism is the emergence of a widespread belief that members of a particular group are well suited for their niche and poorly suited for other alternatives. The other process sustaining ethnic concentrations is employers' preferences for new employees that are recommended by existing ones. Such network hiring entails low recruiting costs, faster training, and better control of workers' performance (Kasinitz and Rosenberg 1996; Waldinger and Lichter 2003).

THE SECOND GENERATION: FROM ETHNIC ECONOMIES TO LABOR MARKET SEGREGATION

If in fact ethnic and racial concentration in the labor market were only the result of skill and language deficiencies that characterize immigrants, then the second-generation as well as non-immigrant ethnic groups would be scattered and dispersed across the labor market. Waldinger (1996: 23), however, argues that the deficiencies are only one factor in the formation of ethnic concentrations, whereas "the continuing importance of ethnic networks shapes a group's employment distribution into the second, and later generations." It suggests, therefore, that the incorporation of the second generation into the labor market takes on a collective form. The second generation is already embedded in communities and networks of organizations and activities that shape their aspirations and create the networks of information. This social organization serves as a mechanism for channeling people into the labor market, and as with their parents, once a favorable niche is established informal recruitment patterns can quickly funnel new hires. As a result, he reports, some groups are more concentrated in the third and fourth generation than their ancestors were as immigrants, although in less stereotypically "immigrant jobs."

Furthermore, the sociological and economic scholarship provides ample evidence to argue that ethnic and racial segregation is not an immigrant-only phenomenon, but rather a major characteristic of the labor market itself. This literature offers four major explanations for segregation in the labor market that resonate with some of the accounts offered by immigration scholars (for reviews of this literature see Reskin and Padavic [1999]). The human capital/skills deficit approach suggest that labor market segmentation is the result of differences between groups in average levels of worker-level characteristics such as education, experience, and skills (Moss and Tilly 2001). The worker preference approach claims that social and cultural differences between groups will lead to different types of labor market position preferences, and thus to segregation by choice (England 1992; Marini and Fan 1997). A third approach stresses the importance of economic and organizational structures (such as firm size and structure, and economic sector) in constraining or facilitating segregation (Reskin 1993; Reskin and McBrier 2000). The final approach argues that processes of stereotyping and queuing segregate workers. Within this approach we find the statistical discrimination argument according to which employers use race, ethnicity, and sex as proxies for productivity, basing hiring decisions on these rather than on personal qualifications (Baron and Bielby 1985; Braddock and McPartland 1987; Reskin and Padavic 1999).

In the following sections I explore two contradictory predictions regarding the differences in the likelihood of working in a co-ethnic setting among second-generation immigrants and their native-born counterparts. The assimilationist logic renders that since concentration is a newcomers' phenomenon, co-ethnic employment patterns among the second generation should be similar to those among the non-immigrant population. On the other hand, some scholars raise concerns regarding the socioeconomic future of the second generation. They point out that many are racial minorities entering a predominantly white society; that some are concentrated in poor urban neighborhoods with troubled school systems; and that discriminatory attitudes and shifts in the structure of the economy may limit their opportunities for economic mobility (Gans 1992; Waters 1999a; Portes and Zhou 1992; Portes and Rumbaut 2001). Thus, according to this perspective, the role of race and ethnicity in determining labor market trajectories remains central for the second generation, leading them to be more concentrated in the labor market, and thus more likely to work in ethnically homogenous environments, compared to their non-immigrant counterparts.

I will explore these predictions by drawing on research on immigrants' economic incorporation and on labor market segregation, and by examining the effect of four factors on shaping the likelihood of working in a co-ethnic environment, namely: human capital characteristics, social networks, organizational characteristics, and labor market opportunity structure.

DATA AND MEASURES

The data for this chapter are derived from the second-generation project and from pooled Current Population Survey (CPS) data of the New York Consolidated Metropolitan Statistics Areas (NYCMSA) from 1998 to 2000. The Second-Generation Project includes two types of data: a telephone survey and in-depth, loosely structured in-person interviews with a 10 percent sub-sample of telephone survey respondents. The survey data include 3,424 interviews with men and women aged eighteen to thirty-two who lived in New York City (except Staten Island) or the inner suburban areas of Nassau and Westchester Counties and Northeastern New Jersey. The respondents represent eight ethno-racial groups: those whose parents were born in China (including Taiwan and Hong Kong), the Dominican Republic, the Anglophone West Indies (including Guyana and Belize), the South American countries of Colombia, Ecuador, and Peru (designated CEP in the remainder of this paper), and Jewish immigrants from the former Soviet Union. For comparison purposes, the data also include respondents whose parents were native-born whites, native-born blacks, and Puerto Ricans. The natives were all born in the U.S. as were their parents (though many Puerto Rican parents were born on the island). About two-thirds of the second-generation respondents were born in the U.S., mostly in New York City, while one-third were born abroad but arrived in the United States by age twelve and have lived there for at least ten years.

The data include information about respondents' family background, the neighborhoods in which they have lived, the schools which they have attended, the kinds of jobs they have held, their experiences with a wide range of official institutions and programs, the activities in which they have participated, the languages they speak, and how they feel about a wide range of issues. These data provide the best picture yet available on the life situations of a representative cross section of the major racial and ethnic groups in metropolitan New York (Kasinitz et al. 2002).

The CPS is a monthly survey of about 50,000 households conducted by the Bureau of the Census for the Bureau of Labor Statistics. It is the primary source of information on the labor force characteristics of the U.S. population. The sample is scientifically selected to represent the civilian non-institutional population. Respondents are interviewed to obtain information about the employment status of each member of the household fifteen years of age and older. Estimates obtained from the CPS include employment, unemployment, earnings, hours of work, and other indicators. They are available by a variety of demographic characteristics including age, sex, race, marital status, and educational attainment. They are also available by occupation, industry, and class of worker. Since the Second-Generation Project is geographically concentrated in the New York Metropolitan Area, I will use CPS data for New York Consolidated Metropolitan Statistical Areas (NYCMSA).

Dependent Variable: Co-ethnic Work Environment

The measure for co-ethnic work environment is based on the question: "What is the race or ethnicity of most of the employees doing the kind of work you do on your job?" If the respondent reports that most of his coworkers are of the same ethnic background, he/she is considered to be working in a co-ethnic environment.

Independent Variables

Job Matching

I use a distinction between formal and informal types of job matching to assess the importance of social networks in finding employment and their effect on the likelihood of working in co-ethnic settings. Information on type of job matching came from the following question: "How did you first hear about this job?" If the respondent said she heard about the job from a parent, sibling, spouse, other relative, friend, coworker or previous employer, the answer was coded as an informal job match. If the respondent heard about the job from a school placement office, a teacher, a guidance counselor, other school official, newspaper or other ad, labor union, state employment agency, private employment agency, America Works, Human Resources (HRA), Internet and the like, the answer was coded as a formal job match.

Ethnic Concentration/Overrepresentation

Because I wish to distinguish between ethnic concentration in an industry and a specific co-ethnic work environment, I include a variable that is based on a calculation of ethnic overrepresentation of the studied groups in the local labor market. Following Logan et al. (1994), I construct a variable of ethnic overrepresentation that is based on data from the CPS. For purposes of analysis I construct a dummy variable that is coded 1 if the respondent is working in an industry where his ethnic group is overrepresented and 0 otherwise.

Workplace Characteristics

I will use two organizational variables that are suggested to affect race and gender composition, *size* and *sector*. Since most studies suggest that the effect of size is nonlinear, I measure it as a set of dummy variables that includes small establishments of 50 or fewer workers, medium firms with 51 to 500 employees, and large organizations with more than 501 workers. Since the *public sector* could be seen as a niche for minority workers (especially African American), I include a dummy variable for public sector employment.

Human Capital Characteristics

Following prior research on ethnic concentration and labor market segregation I include a measure of *educational attainment*. It is operationalized as a set of dummy variables based on self-reported highest educational level attained by the respondent. A central human capital characteristic that is widely discussed in the literature is that of language. But since I am studying the second generation, I assume that language is not a relevant variable. Nevertheless, I do include a distinction between *foreign-born* (1.5ers) and *native-born* children (second-generation) of immigrants, following the argument made in the literature that as time since immigration elapses, immigrants are more likely to behave like natives. I also include dummy indicators for *gender* and *age* as control variables.

RESULTS

Descriptive Statistics

Table 9.1 provides information about the distribution of the second-generation groups and their native-born counterparts across the industries in the New York labor market (in black), about the percent of co-ethnic employment across the industries (in gray italics), and about ethnic overrepresentation across industries (represented by an asterisk). The data in table 9.1 suggest that the distribution of the groups across industries is fairly similar. For most groups the wholesale and retail industry, along with personal and professional services, are the most prevalent. These findings are not surprising given the age of the respondents and nature of the New York City economy. This is where young New Yorkers work, in marked contrast to their parents, who are more concentrated in more "traditional" immigrant industries such as manufacturing for Chinese and Latinos and healthcare for West Indians. It is interesting to note that African Americans tend to work in the public sector (a finding that supports previous research on this group), and that second-generation Chinese are more likely than other groups to work in the Finance Investment and Real Estate industry. When looking at ethnic over-

Table 9.1. Distribution of Groups across Industries

	CEP		Dominican		Puerto Rican		West Indian		Native Black		Chinese		Russian Jews		Native White	
	In COE	In Indus.	In COE	In Indus.	In COE	In Indus.	In COE	In Indus.	In COE	In Indus.	In COE	In Indus.	In COE	In Indus.	In COE	In Indus.
All industries	30, 10.1%		66, 21.5%		90, 30%		68, 23.8%		120, 41%		133, 31.3%		49, 22.5%		75, 24.2%	
Construction	0%	4, 1.3%*	3, 50%	6, 2%	2, 33.3%	6, 2%	2, 50%	4, 1.4%*	5, 29.4%	17, 5.8%	6, 60%	10, 2.4%	1, 20%	5, 2.3%	3, 37.5%	8, 2.6%
Manufacturing	5, 22.7%	22, 7.4%*	5, 25%	20, 6.5%*	5, 38.5%	13, 4.3%	4, 26.7%	15, 5.2%	2, 22.2%	9, 3.1%	11, 30.6%	36, 8.5%*	1, 10%	10, 4.6%	10, 28.6%	35, 11.3%
Transp., Comm. & Pub. Utilities	5, 17.2%	29, 9.7%	3, 11.5%	26, 8.5%	4, 18.2%	22, 7.3%	5, 17.2%	29, 10.1%	10, 35.7%	28, 9.6%*	2, 7.7%	26, 6.1%	2, 28.6%	7, 3.2%	5, 17.2%	29, 9.4%
Wholesale	6, 9%	67, 22.5%	30, 37.5%	80, 26.1%*	28, 32.6%	86, 28.7%	13, 20.6%	63, 22%	19, 45.2%	42, 14.3%	35, 41.7%	84, 19.8%	14, 25.5%	55, 25.2%	8, 16%	50, 16.1%
Retail Trade	5, 11.4%	44, 14.8%	3, 12.5%	24, 7.8%	4, 17.4%	23, 7.7%	6, 20.7%	29, 10.1%	7, 35%	20, 6.8%	11, 15.9%	69, 16.2%	5, 20.8%	24, 11%	14, 35.0%	40, 12.9%*
FIRE																
Busi., Repair & Per. Services	4, 7.8%	51, 17.1%*	10, 22.2%	45, 14.7%	15, 29.4%	51, 17.0%	8, 24.2%	33, 11.5%	27, 45%	60, 20.5%	23, 29.9%	77, 18.1%	12, 26.1%	46, 21.1%	17, 34%	50, 16.1%
Professional Services	5, 7.4%	68, 22.8%	12, 13.0%	92, 30%	29, 34.5%	84, 28%	25, 26.9%	93, 32.5%*	37, 41.1%	90, 30.7%	44, 40%	110, 25.9%	14, 20.6%	68, 31.2%*	16, 20.3%	79, 25.5%*
Public Administration	0, 0%	13, 4.4%	0, 0%	13, 4.2%	3, 20%	15, 5%*	5, 26.3%	19, 6.6%	13, 48.1%	27, 9.2%*	1, 7.7%	13, 3.1%	0, 0%	3, 1.4%	2, 11.1%	18, 5.8%*
Total		298, 100%		307, 100%		300, 100%		286, 100%		293, 100%		425, 100%		218, 100%		310, 100%

Source: Second-Generation Survey.

representation of the groups I find that second-generation CEPs are concentrated in the construction, manufacturing, and personal service industries; that children of Dominican immigrants are overrepresented in manufacturing (although far less so than their immigrant parents), as well as in the wholesale and retail industry; that public administration is an industry where both Puerto Ricans and African Americans are overrepresented, that in the professional services industry second-generation West Indians, Russian Jews, and Native Whites are overrepresented. While overrepresentation was used as a measure of concentration of immigrants, we can see that it is also relevant to their children. Although they might not be concentrated in the same industries or at the same levels as their parents, they are not completely dispersed throughout the labor market.

An additional way to look at the role of race and ethnicity in the labor market is through the composition of the immediate work environment. The first row in the table shows the percentage of each group that works in a co-ethnic work environment, across all industries. As we can see, for most groups about a quarter of all employed respondents work in co-ethnic settings, with the exception of 10 percent of CEPs and 40 percent of African Americans. While it is difficult to evaluate these numbers without any available comparison, I argue that this is not an easily dismissed phenomenon, and thus should be further studied. Some interesting patterns of co-ethnic employment can be seen for particular groups and in specific industries. For purposes of brevity I will only highlight a few. And since some of the cells in the table are very small and thus might not be robust, I will only discuss the cells with more than ten cases. For example, it is worth noting that across all industries African Americans are more likely to work with co-ethnics than West Indians or any of the other immigrant and native groups. This might imply that co-ethnicity is more than just an immigrant phenomenon; it is an inherent feature of the labor market (discrimination against African Americans). Also, the table suggests that CEPs are more likely to be working with co-ethnics in the wholesale and retail trade (where 37.5 percent of those that work in this industry do so with other CEPs) than in the professional services (where only 13 percent of CEPs that work in this industry do so in co-ethnic settings). Furthermore, we can see that although second-generation Chinese are distributed almost equally in the retail, finance, and real estate (FIRE) and personal service industries, they are far more likely to work with co-ethnics in the retail sector (41.7 percent) than in the personal service industry (29.9 percent) or in the FIRE industry (15.9 percent).

Table 9.2 reports the distribution of co-ethnic employment across groups along several key characteristics (gender, age, education, economic sector, company size, method of job matching, and ethnic concentration). The main finding in this table is that there are differences in the percentages of co-ethnic employment across groups along the different variables, but that these patterns are not consistent for all groups, and sometimes they are even opposite in their direction. For example among children of CEPs, Dominicans, Chinese, and Russian Jewish immigrants, males are more likely to work in co-ethnic settings than females, while the opposite is true for Puerto Ricans and African Americans. With regard to age, we can see that while second-generation CEPs, Dominicans, Chinese, and African Americans are less likely to work with co-ethnics, as they get older, the opposite is true for Russian Jews and Native Whites. This could be true due to differences in educational attainment, which is most likely to increase across these age categories. When looking at education we see a similar pattern of decrease in the likelihood of working in co-ethnic settings with an increase in level of education, except for Native Whites, among whom higher education seems to increase the probability of working with co-ethnics. There are some differences between groups with regard to economic sector as well. While African Americans and second-generation West Indians are more likely to work with co-ethnics in the public sector, Native Whites as well as children of Russian Jews and Dominican immigrants are more likely to do so in the private sector. Also, it seems that for most groups working in small firms increases the probability of working with co-ethnics, with the notable exception of Native Whites. The use of social networks in job finding seem to have a similar pattern for almost all groups (with the exception of CEPs), where finding a job though an informal channel increases the chance of working with co-ethnics. Finally, working in an industry where one's ethnic group is overrepresented does not seem to have a uniform effect of co-ethnic employment. While for Dominican and West Indian second-generation immigrants it increases the chances of working in a co-ethnic setting, the opposite is true for Puerto Ricans, and it does not make much of a difference for the other groups.

Multivariate Analysis

To test differences in co-ethnic employment more systematically, I fit a logistic regression model using the variables discussed above as well as a set of dummy variables for the various groups. First I analyze the baseline model of the main effects for all groups. Then I proceed to compare each racial group separately, and lastly I run each group in a separate model.

The results presented in table 9.3 suggest that

1. people with a post-graduate degree are less likely to be working in a co-ethnic environment compared to high school graduates;

Table 9.2.   Distribution of Co-Ethnic Employment along Key Variables

	CEP		Dominican		Puerto Rican		West Indian		Native Black		Chinese		Russian Jews		Native White	
Sex																
Male	20	12%	31	24%	23	18%	32	23%	43	36%	80	34%	27	25%	34	23%
Female	10	7%	35	19%	67	38%	36	24%	83	43%	58	29%	23	20%	43	25%
Age																
18–22 years old	10	9%	33	23%	32	28%	24	20%	35	44%	83	39%	25	20%	11	17%
23–27 years old	10	8%	22	22%	29	29%	28	30%	48	44%	41	26%	16	24%	30	25%
28–32 years old	9	13%	12	16%	30	31%	16	21%	43	36%	15	22%	10	31%	35	27%
Education																
Less than high school	3	9%	17	37%	21	32%	7	27%	22	52%	10	53%	5	40%	2	13%
High school/GED	9	20%	12	20%	24	30%	16	33%	34	41%	15	41%	12	38%	8	21%
Some college/vocational	16	9%	33	22%	30	25%	38	24%	58	45%	81	40%	22	19%	12	15%
BA degree	2	4%	4	9%	15	39%	5	10%	10	24%	28	20%	7	15%	41	34%
More than BA							3	25%	1	10%	4	11%	3	18%	15	22%
Economic Sector																
Private sector	23	10%	40	21%	57	28%	32	17%	57	33%	82	27%	28	18%	54	27%
Public sector			7	9%	21	27%	17	23%	47	46%	24	30%	3	11%	11	15%
Company Size																
Small company (<50)	22	11%	60	29%	71	36%	38	22%	92	48%	120	42%	49	28%	43	24%
Medium company (51–500)	7	11%	6	8%	11	15%	19	26%	24	29%	16	17%	1	3%	18	21%
Large Company (>501)	1	2%	8	25%	10	24%	9	28%	2	4%	1	4%	16	30%		
Job Matching																
Informal job match	14	8%	43	25%	56	35%	41	31%	64	41%	91	46%	25	25%	43	28%
Formal job match	15	12%	22	15%	34	24%	28	18%	61	40%	48	20%	24	20%	34	22%
Ethnic Concentration																
Not CPS concentrated	21	9%	31	15%	87	30%	40	21%	97	41%	121	31%	34	23%	43	25%
CPS concentrated	8	11%	35	35%	3	19%	27	28%	23	42%	11	30%	14	21%	32	23%

Source: Second-Generation Survey.

2. working in a small firm increases the likelihood of working with co-ethnics compared to working in a medium-sized firm; and
3. the odds of people who found their jobs through informal ties working with co-ethnics are 1.55 times higher than for those who found their jobs through formal channels.

In addition, working in an ethnically overrepresented industry increases the odds of working with co-ethnics. Lastly, children of CEP, Dominican, and Russian Jewish immigrants are less likely to work with co-ethnics than are Native Whites. Since the results of this model suggest that even when controlling for all other variables there are group differences in the odds of co-ethnic employment among various groups compared to Native Whites, I ran the same regression model separately for each minority racial group.

The results of the comparison between the Black groups in table 9.4 indicate that among both Native African Americans and West Indians, having a college education reduces the likelihood of working in a co-ethnic environment, while working in the public sector increases that likelihood, as proposed by the literature. Surprisingly, though, controlling for all other variables, the children of West Indian immigrants are still less likely to work with a co-ethnic compared to the Native African Americans with the same characteristics.[6]

When comparing the Latino groups, we learn that different processes are at play. Unlike with the Black groups, among the Latinos it is small firm size and ethnic overrepresentation in the industry that increases the likelihood of working in a co-ethnic environment. However, when holding everything else constant, children of immigrants are less likely to be working with co-ethnics than are "native" minorities, in this case Puerto Ricans.

The results of a separate analysis of each of the groups presented in table 9.5 make even clearer the existence of a different sorting mechanism for each group that affects its members' likelihood to work in co-ethnic settings. Controlling for all other variables in the model, it is college education compared to high school graduation that decreases the chance of working with co-ethnics for second-generation CEPs. Children of Russian Jewish immigrants have to have post-graduate education to lower their odds of working in a co-ethnic setting. Not surprisingly, for Native Whites the opposite is true; having a college degree increases the odds of working in a predominantly white work environment. The other factor that is significant in affecting co-ethnic employment among this group is working in the private sector. By contrast, African Americans are less likely to work with co-ethnics in the private sector compared to the public sector. For all other groups, having a college degree and working in the private sector has no significant effect on co-ethnic

Table 9.3.   Logistic Coefficients Predicting Employment in a Co-ethnic Work Environment (All Groups)

	B	S.E.	Odds Ratios
Age			
18–22 yrs. old	-0.247	0.134	0.78
23–27 yrs. old	(reference)		
28–32 yrs. old	-0.014	0.141	0.99
Sex			
Male	-0.203	0.111	0.82
Female	(reference)		
Education			
Less than HS	0.079	0.214	1.08
HS grad./GED	(reference)		
Some college	0.013	0.154	1.01
BA degree	-0.344	0.192	0.71
More than BA	-0.771**	0.290	0.46
Economic Sector			
Private sector	-0.033	0.130	0.97
Public sector	(reference)		
Company Size			
Small company (>50)	0.616***	0.137	1.85
Medium company (51–500)	(reference)		
Large company (<501)	-0.134	0.206	0.88
Job Matching			
Informal job match	0.439***	0.111	1.55
Formal job match	(reference)		
Ethnic Concentration			
CPS concentrated	0.327*	0.135	1.39
Not CPS concentrated	(reference)		
Group			
Chinese	0.248	0.202	1.28
CEP	-1.341***	0.274	0.26
Dominican	-0.647**	0.230	0.52
Native Black	0.523*	0.212	1.69
Puerto Rican	0.109	0.221	1.11
Russian Jew	-0.613*	0.258	0.54
West Indian	-0.382	0.229	0.68
Native White	(reference)		
Model Summary			
Constant	-1.436***	0.291	0.24
N	2,096		
Chi-square	164.25 (19)***		
Nagelkerke R square	0.114		

Note: *p<.05, **p<.01, ***p<.001.

Table 9.4. Logistic Coefficients Predicting Employment in a Co-ethnic Work Environment (Separately for Blacks and Latinos)

	NB and SG WI			PR and SG CEP and Dom.		
	B	S.E.	Odds Ratios	B	S.E.	Odds Ratios
Age						
18–22 yrs. old	-0.482	0.264	0.62	-0.253	0.232	0.78
23–27 yrs. old	(reference)					
28–32 yrs. old	-0.308	0.252	0.74	0.065	0.256	1.07
Sex						
Male	-0.28	0.219	0.76	-0.38	0.203	0.68
Female	(reference)					
Education						
Less than HS	-0.053	0.394	0.95	0.022	0.308	1.02
HS grad./GED	(reference)					
Some college	0.071	0.271	1.07	-0.122	0.253	0.89
BA degree	-1.033*	0.408	0.36	-0.422	0.37	0.66
More than BA	-0.431	0.643	0.65	-6.51	11.193	0
Economic Sector						
Private sector	-0.604*	0.234	0.55	0.319	0.261	1.38
Public sector	(reference)					
Company Size						
Small company (>50)	0.182	0.244	1.2	0.827**	0.258	2.29
Medium company (51–500)	(reference)					
Large company (<501)	-0.032	0.349	0.97	-0.241	0.45	0.79
Job Matching						
Informal job match	0.27	0.213	1.31	0.195	0.2	1.22
Formal job match	(reference)					
Ethnic Concentration						
CPS concentrated	0.041	0.251	1.04	0.601*	0.256	1.82
Not CPS concentrated	(reference)					
Group						
West Indian (comp to NB)	-0.835***	0.227	0.43			
Dominican (comp to PR)				-0.852**	0.249	0.43
CEP (compared to PR)				-1.506**	0.284	0.22
Model Summary						
Constant	0.098	0.392	1.1	-1.467**	0.441	0.23
N	500			783		
Chi-square	45.1 (13)			81.5 (14)		
Nagelkerke R square	0.124			0.161		

Note: *$p<.05$, **$p<.01$, ***$p<.001$.

employment. Holding all other variables constant, gender has a significant effect on the dependent variable only for Puerto Ricans, whose odds of working in co-ethnic setting are larger in companies that have fewer than fifty employees, compared to those that have fifty-one to five hundred employees. Second-generation Dominicans are also more likely to work with co-ethnics in small companies as well as in industries where their ethnic group is overrepresented. Second-generation Chinese immigrants are less likely to work with co-ethnics in large companies compared to medium ones and, like Native Whites, using informal ties increases their odds of working in co-ethnic settings. Lastly, only for the children of Chinese immigrants does being foreign-born (1.5-generation) significantly increase the chances of working with co-ethnics, compared to being born in the U.S. (second-generation).

DISCUSSION AND CONCLUSION

This is the first study to analyze patterns of economic incorporation among children of post-1965 immigrants, and to examine the role of race and ethnicity in shaping their experiences in the labor market. Based on the findings presented here, it can be argued that co-ethnic employment is a significant experience for second-generation immigrants as well as for their native-born counterparts. Maybe most intriguing is the finding that, controlling for all other variables, Latino and White second-generation immigrants (namely CEPs, Dominicans, and Russian Jews) are less likely to work in ethnically homogenous settings compared to Native Whites with the same characteristic, and that it is African Americans that are the most likely of all groups to work with co-ethnics. Contrary to the predictions of the segmented assimilation theory, West Indians are not significantly different than Native Whites in their likelihood to work with co-ethnics, but are significantly less likely to do so compared to African Americans. These findings suggest that co-ethnic employment is not an immigrant-only phenomenon, but rather a form of segregation that is a characteristic of the labor market itself.

Moreover, the findings indicate that patterns of co-ethnic employment and the factors shaping them vary across groups and industries, pointing to the existence of multiple logics of labor market incorporation. For example, while both African Americans and West Indians are more likely to work with co-ethnics in the public sector, the Hispanic groups are more likely to do so in small firms. And while the former decrease their chances of working with co-ethnics if they have college education, the latter, surprisingly, do so by working in industries where their ethnic group is not overrepresented. Also, social networks that are widely discussed in the literature as affecting the ethnic concentration of immigrants seem to have a significant impact on being co-ethnically employed only among second-generation Chinese and Native Whites.

With regard to the socioeconomic future of the second generation, it seems that since there are different logics at play, we cannot expect the economic consequences of co-ethnicity in the workplace to be uniform across groups. Further research needs to be done to understand when co-ethnicity in the

Table 9.5. Logistic Coefficients Predicting Employment in a Co-ethnic Work Environment (Separately for Each Group)

	CEP	Dominican	Puerto Rican	West Indian	Native Black	Chinese	Russian Jew	Native White
Age								
18–22 yrs. old								
23–27 yrs. old (reference)								
28–32 yrs. old								
Sex								
Male			-1.045***					
Female (reference)								
Education								
Less than HS								
HS grad./GED (reference)								
Some college								
BA degree	-2.413*						-2.780*	1.279*
More than BA								
Economic Sector								
Private sector					-.771**			1.033*
Public sector (reference)								
Company Size								
Small company (>50)		1.418*	.939**					
Medium company (51–500) (reference)								
Large company (<501)						-1.653*		
Job Matching								
Informal job match						.973***		.663*
Formal job match (reference)								
Ethnic Concentration								
CPS concentrated		.828*						
Not CPS concentrated (reference)								
Nativity								
Foreign-born						.718**		
Native-born (reference)								
Model Summary								
N	259	264	259	241	258	374	177	261
Chi-square (df)	26.32 (13)*	42.49 (13)*	30.16 (12)*	21.29 (13)	21.19 (12)*	72.22 (13)*	23.81 (13)*	27.07 (12)*
Nagelkerke R square	0.217	0.248	0.156	0.135	0.108	0.253	0.208	0.146

Note: *p<.05, **p<.01, ***p<.001.

labor market serves as an economic safety net and when it is a springboard to social mobility.

On a more general level, the findings of this study problematize the use of broad racial and panethnic categories, since they highlight the differences between CEPs, Dominicans, and Puerto Ricans as well as those between West Indians and African Americans. The findings also indicate that more research needs to be conducted to test the assumption made in the literature that conclusions about co-ethnicity in the labor market can be drawn only on the basis of ethnic overrepresentation measures in census data. By providing both measures, I make evident that they are not necessarily the same phenomenon. Finally, although the findings of this study provide much insight on the second-generation's paths into the labor market, they mainly point to directions for future research.

NOTES

1. Due to the lack of information on parental place of birth after the 1970 Census and the relative youth of the "new second generation," most studies of this group concentrate on educational outcomes and have been based on gross estimates extrapolated from the available data (for example, Hirschman [1996]; Jensen and Chitose [1996]). Portes and Rumbaut's "Children of Immigrants Longitudinal Study" (CILS) is an important project that collected data specifically on second-generation immigrants. Yet it also concentrates on educational experiences and outcomes, since most of the CILS respondents are still too young to have significant labor market experiences (Portes and Rumbaut 2001).

2. For background on this project, see Philip Kasinitz, Mary Waters, and John Mollenkopf, "The Immigrant Second Generation in New York: A Demographic Overview," at web.gc.cuny.edu/cur/frames/home2.

3. The data include second-generation Dominicans, South Americans, West Indians, Chinese, and Russian Jews. Most of them are children of immigrants that were born in the U.S. (second-generation) others were born abroad but came to the U.S. before the age of twelve (1.5-generation). For comparative purposes data also includes Native Whites, African Americans, and Puerto Ricans.

4. Unlike in the Multi-City Survey of Inequality, the race and ethnicity of coworkers was coded to match their own nation of origin background, rather than a broad ethno-racial code such as "Asian," "Hispanic," or "Black" (for example, see Elliott [2001]).

5. They define the ethnic niche as an industry where groups are represented at rates at least 1.5 times their size in the labor force (Waldinger 1996: 95).

6. For a detailed discussion about African Americans and second-generation West Indians, see Waters (1999b).

REFERENCES

Alba, Richard. 1998. "Assimilation's Quiet Tide." Pp. 327–35 in *Majority and Minority: The Dynamics of Race and Ethnicity in American Life*, ed. Norman R. Yetman. 6th ed. Boston: Allyn and Bacon.

Bailey, Thomas, and Roger Waldinger. 1991. "Primary, Secondary, and Enclave Labor Markets: A Training Systems Approach." *American Sociological Review* 56: 432–45.

Baron, James, and William Bielby. 1985. "Organizational Barriers to Gender Equality: Sex Segregation of Jobs and Opportunities." Pp. 233–51 in *Gender and the Life Course*, ed. Alice Rossi. New York: Aldine DeGruyter.

Braddock, Henry, and James McPartland. 1987. "How Minorities Continue to Be Excluded from Equal Employment Opportunities: Research on Labor Market and Institutional Barriers." *Journal of Social Issues* 43: 5–39.

Elliott, James. 2001. "Referral Hiring and Ethnically Homogenous Jobs: How Prevalent Is the Connection and for Whom." *Social Science Research* 30: 401–25.

England, Paula. 1992. *Comparable Worth: Theory and Evidence*. New York: Aldine DeGruyter.

Farley, Reynolds, and Richard Alba. 2002. "The New Second Generation in the United States." *International Migration Review* 36: 669–701.

Gans, Herbert. 1992. "Second-Generation Decline: Scenarios for the Economic and Ethnic Futures of the Post-1965 American Immigrants." *Ethnic and Racial Studies* 15: 173–92.

Hirschman, Charles. 1996. "Studying Immigrant Adaptation from the 1990 Population Census: From Generational Comparisons to the Process of 'Becoming American.'" Pp. 54–81 in *The New Second Generation*, ed. Alejandro Portes. New York: Russell Sage Foundation.

Jensen, Lief, and Yoshimi Chitose. 1996. "Today's Second Generation: Evidence from the 1990 Census." Pp. 82–107 in *The New Second Generation*, ed. Alejandro Portes. New York: Russell Sage Foundation.

Kasinitz, Philip, and Jan Rosenberg. 1996. "Missing the Connection? Social Isolation and Employment on the Brooklyn Waterfront." *Social Problems* 41, no. 2: 501–19.

Kasinitz, Philip, Mary Waters, and John Mollenkopf. 2002. "Becoming American/Becoming New Yorkers: The Experience of Assimilation in a Majority Minority City." *International Migration Review* 36, no. 4: 1020–36.

Kwong, Peter. 1997. *Forbidden Workers: Illegal Chinese Immigrants and American Labor*. New York: New Press.

Lieberson, Stanley. 1981. "An Asymmetrical Approach to Segregation." Pp. 61–82 in *Ethnic Segregation in Cities*, ed. Ceri Peach, Vaughan Robinson, and Susan Smith. London: Croom Helm.

Lieberson, Stanley, and Mary Waters. 1988. *From Many Strands: Ethnic and Racial Groups in Contemporary America*. New York: Russell Sage Foundation.

Light, Ivan, and Steven Gold. 2000. *Ethnic Economies*. San Diego: Academic Press.

Logan, John, and Richard Alba. 1999. "Minority Niches and Immigrant Enclaves in New York and Los Angeles: Trends and Impacts." Pp. 172–93 in *Immigration and Opportunity: Race, Ethnicity, and Employment in the United States*, ed. Frank Bean and Stephanie Bell-Rose. New York: Russell Sage Foundation.

Logan, John, Richard Alba, and Thomas McNulty. 1994. "Ethnic Economies in Metropolitan Regions: Miami and Beyond." *Social Forces* 72: 691–724.

Marini, Margaret, and Pi-Ling Fan. 1997. "The Gender Gap in Earnings at Career Entry." *American Sociological Review* 62: 588–604.

Model, Suzanne. 1993. "The Ethnic Niches and the Structure of Opportunity: Immigrants and Minorities in New York City." Pp. 161–93 in *The Underclass Debate*, ed. Michael Katz. Princeton, NJ: Princeton University Press.

Moss, Philip, and Chris Tilly. 1997. "Ethnic Economy and Industry in Mid-Twentieth Century Gotham." *Social Problems* 44: 445–64.

———. 2001. *Stories Employers Tell: Race, Skill and Hiring in America*. New York: Russell Sage Foundation.

Perlmann, Joe, and Roger Waldinger. 1999. "Immigrants Past and Present: A Reconsideration." In *The Handbook of International Migration: The American Experience*, ed. Charles Hirschman, Philip Kasinitz, and Josh DeWind. New York: Russell Sage Foundation.

Portes, Alejandro, and Robert Bach. 1985. *Latin Journey: Cuban and Mexican Immigrants in the United States*. Berkeley: University of California Press.

Portes, Alejandro, and Reubén Rumbaut. 2001. *Legacies, The Story of the Immigrant Second Generation*. Berkeley: University of California Press, and New York: Russell Sage Foundation.

Portes, Alejandro, and Min Zhou. 1992. "Gaining the Upper Hand: Economic Mobility among Immigrant and Domestic Minorities." *Ethnic and Racial Studies* 15: 491–522.

———. 1993. "The New Second Generation: Segmented Assimilation and Its Variants." *Annals* 530: 74–96.

Reskin, Barbara. 1993. "Sex Segregation in the Workplace." *Annual Review of Sociology* 19: 241–70.

Reskin, Barbara, and Debra McBrier. 2000. "Why Not Ascription? Organizations' Employment of Male and Female Managers." *American Sociological Review* 65: 210–33.

Reskin, Barbara, and Irene Padavic. 1999. "Sex, Race and Ethnic Inequality in United States Workplaces." Pp. 343–74 in *Handbook of the Sociology of Gender*, ed. Janet Chafetz. New York: Plenum.

Sanders, James, and Victor Nee. 1987. "Limits of Ethnic Solidarity in the Ethnic Enclave Economy." *American Sociological Review* 52: 745–67.

Waldinger, Roger. 1996. *Still the Promised City? African Americans and New Immigrants in Postindustrial New York*. Cambridge, MA: Harvard University Press.

Waldinger, Roger, and Mehdi Bozorgmehr. 1996. *Ethnic Los Angeles*. New York: Russell Sage Foundation.

Waldinger, Roger, and Michael Lichter. 2003. *How the Other Half Works: Immigration and the Social Organization of Labor*. Berkeley: University of California Press.

Waters, Mary. 1999a. "West Indians and African Americans at Work: Structural Differences and Cultural Stereotypes." Pp. 194–227 in *Immigration and Opportunity: Race, Ethnicity, and Employment in the United States*, ed. Frank Bean and Stephanie Bell-Rose. New York: Russell Sage Foundation.

———. 1999b. *Black Identities: West Indian Immigrant Dreams and American Realities*. Cambridge, MA: Harvard University Press.

Wilson, Franklin. 1999. "Ethnic Concentrations and Labor-Market Opportunities." Pp. 106–40 in *Immigration and Opportunity: Race, Ethnicity, and Employment in the United States*, ed. Frank Bean and Stephanie Bell-Rose. New York: Russell Sage Foundation.

Wilson, Julius. 1987. *The Truly Disadvantaged: The Inner City, the Underclass, and Public Policy*. Chicago: Chicago University Press.

Zhou, Min. 1992. *Chinatown: The Socioeconomic Potential of an Urban Enclave*. Philadelphia: Temple University Press.

10

Immigrant Selectivity, Ethnic Capital, and the Reproduction of Educational Inequalities across Borders

Cynthia Feliciano

Research on the second generation—children of immigrants raised in the United States—points to a striking diversity of outcomes that vary by ethnicity, especially in educational achievement and attainment, two of the most important predictors of success in U.S. labor markets (Portes and Rumbaut 2001; Rumbaut and Portes 2001; also see Zeltzer-Zubida, this volume). Previous research has pointed to variability in ethnic resources as an important factor in explaining such disparities, yet most of the literature emphasizes resources in ethnic communities in the host society, rather than the pre-migration sources of ethnic capital (Portes and Zhou 1993; Zhou 1997b; Zhou and Bankston 1994). This chapter argues that pre-migration class background—which varies by immigrant group based on their selectivity—is an ethnic resource that has largely been neglected by previous research, and that variability in immigrant selectivity may help explain educational attainment differences among immigrants' children. In proposing a link between immigrants' educational selectivity—that is, where immigrants ranked within their home country's educational stratification system before migrating—and educational outcomes among immigrants' children, I suggest that ethnic differences in educational success among immigrants' children in the United States can partly be attributed to the reproduction of pre-migration class structures across borders.

IMMIGRANT SELECTIVITY

A universally accepted feature of the migration process is that immigrants are not randomly selected from their home countries[1] (Borjas 1987; Lee 1966;

Ravenstein 1885). Beyond this, however, scholars disagree considerably about how immigrants compare to those left behind, and, surprisingly, current immigration research does not adequately address this basic question of how immigrants compare to those who do not migrate (Gans 2000). Some scholars argue that immigrants are often negatively selected, depending upon the reasons for migration and/or economic conditions in the sending country (Borjas 1990, 1999). Portes, Rumbaut, and other scholars argue, however, that all immigrants represent a positively selected group from their home country (Bray 1984; Portes and Rumbaut 1996: chap. 1).

Immigrant selectivity has been shown to affect earnings (Borjas 1987; Carliner 1980; Chiswick 1978) and health disparities among immigrants (Landale, Oropesa, and Gorman 2000; Weeks, Rumbaut, and Ojeda 1999). However, the impact of selectivity on adaptation processes is understudied (Rumbaut 1999). A relationship between immigrant selectivity and the education of immigrants' children has been suggested by previous research, but not explicitly examined (Borjas 1990; Ogbu 1991). This chapter examines this relationship directly by conceptualizing immigrant selectivity—or pre-migration class background—as a potential ethnic resource that may facilitate immigrant children's educational success.

Most studies incorporating immigrant selectivity do not adequately operationalize the concept due to data limitations. Adjudicating the effects of selectivity requires data comparing non-migrants in the source country with migrants in the receiving society. In other words, data is needed on the home populations in the sending country, as well as comparable data on immigrants from those same countries in the United States. Only a few case studies of specific immigrant groups use such data (Landale et al. 2000; Ortiz 1986; Ramos 1992; Weeks et al. 1999). Existing comparative studies instead use a set of proxies for selectivity, which even they admit are "ad hoc," such as GNP, income inequality, and distance (Borjas 1987; Cobb-Clark 1993; Jasso and Rosenzweig 1986). In contrast, this chapter directly examines the impact of selective migration by using measures that compare the educational attainments of migrants and non-migrants from thirty-two of the top immigrant-sending countries to the United States. Specifically, I address whether differences in the *degree* of positive educational selectivity influence educational outcomes among groups of immigrants' children from different countries. In addressing this question, this chapter seeks to ascertain whether pre-migration resources may be utilized among ethnic groups in the United States to facilitate the next generation's educational success.

REPRODUCING EDUCATIONAL INEQUALITIES ACROSS BORDERS

In proposing a link between immigrant selectivity, on the one hand, and children of immigrants' educational attainment, on the other, I am examining a fundamental problem in educational research. Namely, does education create social mobility, and create opportunities in an open society, or does education merely serve to reproduce the existing social class structure? Scholars such as Bourdieu (1973), Bowles and Gintis (1976), and Willis (1977) argue that, rather than allowing for upward mobility, education actually serves to reproduce the existing social stratification system and perpetuate existing inequalities. According to this view, immigrants who come to the United States seeking better educational opportunities for their children may be disappointed by the realities of limited social mobility.

While immigrants' children often attain more schooling, in absolute terms, than their parents (Farley and Alba 2002), in *relative* terms, immigrants' pre-migration class status may often be reproduced among their U.S.-raised children. Viewing education broadly, it is not just the specific credential, such as whether someone has graduated high school (the absolute level of schooling), which matters. Rather, the context in which education is attained, or how that attainment compares to others, is important. Neglecting educational selectivity, or relative educational attainment, assumes that a high school degree earned in one context (say, a country where only 10 percent of the population has one) has the same meaning as a high school degree earned in another context (say, where 80 percent of the population has one). Because educational opportunities differ substantially by country, immigrants who do not have high educational credentials by American standards may, in fact, be quite selective relative to the general populations in their home countries (Lieberson 1980: 213–14). Stratification models may therefore need to be revised for immigrants' children to reflect the different meanings of educational attainment for different immigrant groups.

Parents' education is the single most important determinant of children's schooling, and not simply because education is related to occupational status and income (Blau and Duncan 1967; Hirschman and Falcon 1985). Rather, educational attainment and educational selectivity often are sources of social, cultural, and ethnic resources or capital. One non-economic benefit of having highly educated parents may be that children perceive more pressure from their parents to continue in school, even if they are not academically oriented (Jencks et al. 1972: 138; Sewell, Haller, and Ohlendorf 1970). Further, children from middle-class or upper-class families may have more cultural capital, which includes resources and advantages such as "values, attitudes, language skills and styles of interaction" that are rewarded in school (Bourdieu 1973; Bourdieu and Passeron 1977). For immigrants, non-economic forms of capital might transfer across borders, even if immigrant parents are not that educated by U.S. standards. Thus, immigrants who were of high status in the home country may facilitate the achievement of the next generation in order to attain a similar class position in the United States.

Ethnic Differences and the Second Generation

Why various American ethnic groups achieve markedly different socioeconomic outcomes is an enduring sociological puzzle. Straight-line assimilation theory predicted a single trajectory of upward mobility over time and across generations in the United States (Gordon 1964; Park 1928), but the reality never fit the theory, even among earlier waves of migration from Europe (Alba and Nee 1997; Perlmann and Waldinger 1997). European immigrant groups moved ahead at divergent rates, with vast differences in educational and occupational attainments among the second generation, even controlling for background factors (Perlmann 1988; Thernstrom 1973). Understanding socioeconomic disparities among second-generation immigrants is particularly important because these disparities may persist across future generations (Borjas 1994; Hirschman and Falcon 1985). Thus, understanding why the second generation succeeds or fails may shed light on why some ethnic groups seem stuck in poverty, why others join the mainstream middle class, and why some, like the Jews and Japanese, achieve extraordinary success (Hirschman and Falcon 1985; Treiman and Lee 1996; Waldinger and Lichter 1996).

Contemporary second-generation national-origin groups differ markedly in educational outcomes. Asian-origin youths tend to be more academically successful than Latin-American-origin youths. For example, in California, 44 percent of Asian high school graduates in 1996 were eligible to attend the University of California (because they had completed the required courses with adequate grades), compared to only 8 percent of Latinos (Lopez and Stanton-Salazar 2001). Such group differences persist even after controlling for parental education and economic resources. Steinberg and his associates (1996), for example, found that, after controlling for family background, ethnic differences persisted in educational achievement, as well as in many beliefs and behaviors related to educational success, such as educational aspirations and time spent on homework (Steinberg 1996; Steinberg, Brown, and Dornbusch 1996).

Many scholars have turned to cultural arguments when class and family background do not seem to explain group differences. In particular, cultural arguments have been invoked to explain the success of "model minority" Asian newcomers, such as the Vietnamese and Chinese, compared to Latinos from countries such as Mexico, the Dominican Republic, and El Salvador. Sowell (1981) attributes the success of Japanese immigrants to valuing reading and education. Others emphasize the "fit" between the value systems in Asian countries and American middle-class values (Caudill and DeVos 1956; Hsu 1971). Some contend that the Confucian culture's reverence for learning drives Asian parents to push their children to succeed, or that Asian families provide environments conducive to school success (Cheng and Yang 1996; Schneider and Lee 1990). However, attributing Asian success to "values" makes little sense when one is lumping together groups from many culturally distinct countries (Steinberg 1981). Cultural arguments ignore the importance of pre-migration characteristics and ethnic community resources in explaining Asian success. The history of Asian exclusion may have made Chinese and Japanese immigration very selective (Cheng and Yang 1996; Hirschman and Wong 1986). In contrast to immigrants with a longer, less restricted, history of migration to the United States, such as Mexicans, many Asian migrants could only begin to migrate under the 1965 Immigration Act's skilled worker provisions because they did not have previous family ties to draw upon for entry. Although in recent decades more Asians have begun to migrate under family provisions, and many Southeast Asians arrived as refugees, the historical pattern for many Asian groups has been one of skilled migration flows.

According to segmented assimilation theory, straight assimilation into the mainstream is one possible outcome of second-generation adaptation; another possibility is downward integration if the children of immigrants fail to attain higher education (Gans 1992; Portes and Zhou 1993; Zhou 1997a). A third possibility is that second-generation immigrants achieve rapid advancement within the ethnic community, using ethnicity as a source of social capital (Coleman 1988; Portes and Zhou 1993; Zhou and Bankston 1998).

This literature suggests that ethnic capital, which is social or cultural capital provided by the ethnic community and characteristic of an entire immigrant group, may influence the next generation's educational success (Portes and Rumbaut 1996, 2001; Zhou and Bankston 1994, 1998). Similarly, Borjas (1992: 126) writes, "persons who grow up in high-quality ethnic environments will, on average, be exposed to social, cultural, and economic factors that increase their productivity when they grow up." Wilson's (1990) work on the underclass also notes the importance of ethnic social resources. He argues that the prospects of young black males in inner city neighborhoods are poor because they are not exposed to "mainstream role models that keep alive the perception that education is meaningful [and] that steady employment is a viable alternative to welfare" (Wilson 1990: 56). Borjas (1992) shows that the skills of the second generation depend not only on the parents' skills, but equally on the average skills of the entire immigrant generation. He finds that ethnic capital, which he measures as the average earnings of the immigrant group, is an important predictor of the earnings of the second generation, and slows down the convergence of ethnic socioeconomic differences across generations (Borjas 1992, 1993).

I argue that the average educational selectivity of the immigrant generation can be thought of as a form of ethnic capital that influences educational attainment among the second generation. This chapter thus brings together ideas from the literatures on immigrant selectivity, class reproduction, and second-generation adaptation to try to understand what accounts for ethnic and racial differences in educational attainment among the new second generation.

ANALYSIS STRATEGY

This chapter addresses two main questions. First, does immigrants' educational selectivity help explain why some ethnic groups obtain higher amounts of schooling, on average, than others? For this question, a group-level analysis is appropriate. Following Borjas (1993), I conduct ordinary least squares regression analyses on aggregate national-origin groups to ascertain whether an immigrant group's educational selectivity affects the average educational attainment of 1.5-generation and second-generation groups, net of the immigrant group's average socioeconomic status. I employ a similar method to Borjas (1993) of using intercensal comparisons so that it is more likely that the groups of immigrants are the parents of the second generation.[2]

Second, I ask a slightly different, although related, question: does immigrants' educational selectivity help explain why individual children of immigrants from certain ethnic/racial groups are more or less likely to attain educational success (as measured by high school graduation and college attendance)? I examine differences across four broad panethnic/racial groups: Whites (European/Canadian origin), Blacks (West Indian origins), Asians (Asian origin), and Latinos (Latin American or Spanish-speaking Caribbean origins). Clearly, these are umbrella terms for very diverse national-origin groups. However, because these groups tend to get lumped together when they come to the United States, these categories are meaningful. For example, the terms "Asian excellence" and "Latino underachievement" are often used in both academic and popular circles. At the individual-level unit of analysis, I conduct logistic regression analyses on 1.5-generation and second-generation adults to ascertain whether including the immigrant group's educational selectivity as an independent variable explains away the significance of membership in a White, Black, Asian, or Latino group.

DATA AND METHODS

The data for this study come from multiple sources. To examine the impact of immigrants' educational selectivity on children of immigrants' educational attainment, I gathered data on the educational attainment of the adult populations of sending countries, data on adult first-generation immigrants in the United States, and data on children of immigrants in the United States.

Measuring Immigrant Selectivity

Measuring immigrants' educational selectivity required data for national-origin groups on both the sending and receiving sides of the migration process. First, I gathered data published by UNESCO (United Nations Educational, Scientific, and Cultural Organization) on the sending countries' average levels of educational attainment, by age, for thirty-one of the top migrant-sending countries to the United States and Puerto Rico.[3] Second, I created extracts on first-generation U.S. immigrants from each of the thirty-two countries from the IPUMS (Integrated Public Use Micro Samples); the IPUMS is a collection of microdata samples of U.S. Census data from multiple years that are coded consistently across time. My selection of the immigrants for each country's sample was guided by three main principles. First, since I wanted measures of educational attainment that would reflect those of the "average" immigrant from that country, I included only those immigrants who migrated within ten years (before or after) of the average year in which a particular immigrant group migrated to the United States. I collected the IPUMS for the closest year available following the average years of migration for that particular national-origin group.[4] This method ensured that I would not overestimate the positive selectivity of immigrants, since it is generally thought that the first waves of migrants are more skilled and educated than later waves (Massey 1988). Further, since return migration is common, using these data limit the possible bias of creating measures based only on long-term immigrants who may be the most successful in the United States and also the most educated. Second, I limited the sample of immigrants to only those who migrated as adults. Thus, I analyzed data from those who migrated at age eighteen plus, so that I could be reasonably sure that most of their education occurred in their home country rather than in the United States.[5] Third, I selected immigrants within the same age range as the home country populations in the published UNESCO data (in most cases, ages 20+ or 25+). This ensured that I was comparing migrants and non-migrants within the same age range.

I constructed the selectivity measures—comparative measures of immigrants' and non-migrants' educational attainments—by calculating "difference" measures of educational attainment (adjusted for age[6]). That is, I calculated the numerical difference between the immigrant groups and the home country populations along several indicators of educational attainment[7] as well as an index of dissimilarity[8] to describe the difference between the educational distributions of the immigrants and their non-migrant counterparts. I calculated seven distinct measures of educational selectivity (six "difference" measures and the index of dissimilarity). Since these measures are highly correlated, I created a more reliable indicator of selectivity by standardizing and summing the "difference" measures and the index of dissimilarity into a selectivity scale ranging from 0 to 1. The scale ranks immigrants from each country according to how positively selected they are relative to their home country's populations, ranging from 0 (Puerto Rico—not positively selected at all) to 1 (India—most positively selected). Table 10.1 lists each national-origin groups' educational selectivity score; this will be the key independent variable.

Measuring Immigrants' Socioeconomic Status

I also used extracts of IPUMS data on immigrants from the thirty-two countries to calculate the average socioeconomic status of the immigrant group, which will be a key control variable. I calculated the average years of schooling among each immigrant group, the average occupational status (Duncan SEI score), and the average income for each national-origin group. Since these variables were all very highly correlated, I standardized and summed these measures into a socioeconomic status scale ranging from 0 to 1. Table 10.1 also lists the average socioeconomic status score of each group.

Educational Attainment among Children of Immigrants

Lastly, I created extracts from the IPUMS and the Current Population Survey (CPS) on children of immigrants ages twenty to forty to measure the dependent variables: college attendance, high school graduation, and years of schooling.[9] I calculated these variables for two different groups of children of immigrants: the 1.5 generation, those who migrated as children before the age of eleven, and the second generation, those who were born in the United States of at least one immigrant parent. The ethnic group of the second gen-

Table 10.1. Means of Independent and Dependent Variables by National Origin

SOURCE COUNTRY	INDEP. VARIABLES		DEPENDENT VARIABLES							
			1990 Census, 1.5 Generation, Ages 20 to 40				1997–2001 CPS, 2nd Generation, Ages 20 to 40			
	Selectivity	SES	Yrs. of School	% HS Grad.	% Some College	N	Yrs. of School	% HS Grad.	% Some College	N
Canada	0.329	0.749	13.65	93.07	67.48	1,227	13.82	93.52	71.09	497
China	0.680	0.380	13.48	85.71	70.33	91	15.39	97.93	90.13	146
Colombia	0.547	0.397	13.46	87.56	68.39	193	13.54	94.99	70.86	105
Cuba	0.330	0.227	13.42	87.87	62.78	1,088	14.22	95.21	70.80	332
Dominican Republic	0.367	0.176	12.57	77.32	54.64	194	13.14	86.90	58.24	190
Ecuador	0.441	0.287	12.96	82.31	60.00	130	13.49	89.97	70.90	62
El Salvador	0.353	0.057	11.92	71.70	50.00	106	13.00	87.11	54.06	183
Greece	0.362	0.271	13.23	82.74	57.87	197	14.03	97.81	74.83	108
Guatemala	0.439	0.062	12.49	74.73	57.14	91	13.12	86.75	61.76	43
Haiti	0.697	0.187	13.49	88.54	72.92	96	14.03	100.00	81.73	42
Honduras	0.437	0.093	12.73	90.38	65.38	52	13.39	95.41	69.84	31
Hong Kong	0.498	0.772	14.43	97.67	85.12	215	13.66	87.85	74.42	23
Hungary	0.728	0.646	14.55	97.96	71.43	49	14.04	97.38	68.63	60
India	1.000	1.000	14.59	97.98	88.38	198	15.36	100.00	90.31	91
Iran	0.962	0.764	13.97	97.01	76.12	67	14.54	90.69	78.83	33
Ireland	0.484	0.699	13.91	94.03	65.67	67	14.44	97.04	79.24	158

Table 10.1. (Continued).

SOURCE COUNTRY	INDEP. VARIABLES		DEPENDENT VARIABLES							
			1990 Census, 1.5 Generation, Ages 20 to 40				1997–2001 CPS, 2nd Generation, Ages 20 to 40			
	Selectivity	SES	Yrs. of School	% HS Grad.	% Some College	N	Yrs. of School	% HS Grad.	% Some College	N
Italy	0.186	0.453	12.97	85.62	53.19	626	14.00	97.52	69.49	459
Jamaica	0.534	0.567	13.37	87.10	62.21	217	13.87	92.47	81.38	62
Japan	0.554	0.766	13.69	93.86	71.74	814	14.26	95.75	74.52	101
Korea	0.426	0.575	13.85	96.33	79.33	300	14.52	100.00	90.06	60
Mexico	0.179	0.000	11.22	59.31	31.87	3,502	12.37	78.54	43.98	2582
Netherlands	0.542	0.861	13.85	94.63	73.15	149	14.39	100.00	88.69	82
Nicaragua	0.726	0.285	12.61	83.33	51.85	54	13.29	91.86	74.89	46
Peru	0.604	0.427	13.12	90.12	69.14	81	13.87	95.37	80.95	57
Philippines	0.578	0.658	13.45	93.26	74.43	653	13.53	96.85	74.16	249
Poland	0.475	0.540	12.76	83.97	51.15	131	14.38	95.71	72.14	113
Portugal	0.178	0.190	12.16	76.73	38.37	245	12.98	86.94	58.77	93
Puerto Rico	0.000	0.088	11.70	63.90	33.77	1,457	12.38	76.94	44.11	1175
Thailand	0.638	0.463	13.03	86.89	59.02	61	13.19	67.84	58.23	30
Russia	0.365	0.776	13.41	94.64	71.43	56	14.28	100.00	82.10	26
Vietnam	0.557	0.423	12.87	85.95	68.60	242	14.14	100.00	90.29	24
Yugoslavia	0.374	0.479	12.99	86.46	57.29	96	13.39	87.30	68.00	47

Source: UNESCO publications; 1990 IPUMS; 1997–2001 Current Population Survey.

eration is defined by the father's place of birth, or, if only the mother was born abroad, the mother's place of birth. For the 1.5 generation, I used 1990 IPUMS data, because it is the only data set with sufficient sample sizes. For the second generation, I used the 1997–2001 CPS because the CPS, unlike the Census, has a question about parents' nativity, which allows me to directly identify U.S.-born children of immigrants. I combined the non-repeated cases across these five years in the CPS to create a dataset of the second generation as of the late 1990s/early 2000s. The means of these variables by national-origin group are also shown in table 10.1.

RESULTS—GROUP-LEVEL ANALYSIS

Descriptive Results

As previously mentioned, table 10.1 shows the main independent and dependent variables used in the group-level analysis, sorted by the country of origin. The table illustrates the substantial variability in socioeconomic status, selectivity, and educational attainment among the thirty-two groups in the study. The relationship between the immigrant groups' educational selectivity score and socioeconomic score is particularly important because immigrant selectivity may not capture anything above and beyond an immigrant groups' socioeconomic status in the United States. Indeed, some groups clearly correspond on both indicators. However, others diverge substantially. For example, some groups, such as Mexicans and Puerto Ricans, have both very low educational selectivity and very low socioeconomic status. Puerto Rican migrants have the lowest selectivity score[10] (0) and the second-lowest socioeconomic status (0.88). Mexicans have the third lowest selectivity score (.179) and the lowest socioeconomic status score (0). Conversely, Indians and Iranians have very high selectivity, and also very high socioeconomic status. Indian immigrants have both the highest educational selectivity (1) and the highest socioeconomic status (1). In contrast, other groups, such as Canadians and Russians, have high socioeconomic status, but low selectivity. These immigrant groups come from countries with high overall educational attainment levels, which, due to a ceiling effect, necessarily means the immigrants will not be that highly selected. Further, some groups are highly selected, but have low overall socioeconomic status; these include immigrants from Nicaragua, Haiti, and China. These immigrants are much more highly educated relative to their home countries' populations, but do not have high educational attainment, occupational statuses or incomes by American standards.

Children of immigrants vary considerably in terms of educational attainment by ethnic group. One-and-one-half-generation and second-generation

Indians have the highest levels of educational attainment, whether measured by mean years of schooling, percent high school graduates, or percent that have attended some college. At the other end of the spectrum, Mexicans have among the lowest levels of attainment. For example, 1.5-generation Indians average 14.59 years of schooling, 98 percent are high school graduates, and 88 percent have attended at least some college. In contrast, 1.5-generation Mexicans average 11.22 years of schooling, only 59 percent are high school graduates, and only 32 percent have at least some college education. For these groups and most others, educational attainment rates are slightly higher among the second generation than the 1.5 generation, most likely because the data for the second generation come from a later time period.

The 1.5 Generation

Table 10.2 shows regression results for the determinants of three educational outcomes among 1.5-generation immigrant groups: mean years of schooling, percent college educated, and percent high school graduates.[11] I begin with a model that includes the average socioeconomic status of the immigrant group as the only predictor of each educational outcome[12] and then add, in model 2, immigrants' educational selectivity to see if it adds any significant explanatory power.[13] Table 10.2, model 1, shows that the immigrant group's average socioeconomic status is a strong predictor of all three educational attainment outcomes for 1.5-generation groups. Thus, the national-origin group with the highest immigrant socioeconomic status score (coded 1), has 2.37 more years of schooling than the group with the lowest socioeconomic status score (coded 0), and this variable explains 67 percent of the variance in average years of schooling among 1.5-generation groups. Less variance in the percent college educated (53 percent) is explained by immigrant socioeconomic status, while socioeconomic status also explains 67 percent of the variance in the percentage of high school graduates. The coefficients reveal that the national-origin group with the highest average immigrant socioeconomic status has nearly 36 percent more college educated persons and 29 percent more high school graduates among the 1.5 generation than those with the lowest immigrant socioeconomic status.

The second models in table 10.2 add immigrants' educational selectivity to the equations. In all cases, this addition increases the explained variance (R^2) and decreases the coefficients of immigrant socioeconomic status. For example, including educational selectivity in the model explains almost three quarters of the variance in mean years of schooling among the 1.5-generation groups. The decline in the coefficients of immigrant socioeconomic status in model 2 indicates that part of the influence of socioeconomic status on aver-

Table 10.2. Coefficients of Models of the Determinants of Educational Attainment among 1.5-Generation Immigrant Groups in the United States, 1990

Independent Variables	Mean Years of Schooling		% Some College		% HS Graduates	
	Model 1	Model 2	Model 1	Model 2	Model 1	Model 2
Immigrant Generation's Socioeconomic Status (Occupational Status, Income, Education)	2.37*** (.30)	1.91*** (.32)	35.63*** (6.14)	24.36*** (6.04)	28.84*** (3.66)	23.80*** (3.94)
Immigrant Generation's Educational Selectivity		1.14** (.40)		27.91*** (7.69)		12.47* (5.01)
Constant	12.13*** (.16)	11.78*** (.19)	47.19*** (3.20)	38.66*** (3.58)	73.62*** (2.00)	69.81*** (2.33)
R-squared	0.67	0.74	0.53	0.68	0.67	0.73

Note:
1. N=32.
2. Standard errors in parentheses.
3. +p<.10, * p<.05, ** p<.01, ***p<.001.
Source: IPUMS 1990.

age group educational outcomes is actually due to its correlation with immigrants' selectivity. Immigrants' educational selectivity significantly affects all of the educational outcomes among the 1.5-generation groups. For example, the most positively selected immigrant group has 1.14 more average years of schooling than the least positively selected group, controlling for average socioeconomic status. The most positively selected group also has almost 28 percent more college educated persons and over 12 percent more high school graduates. Interestingly, immigrants' educational selectivity appears to have the strongest effect on the percent of college educated; adding this to the model increases the explained variance from less than 53 percent to 68 percent.

The Second Generation

Table 10.3 presents similar regression results, but for second-generation groups, those born in the United States of immigrant parents. I first add the average socioeconomic status of the group and then the average educational selectivity of the immigrant group. The findings are similar to the results for the 1.5-generation groups. Net of average socioeconomic status, immigrants' educational selectivity significantly affects the educational attainment of second-generation national-origin groups. There is one exception: educational selectivity does not significantly affect the percentage of second-generation high school graduates, and the effect of immigrants' socioeconomic status on the percentage of high school graduates only borders on significance. This might be due to the fact that there is less variability in percent high school graduates than other educational attainment outcomes, and less variability among the second generation than the 1.5 generation; high school graduation has become the norm. The other difference between second-generation groups as opposed to 1.5-generation groups is that less of the variance in educational attainment is explained by the variables included in the analysis. For example, 51 percent of the variance in percent college educated is explained for second-generation groups, compared to 68 percent for 1.5-generation groups. Similarly, slightly over half of the variability in average years of schooling is explained for the second generation, while almost three quarters of the variability is explained for the 1.5-generation groups. This finding most likely reflects the different experiences of the 1.5 and second generation. Having grown up entirely in the United States, the second generation is less likely to be as influenced by the migration experiences and characteristics of the immigrant generation.

Table 10.3. Coefficients of Models of the Determinants of Educational Attainment among Second-Generation Immigrant Groups in the United States, 1997–2001

Independent Variables	Mean Years of Schooling		% Some College		% HS Graduates	
	Model 1	Model 2	Model 1	Model 2	Model 1	Model 2
Immigrant Generation's Socioeconomic Status (Occupational Status, Income, Education)	1.75***	1.28**	28.65***	19.42**	11.92*	9.73+
	(.35)	(.38)	(6.43)	(6.85)	(4.60)	(5.40)
Immigrant Generation's Educational Selectivity		1.18*		22.85*		5.41
		(.49)		(8.73)		(6.87)
Constant	13.03***	12.67***	59.60***	52.61***	87.22***	85.56***
	(.18)	(.23)	(3.35)	(4.06)	(2.39)	(3.20)
R-squared	0.45	0.54	0.40	0.51	0.18	0.20

Note:
1. N=32.
2. Standard errors in parentheses.
3. +p<.10, *p<.05, **p<.01, ***p<.001.
Source: March CPS, 1997–2001.

RESULTS—INDIVIDUAL-LEVEL ANALYSIS:
ETHNIC/RACIAL DIFFERENCES

Descriptive Statistics

Having shown that educational selectivity is an important variable affecting group-level differences in educational attainment outcomes among children of immigrants, I now turn to individual-level analyses. I address the question of whether immigrants' educational selectivity contributes to explaining the advantages or disadvantages associated with panethnic group membership for children of immigrants. Specifically, I consider Whites (consisting of children of immigrants with national origins in Europe or Canada), Blacks (national origins in Haiti, Jamaica), Asians (national origins in Asia), and Latinos (national origins in Latin America or Spanish-speaking Caribbean). I examine two educational transitions that are crucial influences on subsequent labor market outcomes: high school graduation and college attendance.

Table 10.4 shows the means and standard deviations of the variables included in this analysis by race/ethnicity for the 1.5 generation and the second generation. The table shows that there are sharp disparities in educational outcomes among the groups, and particularly between Asians and Latinos. Generally, Asians have the highest levels of educational attainment, while Latinos have the lowest. Whites and Blacks also have much higher attainment than Latinos, although not as high as Asians. For example, 76 percent of 1.5-generation Asians have some college schooling, compared to only 40 percent of 1.5-generation Latinos. One-and-one-half-generation Whites and Blacks have similar levels of educational attainment.

Among the second generation, Asians are also the most educated. Second-generation Latinos again have the lowest levels of attainment: only 80 percent are high school graduates and only 48 percent have some college education.

The independent variables in the analysis include age, age at migration, sex, central city residence, and immigrants' socioeconomic status and educational selectivity, both defined at the level of the national-origin group.[14] The table shows that among both the 1.5 generation and the second generation, Blacks are more likely to be female (63 percent among the second generation), and also more often reside in central cities than the other groups. Whites are the least urban (only 24 percent of second-generation Whites are located in central cities, compared to over half of Blacks). As for the immigrant groups' socioeconomic status and selectivity, Latinos tend to come from immigrant groups with the lowest socioeconomic statuses and with the least positive selectivity, while Asians tend to have higher socioeconomic status and higher selectivity. Blacks and Whites fall in between. Whites tend to have high socioeconomic status but are less selective than Asians or Blacks. Blacks

Table 10.4. Means and Standard Deviations of Variables Included in Individual-Level Analysis by Ethnic/Racial Group, Ages 20 to 40

	White	Black	Asian	Latino
1.5 Generation, 1990 Census				
College-educated	0.62	0.66	0.76	0.4
High School Graduate	0.90	0.88	0.93	0.67
Age	30.03	25.87	26.71	27.97
	(5.82)	(4.52)	(5.57)	(5.69)
Age at Immigration	3.84	6.14	4.38	4.78
	(3.22)	(3.14)	(3.40)	(3.35)
Female	0.48	0.56	0.51	0.51
Central City	0.33	0.55	0.38	0.48
Immigrant Group's Socioeconomic Status	0.60	0.46	0.68	0.09
(Occupational Status, Income, Education)	(.19)	(.18)	(.15)	(.13)
Immigrant Group's Educational Selectivity	0.35	0.57	0.58	0.21
	(.16)	(.11)	(.13)	(.15)
N	2,058	272	1,881	5,621
2nd Generation, 1997–2001 CPS				
College-educated	0.69	0.75	0.79	0.48
High School Graduate	0.94	0.89	0.98	0.80
Age	30.99	26.37	27.27	28.37
	(6.03)	(4.78)	(5.66)	(5.93)
Female	0.51	0.63	0.51	0.54
Central City	0.24	0.51	0.40	0.40
Immigrant Group's Socioeconomic Status	0.50	0.39	0.60	0.07
(Occupational Status, Income, Education)	(.25)	(.24)	(.20)	(.12)
Immigrant Group's Educational Selectivity	0.35	0.48	0.62	0.18
	(.18)	(.18)	(.15)	(.15)
N	1,162	65	255	2,036

have lower socioeconomic status than Whites or Asians, but have higher selectivity than Whites and Latinos.

Multivariate Analysis

High School Graduation

Tables 10.5 and 10.6 show odds ratios of the determinants of high school graduation among 1.5- and second-generation adults in the United States. The significance levels reflect the use of robust standard errors, to correct for the clustering at the level of the immigrant group. Model 1 includes only the broad ethnic/racial groups as predictors of high school graduation, with Whites as the comparison group. These results show that for the 1.5 generation (table 10.5), Blacks do not differ significantly from Whites in rates of

Table 10.5. Odds Ratios of Models of the Determinants of High School Graduation among 1.5-Generation Persons Aged 20 to 40 in the United States, 1990

	Model 1	Model 2	Model 3
Black	0.820	1.587	0.920
Asian	1.676*	1.335	0.978
Latino	0.239**	1.335	1.194
Age		1.017+	1.022*
Age at Immigration (approximate)		.962***	0.951**
Female		1.239**	1.244***
Central City		.702*	0.732*
Immigrant Group's Socioeconomic Status (Occupational Status, Income, Education)		33.222***	15.637**
Immigrant Group's Educational Selectivity			5.362**
Observations	9,832	9,832	9,832

Note: Robust standard errors, adjusted for clustering at national-origin group level: +p<.10, *p<.05, **p<.01, ***p<.001.
Source: IPUMS 1990.

high school completion. Asians, however, are 1.7 times as likely to graduate high school as Whites; Latinos are approximately 75 percent less likely to graduate high school as White 1.5-generation adults. Among the second generation (table 10.6), Asians are over two times as likely as Whites to graduate high school. Second-generation Latinos are less likely to graduate high school than Whites.

Model 2 adds individual-level controls to the analysis as well as the average socioeconomic status of the immigrant group. These variables generally have results consistent with the literature. Age has little effect for the 1.5 and second generation (reflecting little variation in age in the sample). Age at migration has a negative effect for the 1.5 generation. Women are slightly more likely to graduate high school than men among the 1.5 and second generation.

Central city residence has a negative influence on the odds of high school completion for both the 1.5 generation and the second generation. The immigrant group's average socioeconomic status has a large effect: among the 1.5 generation, those from immigrant groups with the highest socioeconomic status are thirty-three times as likely to graduate high school as those from groups with the lowest socioeconomic status; among the second generation, those from immigrant groups with the highest socioeconomic status are over nine times as likely to graduate high school as those with the lowest socioeconomic status.

Adding the factors in model 2 also changes some of the racial/ethnic group membership findings. The Asian advantage is partly explained by these factors. Among the 1.5 generation, Asians are still slightly more likely to graduate high school than Whites, but the advantage decreases from 1.7 to 1.3

Table 10.6. Odds Ratios of Models of the Determinants of High School Graduation among Second-Generation Persons Aged 20 to 40 in the United States, 1997–2001

	Model 1	Model 2	Model 3
Black	0.465	0.700	0.553
Asian	2.634***	2.291**	1.669+
Latino	0.247***	0.626*	0.627*
Age		1.020**	1.025**
Female		1.270***	1.290***
Central City		0.671*	0.701**
Immigrant Group's Socioeconomic Status (Occupational Status, Income, Education)		9.042***	4.855**
Immigrant Group's Educational Selectivity			4.356***
Observations	7,289	7,289	7,289

Note: Robust standard errors, adjusted for clustering at national-origin group level: +p<.10, *p<.05, **p<.01, ***p<.001.
Source: March CPS 1997–2001.

times as likely, and is no longer statistically significant. Among the second generation (table 10.6), the Asian advantage is partly explained, as the odds ratio declines from 2.6 to 2.3, net of the factors in model 2. For Latinos, these factors explain the disadvantage among the 1.5 generation; net of these factors, Latinos do not significantly differ from Whites in their likelihood of graduating from high school. For the second generation, adding these controls substantially decreases the Latino disadvantage relative to Whites (the odds ratio changes from .247 to .626). Therefore, the lower socioeconomic status of Latino immigrants explains part of the Latino disadvantage in high school graduation rates relative to Whites.

Model 3 adds immigrants' educational selectivity to the models in tables 10.5 and 10.6. Immigrants' educational selectivity is an important predictor of high school graduation, net of other factors for the 1.5 generation; those from immigrant groups with the highest educational selectivity are approximately 5.4 times as likely to graduate high school as those from immigrant groups with the lowest educational selectivity. Among the second generation, those from immigrant groups with the highest selectivity are approximately 4.4 times as likely to graduate high school as those from immigrant groups with the lowest selectivity. Adding the immigrant group's educational selectivity in model 3 also decreases the odds ratio on immigrant group socioeconomic status substantially (from 33.22 to 15.64 for the 1.5 generation, and from 9.04 to 4.86 for the second generation). This indicates that part of the influence of immigrant group socioeconomic status is actually due to its correlation with selectivity.

Adding immigrants' educational selectivity partly explains some of the racial/ethnic group findings. The Asian 1.5 generation's differences from

Whites were explained previously, but the odds ratio does decline even further. However, adding immigrants' selectivity to the model explains Asians' advantage over Whites for the second generation (the odds ratio, 1.67, only borders on significance). This suggests that Asians' high educational selectivity explains their advantage over Whites in terms of high school graduation rates.

College Attendance

Tables 10.7 and 10.8 examine the effects of the included variables on the odds of college attendance. Model 1 shows that, among the 1.5 generation, Blacks do not differ significantly from Whites in the odds of attending college, while Asians are 1.9 times more likely to attend college than Whites, and Latinos are less than half as likely to attend college as Whites. Among the second generation, Asians are over two times as likely to attend college as Whites, while Latinos are less likely to attend college.

Model 2 adds the individual-level controls as well as immigrants' socioeconomic status. For both the Asian 1.5 and second generation, part of their advantage over Whites is explained by these factors, most importantly, the higher socioeconomic status of the immigrant generation. Nevertheless, even controlling for these factors, both 1.5- and second-generation Asians are still more likely than Whites to attend college. In contrast, the disadvantage of the Latino 1.5 generation, and part of the disadvantage of the second generation, is explained by including individual background variables and immigrants' socioeconomic status.

Table 10.7. Odds Ratios of Models of the Determinants of College Education among 1.5-Generation Persons Ages 20 to 40 in the United States, 1990

	Model 1	Model 2	Model 3
Black	1.202	1.928	1.156
Asian	1.897**	1.765**	1.271
Latino	0.418**	1.434	1.193
Age		1.025*	1.031**
Age at Immigration (approximate)		0.984	0.973*
Female		1.172**	1.177**
Central City		0.931	0.966
Immigrant Group's Socioeconomic Status		10.512**	4.377**
(Occupational Status, Income, Education)			
Immigrant Group's Educational Selectivity			6.204**
Observations	9,832	9,832	9,832

Note: Robust standard errors, adjusted for clustering at national-origin group level: +p<.10, *p<.05, **p<.01, ***p<.001.

Table 10.8. Odds Ratios of Models of the Determinants of College Attendance among Second-Generation Persons Ages 20 to 40 in the United States, 1997–2001

	Model 1	Model 2	Model 3
Black	0.903	1.086	0.861
Asian	2.035**	1.841*	1.366
Latino	0.391**	0.677*	0.656**
Age		1.003	1.007
Female		1.348**	1.367**
Central City		0.920	0.949
Immigrant Group's Socioeconomic Status (Occupational Status, Income, Education)		3.618**	1.929+
Immigrant Group's Educational Selectivity			4.063**
Observations	7,289	7,289	7,289

Note: Robust standard errors, adjusted for clustering at national-origin group level: +p<.10, *p<.05, **p<.01, ***p<.001.
Source: March CPS 1997–2001.

Model 3 introduces immigrants' educational selectivity to the model. For Blacks and Latinos, immigrants' educational selectivity does not change the substantive results. For the Asian 1.5 and second generation, however, immigrants' selectivity is an important factor explaining their advantage in terms of college attendance. Once selectivity is introduced into the model, the odds ratio of Asians attending college decreases from 1.8 times as likely as Whites, to 1.3 times as likely among the 1.5 generation, which is not significantly different from Whites. Among the second generation, the Asian advantage in terms of college attendance relative to Whites is also explained by the higher educational selectivity of the immigrant generation.

DISCUSSION AND CONCLUSION

In tackling the long-standing question of how to explain ethnic group differences in educational outcomes, this study highlights the influence of immigrant selectivity—a previously neglected factor. I find that the average educational selectivity of the immigrant group significantly affects the mean years of schooling, percent high school graduates, and percent who have attended college among 1.5- and second-generation children of immigrants, at the ethnic group level of analysis. Educational selectivity explains a substantial portion of the variance in ethnic group differences in average years of schooling, percent with some college schooling, and high school graduation rates. Even controlling for immigrants' average socioeconomic status, higher educational selectivity among the immigrant generation is associated with higher educational attainment among the next generation. I also show that immigrant selectivity is a significant predictor of educational attainment among immigrants' children at the individual level. Furthermore, immigrant selectivity is an important factor contributing to broad ethnic/racial group differences in educational attainment, especially college attendance rates. In particular, it helps to explain the high college attendance rates among Asians.

There are multiple implications of these findings for the study of ethnicity and immigration. By directly measuring selectivity using compiled educational attainment data on both immigrants *and* non-migrants in their homelands, the study points to the importance of examining pre-migration factors as sources of ethnic resources and/or vulnerabilities. Using measures that incorporate migrants' experiences prior to migrating may help illuminate the incorporation processes of both immigrants and their children after crossing borders into the United States. In other words, not only are ethnic resources that are mobilized after migration important (such as the formation of supportive ethnic communities and enclaves, financial resources, and social networks) but there may be intangible ethnic resources that immigrants carry with them from the origin country that help to explain adaptation outcomes.

Like Shih's chapter in this volume, this chapter suggests that immigrants transport non-economic forms of capital, such as social and cultural capital, across borders, which they then mobilize as ethnic resources in the United States. Since immigrant selectivity matters above and beyond the absolute level of schooling, occupational status or income of the immigrant groups, this suggests that selectivity matters for the non-economic benefits it is capturing. These findings are consistent with theories of ethnic, social, and cultural capital. That is, educational selectivity (as well as educational attainment) may capture less tangible forms of ethnic capital that either hinder or facilitate success in school. For example, highly selected immigrant groups' children may be *expected* to attain a certain level of schooling, comparable to the relative level the immigrants themselves attained in the home country. The finding that selectivity appears to have a stronger effect on college attendance rates than high school graduation rates is consistent with theories of non-economic capital. Given that I control for income and occupational status, this suggests that it is not only economic differences that determine who among the second generation will attend college. Instead, my results are consistent with the argument that some immigrant parents are pushing their children to rise to a higher than average class position, and to do so, the second generation must attend college. After all, it is the transition to college that is most crucial in contemporary American society, separating those who are likely to attain above average labor market outcomes from the rest. Thus, highly selective immigrant groups, even if they are not economically well-off in the United States, may be able to draw upon ethnic capital in the form of high collective expectations for the next generation's educational success (a form of cultural capital), or they may mobilize social networks to spread information about opportunities and resources (a form of social capital) to facilitate the next generation's transitions to college.

These findings challenge cultural explanations for ethnic group differences in educational outcomes in two ways. First, the study counters suggestions that certain national groups intrinsically value education more than others by showing that there is a selection process occurring: only select segments of these home countries' populations come to the United States, and they are not necessarily representative of their national cultures. Second, while some scholars privilege the development of "oppositional cultures" in the United States as an explanation for ethnic group differences (Ogbu 1991), I suggest that a structural characteristic of immigrant groups prior to migration—their pre-migration class position—is important, insofar as it can be mobilized as an ethnic resource in the United States.

Consistent with theories of class reproduction (Bourdieu 1973; Bowles and Gintes 1976; Willis 1977), this chapter suggests that education is not often a vehicle for upward mobility among immigrant groups. Rather, education often serves to reproduce existing stratification systems, even those carried across borders from other countries. That is, relative class position, measured by the relative pre-migration educational attainment of the immigrant generation, is often reproduced among the next generation in the United States. My findings suggest that when education is conceptualized in a broad sense, such that more than the degree attained is considered, the importance of *relative* educational attainment (or educational selectivity) becomes clear. For immigrants, understanding where they were situated in their home country's system of educational stratification prior to migration can help explain where their children end up in the American educational stratification system. Future research should be directed toward better understanding the mechanisms through which pre-migration characteristics are utilized as ethnic resources in the United States to facilitate the second-generation's success in educational attainment, as well as in the labor market.

NOTES

1. Immigrant selection occurs on several complex and interrelated levels. For example, immigrants self-select themselves, since only some people wish to migrate or have the resources to do so. Further, some countries have historically had restrictive exit policies allowing only select individuals to emigrate (Foner 2000). The nature of

migration flows are also influenced by political and economic conditions in the sending country (the contexts of exit) (Massey 1999; Menjivar 1993; Rumbaut 1997), the historical relationship between the United States and potential sending countries (Rumbaut 1995, 1997), and U.S. immigration policy (Green 1999). Investigating such causes of immigrant selection are beyond the scope of this chapter; instead, this chapter focuses on the *impact* of these selection processes on children of immigrants' educational outcomes.

2. Borjas (1993) found that earnings of second-generation workers are more heavily influenced by the earnings of their parents' generation than by the earnings of current immigrants from the same source country. To this end, I followed Borjas's method of using younger aged children of immigrants (ages 20 to 40), and earlier data from the immigrant generation, to ensure that there was overlap of parents and children in the analysis.

3. I searched for data from the top thirty-eight sending countries and found acceptable data (for the appropriate years for that country, by age) for thirty-two national-origin groups. Most of the country of origin data was available through UNESCO (United Nations Educational, Scientific, and Cultural Organization) publications. UNESCO data accounts for the different educational systems in different countries because data are compiled in six educational categories that are comparable across nations. For Puerto Rico, I used data published by the U.S. Census. I selected the year of the data by choosing the closest year (for which there was available data) to the average year of immigration of the U.S. immigrants from that country (calculated from the 1990 Census). A table of specific data sources for each country is available from the author by request.

4. In most cases, this meant I used IPUMS data from two decades. For example, if the average year of immigration for immigrants from a certain country was 1980–1981, I selected immigrants from that country who migrated from 1975–1980 using IPUMS data from 1980, and I selected immigrants from that country who migrated from 1980–1986 using IPUMS data from 1990.

5. To be more precise, I chose eighteen-plus as the cutoff to ensure that all of the immigrants' primary and secondary schooling occurred in the home country. Some of the immigrants, especially those between the ages of eighteen and twenty-five, may have attended college in the United States, however. In general, this is not a high percentage of immigrants. For example, only a slightly higher percentage of those who migrated before age twenty-five have attended college compared to those who migrated after age twenty-five (37 percent vs. 32 percent). This difference varies across immigrant groups, with the more educated groups appearing to have completed some college education in the United States. Given that international students are adult immigrants who often end up settling in the United States, however, it makes sense to include these immigrants in measuring educational selectivity.

6. To adjust for the different age distributions of the immigrants and the home country populations, I used direct standardization; the age structure of each immigrant group was used to calculate the six measures for the populations of the corresponding country. This standardization is important because immigrants are selected by age as well as education, and because age and educational attainment are related. In most cases, immigrants tend to be younger than those who remain in the homeland. Since

most populations are becoming more educated over time, younger adult persons are generally more educated than older persons from the same country. Not accounting for the differing age distributions would have overestimated the degree of positive selectivity simply because immigrants tend to be younger than non-migrants.

7. These indicators were:

1. percent with at least some college education,
2. percent with at least some secondary schooling or higher,
3. percent with at least some secondary, second level schooling or higher (11th grade or higher),
4. percent with no schooling,
5. mean years of schooling, and
6. median years of schooling.

8. The index of dissimilarity (D) is most often used to study residential segregation, but I use it here to compare the distributions of educational attainment between immigrants and home country populations. In order to calculate D, I used the educational categories that the countries' populations and immigrants were divided into ("no schooling/illiterate," "first level incomplete," "first level completed," "second level 1st cycle," "second level, second cycle," and "post-secondary schooling or higher"). If D equals 0, it would mean that the educational attainment distributions of immigrants and non-migrants were exactly the same; if D equals 1, it would mean that the educational distributions of the two groups had no overlap. An intermediate value, say .55, would indicate that 55 percent of the two groups would need to exchange educational attainment values in order to make their distributions identical.

9. I included only adults ages twenty to forty, so that they are old enough to have at least attended some college, yet young enough to be the children of the immigrant generation.

10. Puerto Ricans are actually the only group in the study that was negatively selected on certain measures of educational attainment (mean years of schooling and percent college educated).

11. Since the number of cases is only thirty-two, I investigated whether any one national-origin group, such as Mexicans or Puerto Ricans, was driving the results. I ran the regressions excluding each of the thirty-two countries to examine whether the results would differ if any one country was not included in the sample. I found that the substantive results did not change.

12. Since the number of cases is only thirty-two, the model would be highly unstable if I included more than two to three predictors. However, I did try the analysis with a number of other possible predictors of 1.5-generation groups' educational attainment, none of which was significant: mean age of 1.5 generation in sample, country distance from United States, source country income inequality, and per capita GDP in the source country. Two additional source country characteristics did influence educational attainment among children of immigrants, but only through their effects on immigrants' socioeconomic status and selectivity. The literacy rate is, contrary to what one might expect, negatively related to educational attainment among children of

immigrants: children of immigrants from countries with higher literacy rates had lower educational attainment. This counterintuitive finding is entirely explained away by immigrants' selectivity, since immigrants from countries with higher educational attainment levels are more likely to be less positively selected. Those from countries where English is spoken have higher educational attainment, but this is because immigrants from these countries have higher socioeconomic statuses in the United States.

13. The substantive results did not change when I used different codings of immigrants' educational selectivity. For example, I tried the analyses using a less robust measure, simply the difference between the average years of schooling between the immigrant groups and their home country populations, and found substantively similar results.

14. The findings in this section should be treated as tentative given that I cannot control for family background factors, such as parents' educational attainment, which have been found to be important predictors of educational attainment.

REFERENCES

Alba, Richard D., and Victor Nee. 1997. "Rethinking Assimilation Theory for a New Era of Immigration." *International Migration Review* 31: 826–74.

Blau, Peter Michael, and Otis Dudley Duncan. 1967. *The American Occupational Structure*. New York: Wiley.

Borjas, George J. 1987. "Self-Selection and the Earnings of Immigrants." *American Economic Review* 77: 531–53.

———. 1990. *Friends or Strangers: The Impact of Immigrants on the U.S. Economy*. New York: Basic Books.

———. 1992. "Ethnic Capital and Intergenerational Mobility." *Quarterly Journal of Economics* 107: 123–50.

———. 1993. "The Intergenerational Mobility of Immigrants." *Journal of Labor Economics* 11: 113–35.

———. 1994. "Long-run Convergence of Ethnic Skill Differentials: The Children and Grandchildren of the Great Migration." *Industrial and Labor Relations Review* 47:553–73.

———. 1999. *Heaven's Door: Immigration Policy and the American Economy*. Princeton, NJ: Princeton University Press.

Bourdieu, Pierre. 1973. "Cultural Reproduction and Social Reproduction." Pp. 71–112 in *Knowledge, Education, and Cultural Change*, ed. Richard Brown. London: Tavistock.

Bourdieu, Pierre, and Jean Claude Passeron. 1977. *Reproduction in Education, Society and Culture*. London; Beverly Hills: Sage Publications.

Bowles, Samuel, and Herbert Gintis. 1976. *Schooling in Capitalist America: Educational Reform and the Contradictions of Economic Life*. New York: Basic Books.

Bray, David. 1984. "Economic Development: The Middle Class and International Migration in the Dominican Republic." *International Migration Review* 18: 217–36.

Carliner, Geoffrey. 1980. "Wages, Earnings, and Hours of 1st, 2nd, and 3rd Generation American Males." *Economic Inquiry* 18: 87–102.

Caudill, William, and George DeVos. 1956. "Achievement, Culture and Personality: The Case of the Japanese Americans." *American Anthropologist* 58: 1102–26.

Cheng, Lucie, and Philip Q. Yang. 1996. "Asians: The 'Model Minority' Deconstructed." Pp. 305–44 in *Ethnic Los Angeles*, ed. Roger Waldinger and Mehdi Bozorgmehr. New York: Russell Sage Foundation.

Chiswick, Barry R. 1978. "The Effect of Americanization on the Earnings of Foreign-born Men." *Journal of Political Economy* 86: 897–921.

Cobb-Clark, Deborah A. 1993. "Immigrant Selectivity and Wages: The Evidence for Women." *American Economic Review* 83: 986–93.

Coleman, James S. 1988. "Social Capital in the Creation of Human Capital." *American Journal of Sociology* 94: S95–S120.

Farley, Reynolds, and Richard Alba. 2002. "The New Second Generation in the United States." *International Migration Review* 36: 669–701.

Foner, Nancy. 2000. *From Ellis Island to JFK: New York's Two Great Waves of Immigration*. New Haven, CT, and New York: Yale University Press and Russell Sage Foundation.

Gans, Herbert J. 1992. "Second Generation Decline: Scenarios for the Economic and Ethnic Futures of the Post-1965 American Immigrants." *Ethnic and Racial Studies* 15: 173–92.

———. 2000. "Filling in Some Holes: Six Areas of Needed Immigration Research." Pp. 76–89 in *Immigration Research for a New Century*, ed. Nancy Foner, Rubén G. Rumbaut, and Steven J. Gold. New York: Russell Sage Foundation.

Gordon, Milton Myron. 1964. *Assimilation in American Life: The Role of Race, Religion, and National Origins*. New York: Oxford University Press.

Green, David A. 1999. "Immigrant Occupational Attainment: Assimilation and Mobility over Time." *Journal of Labor Economics* 17: 49–79.

Hirschman, Charles, and Luis M. Falcon. 1985. "The Educational Attainment of Religio-Ethnic Groups in the United States." *Research in Sociology of Education and Socialization* 5: 83–120.

Hirschman, Charles, and Morrison G. Wong. 1986. "The Extraordinary Educational Attainment of Asian-Americans: A Search for Historical Evidence and Explanations." *Social Forces* 65: 1–27.

Hsu, Francis. 1971. *The Challenge of the American Dream: The Chinese in the United States*. Belmont, CA: Wadsworth.

Jasso, Guillermina, and Mark R. Rosenzweig. 1986. "What's In a Name? Country-of-origin Influences on the Earnings of Immigrants in the Untied States." *Research in Human Capital and Development* 4: 75–106.

Jencks, Christopher, Marshall Smith, Henry Acland, Mary Jo Bane, David Cohen, Herbert Gintis, Barbara Heyns, and Stephan Michelson. 1972. *Inequality: A Reassessment of the Effect of Family and Schooling in America*. New York: Harper & Row.

Landale, Nancy S., R. S. Oropesa, and Bridget K. Gorman. 2000. "Migration and Infant Death: Assimilation or Selective Migration among Puerto Ricans?" *American Sociological Review* 65: 888–909.

Lee, Everett S. 1966. "Theory of Migration." *Demography* 3: 47–57.

Lieberson, Stanley. 1980. *A Piece of the Pie: Black and White Immigrants since 1880*. Berkeley: University of California Press.

Lopez, David E., and Ricardo D. Stanton-Salazar. 2001. " Mexican-Americans: A Second Generation at Risk." Pp. 57–90 in *Ethnicities: Children of Immigrants in America*, ed. Rubén G. Rumbaut and Alejandro Portes. Berkeley: University of California Press.

Massey, Douglas S. 1988. "Economic Development and International Migration in Comparative Perspective." *Population and Development Review* 14: 383–413.

——. 1999. "Why Does Immigration Occur? A Theoretical Synthesis." Pp. 34–52 in *Handbook of International Migration: The American Experience*, ed. Charles Hirschman, Philip Kasinitz, and Josh DeWind. New York: Russell Sage Foundation.

Menjívar, Cecilia. 1993. "History, Economy and Politics: Macro- and Micro-Level Factors in Recent Salvadorean Migration to the U.S." *Journal of Refugee Studies* 6: 350–71.

Ogbu, John U. 1991. "Immigrant and Involuntary Minorities in Comparative Perspective." Pp. 3–33 in *Minority Status and Schooling: A Comparative Study of Immigrant and Involuntary Minorities*, ed. Margaret A. Gibson and John U. Ogbu. New York: Garland Publishing.

Ortiz, Vilma. 1986. "Changes in the Characteristics of Puerto Rican Migrants from 1955 to 1980." *International Migration Review* 20: 612–28.

Park, Robert. 1928. "Human Migration and the Marginal Man." *American Journal of Sociology* 33: 881–93.

Perlmann, Joel. 1988. *Ethnic Differences: Schooling and Social Structure among the Irish, Italians, Jews, and Blacks in an American City, 1880–1935*. Cambridge and New York: Cambridge University Press.

Perlmann, Joel, and Roger Waldinger. 1997. "Second-generation Decline? Children of Immigrants, Past and Present: A Reconsideration." *International Migration Review* 31: 893–922.

Portes, Alejandro, and Rubén G. Rumbaut. 1996. *Immigrant America: A Portrait*. Berkeley: University of California Press.

——. 2001. *Legacies: The Story of the Immigrant Second Generation*. Berkeley and New York: University of California Press and Russell Sage Foundation.

Portes, Alejandro, and Min Zhou. 1993. "The New Second Generation: Segmented Assimilation and Its Variants." *Annals of the American Academy of Political and Social Science* 530: 74–96.

Ramos, Fernando. 1992. "Out-Migration and Return Migration of Puerto Ricans." Pp. 49–66 in *Immigration and the Work Force: Economic Consequences for the United States and Source Areas*, ed. George J. Borjas and Richard B. Freeman. Chicago: University of Chicago Press.

Ravenstein, E. G. 1885. "The Laws of Migration." *Journal of the Royal Statistical Society* 48: 167–227.

Rumbaut, Rubén G. 1995. "The New Californians: Comparative Research Findings on the Educational Progress of Immigrant Children." Pp. 17–69 in *California's Im-*

migrant Children: Theory, Research, and Implications for Educational Policy, ed. Rubén G. Rumbaut and Wayne A. Cornelius. San Diego: Center for U.S.-Mexican Studies, University of California, San Diego.

———. 1997. "Ties That Bind: Immigration and Immigrant Families in the United States." Pp. 3–46 in *Immigration and the Family: Research and Policy on U.S. Immigrants*, ed. Alan Booth, Ann C. Crouter, and Nancy Landale. Mahwah, NJ: Lawrence Erlbaum Associates.

———. 1999. "Assimilation and Its Discontents." Pp. 172–95 in *The Handbook of International Migration: The American Experience*, ed. Charles Hirschman, Philip Kasinitz, and Josh DeWind. New York: Russell Sage Foundation.

Rumbaut, Rubén G., and Alejandro Portes. 2001. *Ethnicities: Children of Immigrants in America*. Berkeley: University of California Press.

Schneider, Barbara, and Yongsook Lee. 1990. "A Model for Academic Success: The School and Home Environment of East Asian Students." *Anthropology and Education Quarterly* 21, no. 4: 358–77.

Sewell, William H., Archibald O. Haller, and George W. Ohlendorf. 1970. "The Educational and Early Occupational Status Attainment Process: Replication and Revision." *American Sociological Review* 35: 1014–27.

Sowell, Thomas. 1981. *Ethnic America: A History*. New York: Basic Books.

Steinberg, Laurence. 1996. "Ethnicity and Educational Achievement." *American Educator* (Summer).

Steinberg, Laurence D., B. Bradford Brown, and Sanford M. Dornbusch. 1996. *Beyond the Classroom: Why School Reform Has Failed and What Parents Need to Do*. New York: Simon & Schuster.

Steinberg, Stephen. 1981. *The Ethnic Myth: Race, Ethnicity, and Class in America*. New York: Atheneum.

Thernstrom, Stephan. 1973. *The Other Bostonians; Poverty and Progress in the American Metropolis, 1880–1970*. Cambridge, MA: Harvard University Press.

Treiman, Donald J., and Hye-kyung Lee. 1996. "Income Differences among 31 Ethnic Groups in Los Angeles." Pp. 37–82 in *Social Differentiation and Social Inequality: Essays in Honor of John Pock*, ed. James N. Baron, David B. Grusky, and Donald J. Treiman. Boulder, CO: Westview Press.

Waldinger, Roger, and Michael Lichter. 1996. "Anglos: Beyond Ethnicity?" Pp. 413–41 in *Ethnic Los Angeles*, ed. Roger Waldinger and Mehdi Bozorgmehr. New York: Russell Sage Foundation.

Weeks, John R., Rubén G. Rumbaut, and Norma Ojeda. 1999. "Reproductive Outcomes among Mexico-Born Women in San Diego and Tijuana: Testing the Migration Selectivity Hypothesis." *Journal of Immigrant Health* 1: 77–90.

Willis, Paul E. 1977. *Learning To Labour: How Working Class Kids Get Working Class Jobs*. Farnborough, England: Saxon House.

Wilson, William J. 1990. *The Truly Disadvantaged: The Inner City, the Underclass, and Public Policy*. Chicago: University of Chicago Press.

Zhou, Min. 1997a. "Growing Up American: The Challenge Confronting Immigrant Children and Children of Immigrants." *Annual Review of Sociology* 23: 63–95.

————. 1997b. "Social Capital in Chinatown: The Role of Community-Based Organizations and Families in the Adaptation of the Younger Generation." Pp. 181–205 in *Beyond Black and White: New Faces and Voices in U.S. Schools*, ed. Maxine Seller and Lois Weis. Albany: State University of New York Press.

Zhou, Min, and Carl Bankston. 1994. "Social Capital and the Adaptation of the Second Generation: The Case of Vietnamese Youth in New Orleans." *International Migration Review* 28: 821–45.

————. 1998. *Growing Up American: How Vietnamese Children Adapt to Life in the United States*. New York: Russell Sage Foundation.

Index

About the Editor and Contributors

Caroline B. Brettell is Dedman Family Distinguished Professor in the department of anthropology at Southern Methodist University. She served as chair of the department from 1994 to 2004. In addition to numerous book chapters and articles, she is the author of *Men Who Migrate, Women Who Wait: Population and History in a Portuguese Parish* (1986), *We Have Already Cried Many Tears: The Stories of Three Portuguese Migrant Women* (1982, 1995), *Writing against the Wind: A Mother's Life History* (1999) and *Anthropology and Migration: Essays on Transnationalism, Ethnicity and Identity* (2003); coauthor with Richard Brettell of *Painters and Peasants in the 19th* Century (1983); editor of *When They Read What We Write: The Politics of Ethnography* (1993); coeditor of *International Migration: The Female Experience* (1986), *Gender in Cross-Cultural Perspective* (1993, 1997, 2001, 2005), *Gender and Health: An International Perspective* (1996), and *Migration Theory: Talking across Disciplines* (2000). She currently is principal investigator on a project funded through the Cultural Anthropology Program of the National Science Foundation titled "Immigrants, Rights, and Incorporation in a Suburban Metropolis."

Alexander X. Byrd is assistant professor of history at Rice University. He is completing a manuscript on free and forced transatlantic black migration in the late eighteenth century entitled *Captives and Voyagers: Black Migrants across the Eighteenth-Century British Atlantic World*. For supporting the larger work on which his contribution to this volume is based, he is grateful to the Social Science Research Council International Migration program, the ACLS/Andrew Mellon Fellowship for Junior Faculty, the Shelby Cullom

Davis Center for Historical Studies, the Woodrow Wilson Fellowship Foundation, the Ford Foundation, and the School of Humanities' Paula and John Mosle Fund.

Cynthia Feliciano is assistant professor of sociology and Chicano/Latino studies at the University of California, Irvine. Previously, she was a University of California President's Postdoctoral Fellow. She earned her Ph.D. from the University of California, Los Angeles, where she was awarded fellowships from the Ford Foundation and the Social Science Research Council. Her research focuses on the intersections of race and ethnicity, education, and immigration. Her articles have appeared in journals such as *Demography*, *International Migration Review*, *Ethnic and Racial Studies*, and *Social Science Quarterly*. Her book, *Unequal Origins: Immigrant Selection and the Education of the Second Generation*, was recently published by LFB Scholarly Publishing.

Norma Fuentes is assistant professor in the department of sociology and anthropology at Fordham University, New York. Her research interests include immigration and gender and racial, class, and ethnic stratification among Latina immigrant women in New York City. Her current research project examines the process of work integration and immigrant adjustment among Dominican and Mexican women and the role of race and ethnicity in employers' selection and racial and ethnic stratification of the women at work. She is currently writing a chapter, "The Challenges of Combining Ethnography and Survey Methods among Immigrant Populations in New York City," to appear in a book tentatively titled *Research Methods Choices in Interdisciplinary Contexts: War Stories of New Scholars*. She was recently awarded a Postdoctoral Fellowship by the Social Science Research Council to participate in a collaborative research project entitled "PIRE, Children of Immigrants in Schools," to conduct field research among Muslim children and their mothers in Amsterdam and for future comparison with Dominican women in New York.

Alana C. Hackshaw is completing a Ph.D. in political science at the University of Michigan. She holds an MA from the University of Michigan and a BA in History and Political Science from the University of Rochester. Her dissertation is titled "Negotiating the Boundaries of Racial Community: The Political Significance of Identity Politics among African Americans and West Indians." Her research interests focus on immigrant political incorporation and socialization, and racial politics. In 2003–2004 she was a Visiting Scholar at the Center for Urban Research, City University of New York Graduate Center.

David Manuel Hernández is assistant professor and President's Postdoctoral Fellow in the department of Chicana and Chicano studies at the University of California, Los Angeles. He completed his Ph.D. in comparative ethnic studies at the University of California, Berkeley, where he was awarded fellowships from the National Science Foundation and the Social Science Research Council. He is currently revising his dissertation project, entitled "Undue Process: Immigrant Detention, Due Process, and Lesser Citizenship," into a book manuscript.

Jamillah Karim is assistant professor of religion at Spelman College. She obtained her Ph.D. in Islamic studies at Duke University. She specializes in Islam in America, women and Islam, race and Islam, and Muslim immigration. She is currently a postdoctoral fellow at the University of Virginia working on a book project, *Crossing Ethnic and Gender Lines: African American and South Asian Muslim Women in the American Ummah*. Her most recent publications include "Voices of Faith, Faces of Beauty: Connecting American Muslim Women through Azizah Magazine," in *Muslim Networks from Hajj to Hip Hop* (Miriam Cooke and Bruce B. Lawrence, eds.) and "Between Immigrant Islam and Black Liberation: Young Muslims Inherit Global Muslim and African American Legacies," *The Muslim World* 95, no. 4 (October 2005).

Mariel Rose is completing a Ph.D. in American studies at New York University. Her research interests span the politics of narrative and commemoration in Southern history, new immigration in the Southern Appalachians, and the cultural implications of neoliberal capitalism. She has published an article in the journal *Ethnohistory* and has contributed a chapter to the pending book *Moving Workers in the Modern South*, edited by Robert Cassanello and Colin Davis.

Johanna Shih received her doctoral degree in sociology at the University of California, Los Angeles, and is currently assistant professor at Hofstra University. Her research interests include issues of work and inequality in organizations, racial and nativist attitudes among employers and among white Americans more generally, and communities where post-1965 immigration has effected changing ethnic and racial relations.

Zulema Valdez earned her Ph.D. from the department of sociology at the University of California, Los Angeles. Currently, she is assistant professor of sociology at Texas A&M University. Previously, she was a postdoctoral research fellow at the Gerald R. Ford School of Public Policy, University of

Michigan, and at the Center for Comparative Immigration Studies, University of California, San Diego. Her interests include race and ethnic relations, economic sociology, immigration and poverty; her work focuses on understanding the relationship between social group membership and economic inequality in capitalism. She has been awarded grants from the Ford Foundation, the Social Science Research Council, and ASA/NSF. Her most recent publication is "Segmented and Socioeconomic Assimilation among Mexicans in the Southwest," forthcoming in *The Sociological Quarterly*.

Aviva Zeltzer-Zubida is assistant professor of sociology at Brooklyn College of the City University of New York. She received a Ph.D. in sociology from the City University of New York Graduate Center. Her research interests include social inequality, race and ethnicity, immigration, and labor markets. She has published several articles on identity formation among the children of Russian Jewish immigrants. Her current research centers on the role of race and ethnicity in shaping labor market trajectories of second-generation immigrants in the metropolitan New York area.